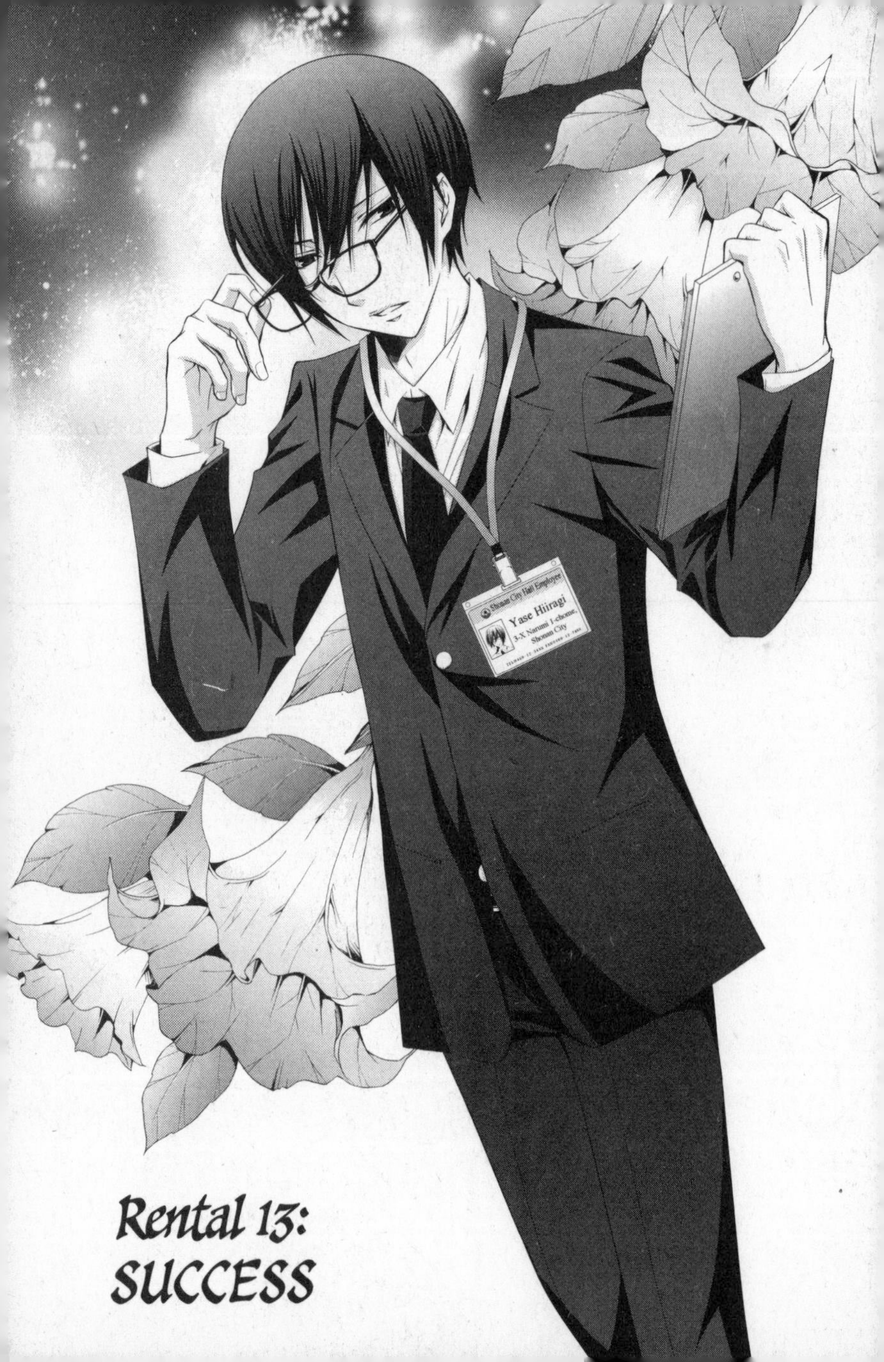
Shonan City Hall Employee
Yase Hiiragi
3-X Narumi 1-chome, Shonan City

Rental 13: SUCCESS

THIS MAN IS MY FATHER?!

THE YOKAI AREN'T OBEYING BANDAGES' COMMANDS.

THEY'RE KNEELING TO DAD INSTEAD...

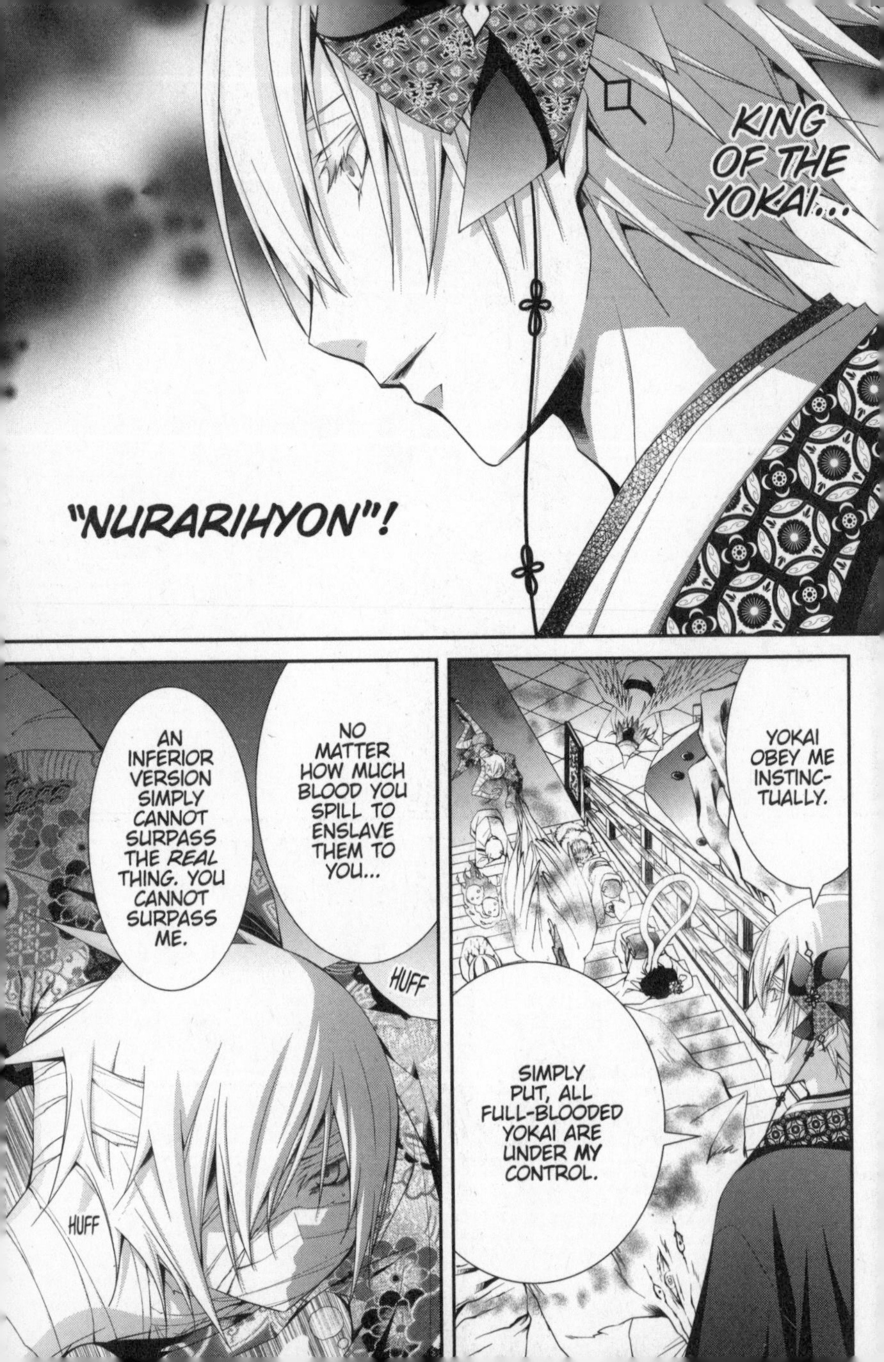
KING OF THE YOKAI...
"NURARIHYON"!
YOKAI OBEY ME INSTINCTUALLY.
SIMPLY PUT, ALL FULL-BLOODED YOKAI ARE UNDER MY CONTROL.
NO MATTER HOW MUCH BLOOD YOU SPILL TO ENSLAVE THEM TO YOU...
AN INFERIOR VERSION SIMPLY CANNOT SURPASS THE *REAL* THING. YOU CANNOT SURPASS ME.
HUFF
HUFF

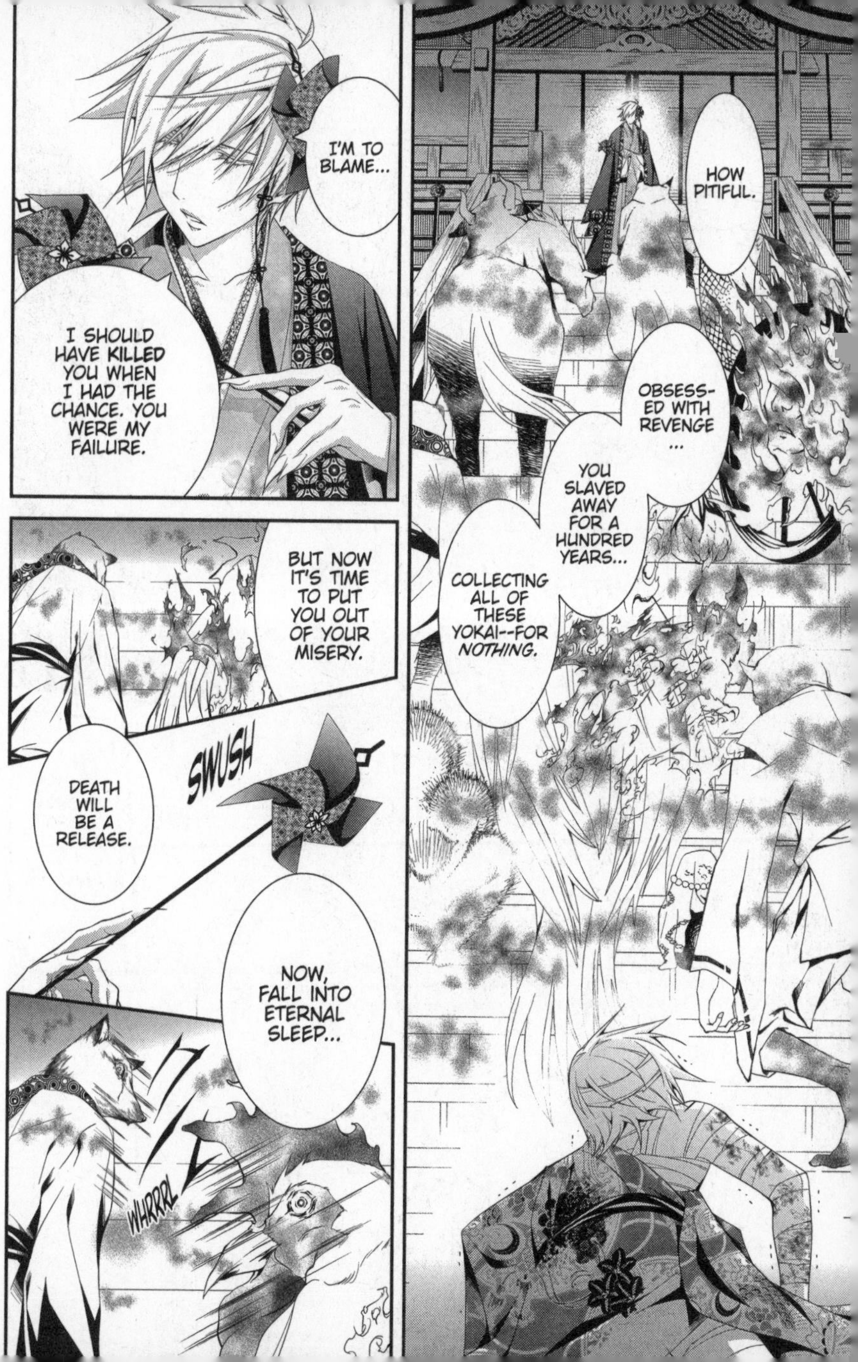
HOW PITIFUL.
OBSESS-ED WITH REVENGE ...
YOU SLAVED AWAY FOR A HUNDRED YEARS...
COLLECTING ALL OF THESE YOKAI--FOR *NOTHING*.
I'M TO BLAME...
I SHOULD HAVE KILLED YOU WHEN I HAD THE CHANCE. YOU WERE MY FAILURE.
BUT NOW IT'S TIME TO PUT YOU OUT OF YOUR MISERY.
SWUSH
DEATH WILL BE A RELEASE.
NOW, FALL INTO ETERNAL SLEEP...
WHRRRL

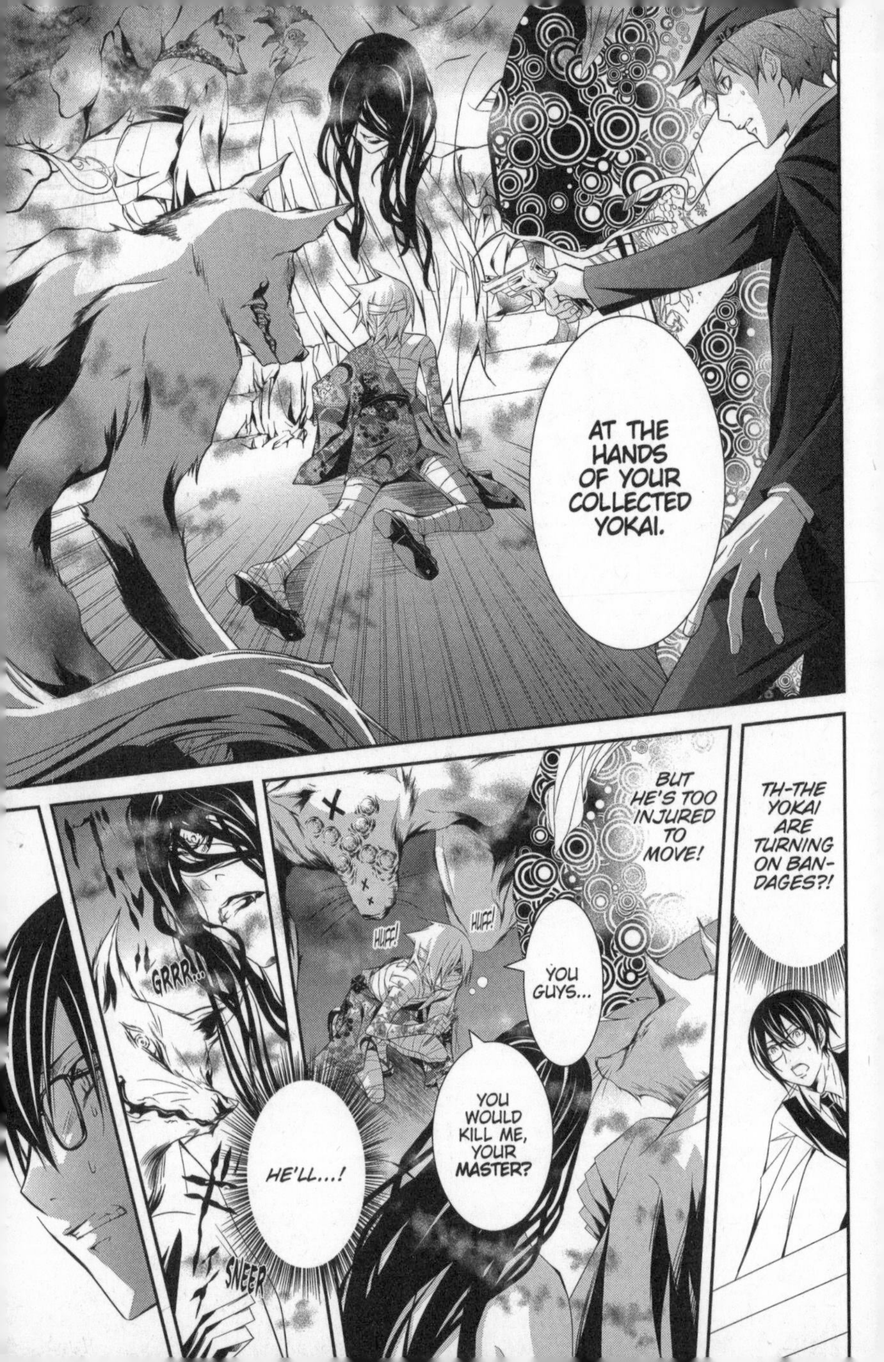
AT THE HANDS OF YOUR COLLECTED YOKAI.
TH-THE YOKAI ARE TURNING ON BAN-DAGES?!
BUT HE'S TOO INJURED TO MOVE!
HUFF!
HUFF!
YOU GUYS...
YOU WOULD KILL ME, YOUR MASTER?
GRRR...
HE'LL...!
SNEER

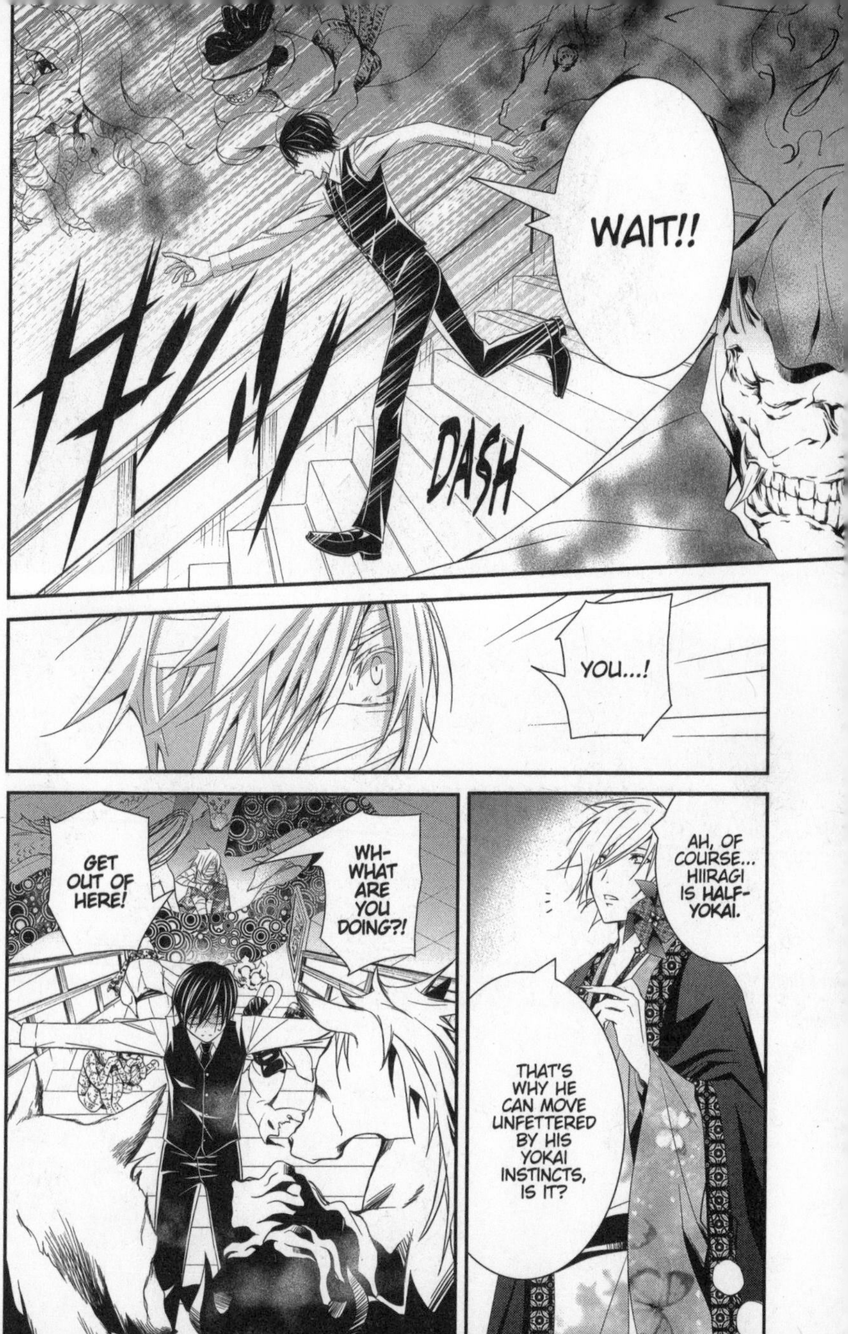
WAIT!!
DASH
YOU...!
AH, OF COURSE... HIIRAGI IS HALF-YOKAI.
THAT'S WHY HE CAN MOVE UNFETTERED BY HIS YOKAI INSTINCTS, IS IT?
WH-WHAT ARE YOU DOING?!
GET OUT OF HERE!

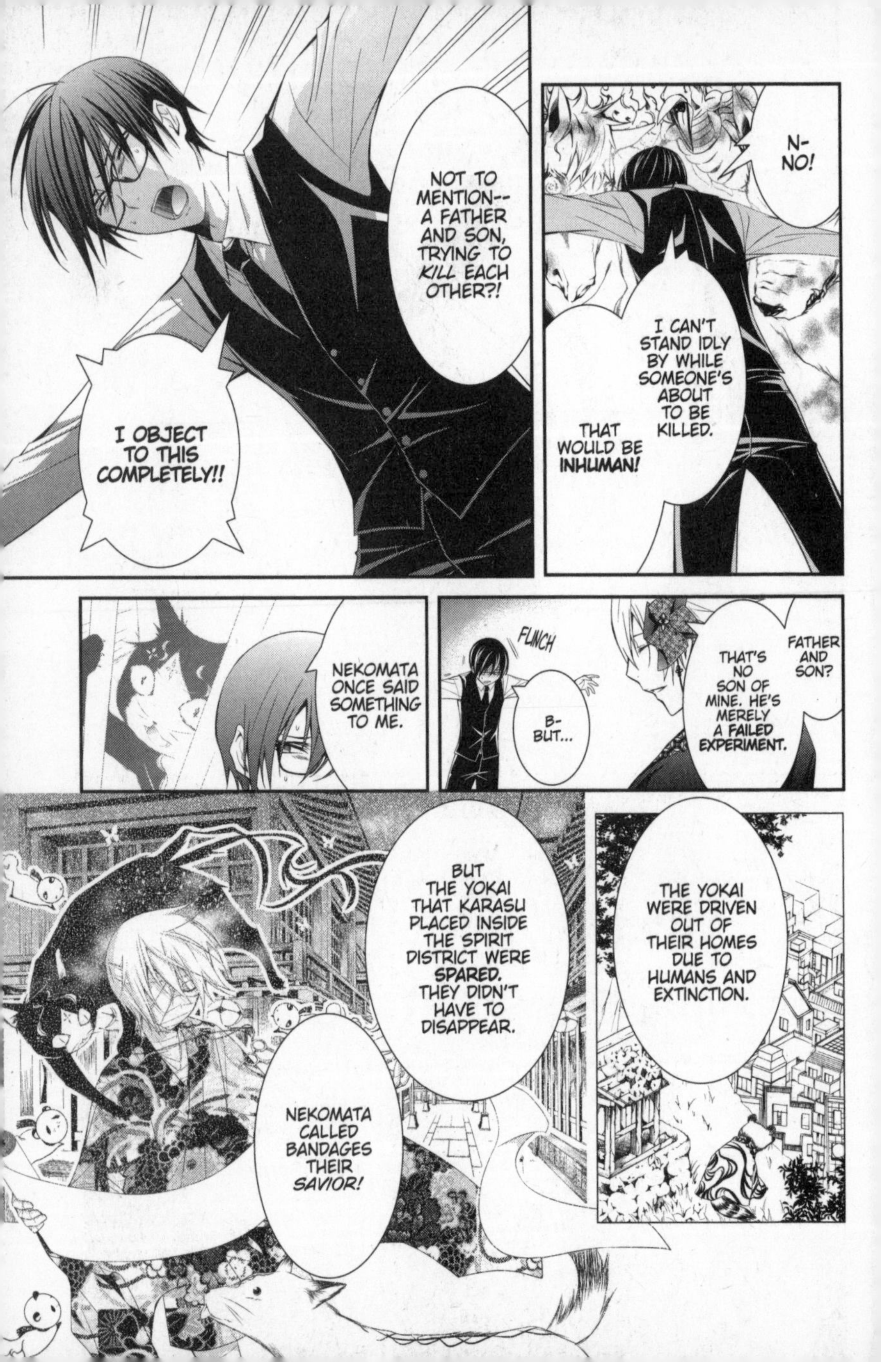
N-NO!
I CAN'T STAND IDLY BY WHILE SOMEONE'S ABOUT TO BE KILLED.
THAT WOULD BE INHUMAN!
NOT TO MENTION-- A FATHER AND SON, TRYING TO *KILL* EACH OTHER?!
I OBJECT TO THIS COMPLETELY!!
FATHER AND SON?
THAT'S NO SON OF MINE. HE'S MERELY A FAILED EXPERIMENT.
FLINCH
B-BUT...
NEKOMATA ONCE SAID SOMETHING TO ME.
THE YOKAI WERE DRIVEN OUT OF THEIR HOMES DUE TO HUMANS AND EXTINCTION.
BUT THE YOKAI THAT KARASU PLACED INSIDE THE SPIRIT DISTRICT WERE SPARED. THEY DIDN'T HAVE TO DISAPPEAR.
NEKOMATA CALLED BANDAGES THEIR *SAVIOR!*

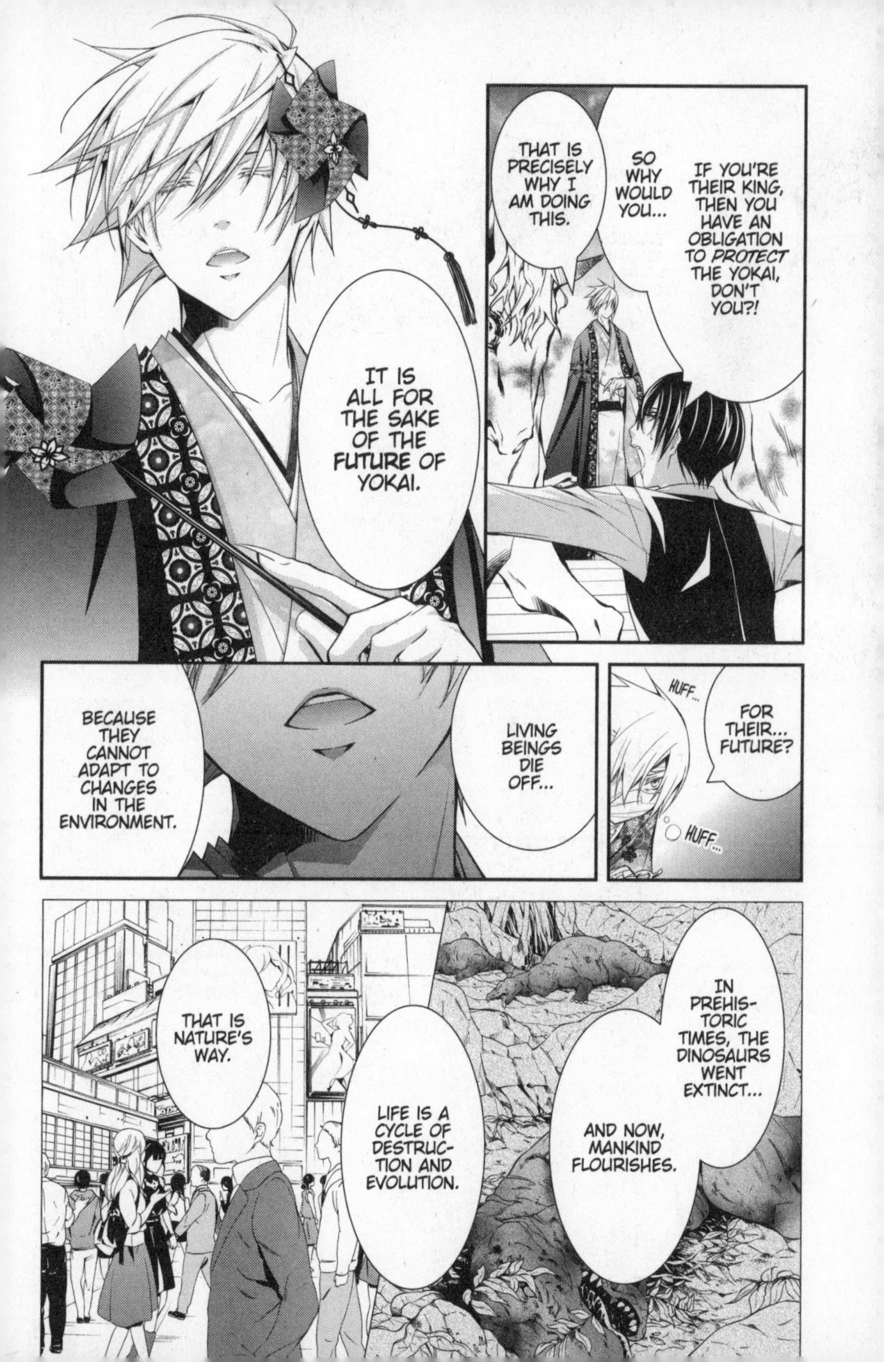
IF YOU'RE THEIR KING, THEN YOU HAVE AN OBLIGATION TO *PROTECT* THE YOKAI, DON'T YOU?!
SO WHY WOULD YOU...
THAT IS PRECISELY WHY I AM DOING THIS.
IT IS ALL FOR THE SAKE OF THE FUTURE OF YOKAI.
HUFF...
FOR THEIR... FUTURE?
HUFF...
LIVING BEINGS DIE OFF...
BECAUSE THEY CANNOT ADAPT TO CHANGES IN THE ENVIRONMENT.
IN PREHISTORIC TIMES, THE DINOSAURS WENT EXTINCT...
AND NOW, MANKIND FLOURISHES.
LIFE IS A CYCLE OF DESTRUCTION AND EVOLUTION.
THAT IS NATURE'S WAY.

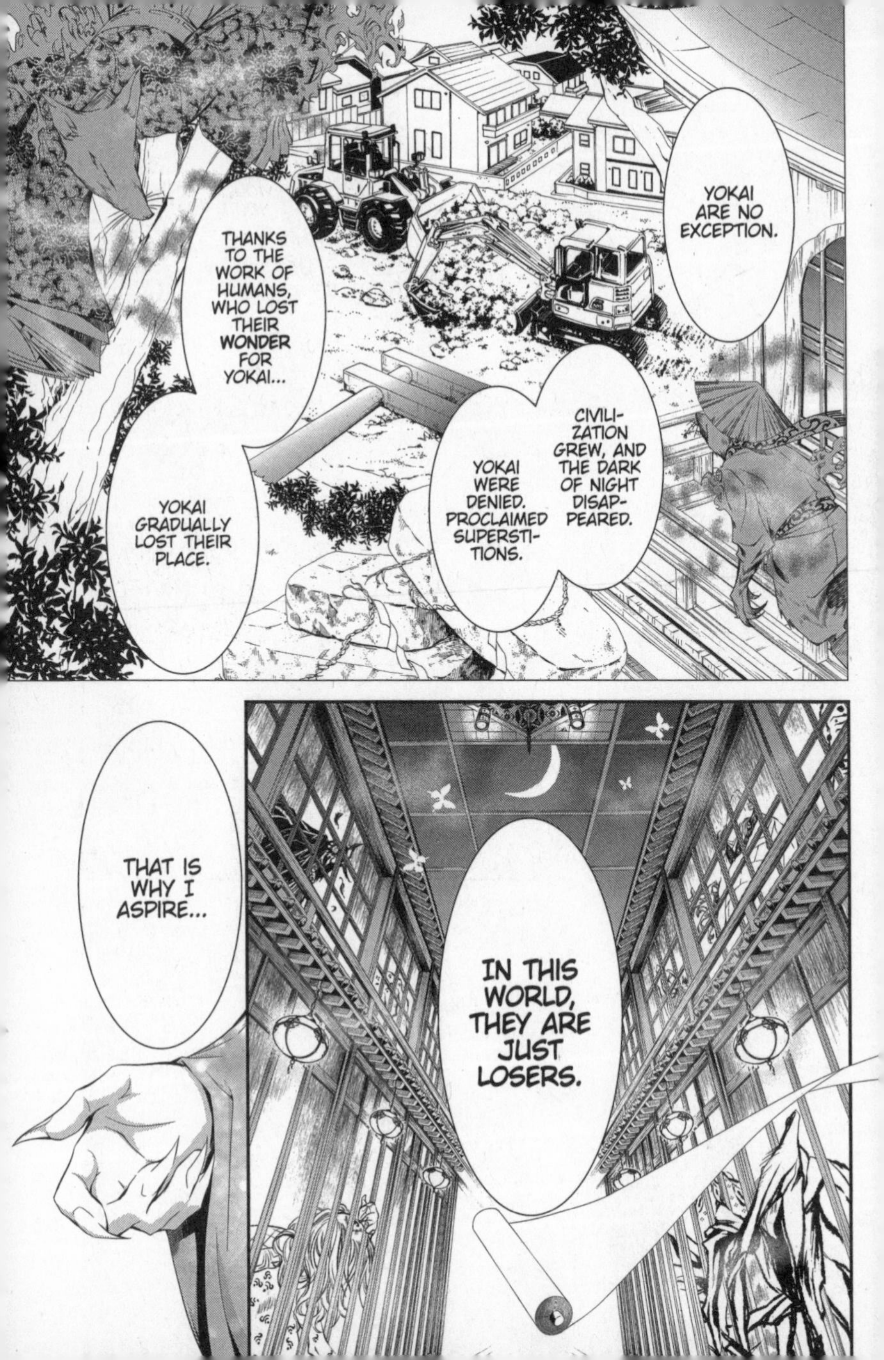
YOKAI ARE NO EXCEPTION.
CIVILIZATION GREW, AND THE DARK OF NIGHT DISAPPEARED.
YOKAI WERE DENIED. PROCLAIMED SUPERSTITIONS.
THANKS TO THE WORK OF HUMANS, WHO LOST THEIR WONDER FOR YOKAI...
YOKAI GRADUALLY LOST THEIR PLACE.
IN THIS WORLD, THEY ARE JUST LOSERS.
THAT IS WHY I ASPIRE...

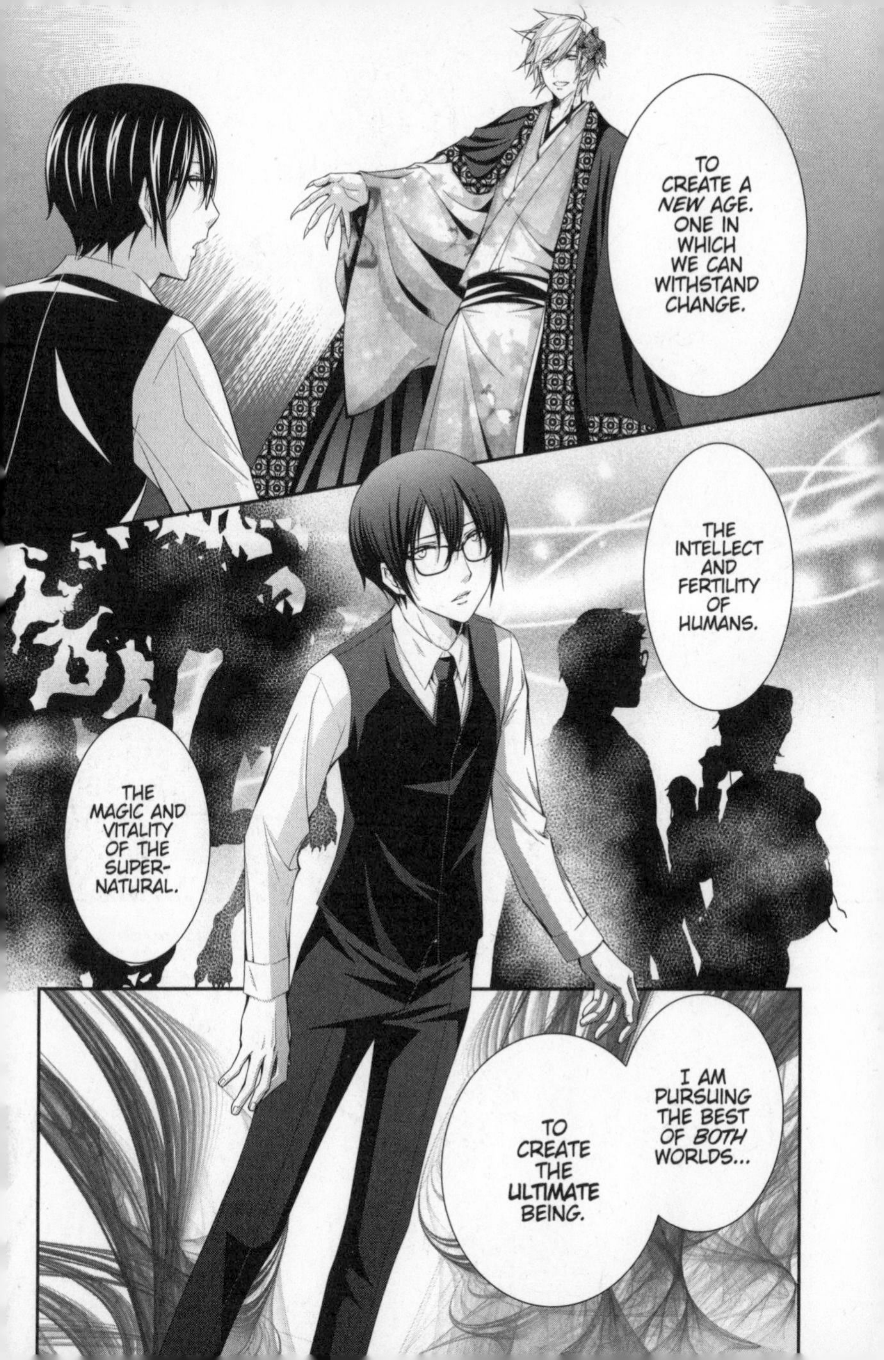
TO CREATE A *NEW AGE*. ONE IN WHICH WE CAN WITHSTAND CHANGE.
THE INTELLECT AND FERTILITY OF HUMANS.
THE MAGIC AND VITALITY OF THE SUPER-NATURAL.
I AM PURSUING THE BEST OF *BOTH* WORLDS...
TO CREATE THE ULTIMATE BEING.

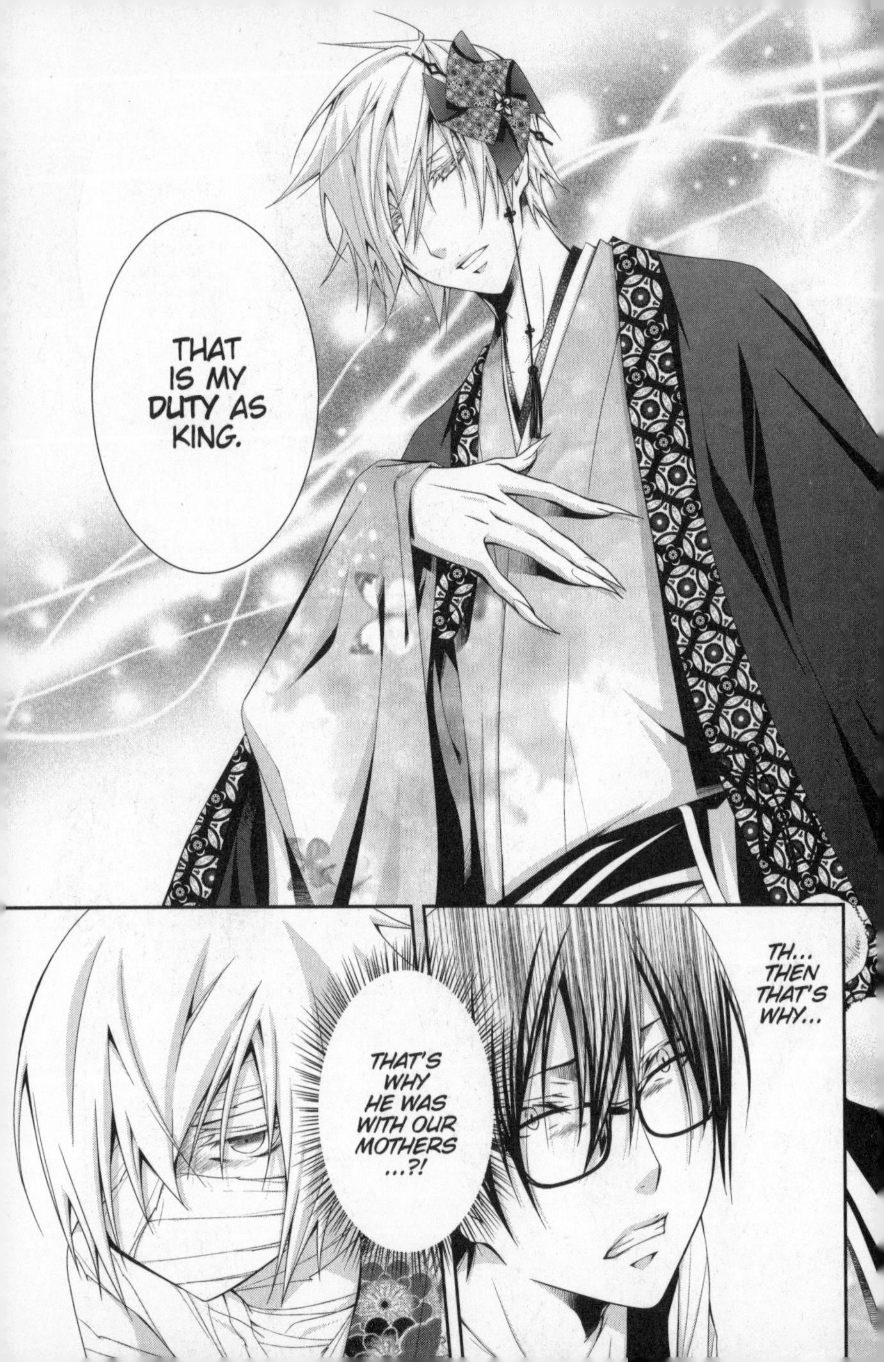
THAT IS MY DUTY AS KING.
TH... THEN THAT'S WHY...
THAT'S WHY HE WAS WITH OUR MOTHERS ...?!

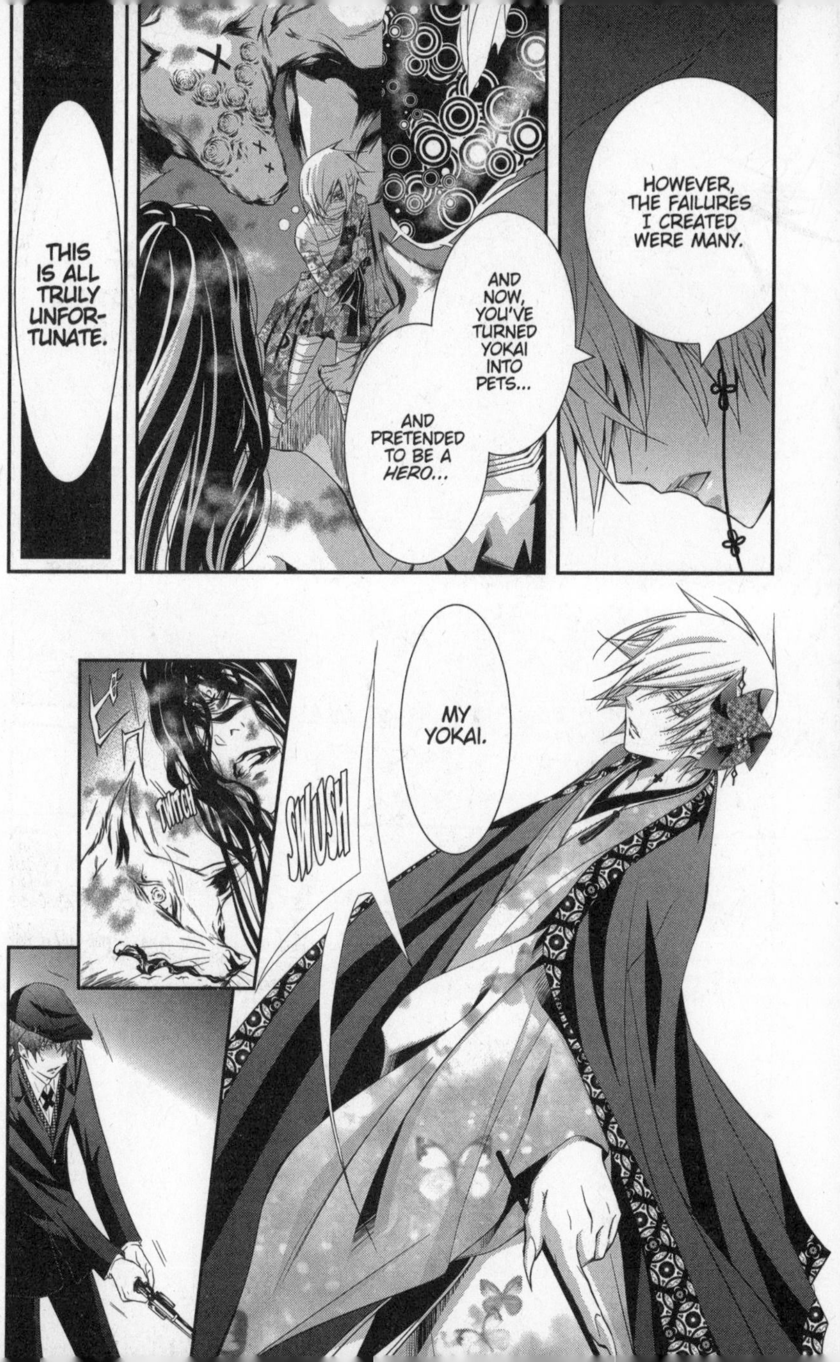
HOWEVER, THE FAILURES I CREATED WERE MANY.
AND NOW, YOU'VE TURNED YOKAI INTO PETS...
AND PRETENDED TO BE A *HERO*...
THIS IS ALL TRULY UNFOR-TUNATE.
MY YOKAI.
SWOSH
TWITCH

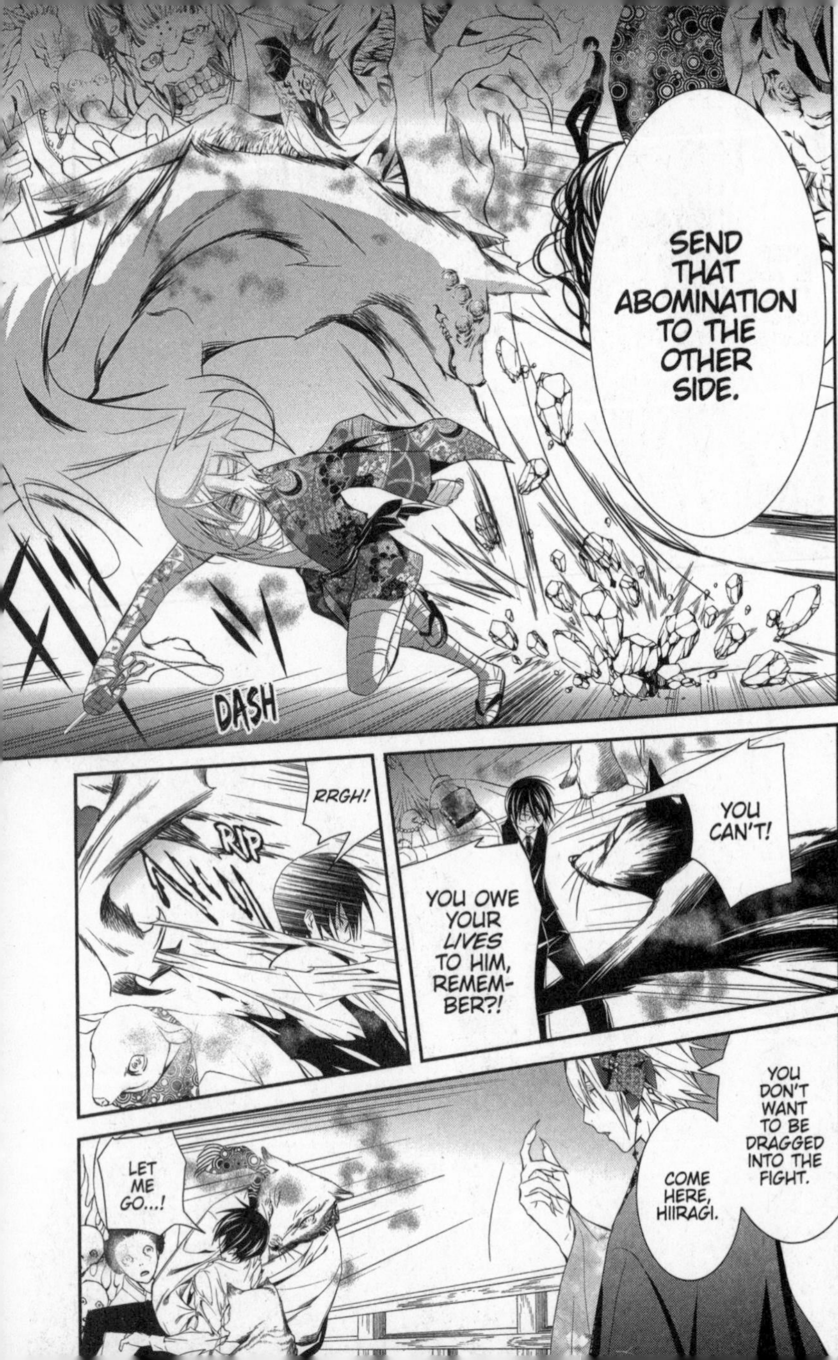
SEND THAT ABOMINATION TO THE OTHER SIDE.
DASH
YOU CAN'T!
YOU OWE YOUR *LIVES* TO HIM, REMEMBER?!
RRGH!
RIP
YOU DON'T WANT TO BE DRAGGED INTO THE FIGHT.
COME HERE, HIIRAGI.
LET ME GO...!

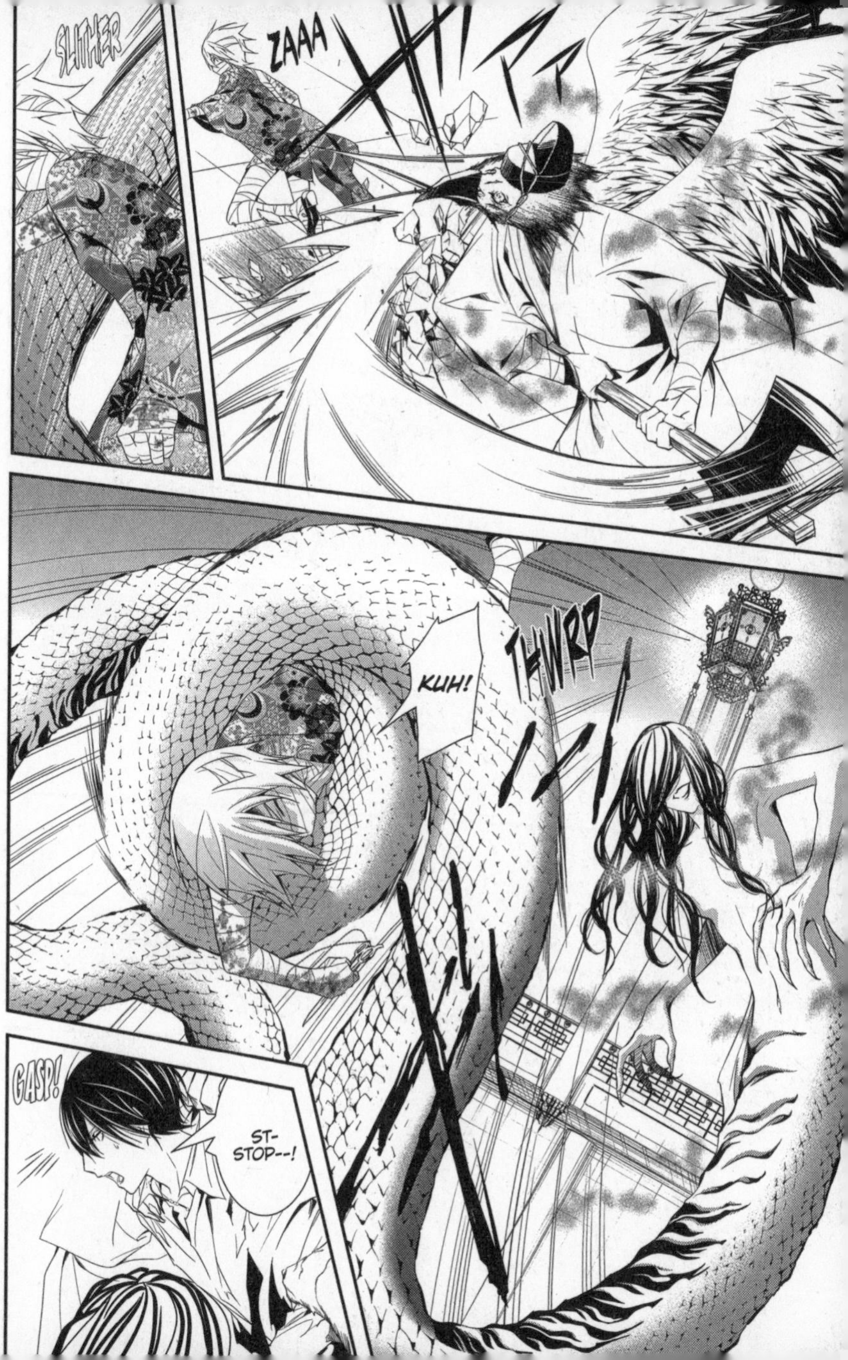
ZAAA
SLITHER
THWRP
KUH!
GASP!
ST-
STOP--!

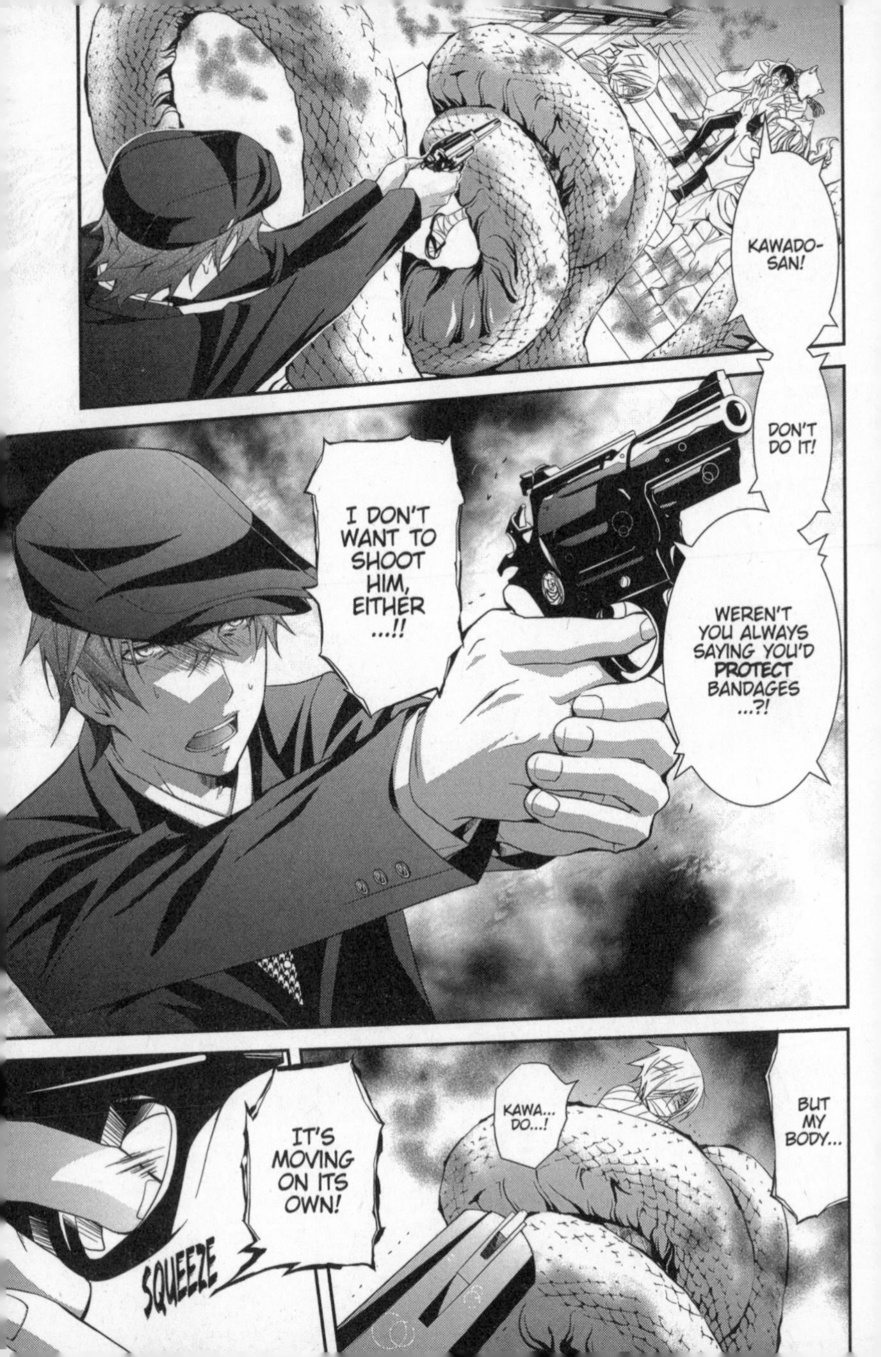
KAWADO-SAN!
DON'T DO IT!
WEREN'T YOU ALWAYS SAYING YOU'D PROTECT BANDAGES ...?!
I DON'T WANT TO SHOOT HIM, EITHER ...!!
BUT MY BODY...
KAWA... DO...!
IT'S MOVING ON ITS OWN!
SQUEEZE

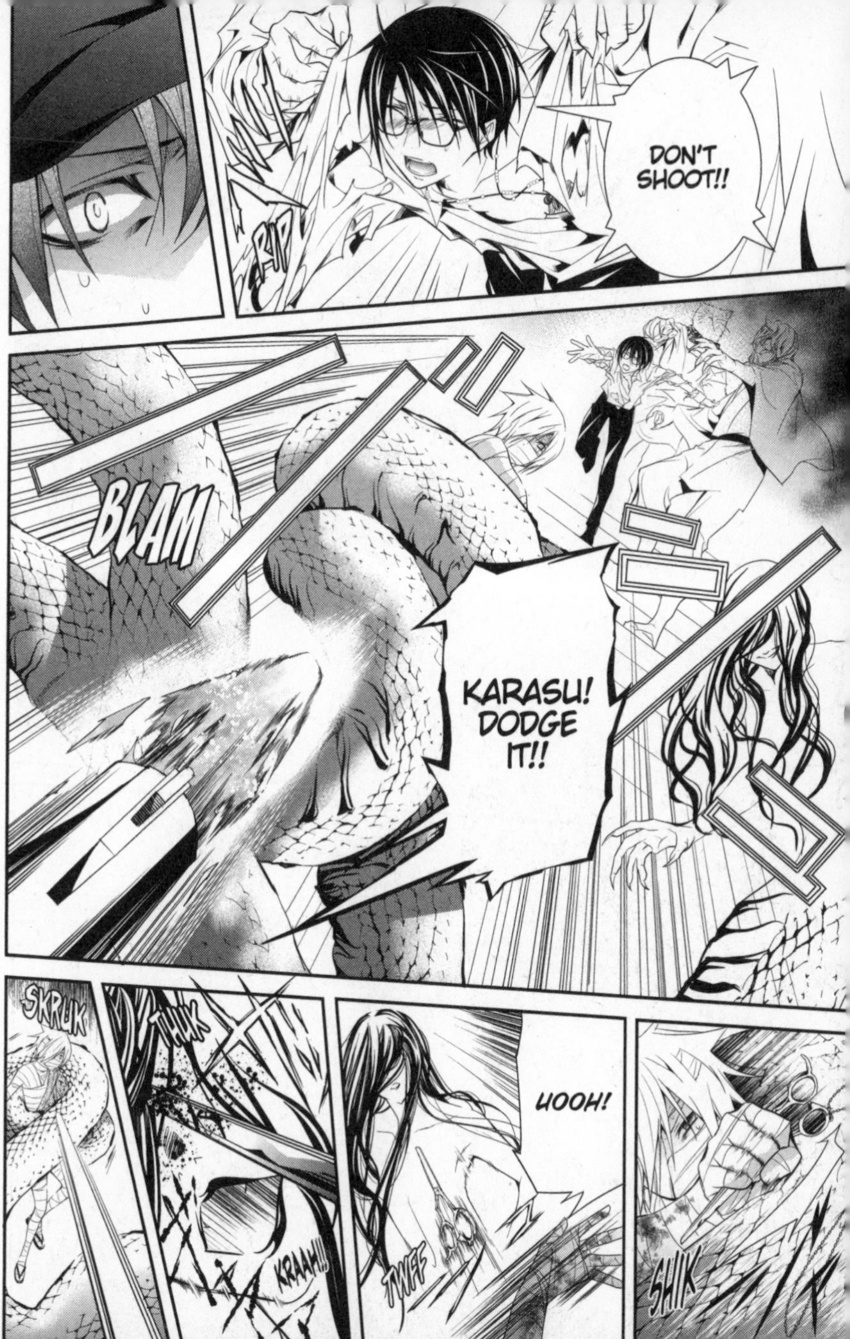
DON'T SHOOT!!
RIP
KARASU! DODGE IT!!
BLAM
SHIK
UOOH!
TWFF
THUK
KRAAH!!
SKRUK

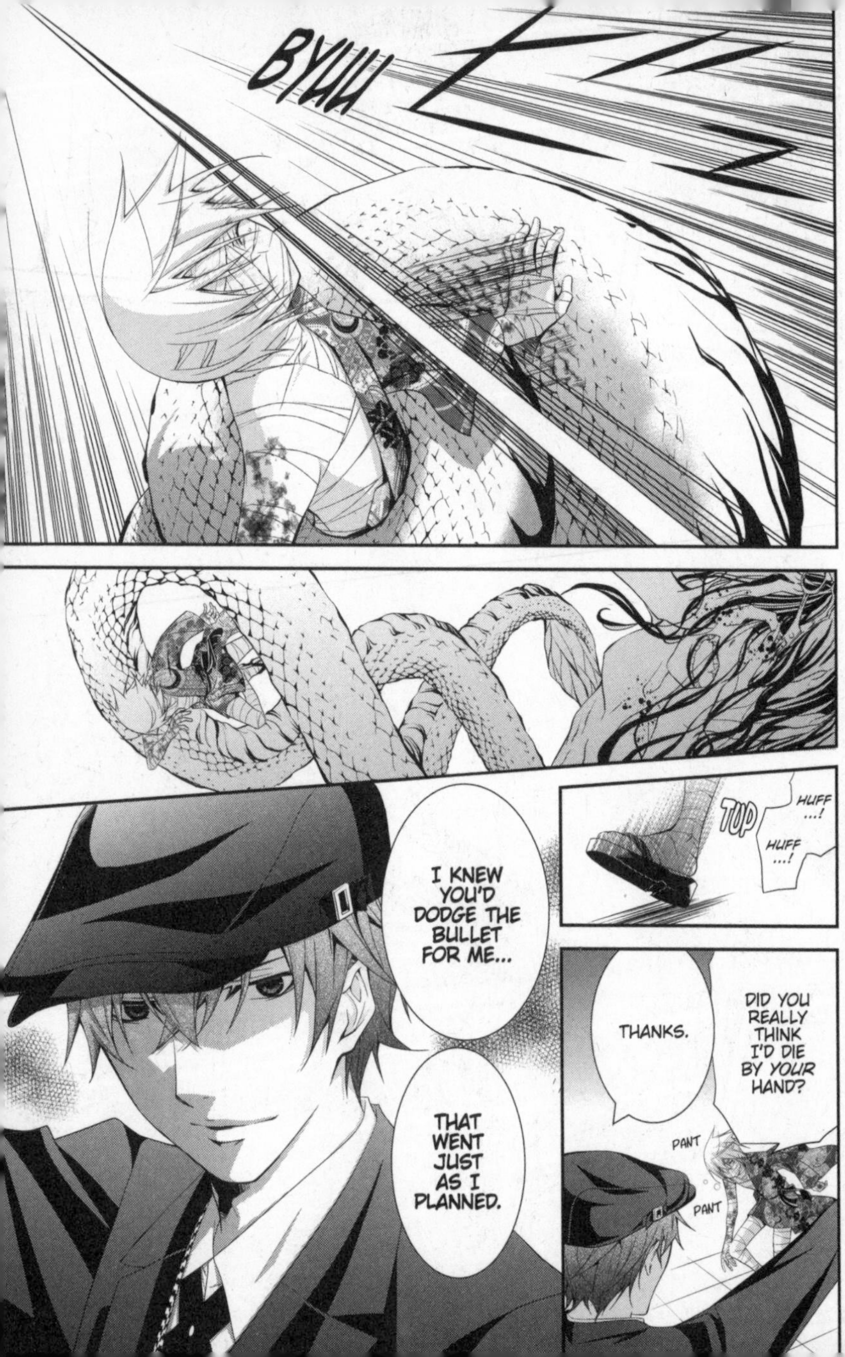
BYUU
TUP
HUFF...!
HUFF...!
DID YOU REALLY THINK I'D DIE BY YOUR HAND?
THANKS.
PANT
PANT
I KNEW YOU'D DODGE THE BULLET FOR ME...
THAT WENT JUST AS I PLANNED.

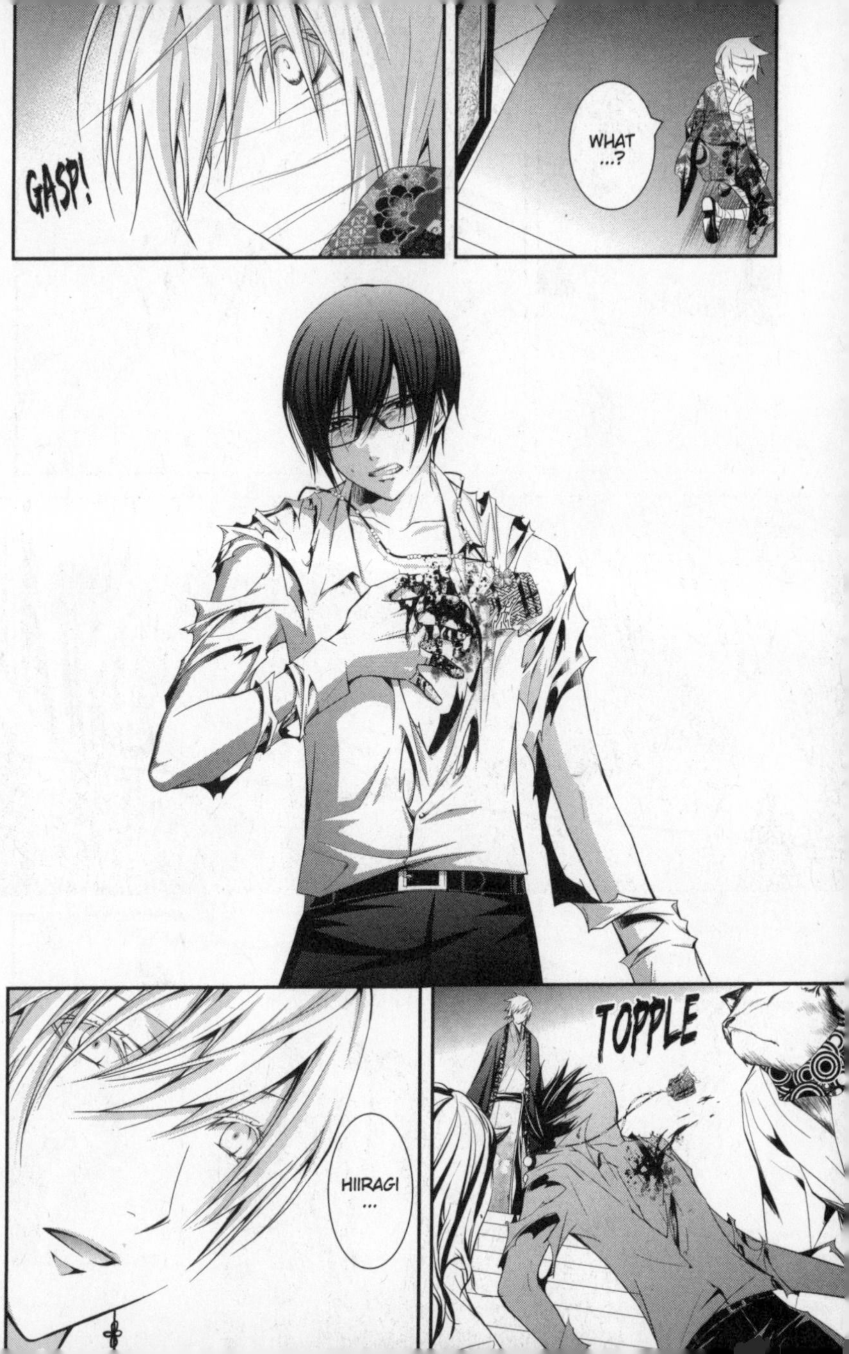
WHAT ...?
GASP!
TOPPLE
HIIRAGI ...

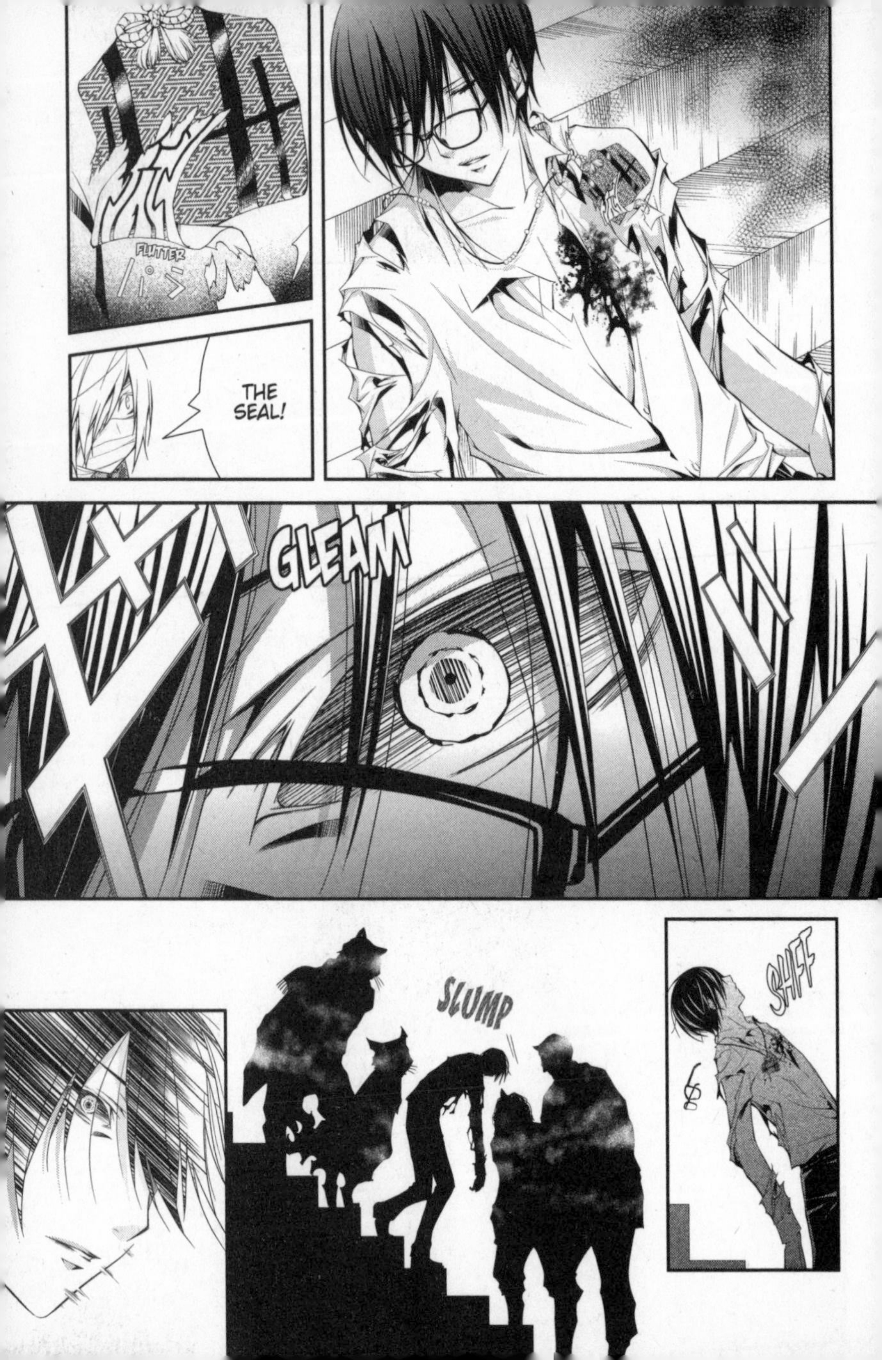
FLUTTER
THE SEAL!
GLEAM
SHFF
SLUMP

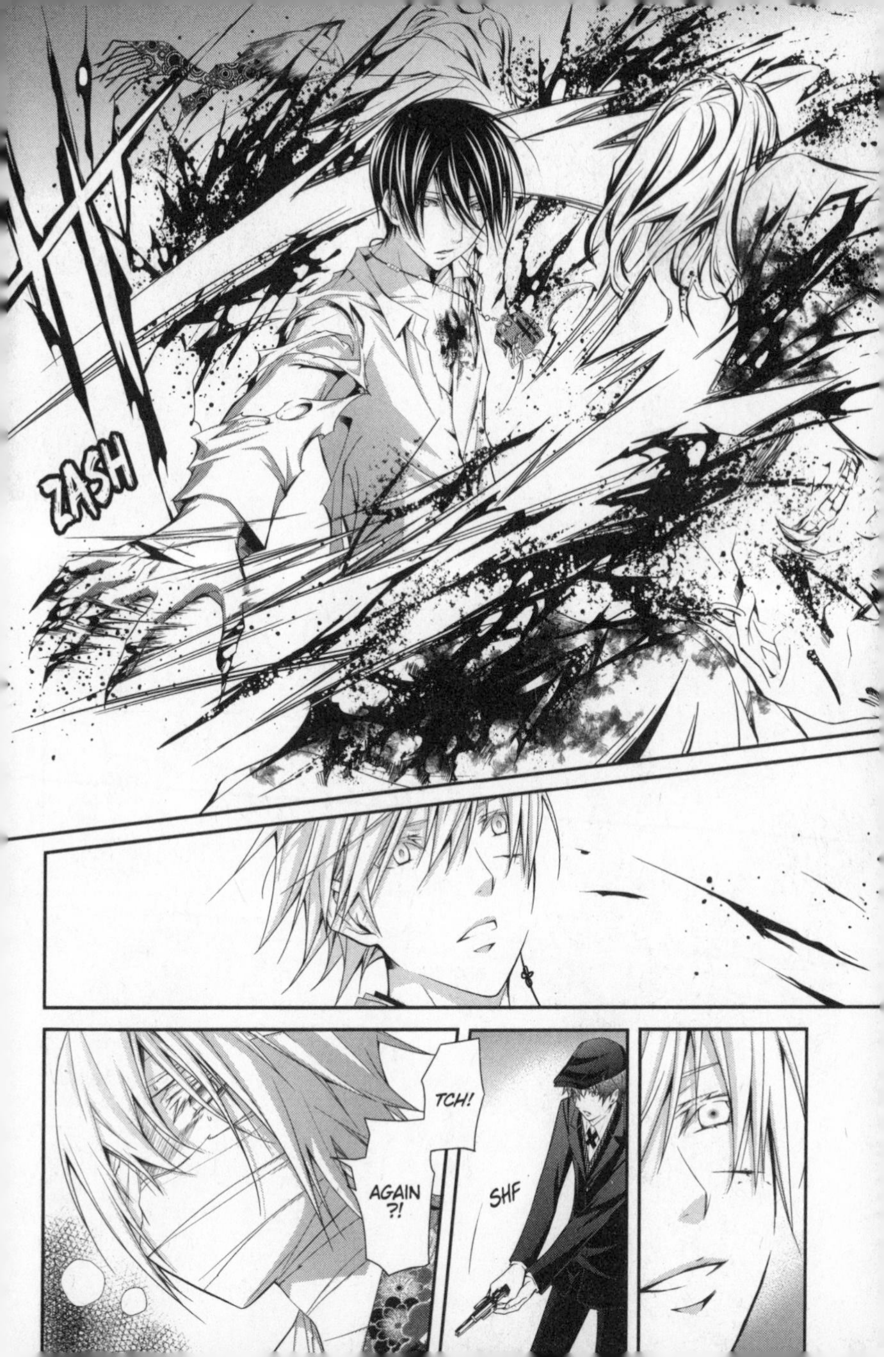
ZASH
TCH!
SHF
AGAIN ?!

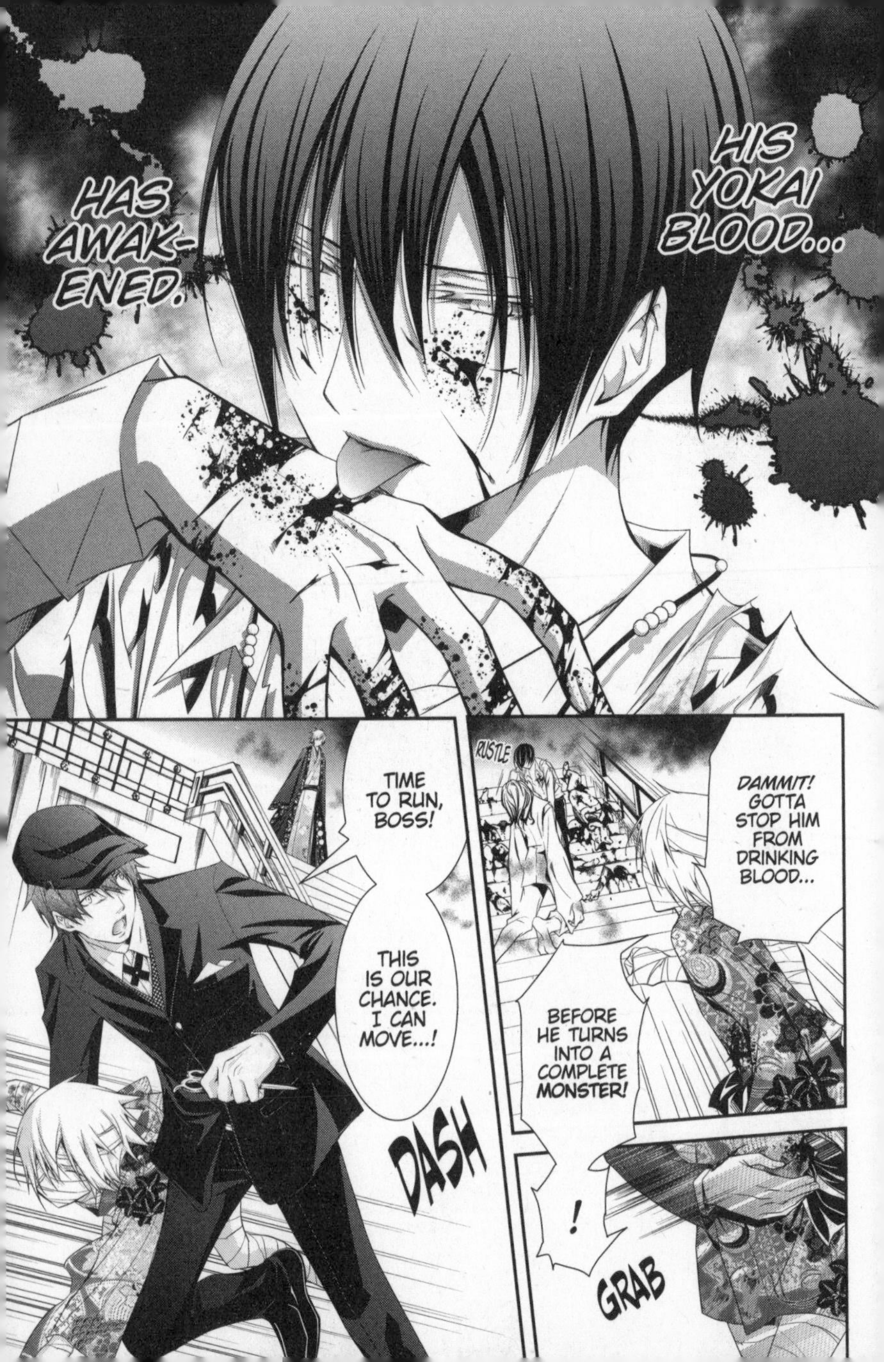
HIS YOKAI BLOOD...
HAS AWAK-ENED.
RUSTLE
DAMMIT! GOTTA STOP HIM FROM DRINKING BLOOD...
BEFORE HE TURNS INTO A COMPLETE MONSTER!
!
GRAB
TIME TO RUN, BOSS!
THIS IS OUR CHANCE. I CAN MOVE...!
DASH

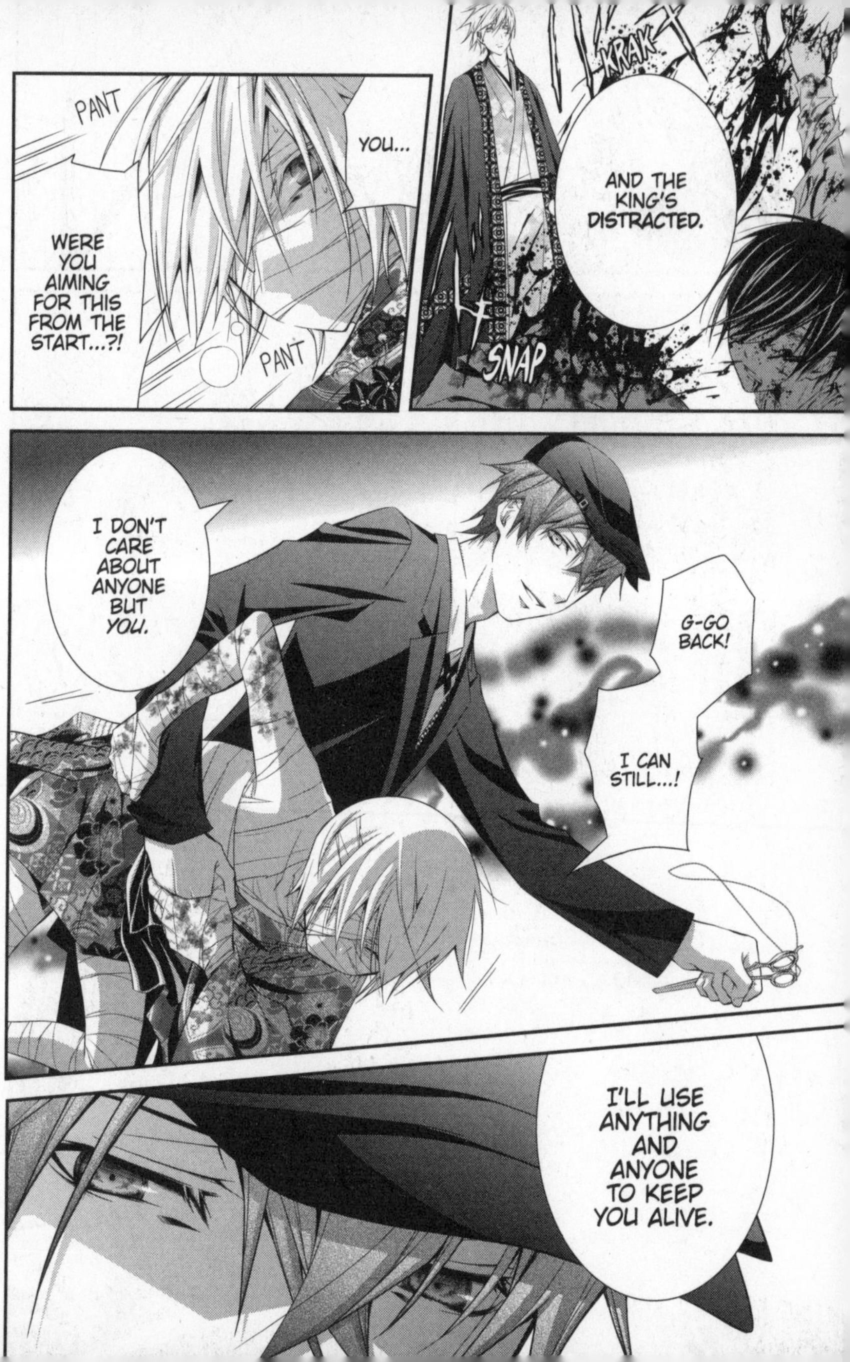
KRAK
AND THE KING'S DISTRACTED.
SNAP
PANT
YOU...
WERE YOU AIMING FOR THIS FROM THE START...?!
PANT
G-GO BACK!
I CAN STILL...!
I DON'T CARE ABOUT ANYONE BUT *YOU.*
I'LL USE ANYTHING AND ANYONE TO KEEP YOU ALIVE.

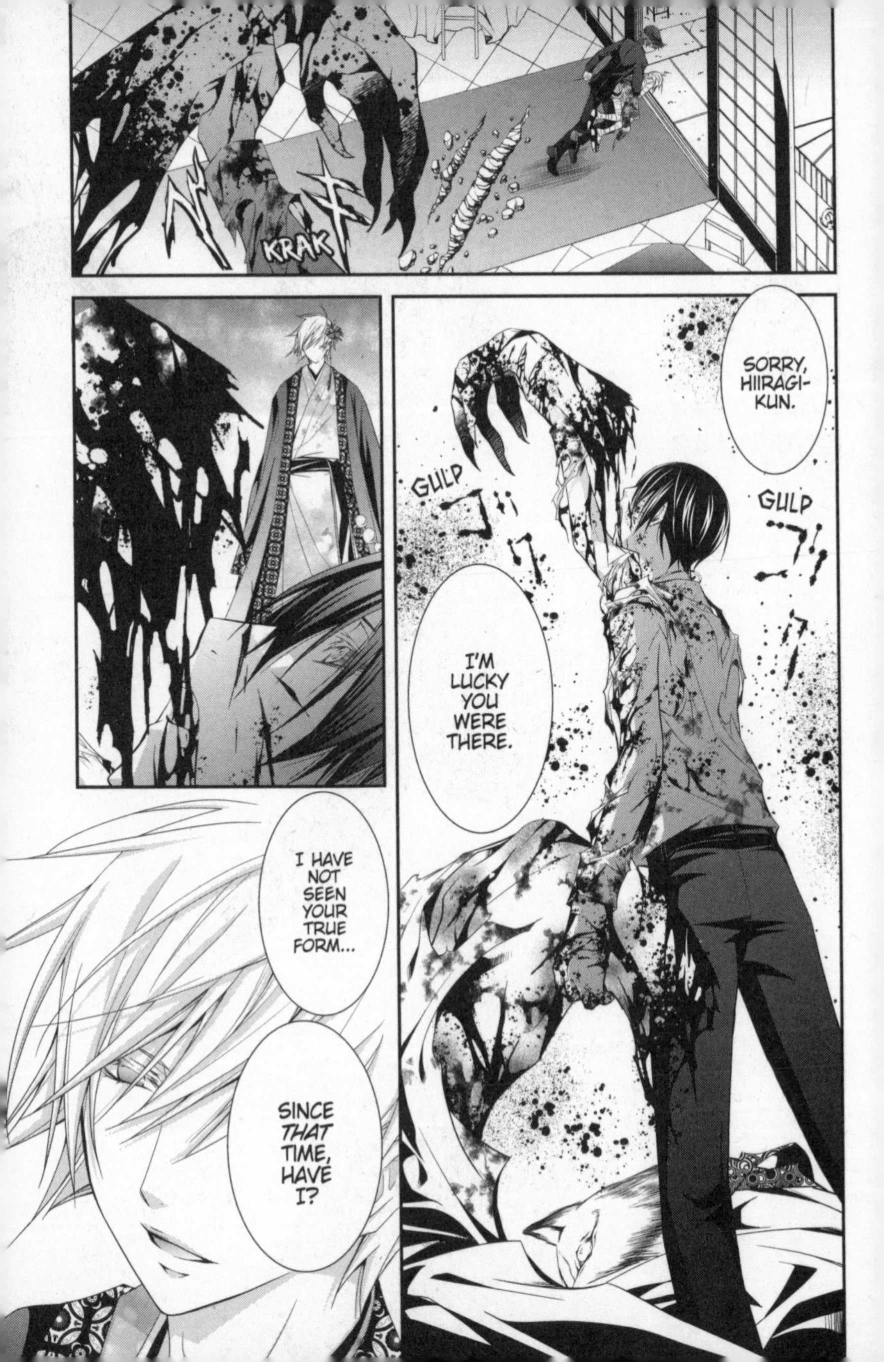
KRAK
SORRY, HIIRAGI-KUN.
GULP
GULP
I'M LUCKY YOU WERE THERE.
I HAVE NOT SEEN YOUR TRUE FORM...
SINCE *THAT* TIME, HAVE I?

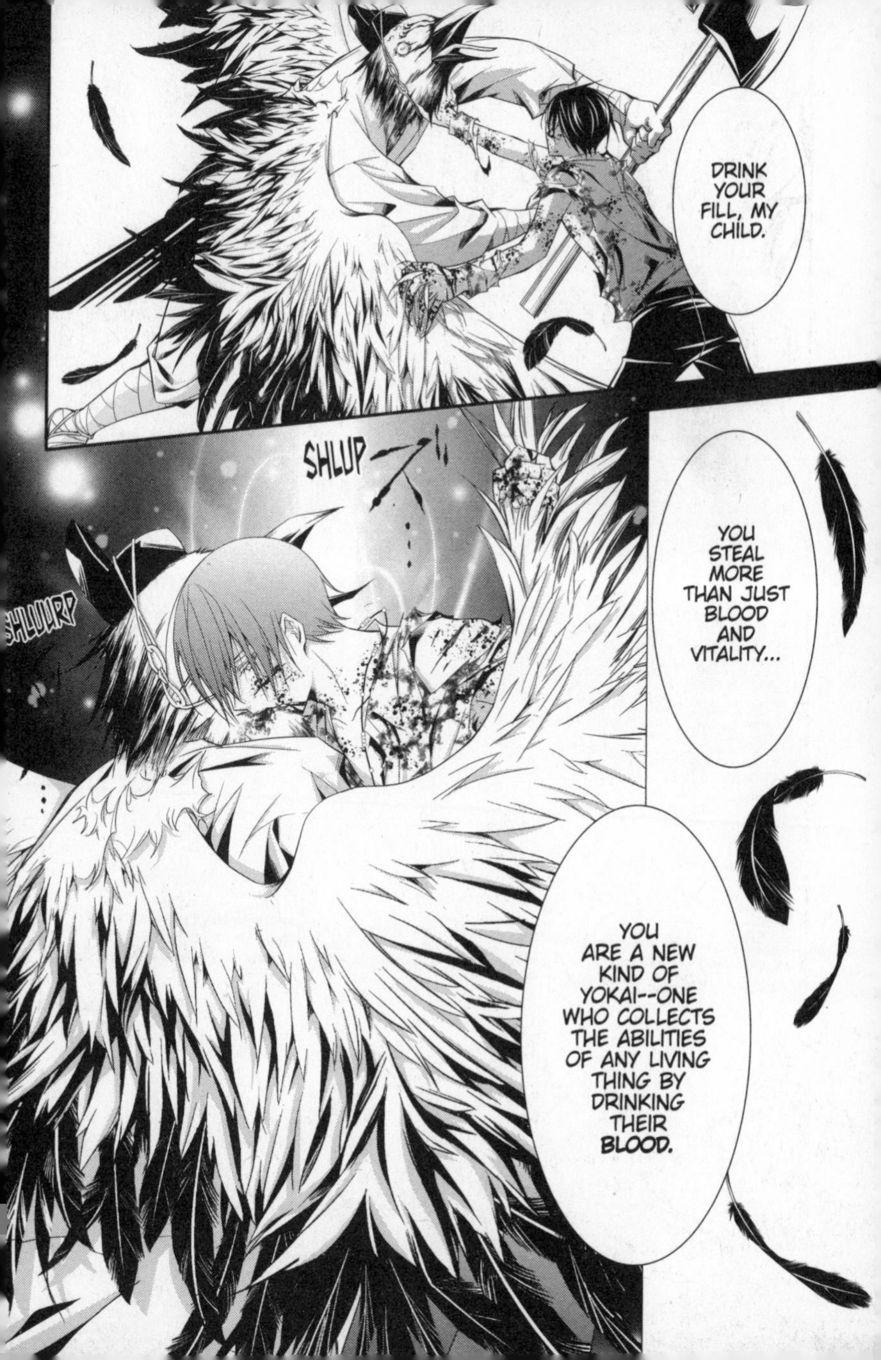
DRINK YOUR FILL, MY CHILD.
YOU STEAL MORE THAN JUST BLOOD AND VITALITY...
SHLUP
SHLUURP
YOU ARE A NEW KIND OF YOKAI--ONE WHO COLLECTS THE ABILITIES OF ANY LIVING THING BY DRINKING THEIR BLOOD.

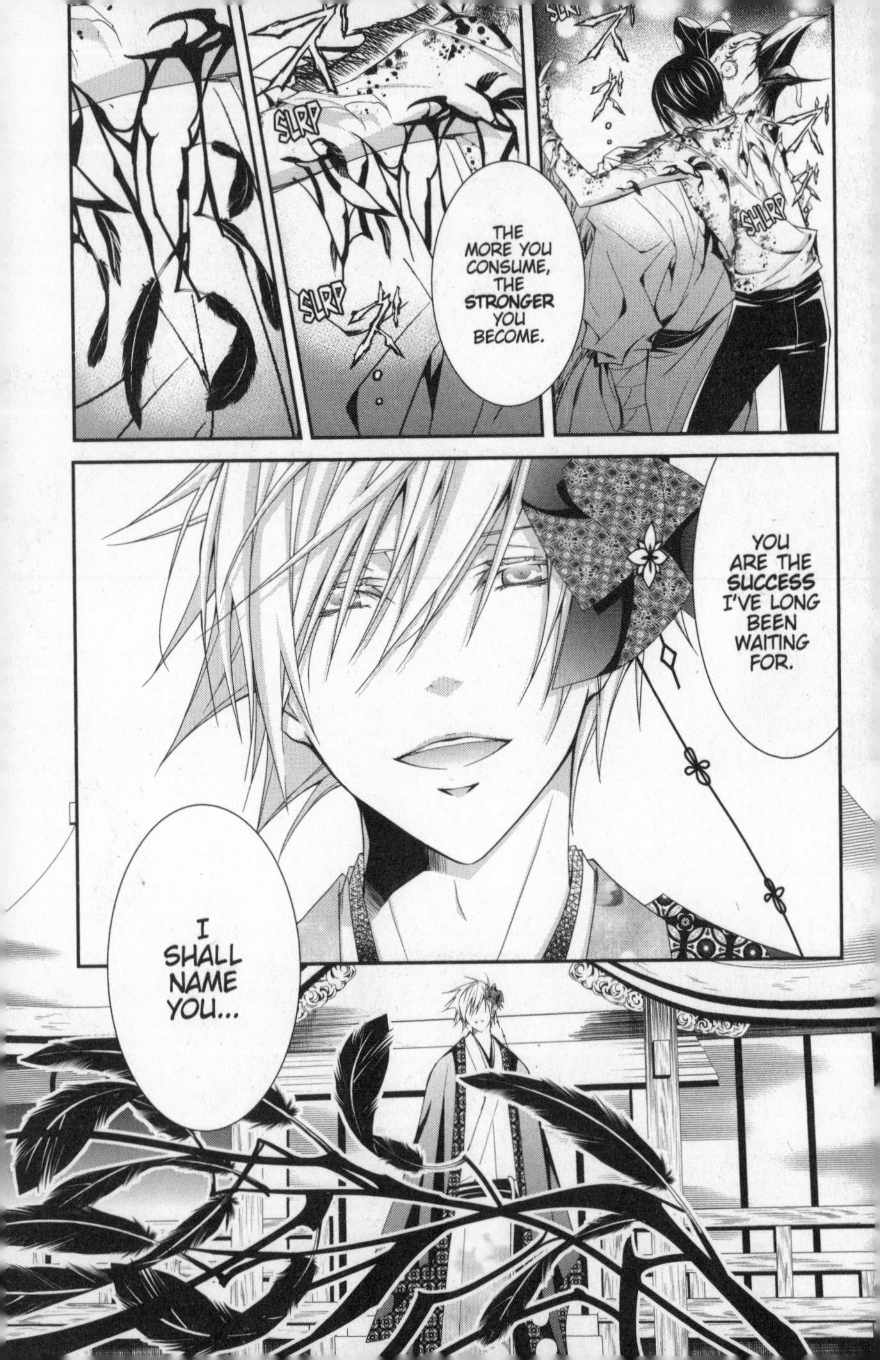
SHLRP
SLRP
THE MORE YOU CONSUME, THE STRONGER YOU BECOME.
SLRP
YOU ARE THE SUCCESS I'VE LONG BEEN WAITING FOR.
I SHALL NAME YOU...

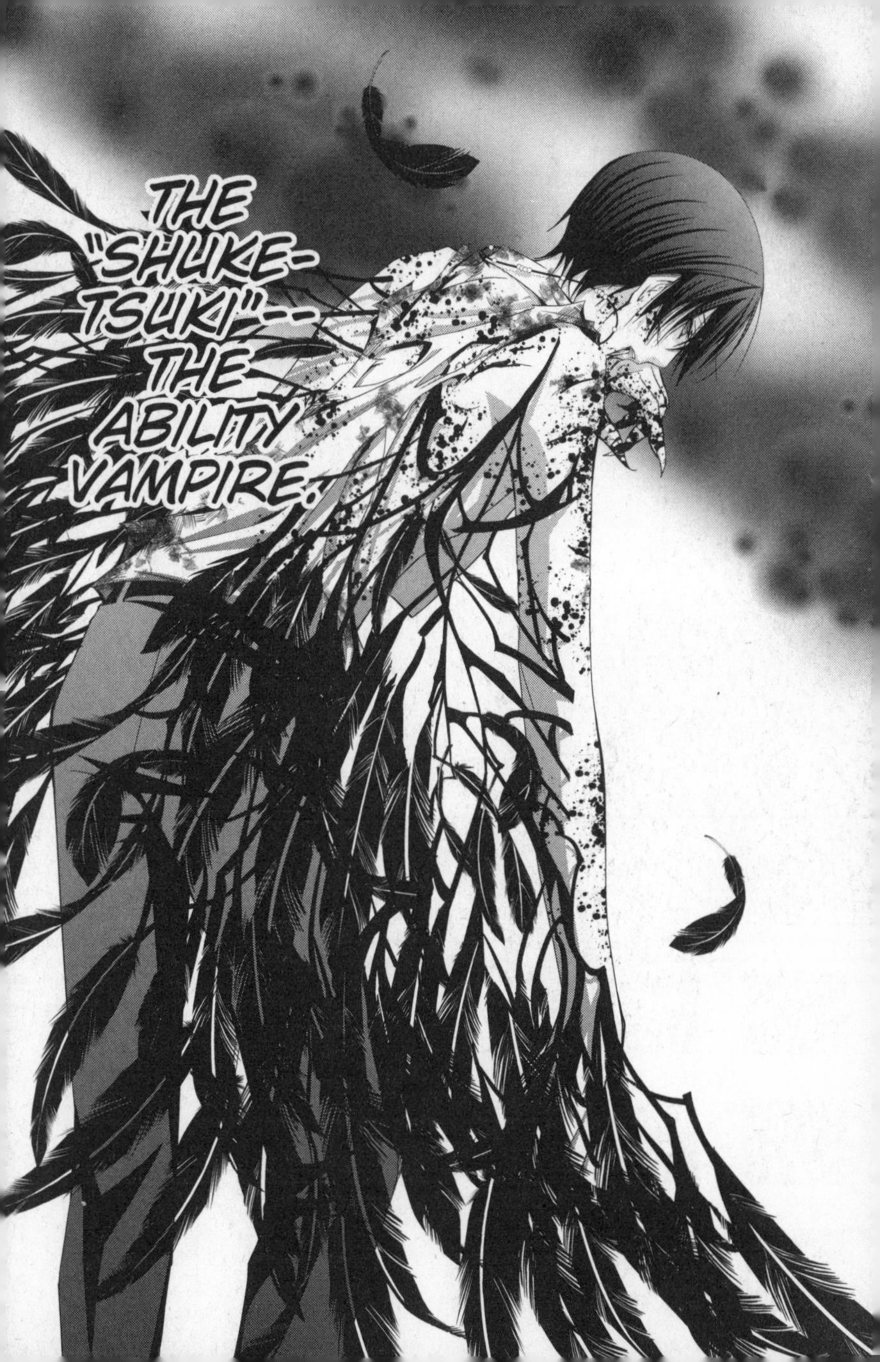
THE "SHUKE-TSUKI"-- THE ABILITY VAMPIRE.

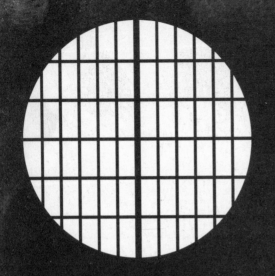

Yōkai Rental Shop

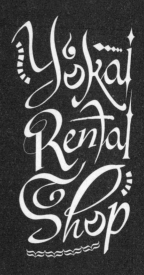

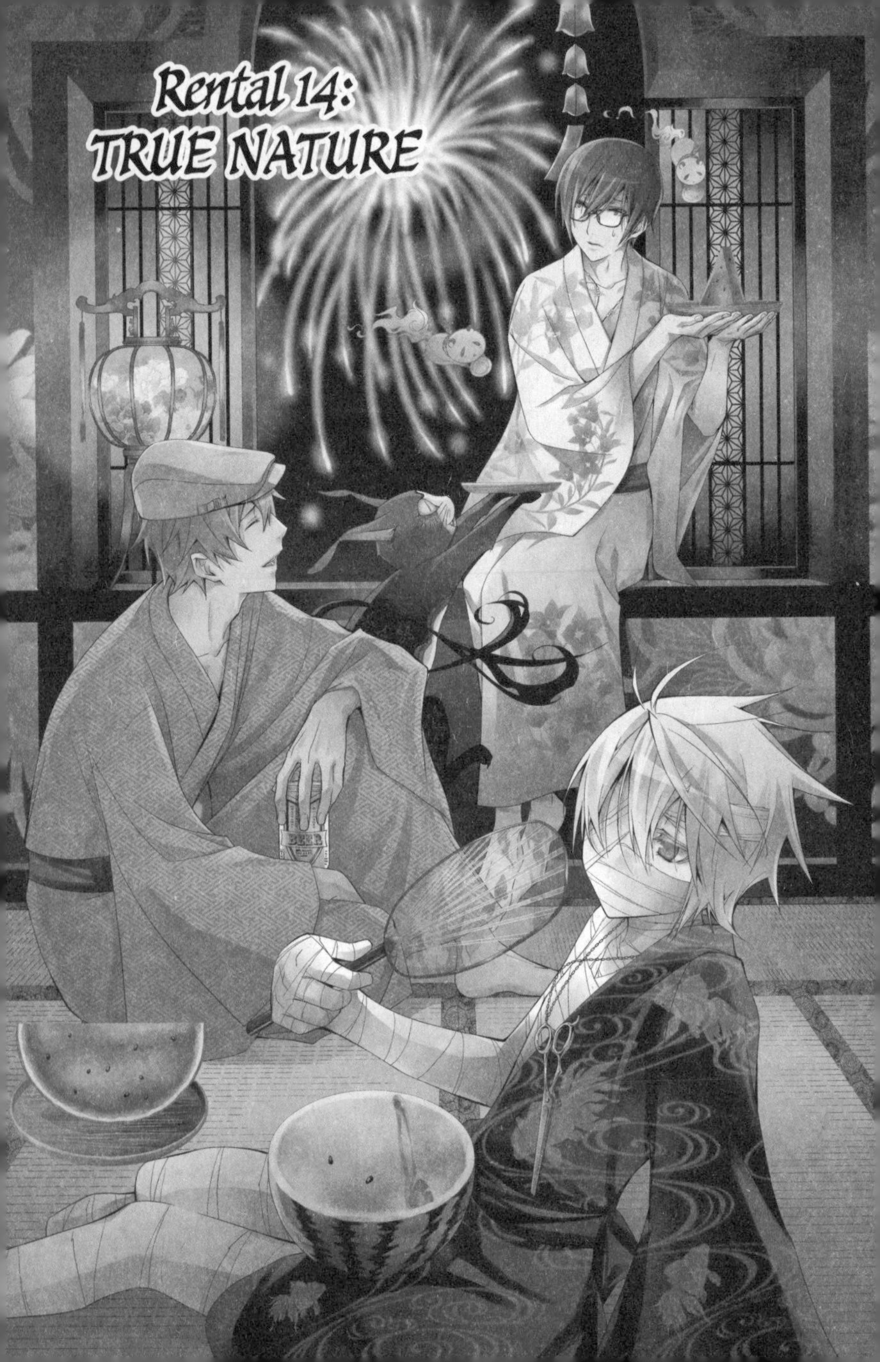
Rental 14:
TRUE NATURE
BEER

Yōkai Rental Shop

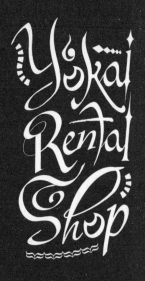

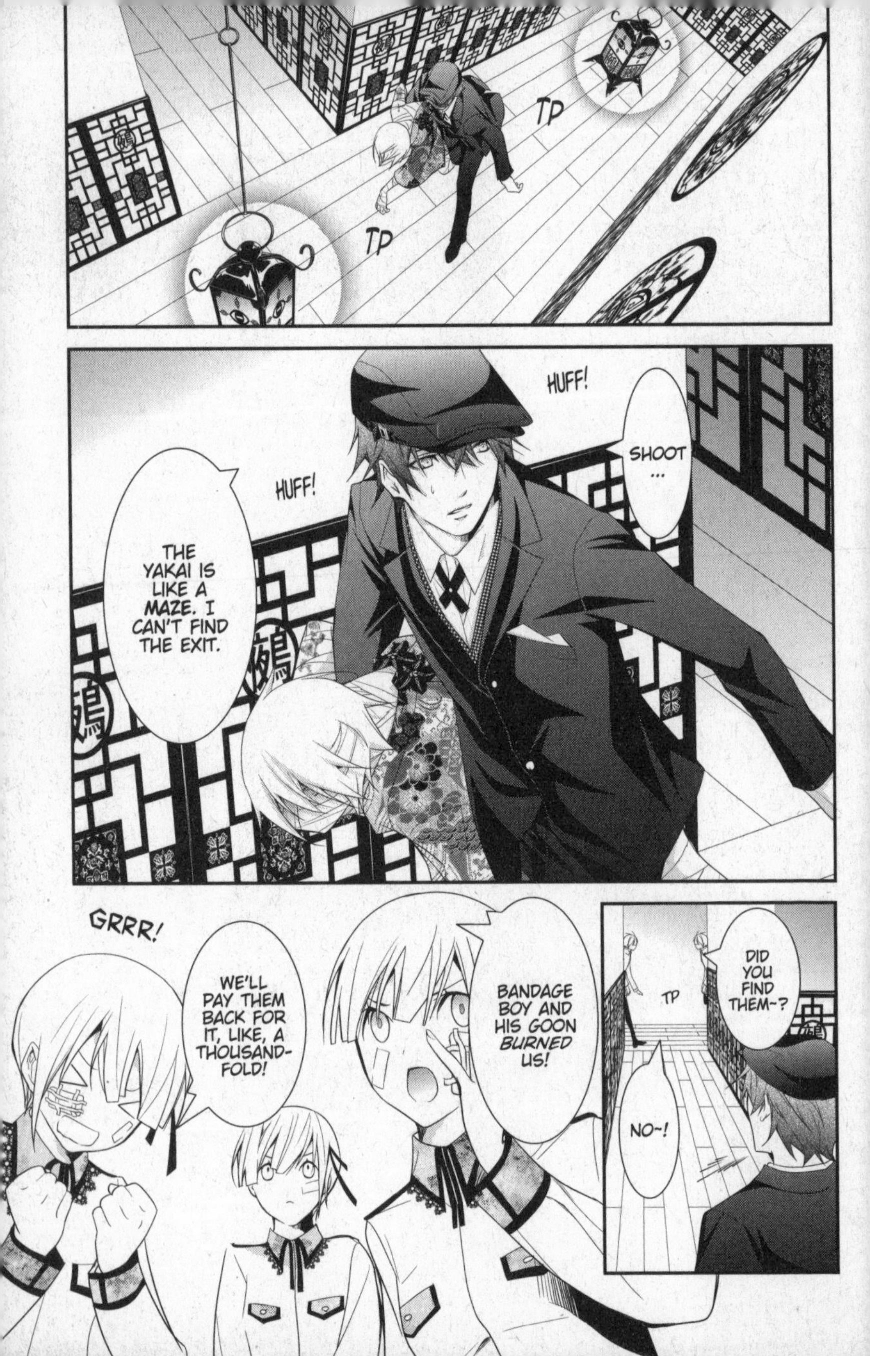
TP
TP
HUFF!
SHOOT ...
HUFF!
THE YAKAI IS LIKE A MAZE. I CAN'T FIND THE EXIT.
DID YOU FIND THEM~?
TP
NO~!
BANDAGE BOY AND HIS GOON *BURNED* US!
WE'LL PAY THEM BACK FOR IT, LIKE, A THOUSAND-FOLD!
GRRR!

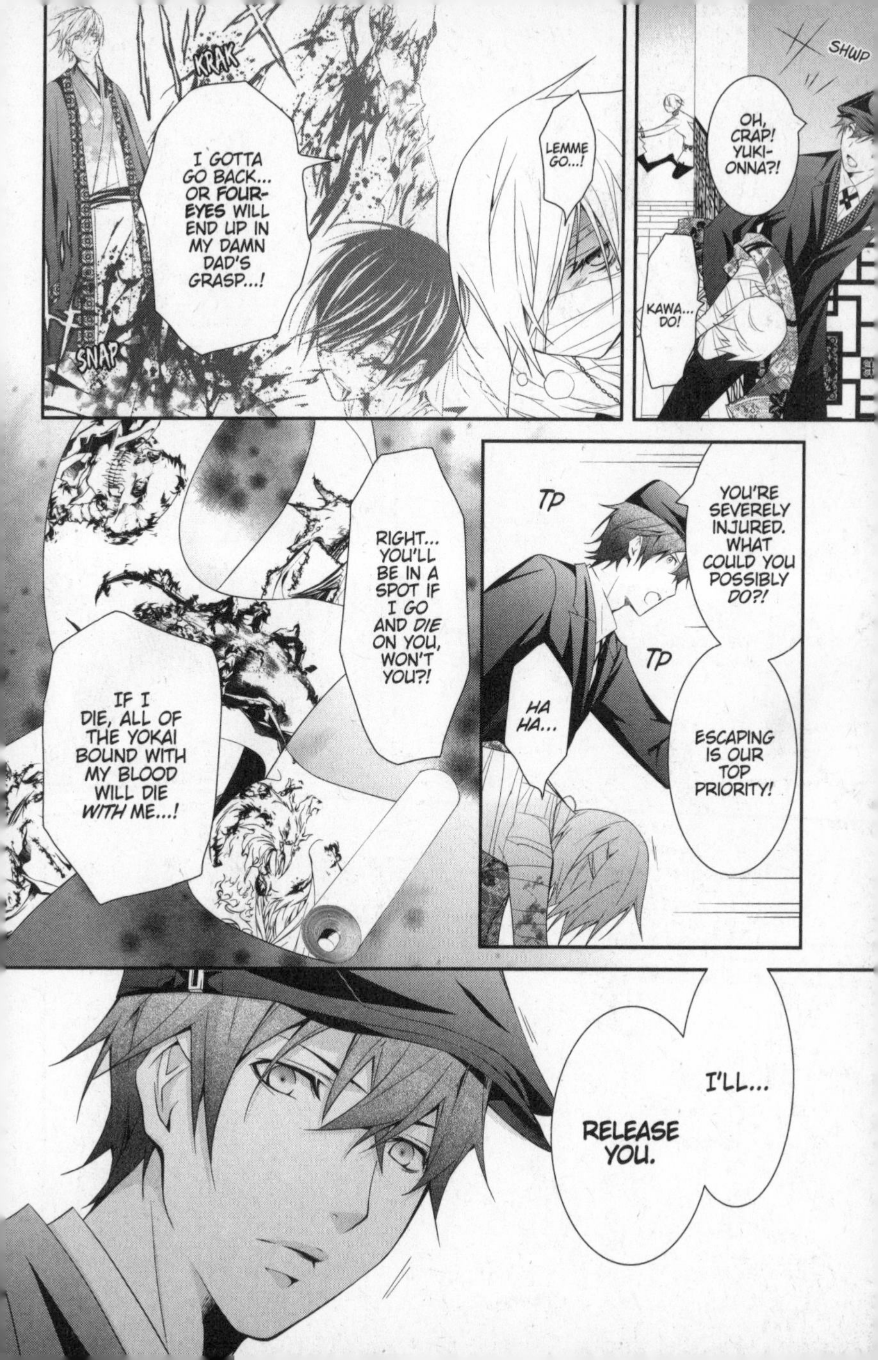
SHWP
OH, CRAP! YUKI-ONNA?!
KAWA... DO!
LEMME GO...!
KRAK
I GOTTA GO BACK... OR FOUR-EYES WILL END UP IN MY DAMN DAD'S GRASP...!
SNAP
TP
YOU'RE SEVERELY INJURED. WHAT COULD YOU POSSIBLY *DO*?!
TP
ESCAPING IS OUR TOP PRIORITY!
HA HA...
RIGHT... YOU'LL BE IN A SPOT IF I GO AND *DIE* ON YOU, WON'T YOU?!
IF I DIE, ALL OF THE YOKAI BOUND WITH MY BLOOD WILL DIE *WITH* ME...!
I'LL...
RELEASE YOU.

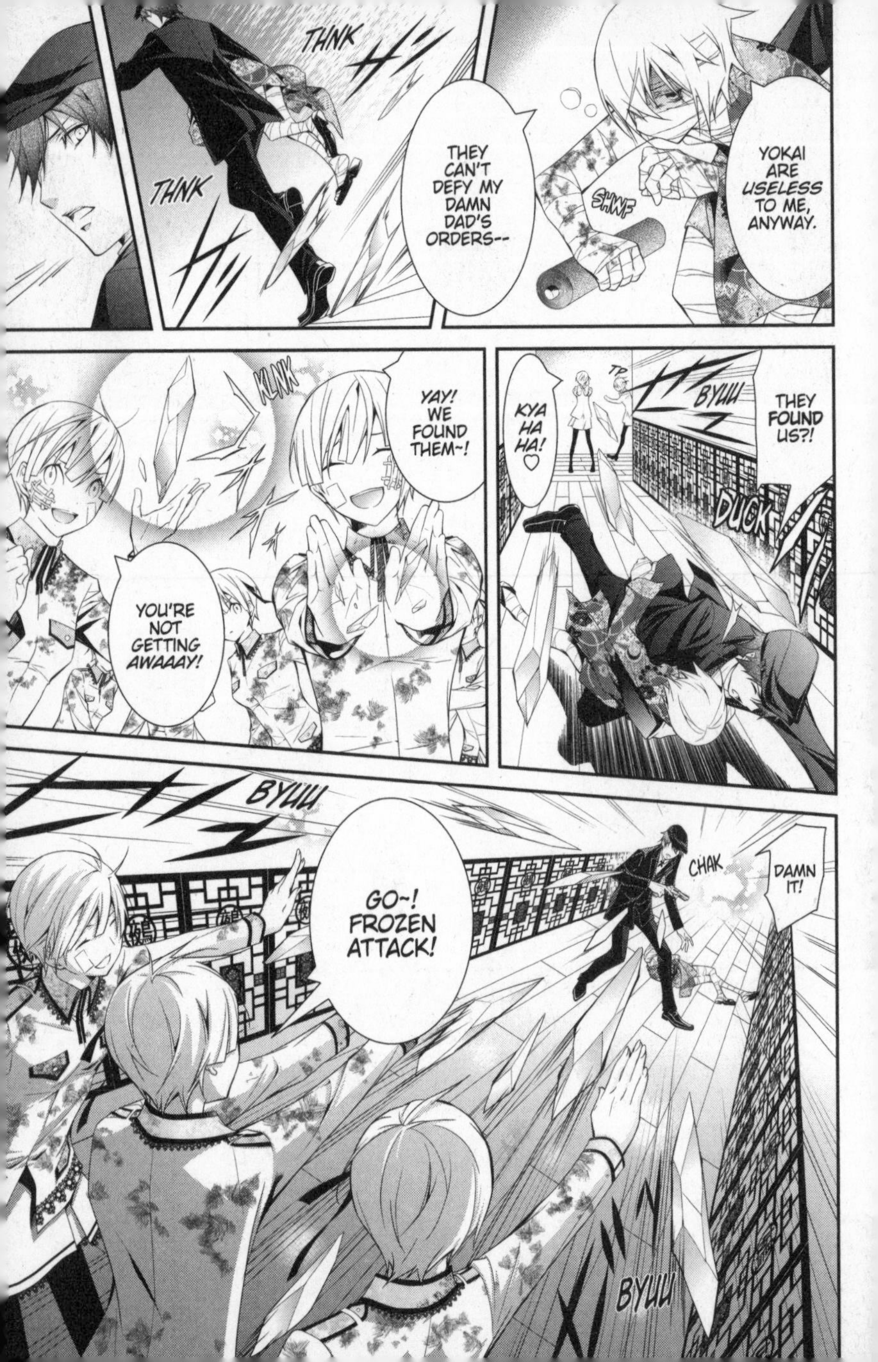
YOKAI ARE USELESS TO ME, ANYWAY.
SHWF
THEY CAN'T DEFY MY DAMN DAD'S ORDERS--
THNK
THNK
THEY FOUND US?!
BYUU
TP
KYA HA HA! ♡
DUCK
YAY! WE FOUND THEM~!
KLNK
YOU'RE NOT GETTING AWAAAY!
DAMN IT!
CHAK
GO~! FROZEN ATTACK!
BYUU
BYUU

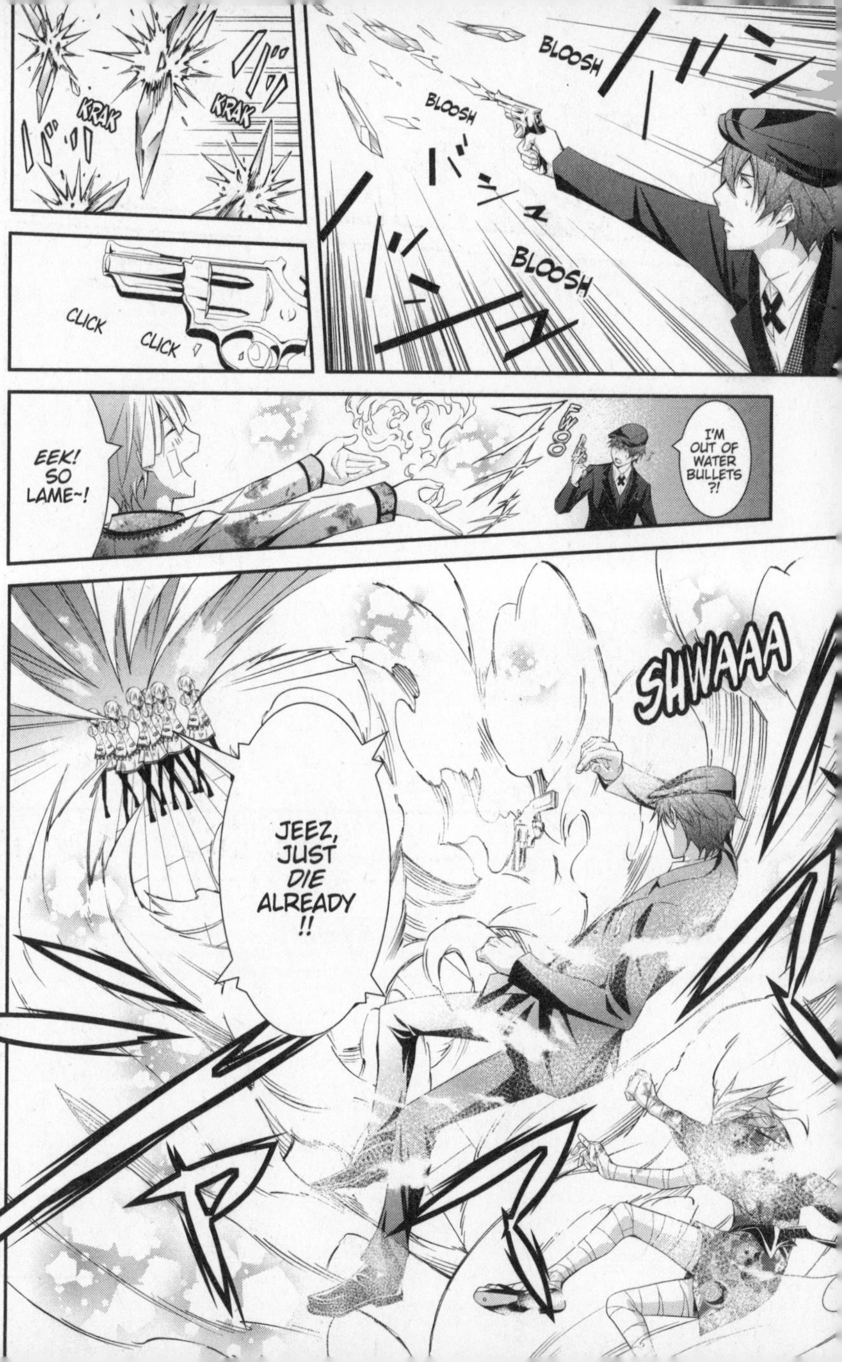

BLOOSH
BLOOSH
BLOOSH
KRAK
KRAK
CLICK
CLICK
I'M OUT OF WATER BULLETS?!
FWOO
EEK! SO LAME~!
SHWAAA
JEEZ, JUST DIE ALREADY!!

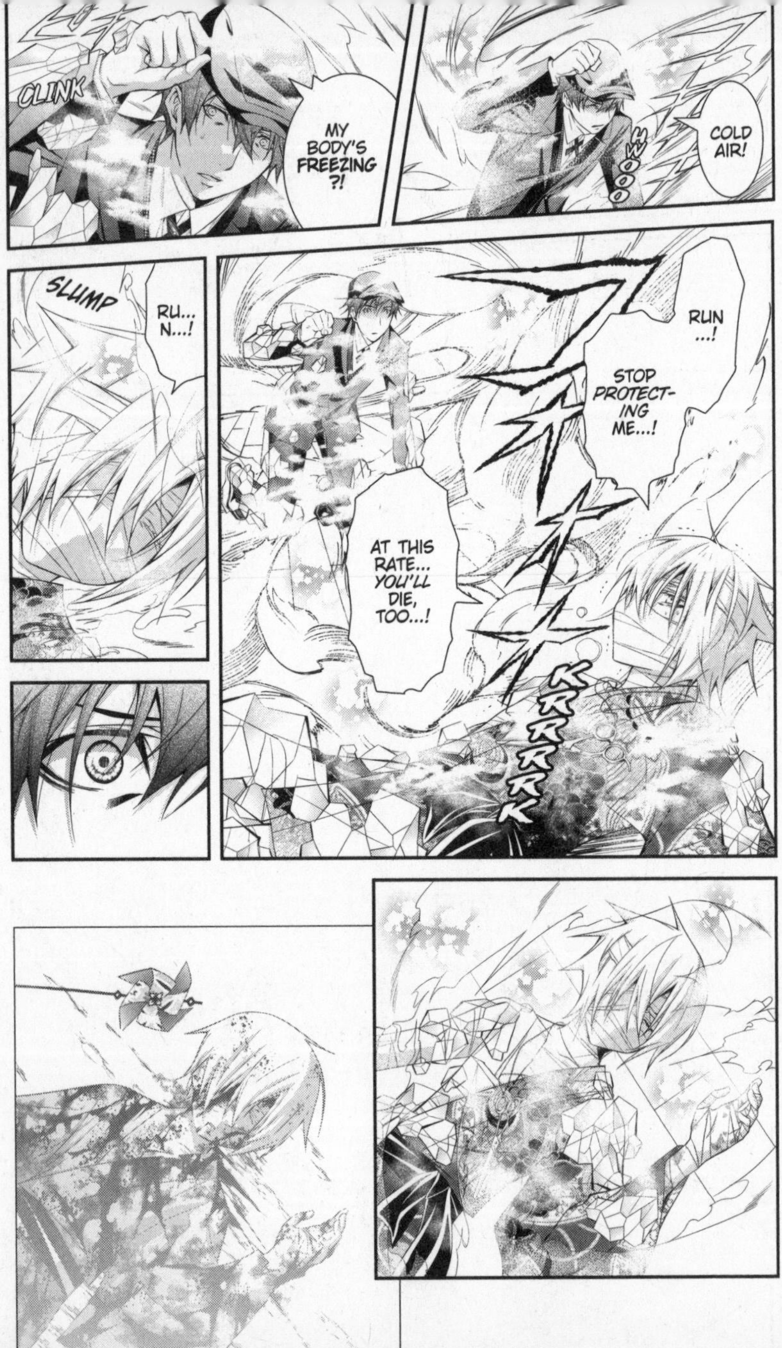
HWOOO
COLD AIR!
CLINK
MY BODY'S FREEZING ?!
RUN ...!
STOP PROTECTING ME...!
AT THIS RATE... YOU'LL DIE, TOO...!
KRRRRRK
SLUMP
RU... N...!

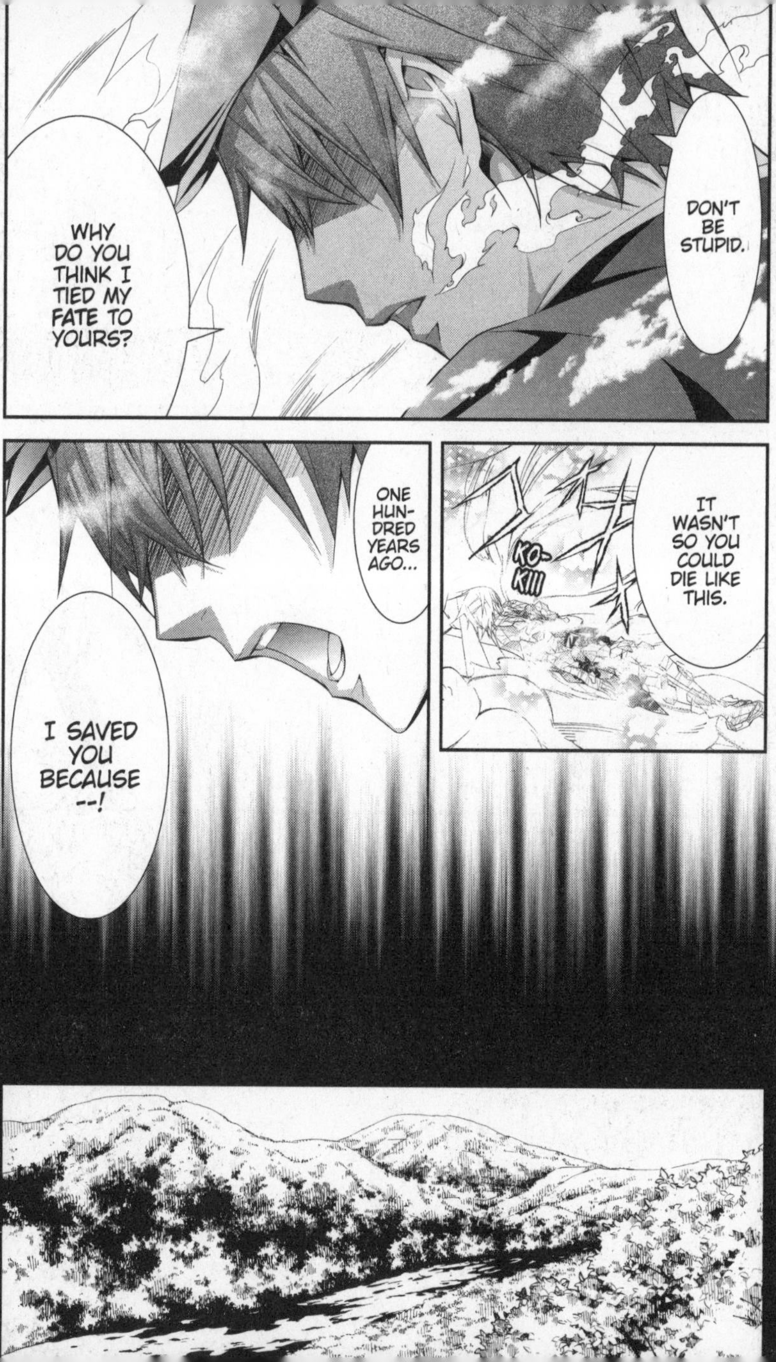
DON'T BE STUPID.
WHY DO YOU THINK I TIED MY FATE TO YOURS?
IT WASN'T SO YOU COULD DIE LIKE THIS.
KO-KIII
ONE HUN-DRED YEARS AGO...
I SAVED YOU BECAUSE --!

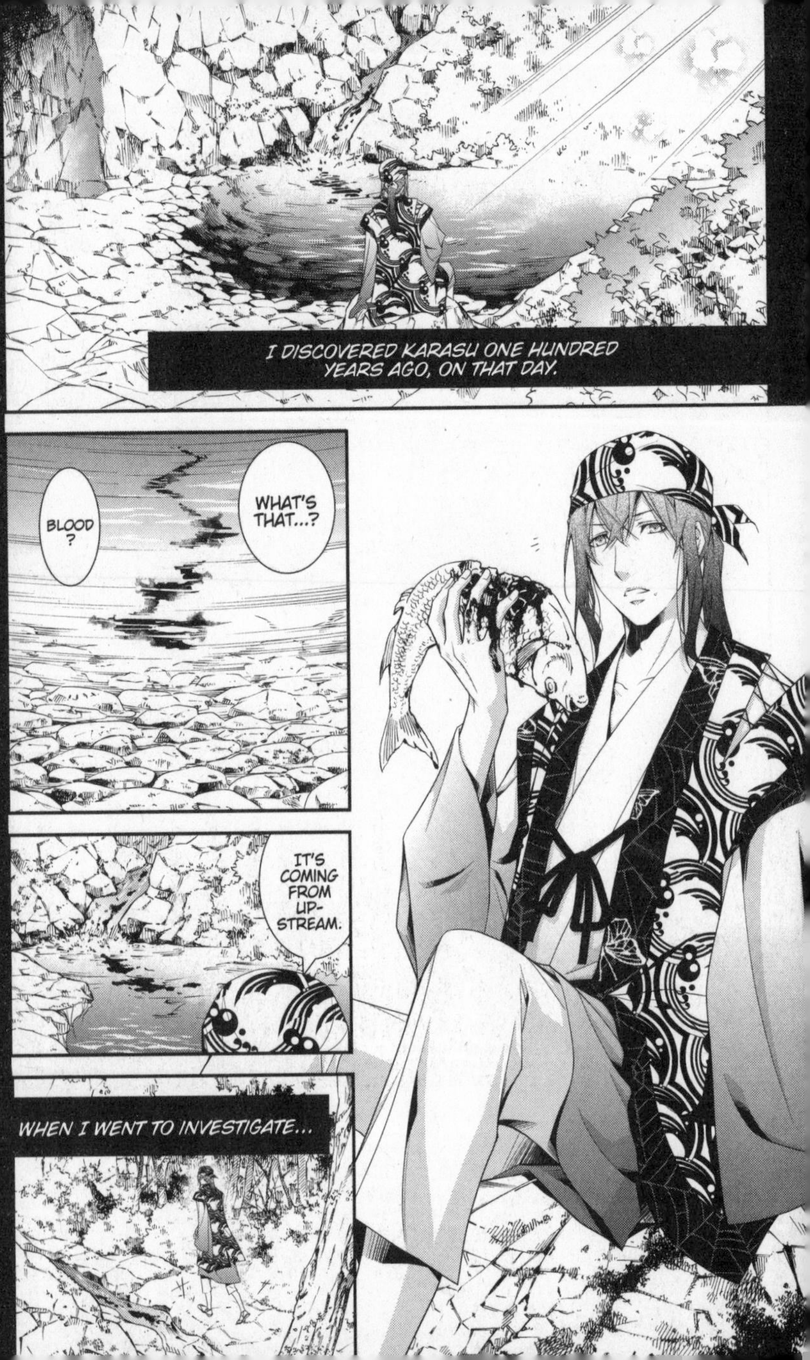
I DISCOVERED KARASU ONE HUNDRED YEARS AGO, ON THAT DAY.
WHAT'S THAT...?
BLOOD?
IT'S COMING FROM UPSTREAM.
WHEN I WENT TO INVESTIGATE...

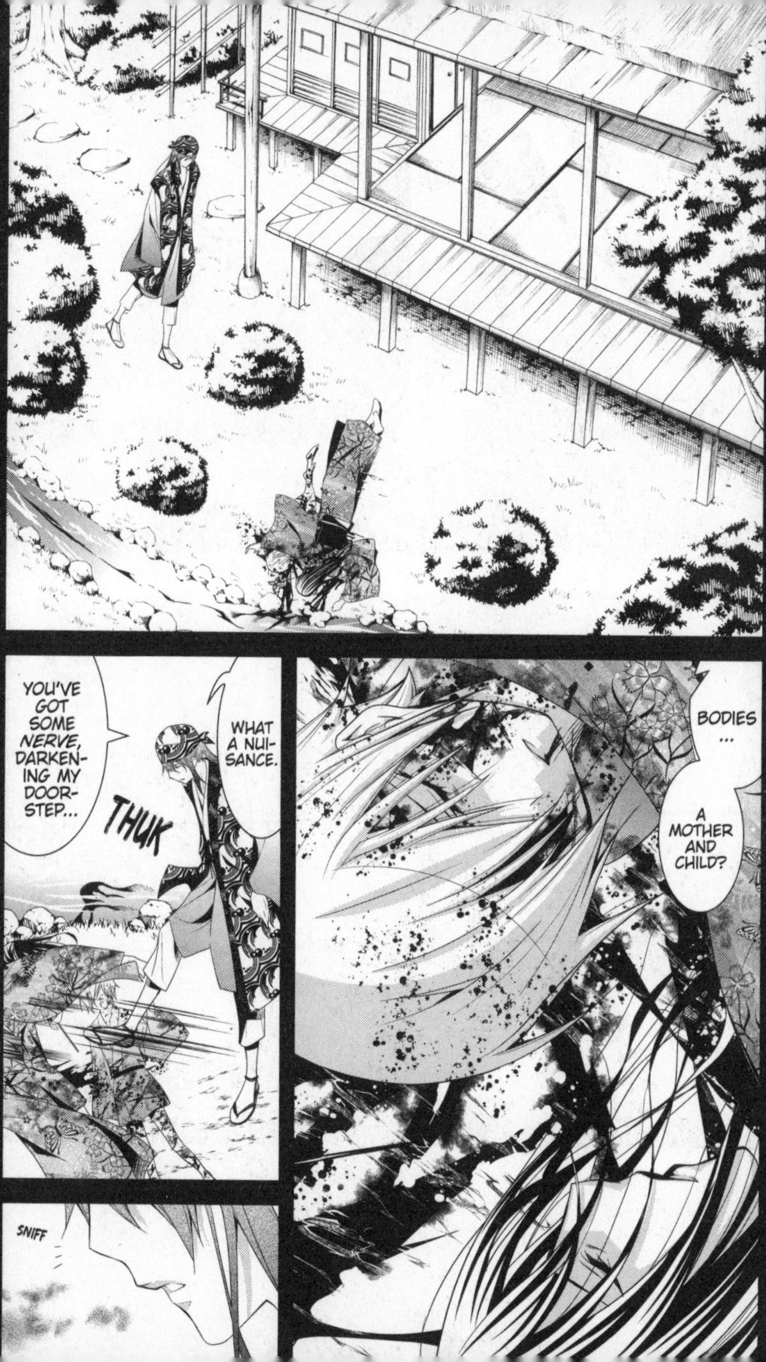
BODIES...
A MOTHER AND CHILD?
WHAT A NUISANCE.
YOU'VE GOT SOME NERVE, DARKENING MY DOORSTEP...
THUK
SNIFF

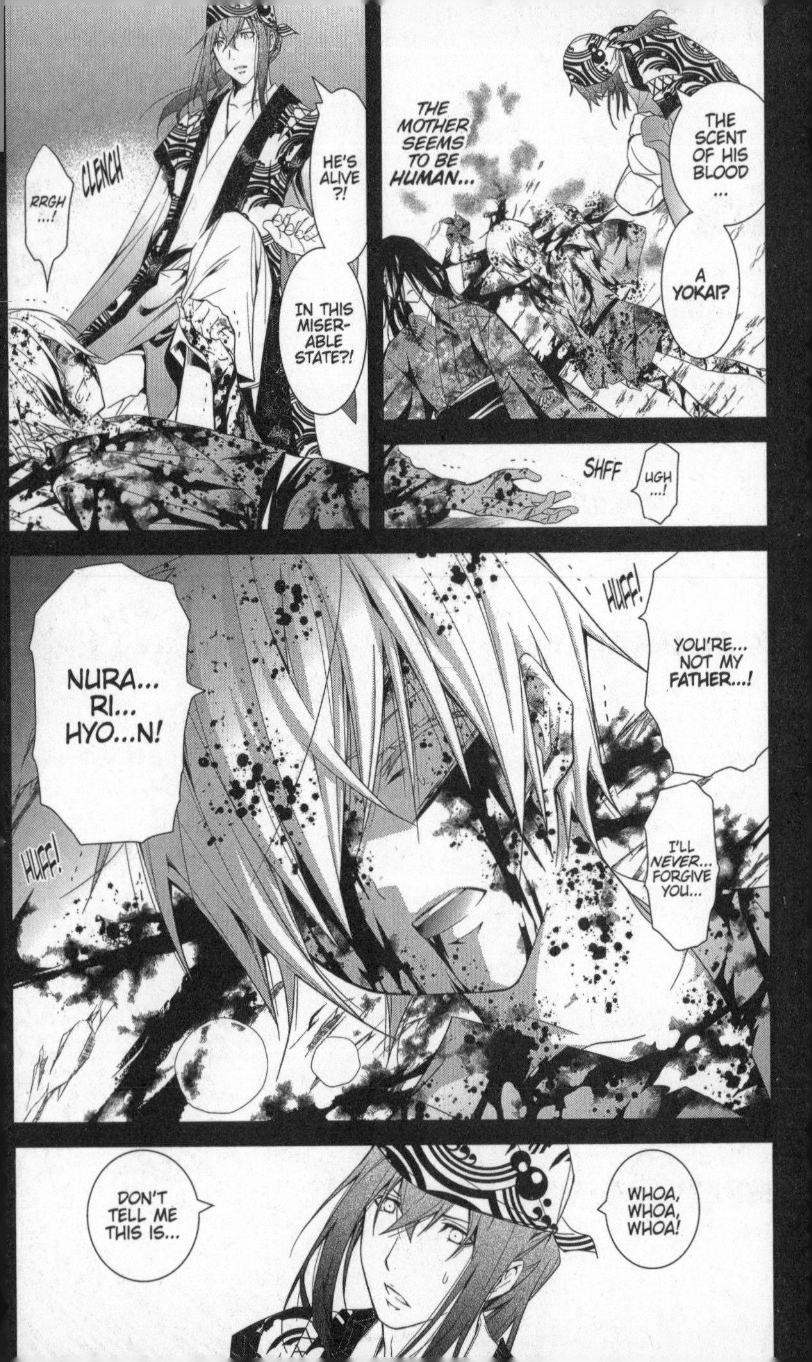
THE SCENT OF HIS BLOOD...
A YOKAI?
THE MOTHER SEEMS TO BE HUMAN...
SHFF
UGH...!
HE'S ALIVE?!
IN THIS MISERABLE STATE?!
CLENCH
RRGH...!
HUFF!
YOU'RE... NOT MY FATHER...!
I'LL NEVER... FORGIVE YOU...
NURA... RI... HYO...N!
HUFF!
WHOA, WHOA, WHOA!
DON'T TELL ME THIS IS...

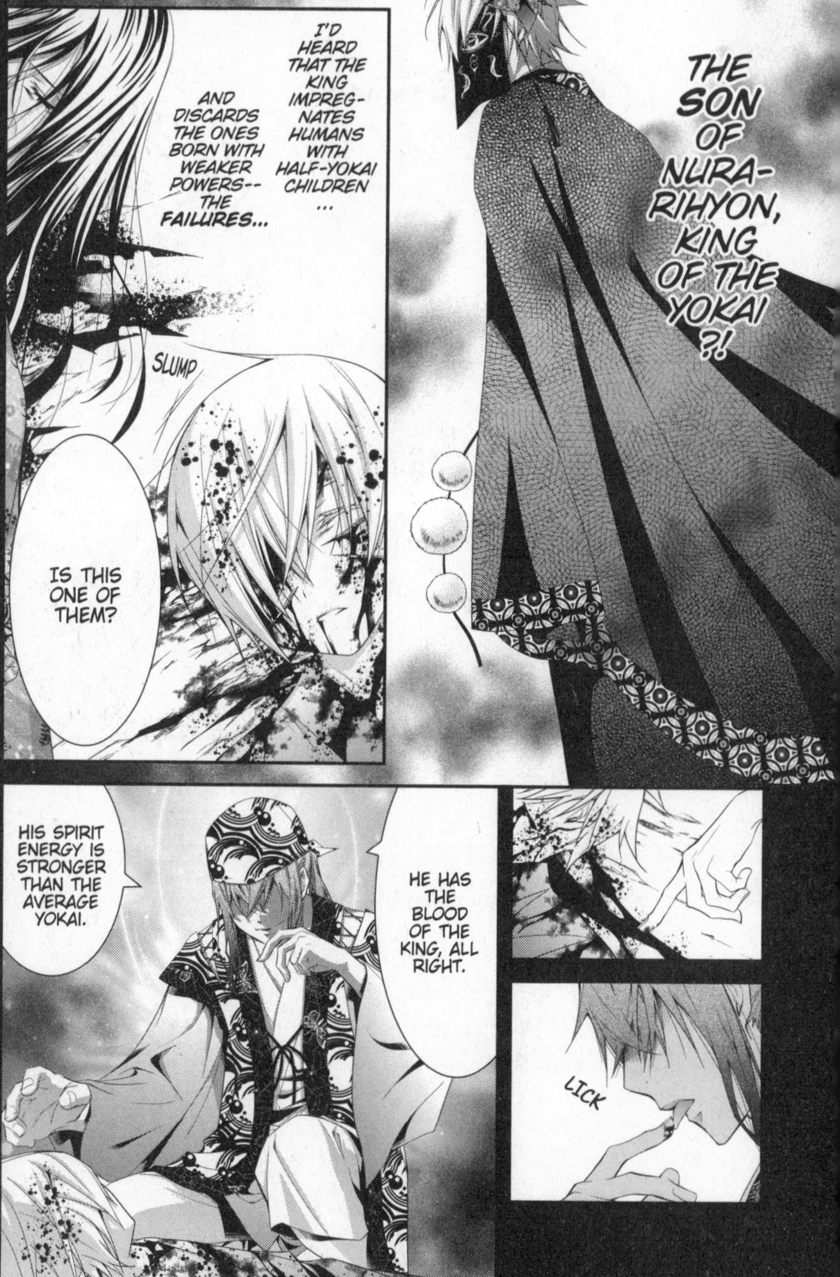
THE SON OF NURA-RIHYON, KING OF THE YOKAI ?!
I'D HEARD THAT THE KING IMPREG-NATES HUMANS WITH HALF-YOKAI CHILDREN ...
AND DISCARDS THE ONES BORN WITH WEAKER POWERS-- THE FAILURES...
SLUMP
IS THIS ONE OF THEM?
LICK
HE HAS THE BLOOD OF THE KING, ALL RIGHT.
HIS SPIRIT ENERGY IS STRONGER THAN THE AVERAGE YOKAI.

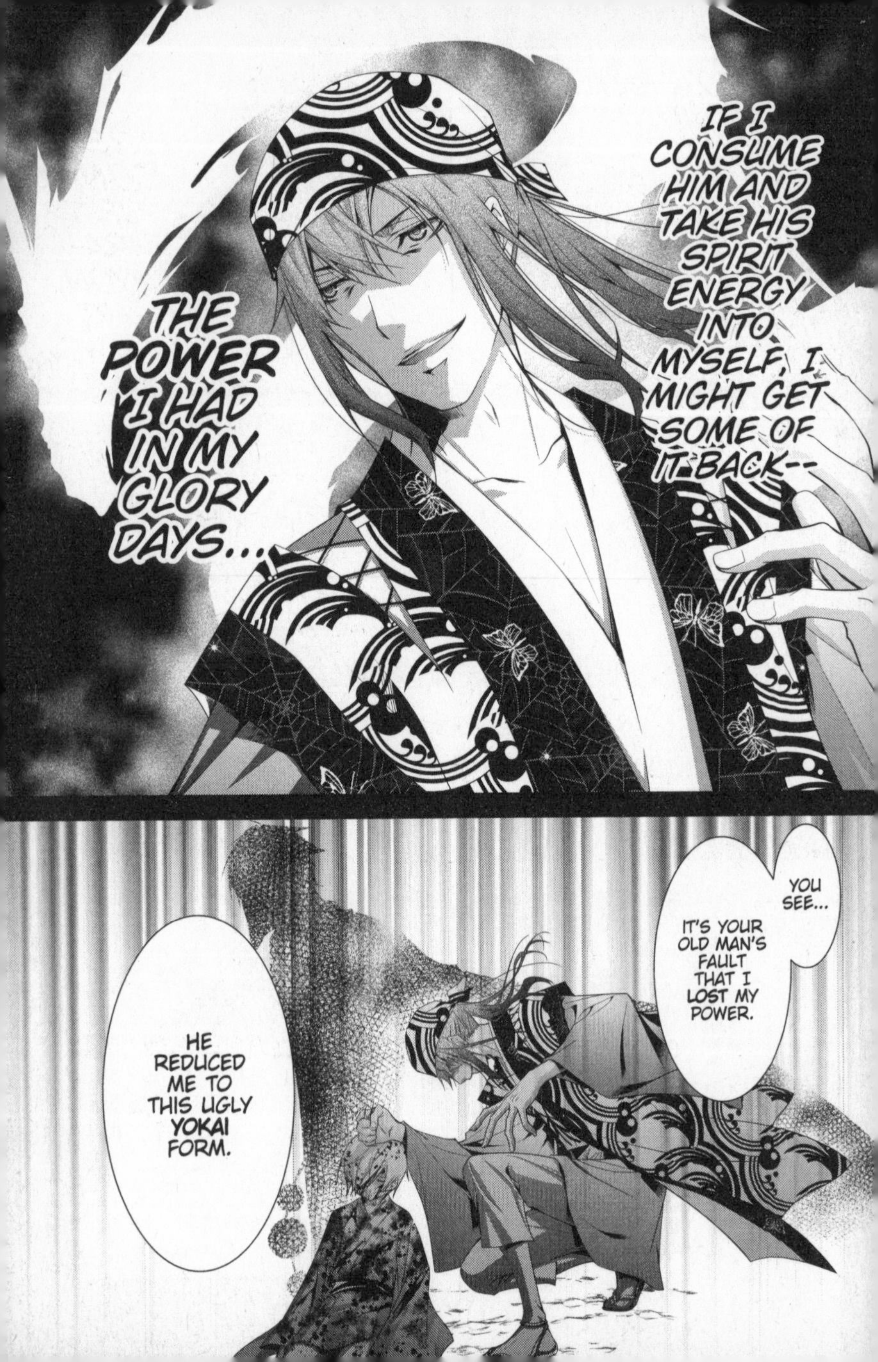
IF I CONSUME HIM AND TAKE HIS SPIRIT ENERGY INTO MYSELF, I MIGHT GET SOME OF IT BACK--
THE POWER I HAD IN MY GLORY DAYS...
YOU SEE...
IT'S YOUR OLD MAN'S FAULT THAT I LOST MY POWER.
HE REDUCED ME TO THIS UGLY YOKAI FORM.

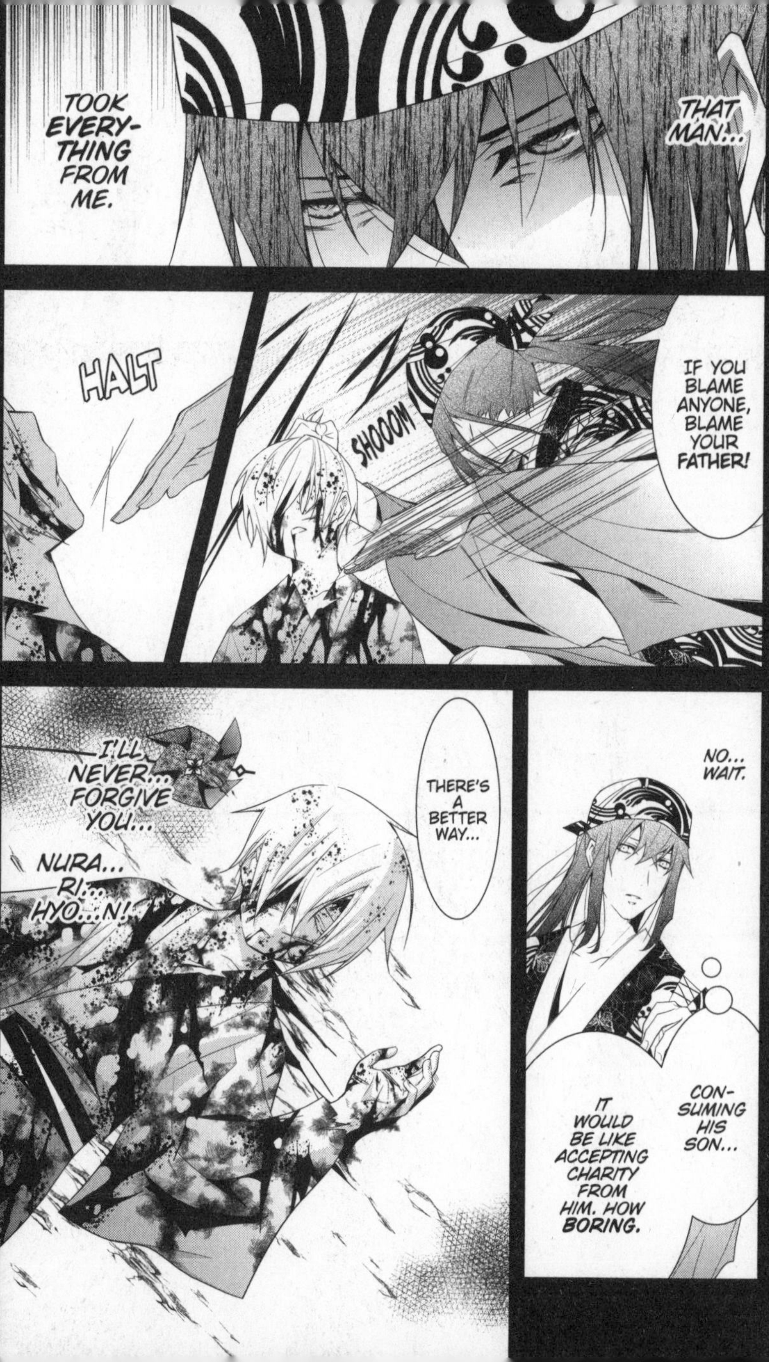
THAT MAN...
TOOK EVERY-THING FROM ME.
IF YOU BLAME ANYONE, BLAME YOUR FATHER!
SHOOOM
HALT
NO... WAIT.
CON-SUMING HIS SON...
IT WOULD BE LIKE ACCEPTING CHARITY FROM HIM. HOW BORING.
THERE'S A BETTER WAY...
I'LL NEVER... FORGIVE YOU...
NURA... RI... HYO...N!

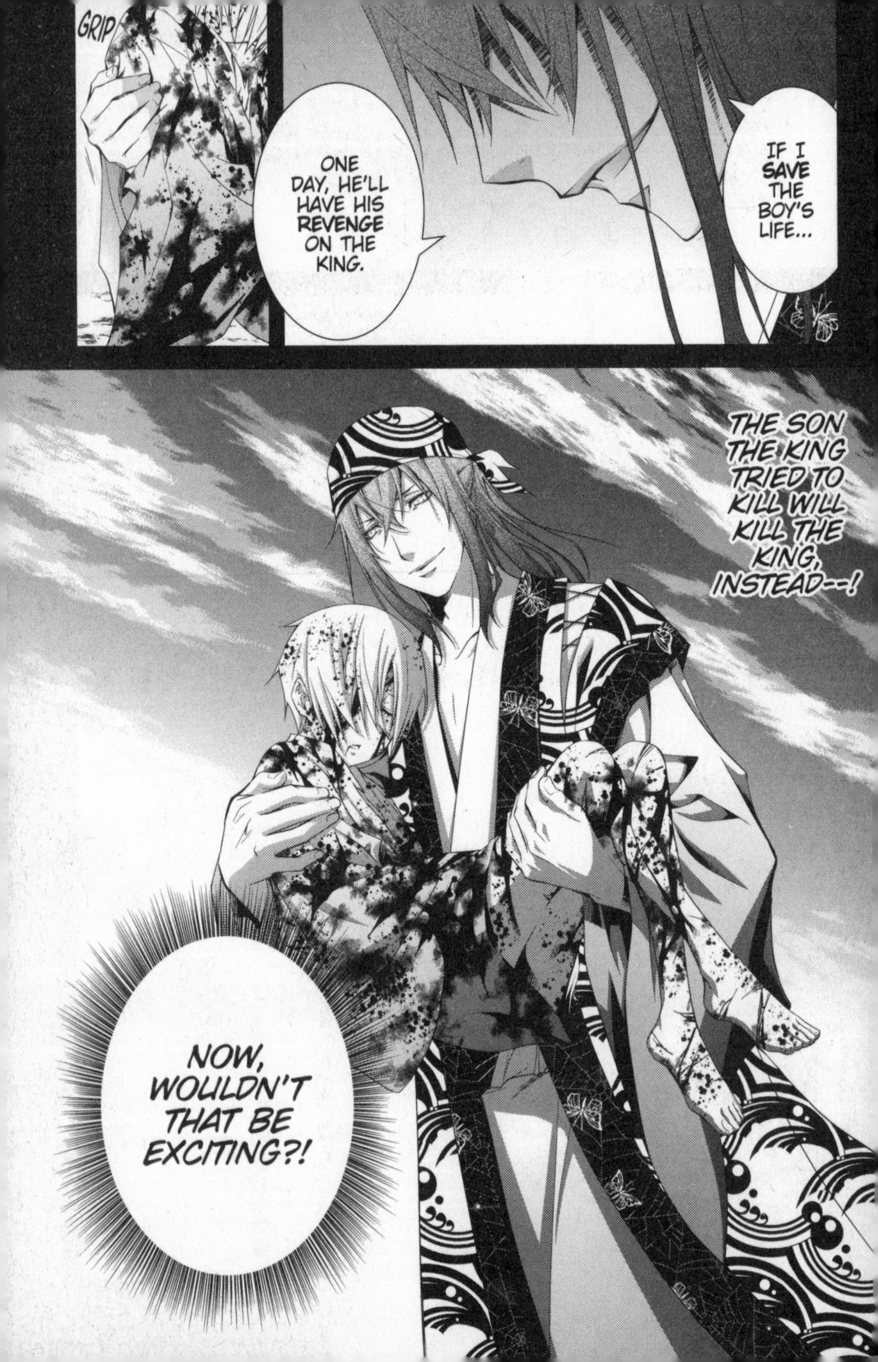
IF I SAVE THE BOY'S LIFE...
ONE DAY, HE'LL HAVE HIS REVENGE ON THE KING.
GRIP
THE SON THE KING TRIED TO KILL WILL KILL THE KING, INSTEAD--!
NOW, WOULDN'T THAT BE EXCITING?!

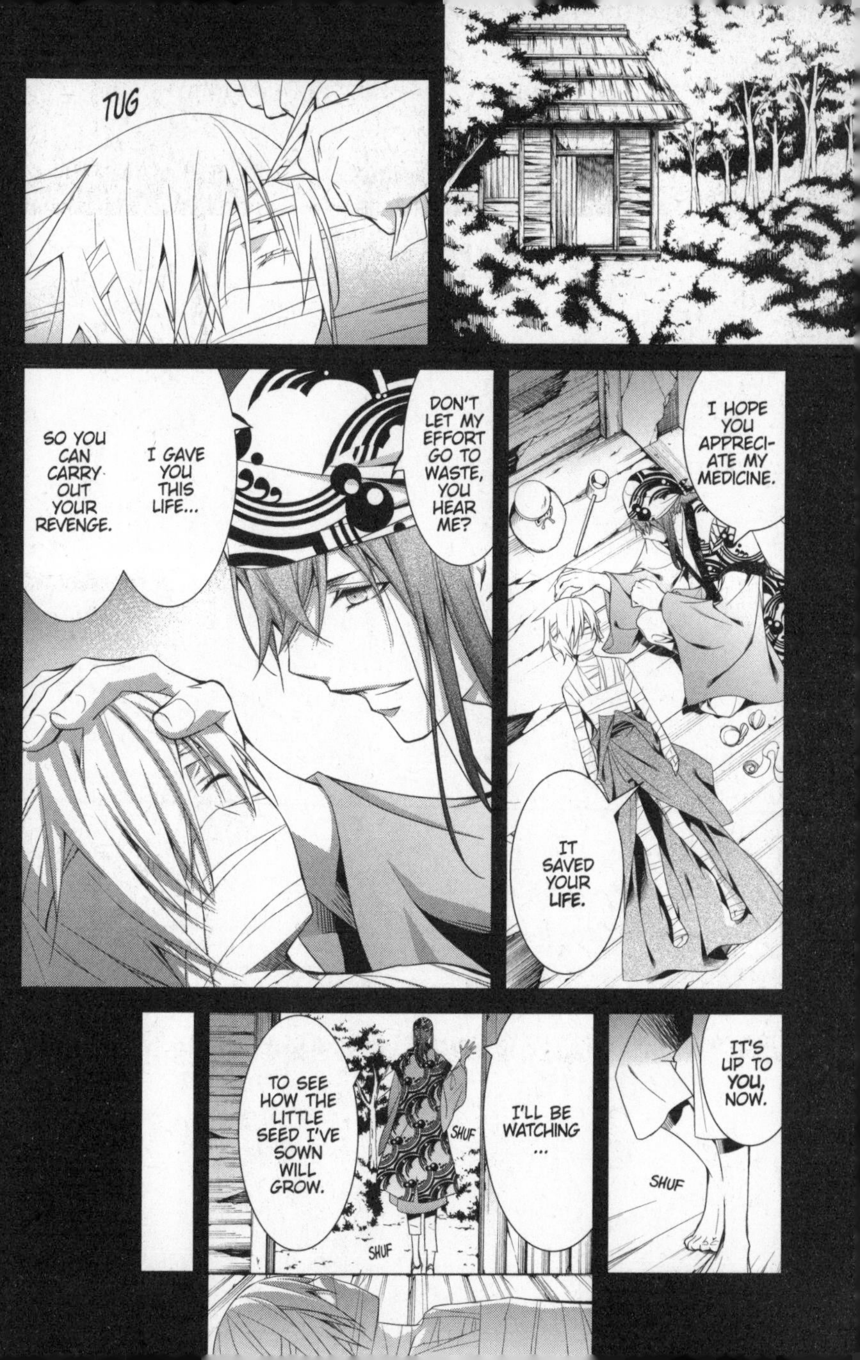
TUG
I HOPE YOU APPRECIATE MY MEDICINE.
IT SAVED YOUR LIFE.
DON'T LET MY EFFORT GO TO WASTE, YOU HEAR ME?
I GAVE YOU THIS LIFE...
SO YOU CAN CARRY OUT YOUR REVENGE.
IT'S UP TO YOU, NOW.
SHUF
I'LL BE WATCHING ...
SHUF
TO SEE HOW THE LITTLE SEED I'VE SOWN WILL GROW.
SHUF

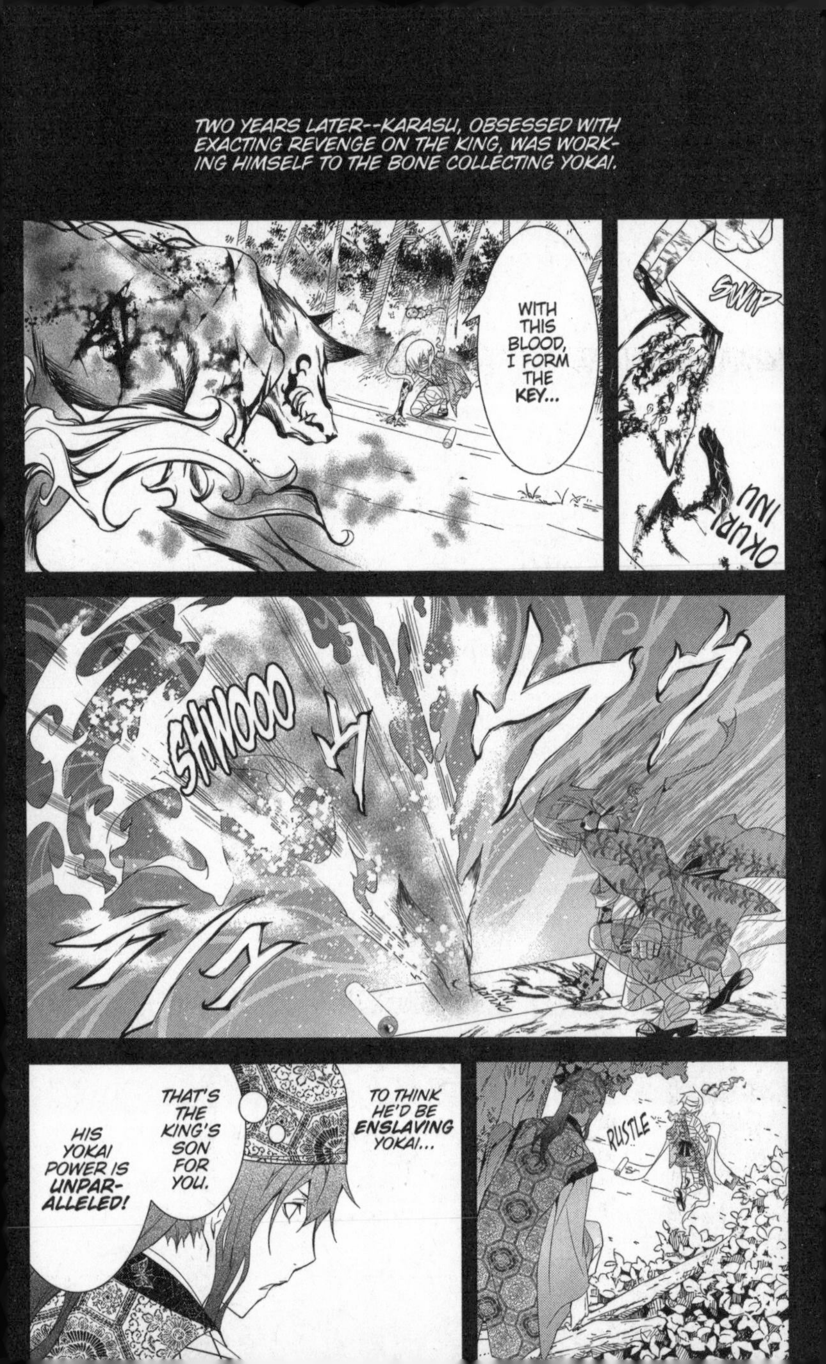
TWO YEARS LATER--KARASU, OBSESSED WITH EXACTING REVENGE ON THE KING, WAS WORKING HIMSELF TO THE BONE COLLECTING YOKAI.
SWIP
OKURI INU
WITH THIS BLOOD, I FORM THE KEY...
SHWOOO
RUSTLE
TO THINK HE'D BE ENSLAVING YOKAI...
THAT'S THE KING'S SON FOR YOU.
HIS YOKAI POWER IS UNPARALLELED!

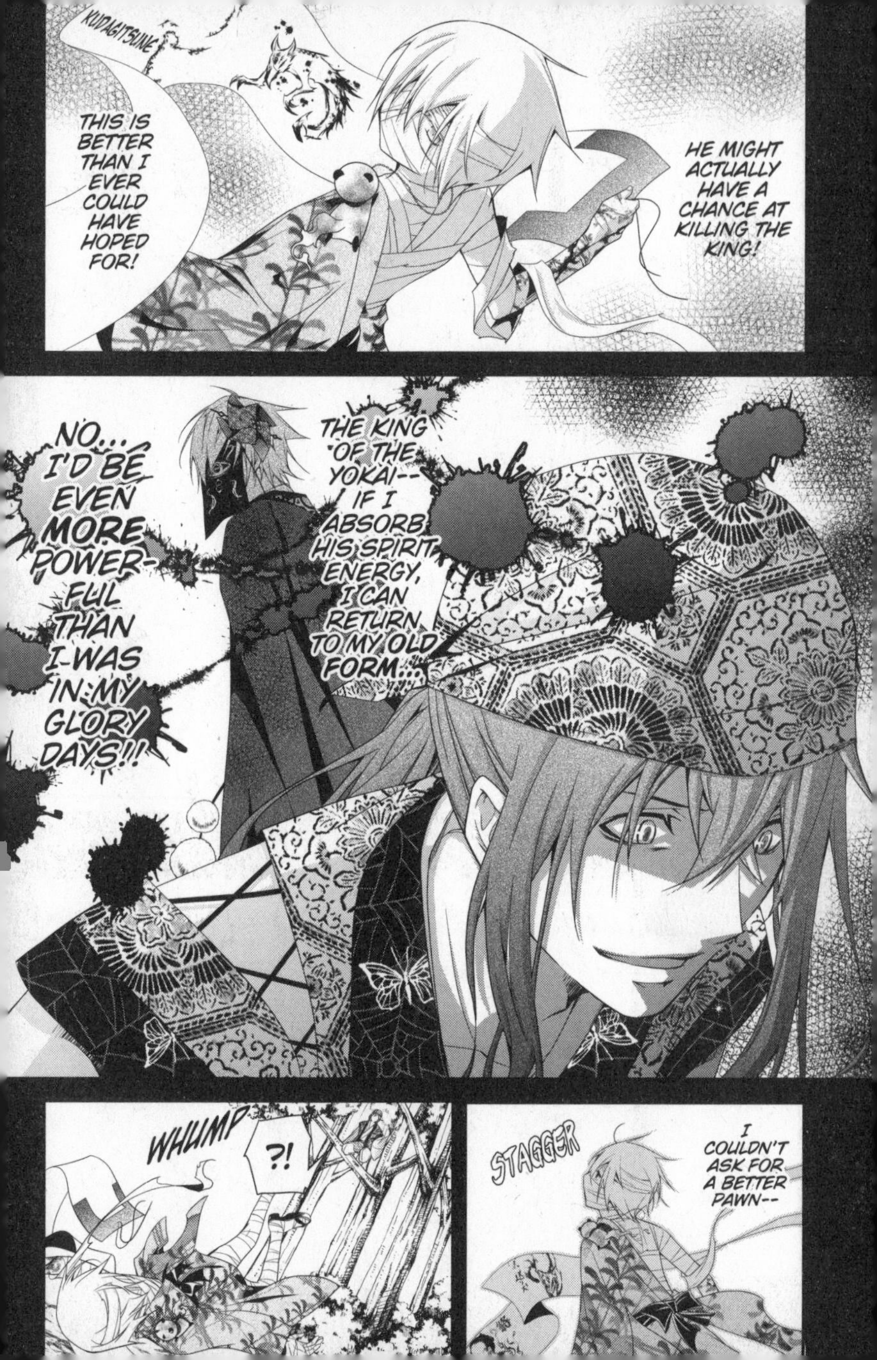
HE MIGHT ACTUALLY HAVE A CHANCE AT KILLING THE KING!
KUDAGITSUNE
THIS IS BETTER THAN I EVER COULD HAVE HOPED FOR!
THE KING OF THE YOKAI--IF I ABSORB HIS SPIRIT ENERGY, I CAN RETURN TO MY OLD FORM...
NO... I'D BE EVEN MORE POWER-FUL THAN I WAS IN MY GLORY DAYS!!
I COULDN'T ASK FOR A BETTER PAWN--
STAGGER
WHUMP
?!

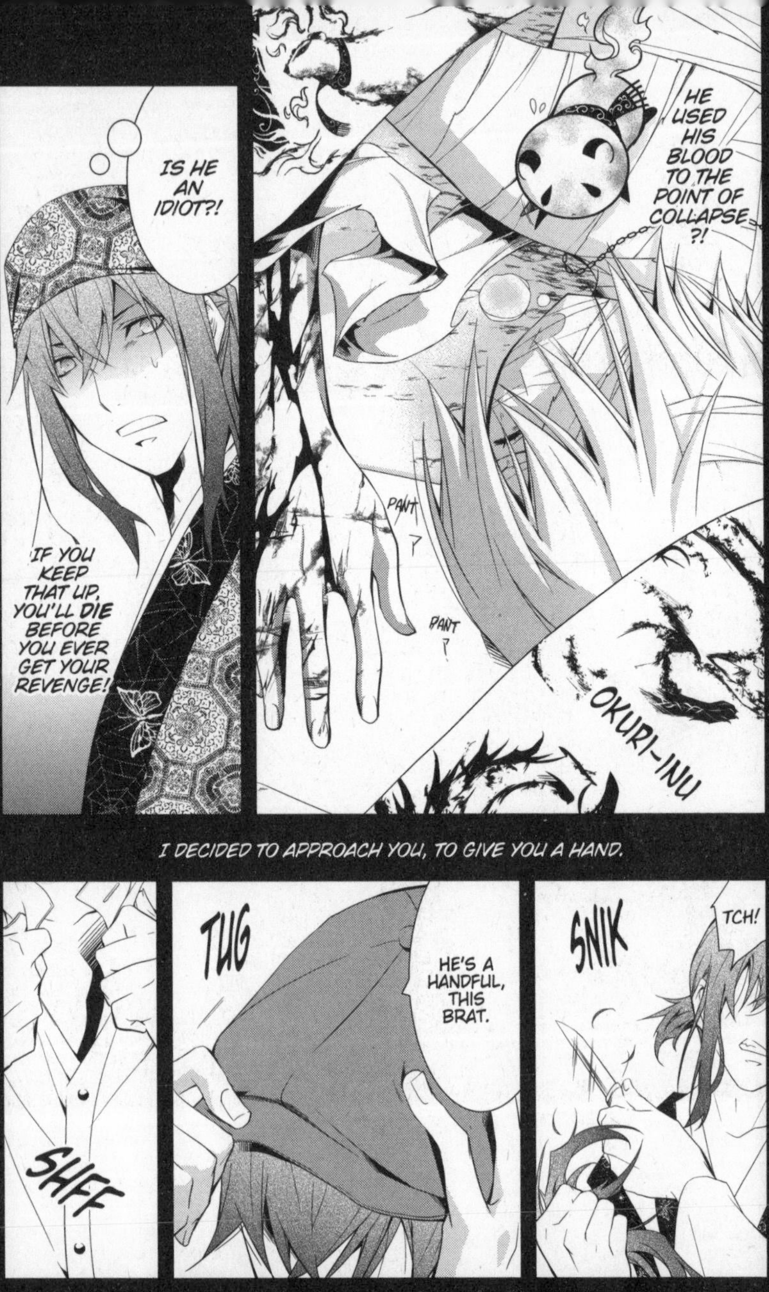
HE USED HIS BLOOD TO THE POINT OF COLLAPSE?!
PANT
PANT
OKURI-INU
IS HE AN IDIOT?!
IF YOU KEEP THAT UP, YOU'LL DIE BEFORE YOU EVER GET YOUR REVENGE!
I DECIDED TO APPROACH YOU, TO GIVE YOU A HAND.
SNIK
TCH!
TUG
HE'S A HANDFUL, THIS BRAT.
SHFF

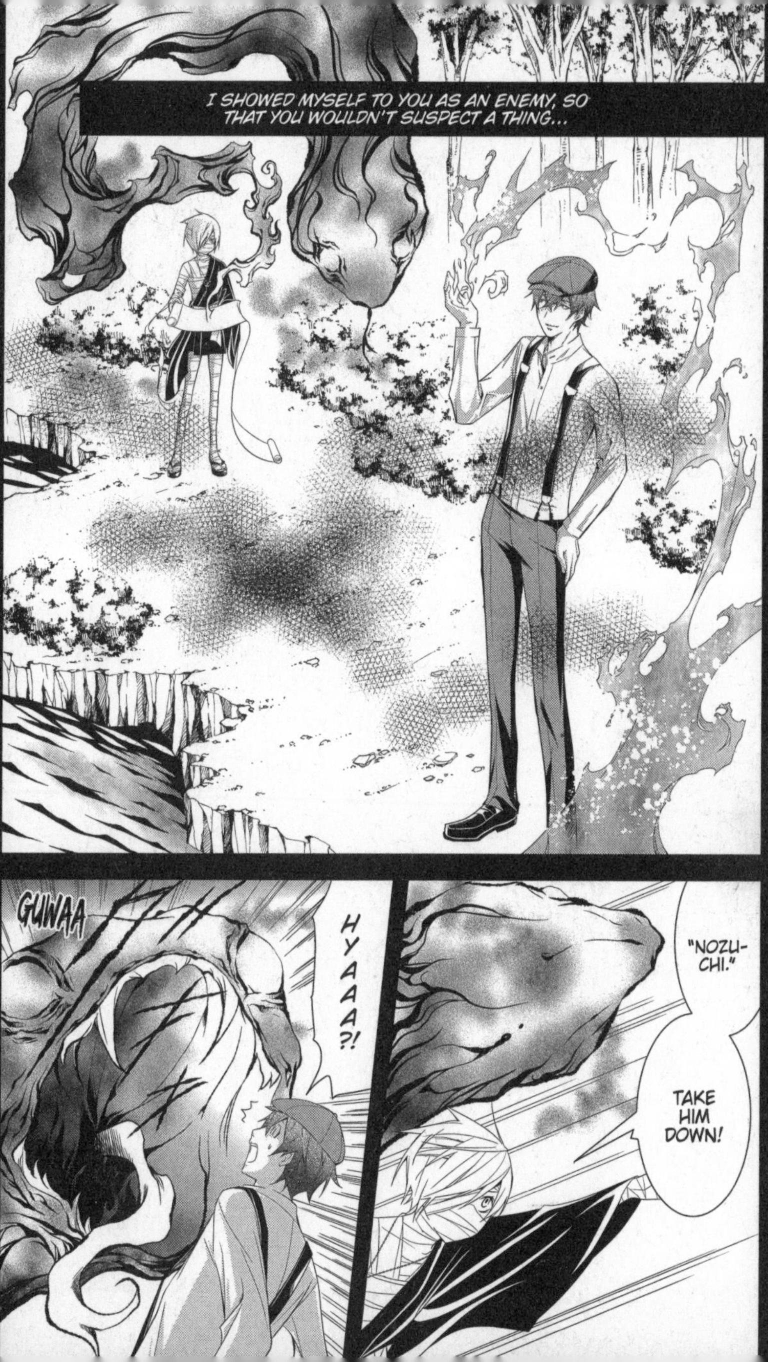
I SHOWED MYSELF TO YOU AS AN ENEMY, SO THAT YOU WOULDN'T SUSPECT A THING...
"NOZU-CHI."
TAKE HIM DOWN!
HYAAAA?!
GUWAA

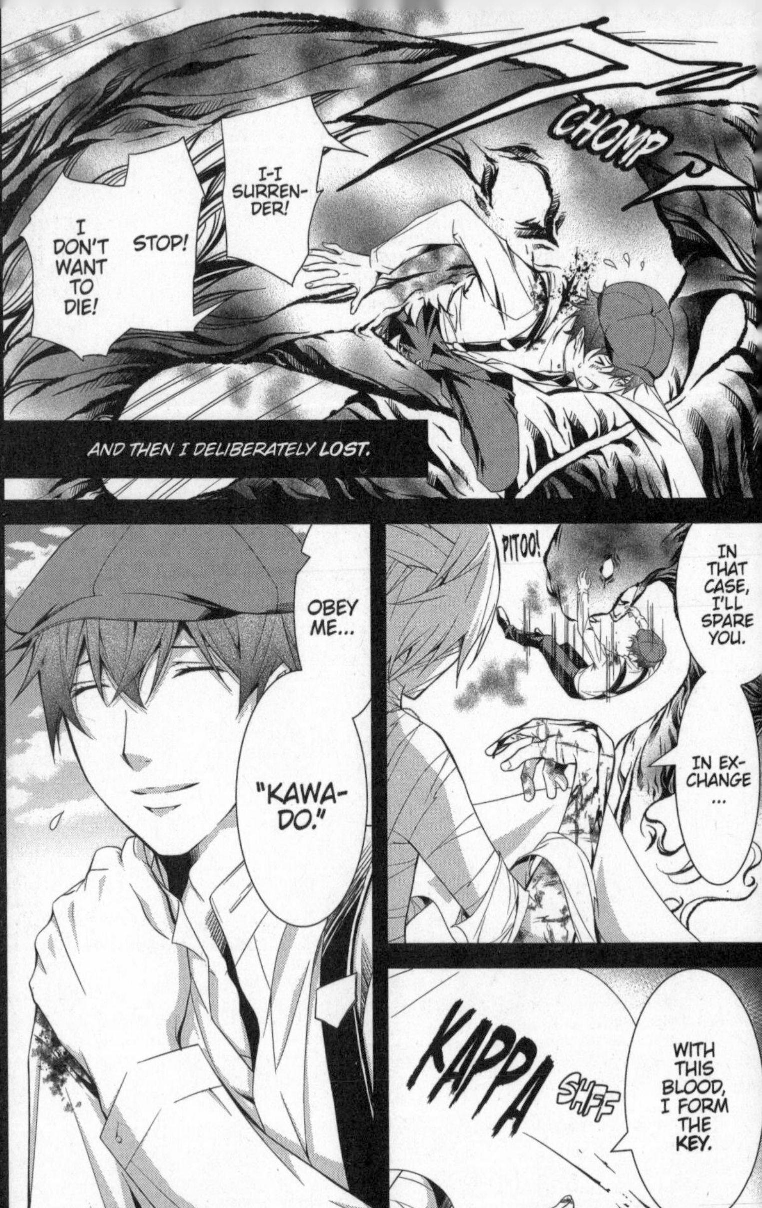
CHOMP
I-I SURRENDER!
STOP!
I DON'T WANT TO DIE!
AND THEN I DELIBERATELY LOST.
IN THAT CASE, I'LL SPARE YOU.
PITOO!
IN EXCHANGE...
WITH THIS BLOOD, I FORM THE KEY.
SHFF
KAPPA
OBEY ME...
"KAWADO."

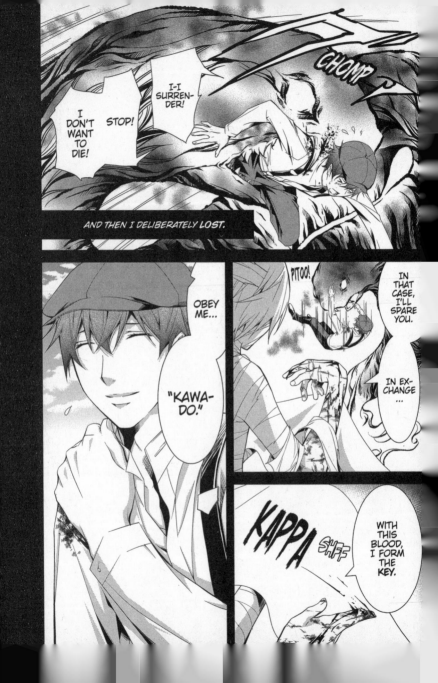

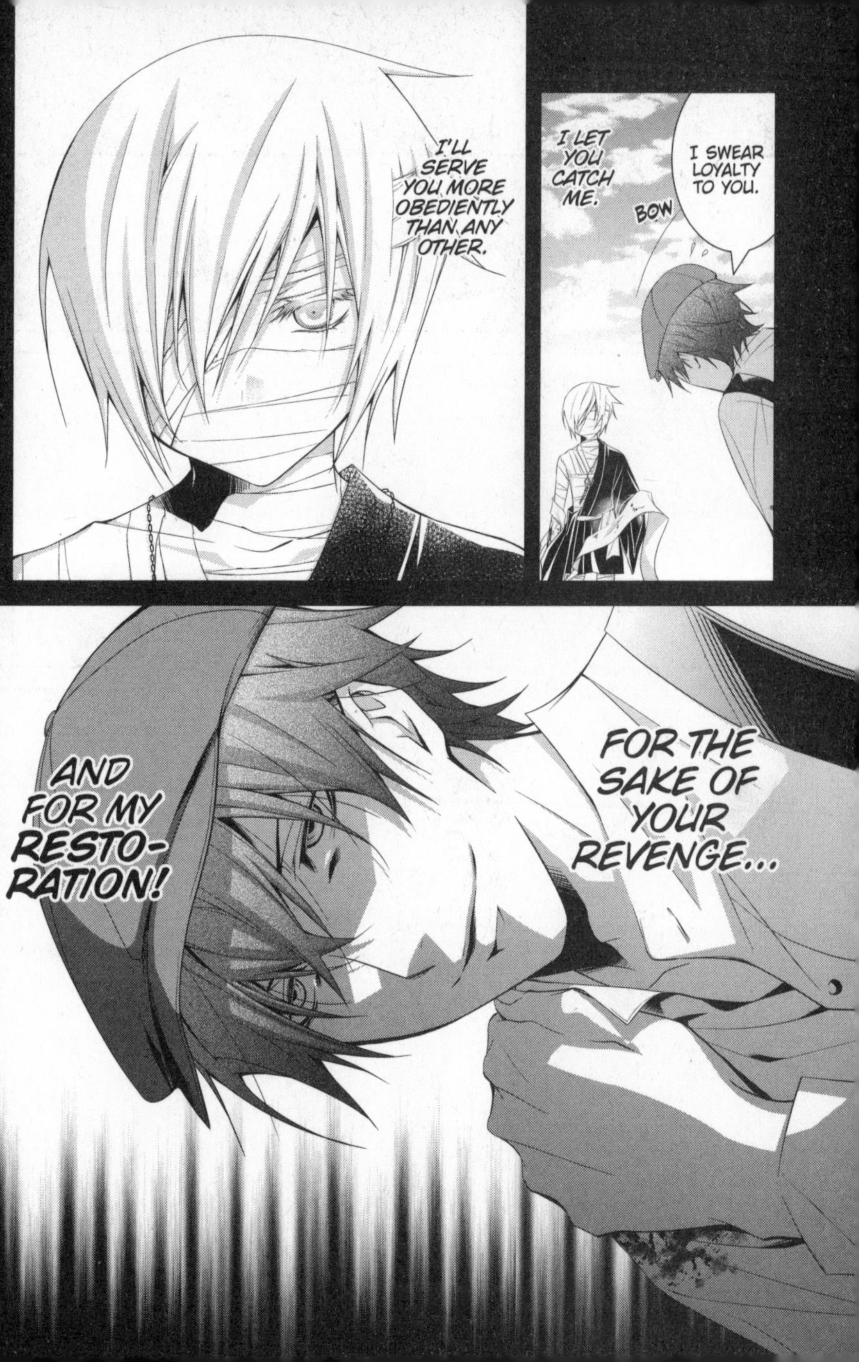
I SWEAR LOYALTY TO YOU.
BOW
I LET YOU CATCH ME.
I'LL SERVE YOU MORE OBEDIENTLY THAN ANY OTHER.
FOR THE SAKE OF YOUR REVENGE...
AND FOR MY RESTO-RATION!

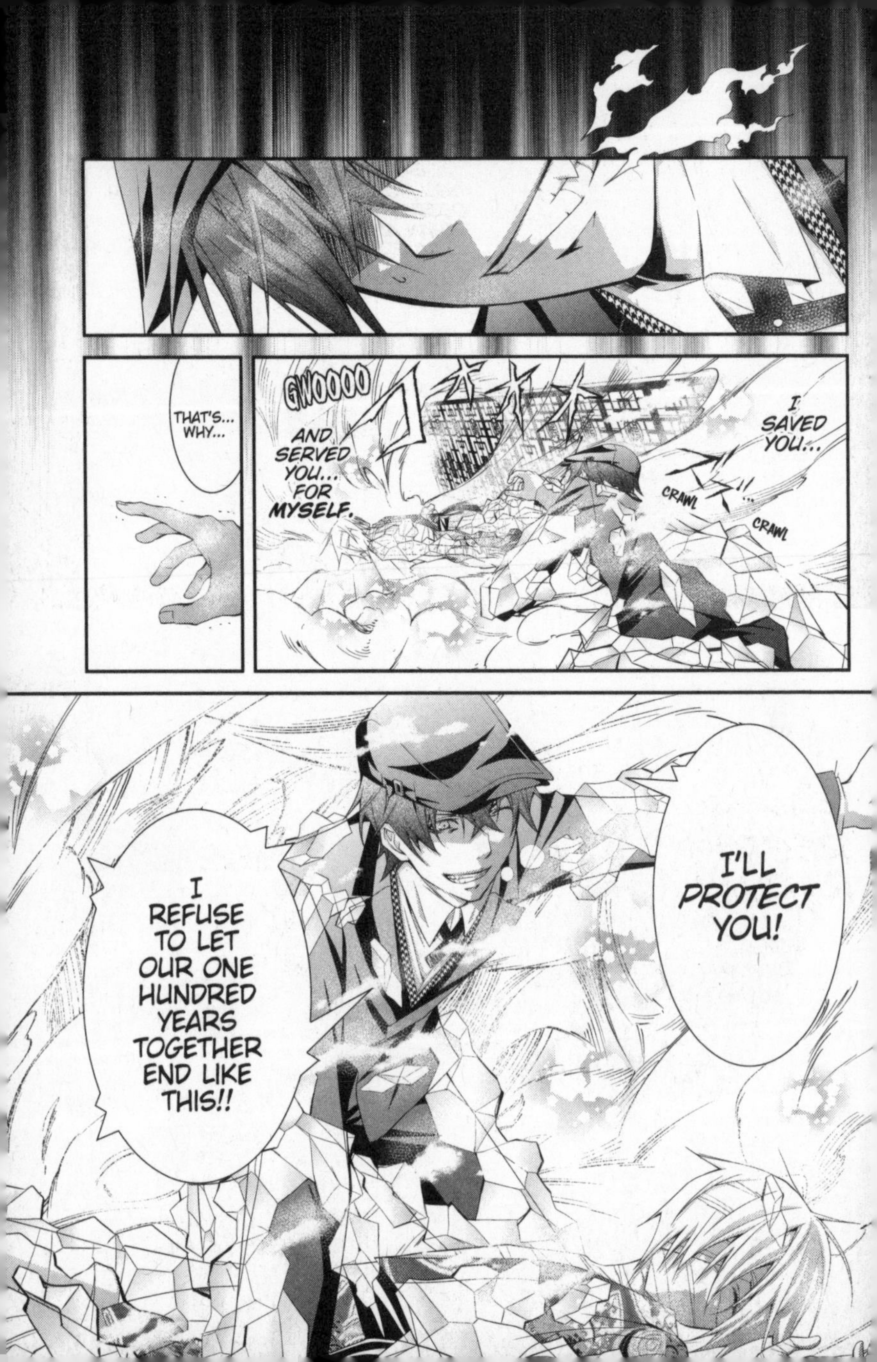
I SAVED YOU...
GWOOOO
AND SERVED YOU... FOR MYSELF.
CRAWL
CRAWL
THAT'S... WHY...
I'LL PROTECT YOU!
I REFUSE TO LET OUR ONE HUNDRED YEARS TOGETHER END LIKE THIS!!

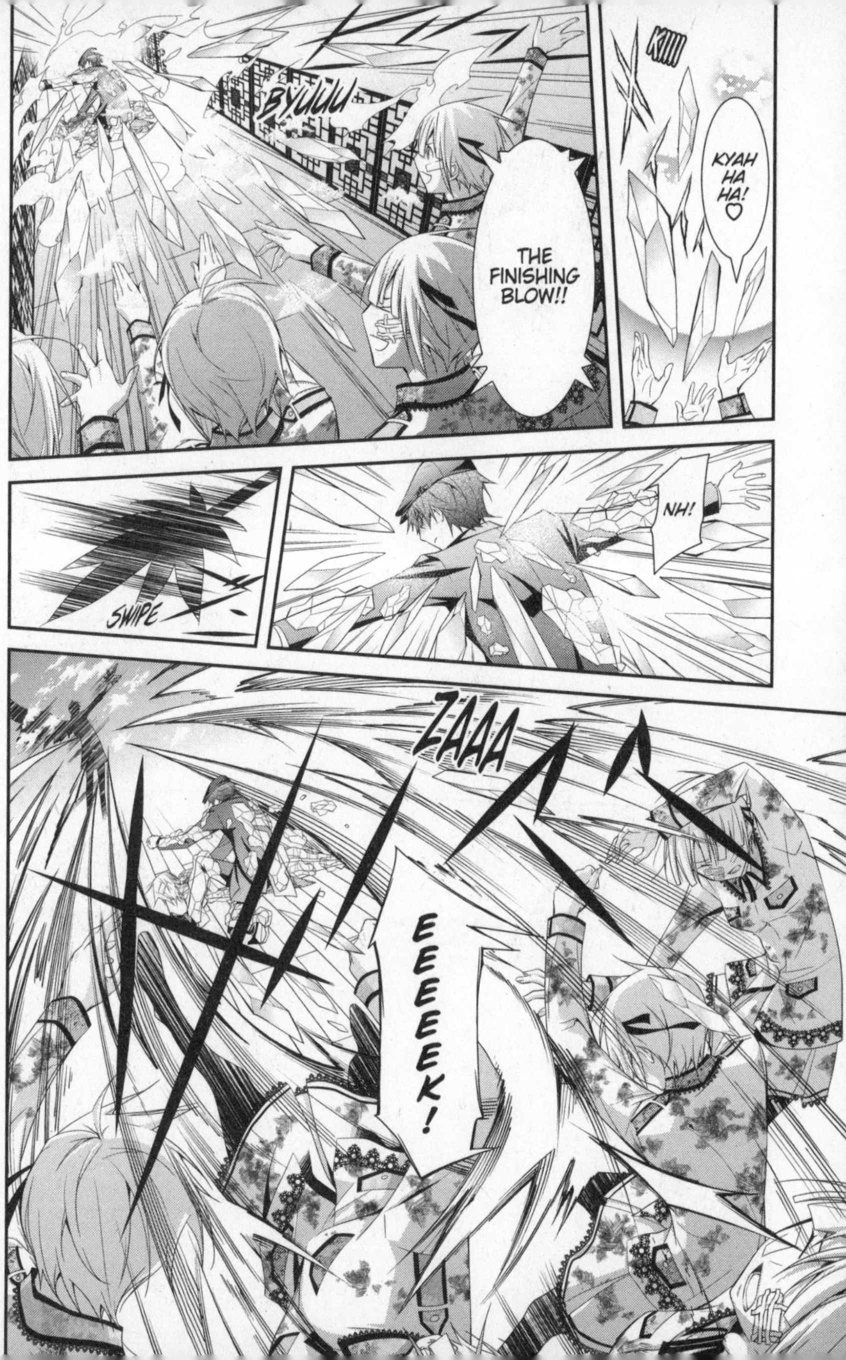
KIII
KYAH HA HA! ♡
BYUUU
THE FINISHING BLOW!!
NH!
SWIPE
ZAAA
EEEEEEK!

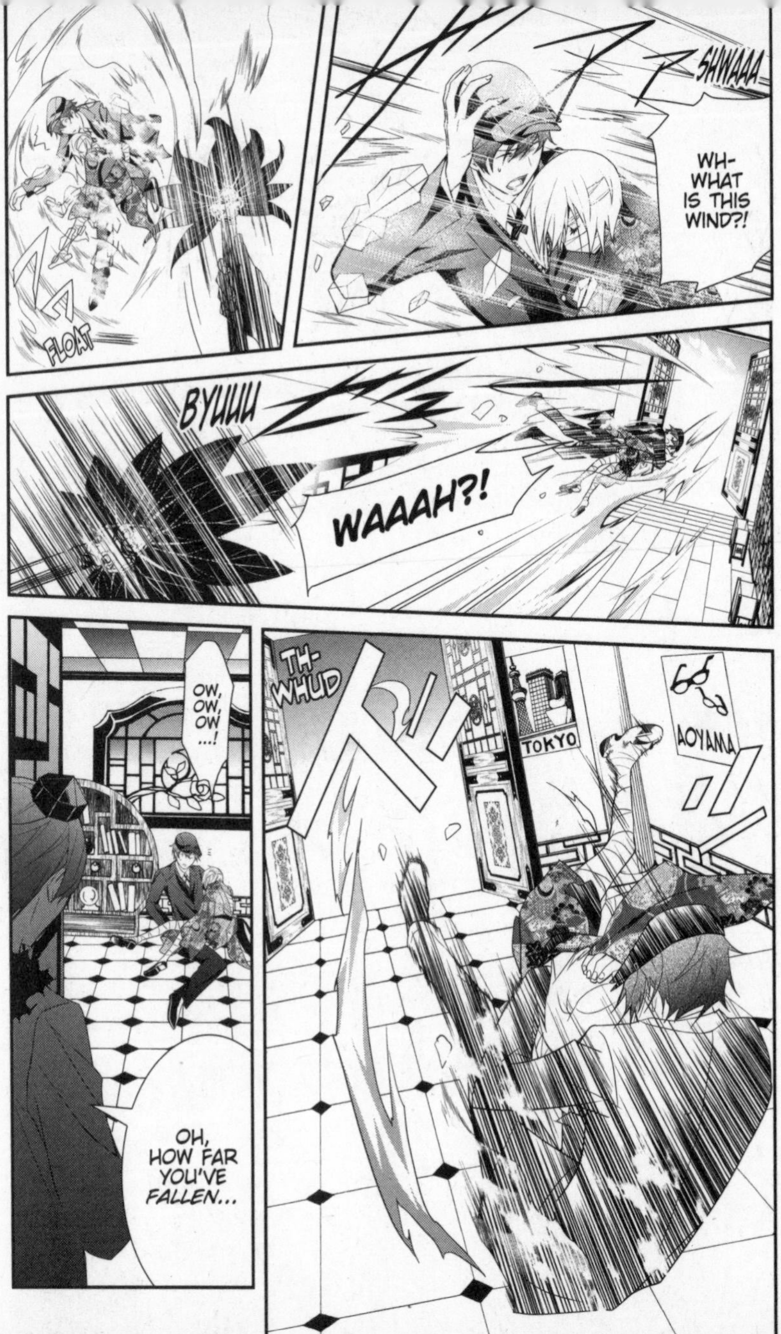
SHWAAA
WH- WHAT IS THIS WIND?!
FLOAT
BYUUU
WAAAH?!
TH-WHUD
TOKYO
AOYAMA
OW, OW, OW ...!
OH, HOW FAR YOU'VE FALLEN...

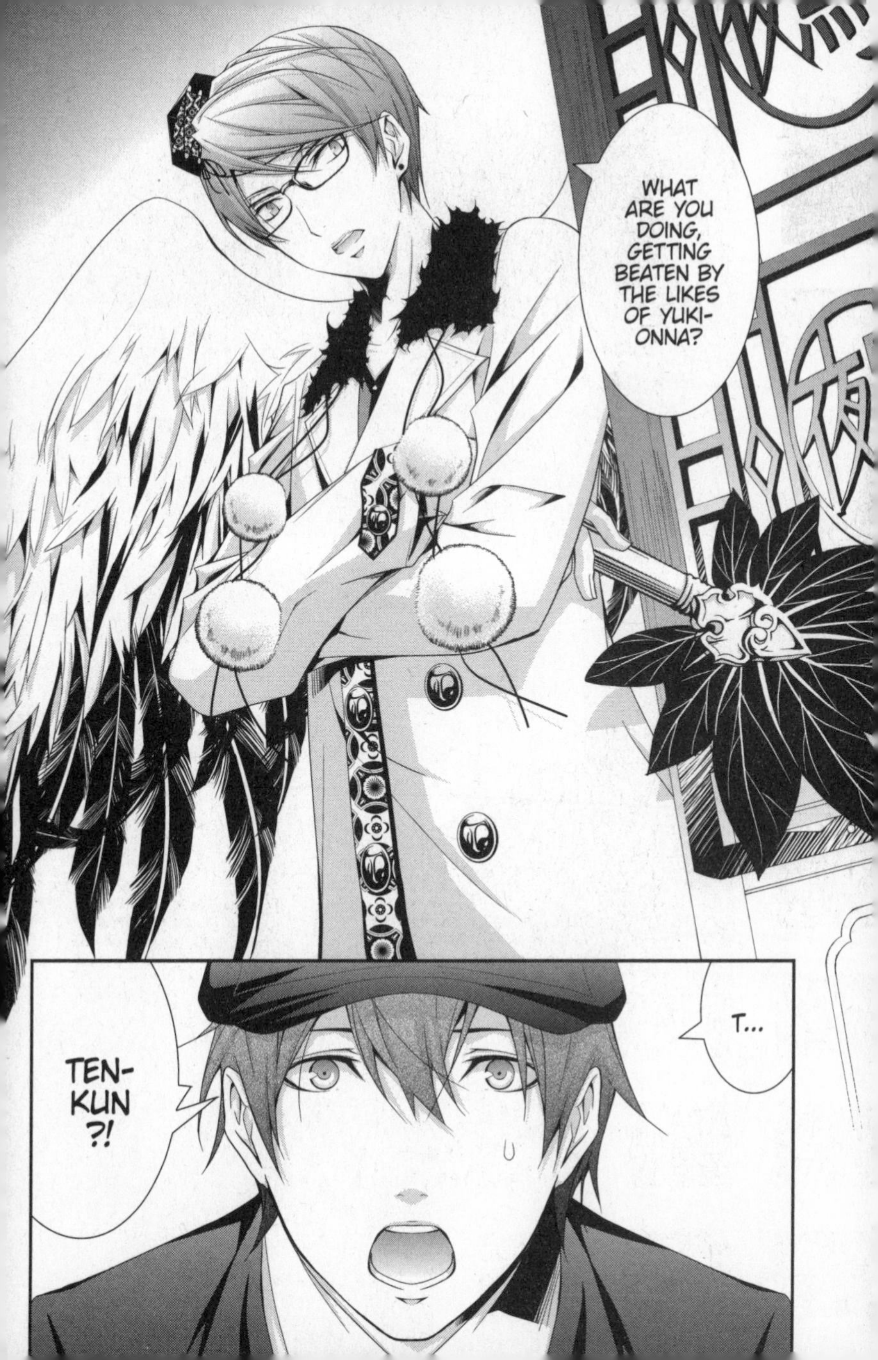
WHAT ARE YOU DOING, GETTING BEATEN BY THE LIKES OF YUKI-ONNA?
T...
TEN-KUN?!

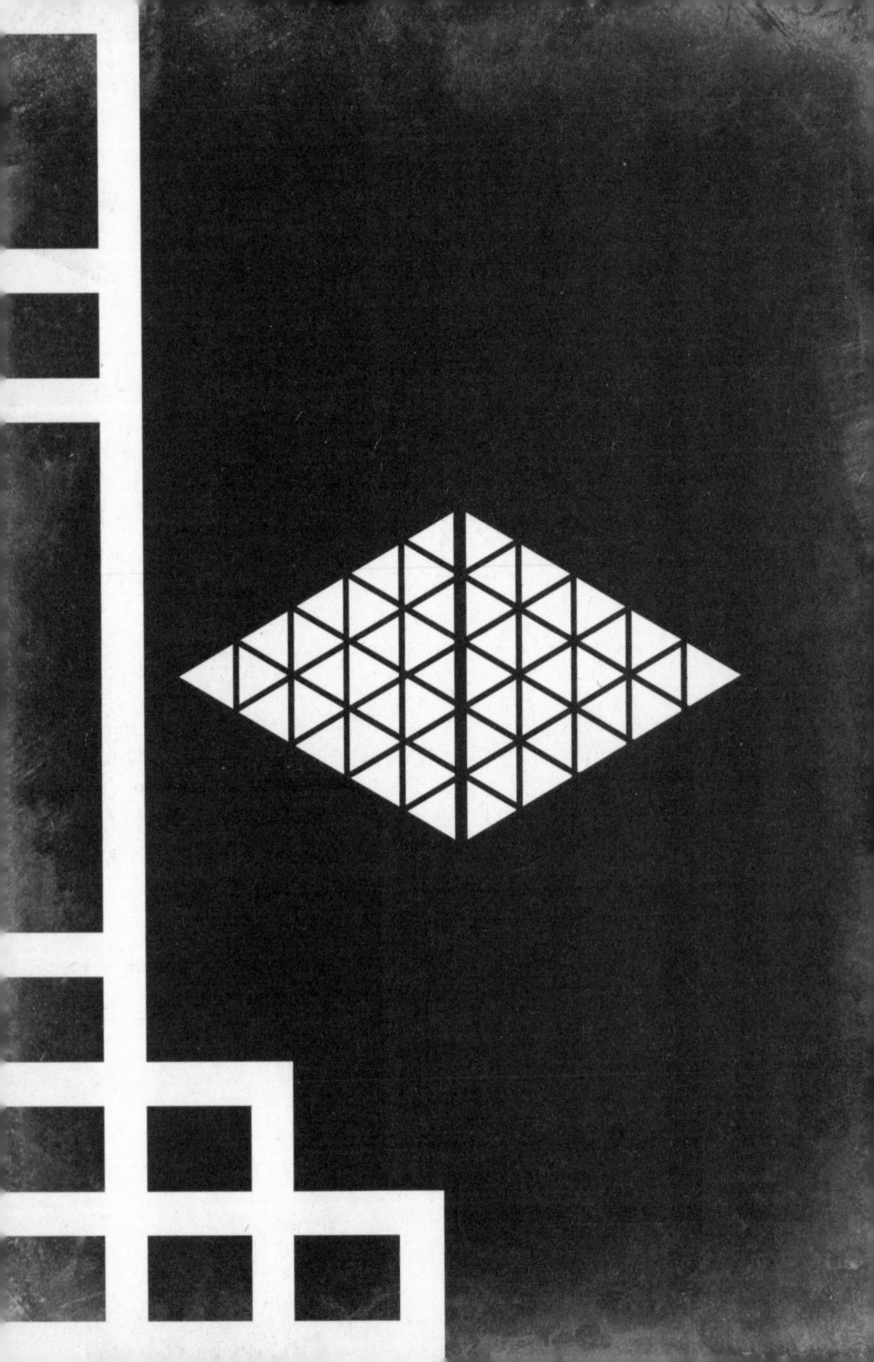

Yokai Rental Shop

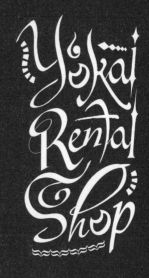

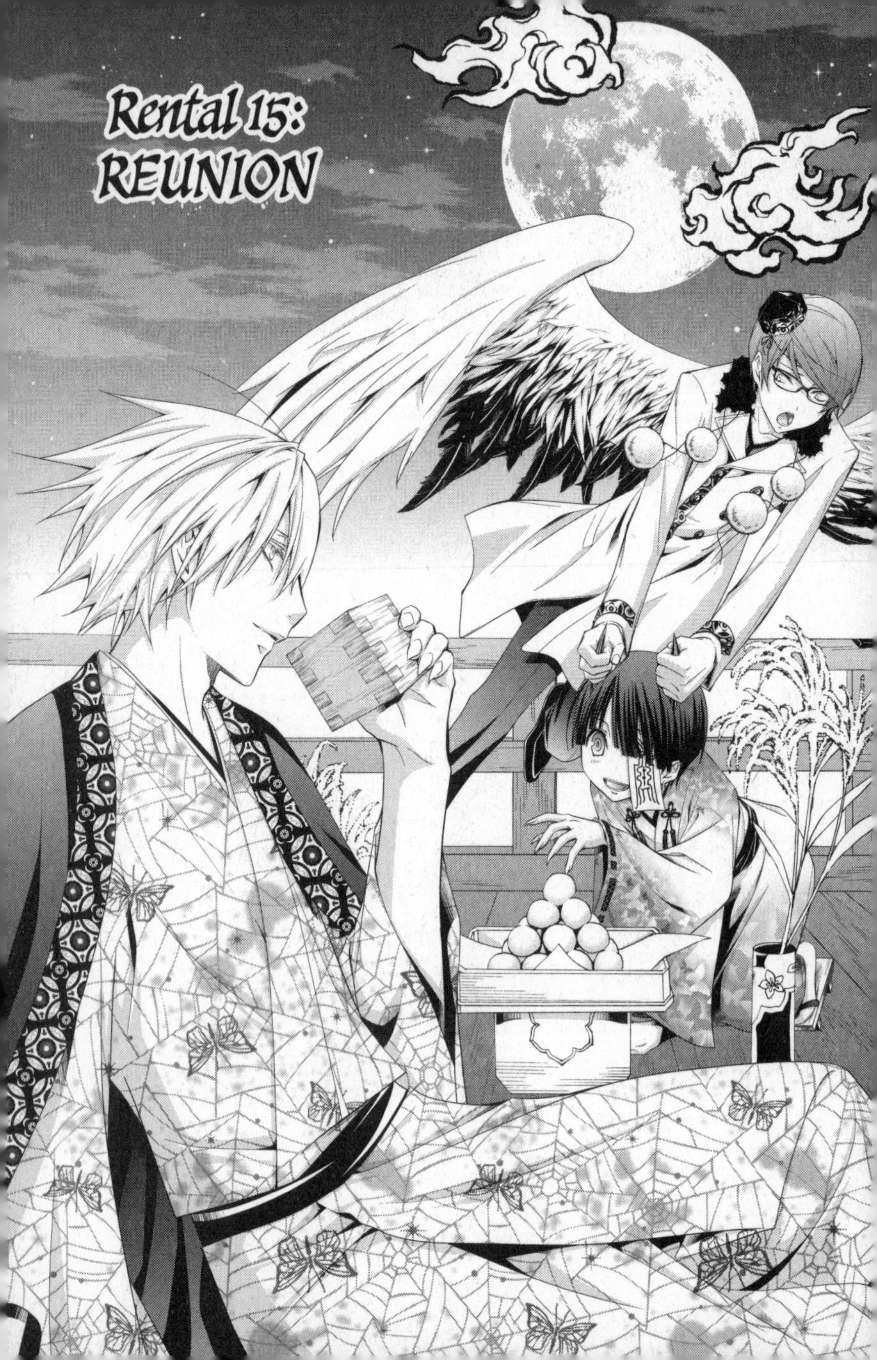
Rental 15:
REUNION

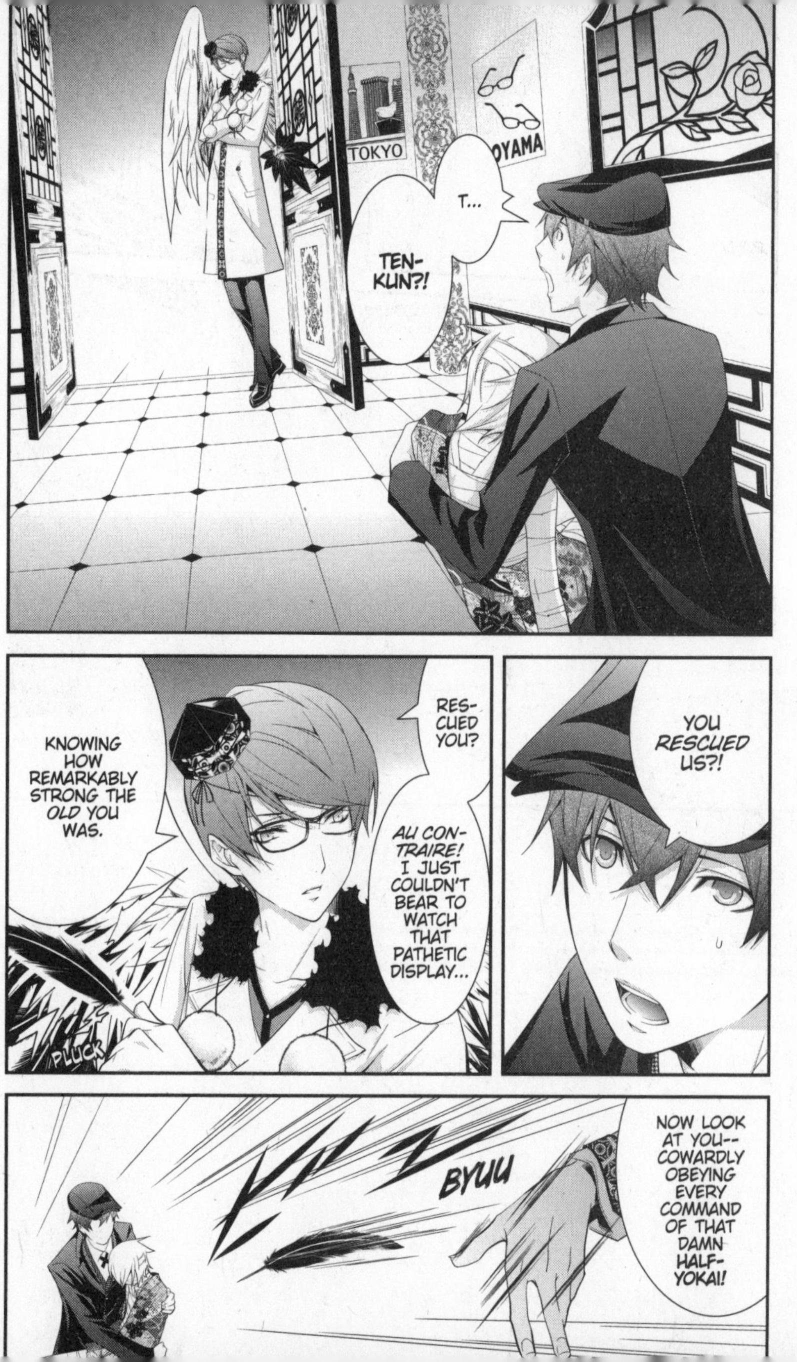
OYAMA
TOKYO
T...
TEN-KUN?!
YOU *RESCUED* US?!
RES-CUED YOU?
AU CON-TRAIRE! I JUST COULDN'T BEAR TO WATCH THAT PATHETIC DISPLAY...
KNOWING HOW REMARKABLY STRONG THE *OLD* YOU WAS.
PLUCK
NOW LOOK AT YOU-- COWARDLY OBEYING EVERY COMMAND OF THAT DAMN HALF-YOKAI!
BYUU

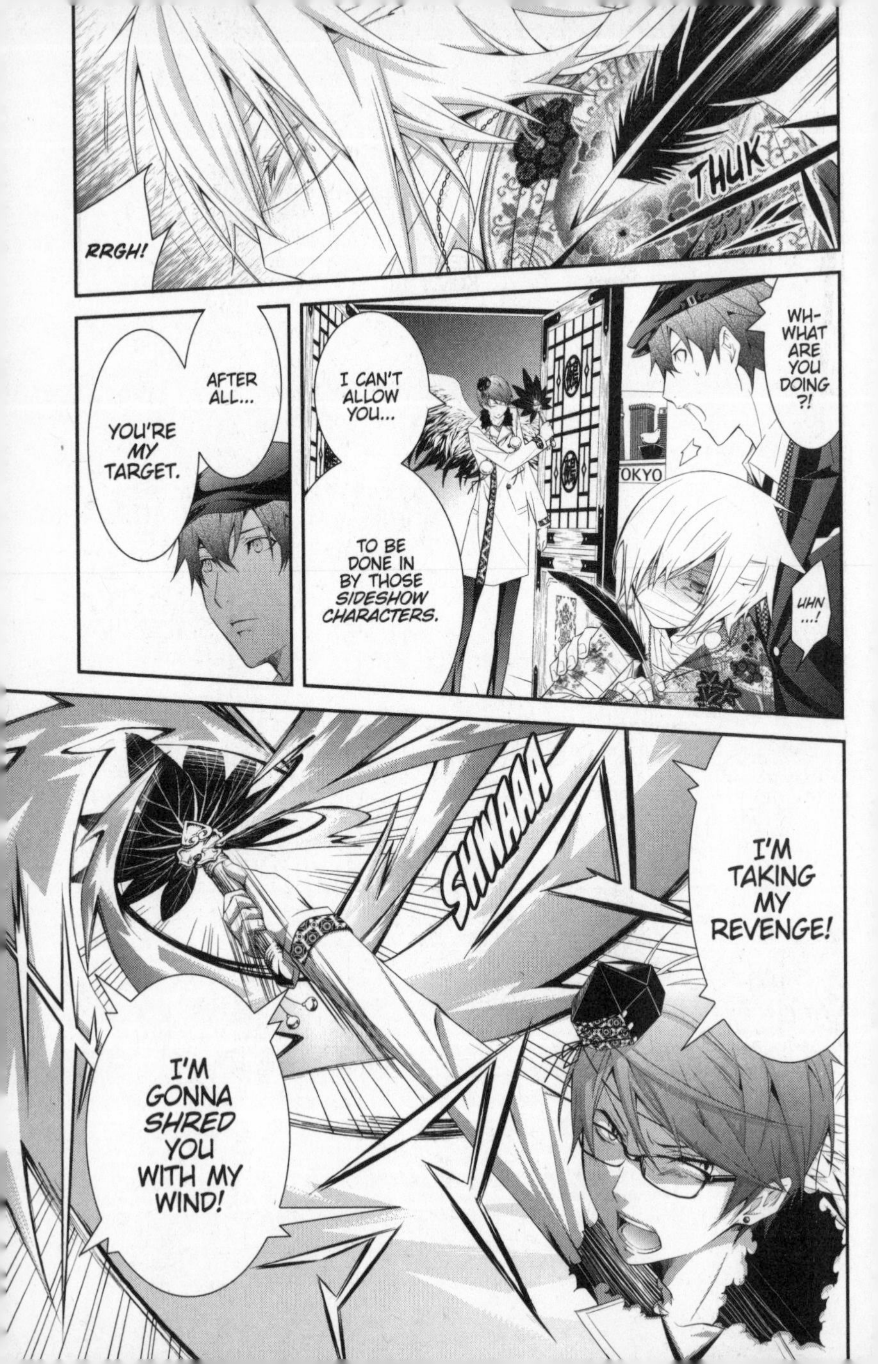
THUK
RRGH!
WH-WHAT ARE YOU DOING?!
I CAN'T ALLOW YOU...
TO BE DONE IN BY THOSE SIDESHOW CHARACTERS.
UHN...!
AFTER ALL...
YOU'RE MY TARGET.
SHWAAA
I'M TAKING MY REVENGE!
I'M GONNA SHRED YOU WITH MY WIND!

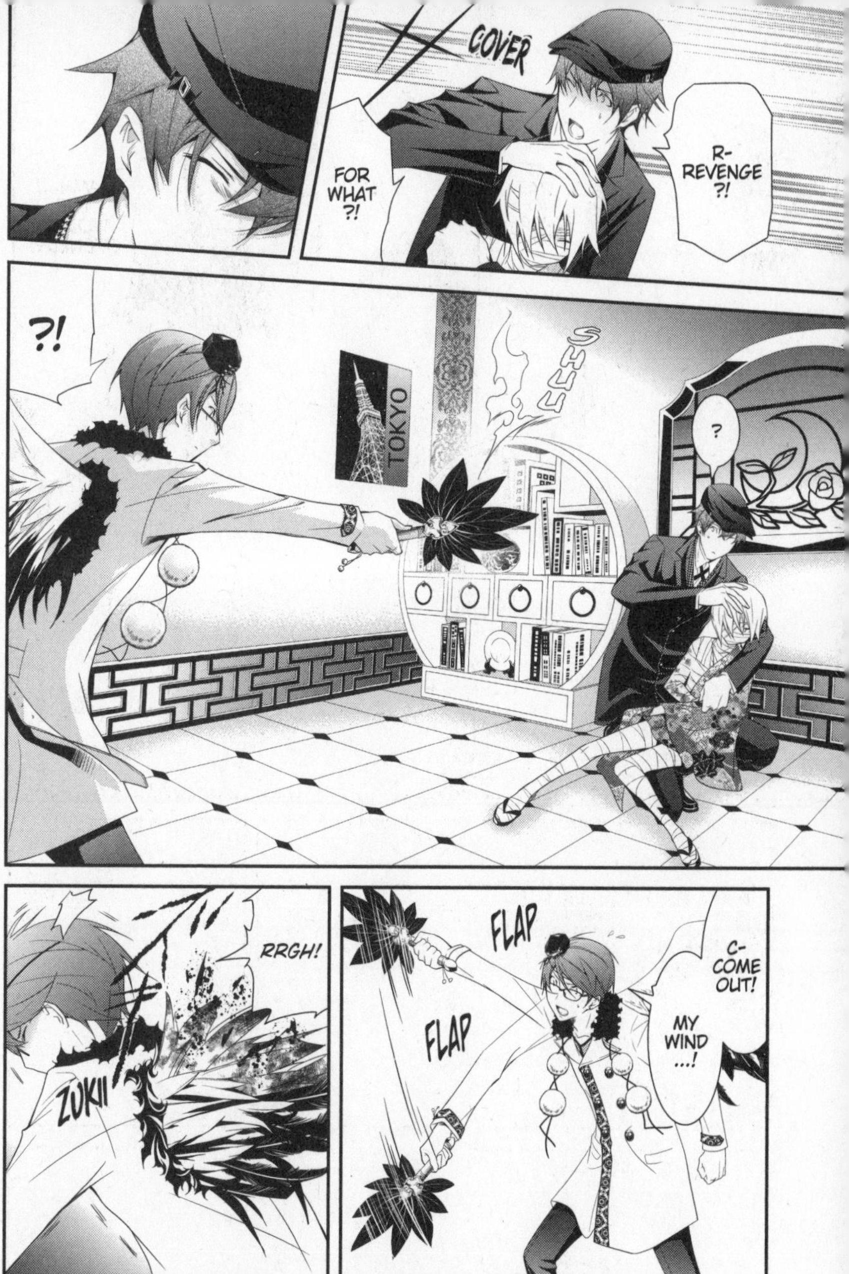
COVER
R-REVENGE?!
FOR WHAT?!
SHUU
?
?!
C-COME OUT!
MY WIND...!
FLAP
FLAP
RRGH!
ZUKII

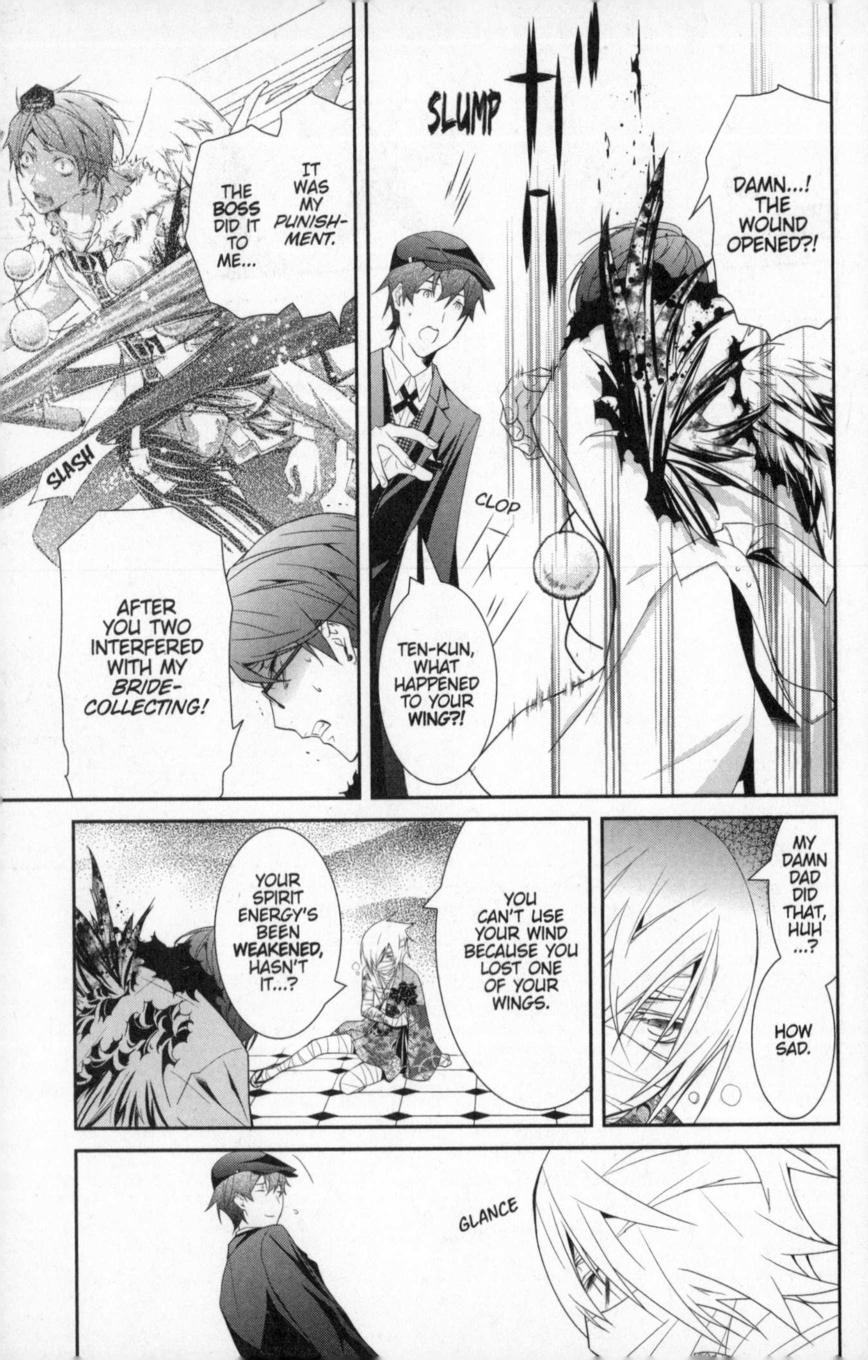
SLUMP
DAMN...! THE WOUND OPENED?!
CLOP
TEN-KUN, WHAT HAPPENED TO YOUR WING?!
IT WAS MY PUNISHMENT.
THE BOSS DID IT TO ME...
SLASH
AFTER YOU TWO INTERFERED WITH MY BRIDE-COLLECTING!
MY DAMN DAD DID THAT, HUH...?
HOW SAD.
YOU CAN'T USE YOUR WIND BECAUSE YOU LOST ONE OF YOUR WINGS.
YOUR SPIRIT ENERGY'S BEEN WEAKENED, HASN'T IT...?
GLANCE

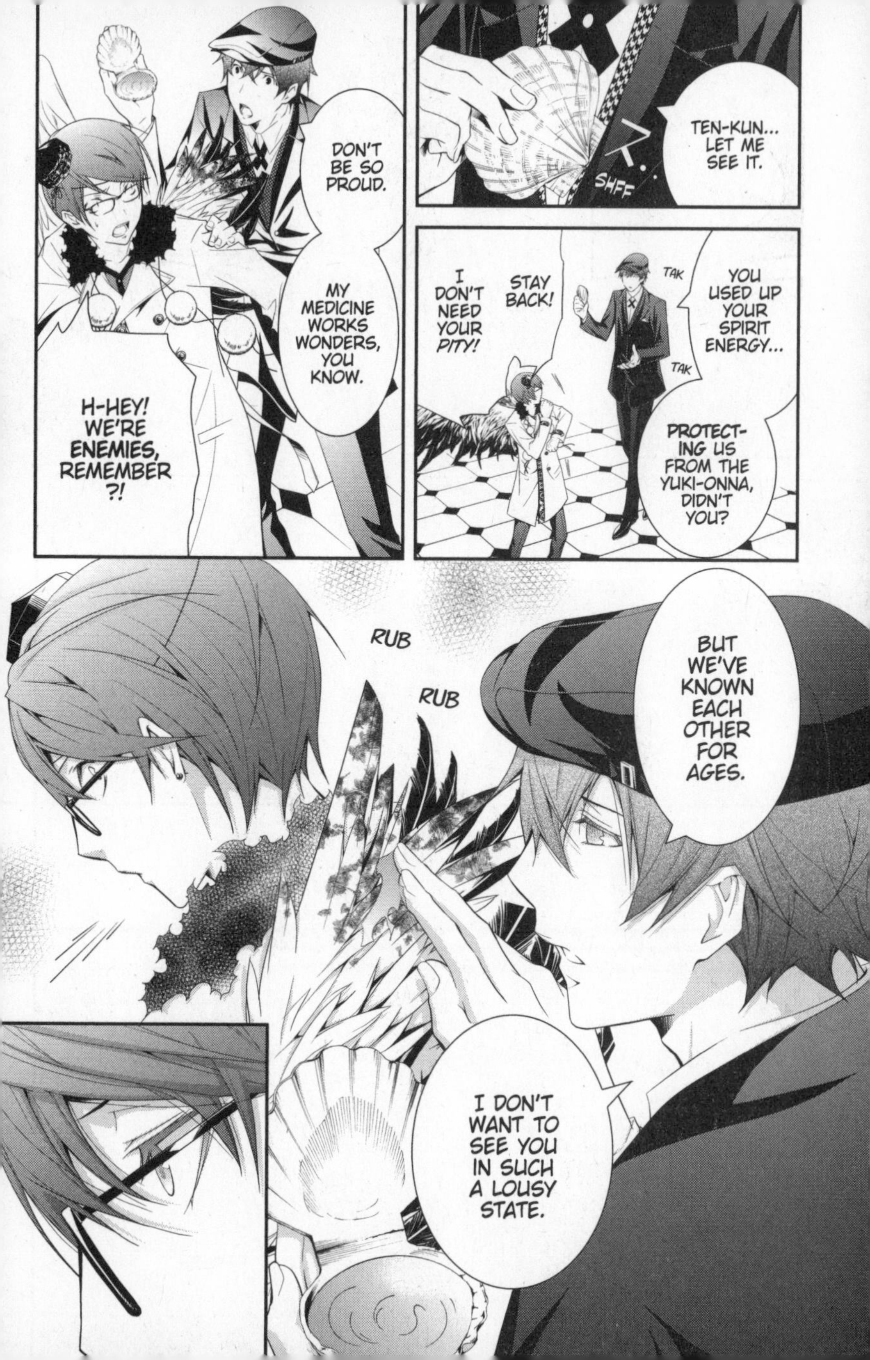
TEN-KUN... LET ME SEE IT.
SHFF
YOU USED UP YOUR SPIRIT ENERGY...
TAK
TAK
PROTECTING US FROM THE YUKI-ONNA, DIDN'T YOU?
STAY BACK!
I DON'T NEED YOUR PITY!
DON'T BE SO PROUD.
MY MEDICINE WORKS WONDERS, YOU KNOW.
H-HEY! WE'RE ENEMIES, REMEMBER?!
BUT WE'VE KNOWN EACH OTHER FOR AGES.
RUB
RUB
I DON'T WANT TO SEE YOU IN SUCH A LOUSY STATE.

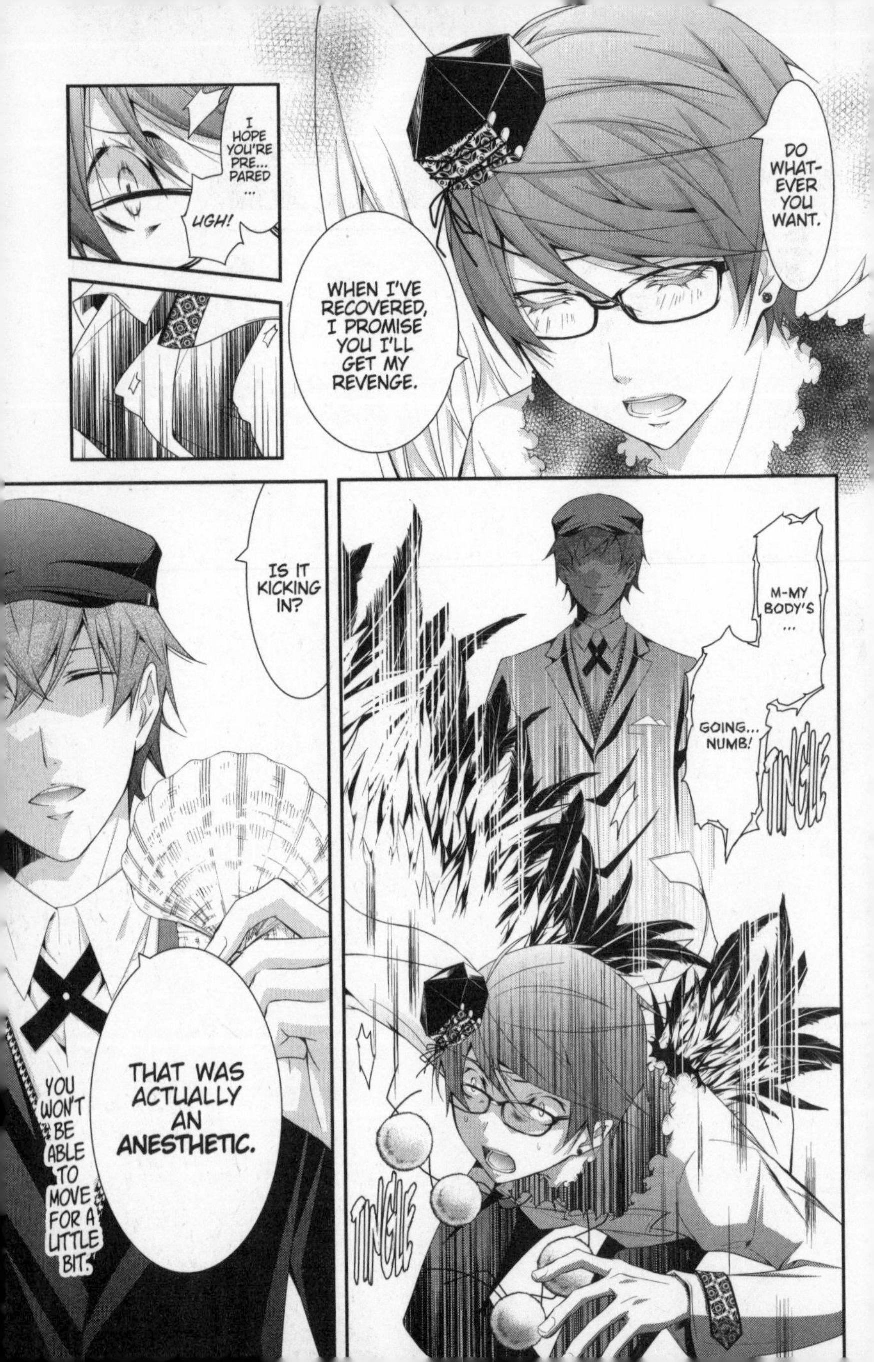
DO WHATEVER YOU WANT.
WHEN I'VE RECOVERED, I PROMISE YOU I'LL GET MY REVENGE.
I HOPE YOU'RE PRE... PARED...
UGH!
M-MY BODY'S...
GOING... NUMB!
TINGLE
TINGLE
IS IT KICKING IN?
THAT WAS ACTUALLY AN ANESTHETIC.
YOU WON'T BE ABLE TO MOVE FOR A LITTLE BIT.

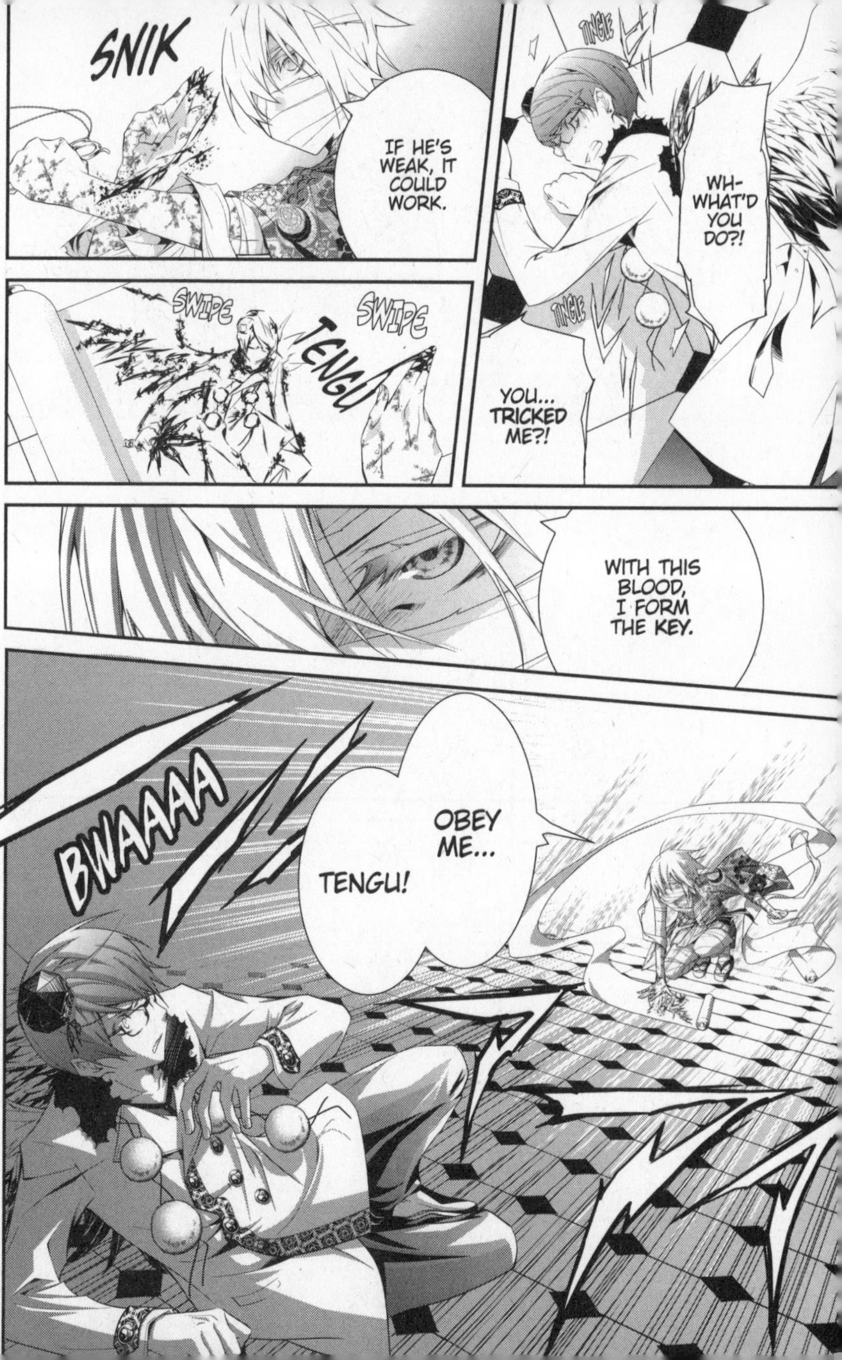
TINGLE
WH-WHAT'D YOU DO?!
TINGLE
YOU... TRICKED ME?!
SNIK
IF HE'S WEAK, IT COULD WORK.
SWIPE
SWIPE
TENGU
WITH THIS BLOOD, I FORM THE KEY.
OBEY ME...
TENGU!
BWAAAA

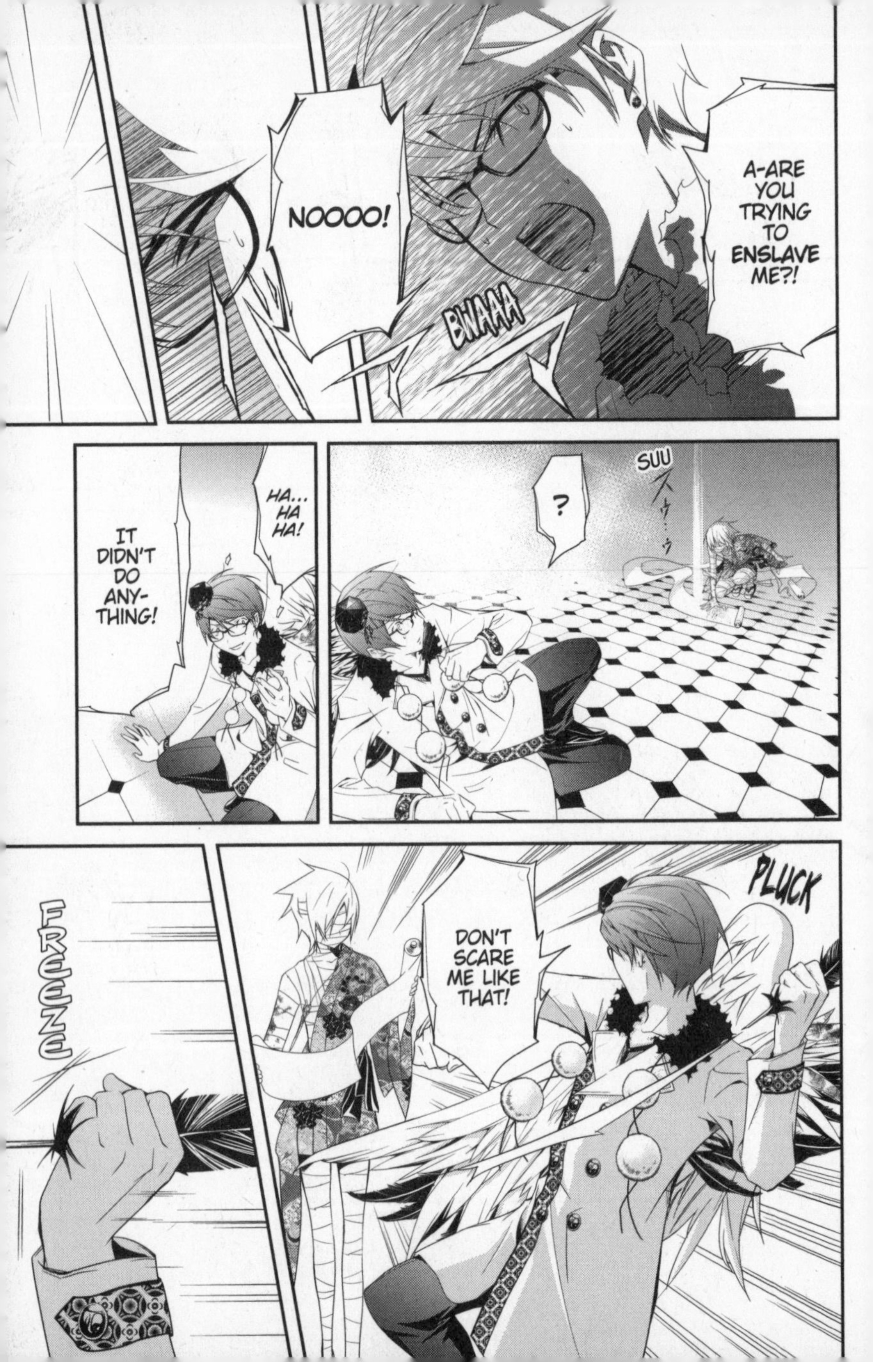
A-ARE YOU TRYING TO ENSLAVE ME?!
NOOOO!
BWAAA
SUU
?
HA... HA HA!
IT DIDN'T DO ANY-THING!
PLUCK
DON'T SCARE ME LIKE THAT!
FREEZE

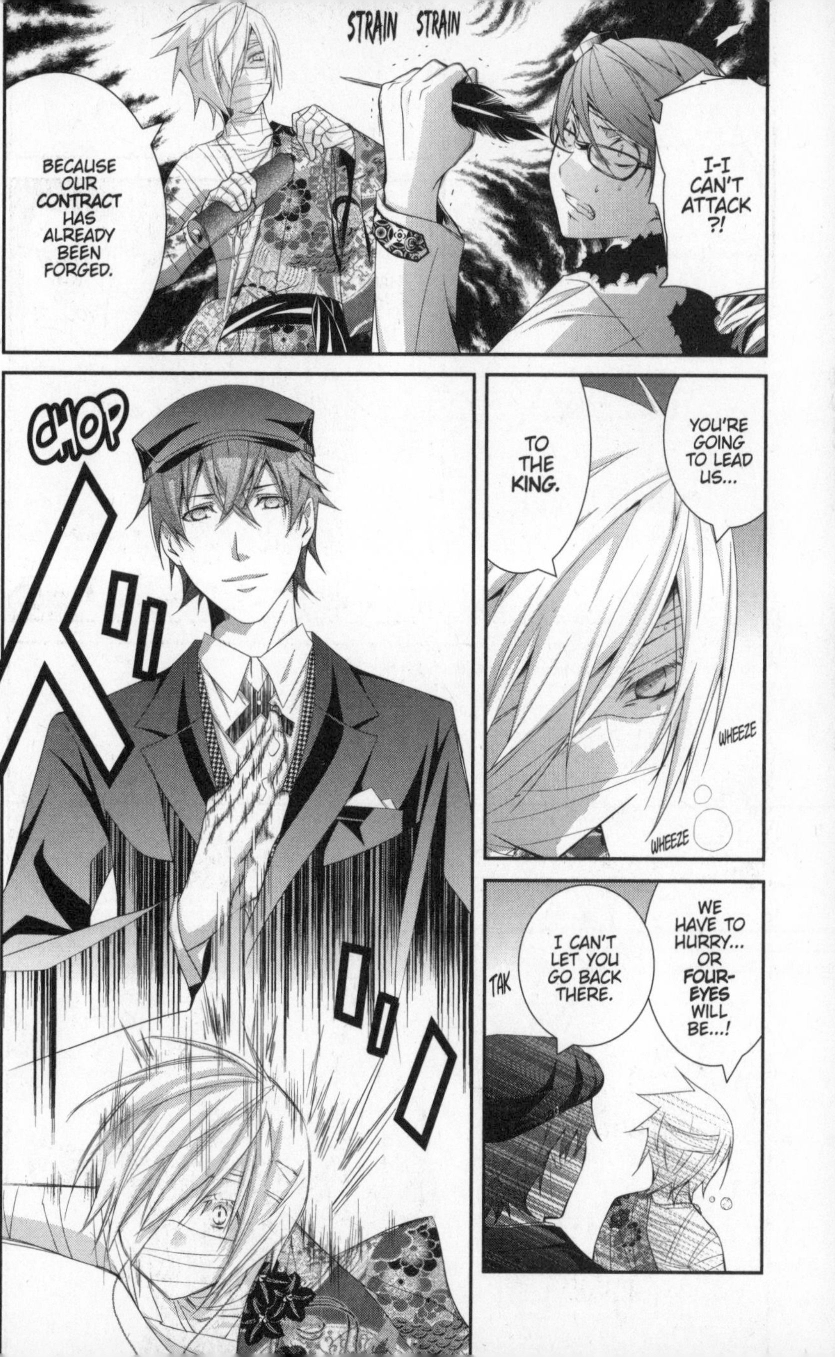
STRAIN STRAIN
I-I CAN'T ATTACK ?!
BECAUSE OUR CONTRACT HAS ALREADY BEEN FORGED.
YOU'RE GOING TO LEAD US...
TO THE KING.
WHEEZE
WHEEZE
WE HAVE TO HURRY... OR FOUR-EYES WILL BE...!
I CAN'T LET YOU GO BACK THERE.
TAK
CHOP

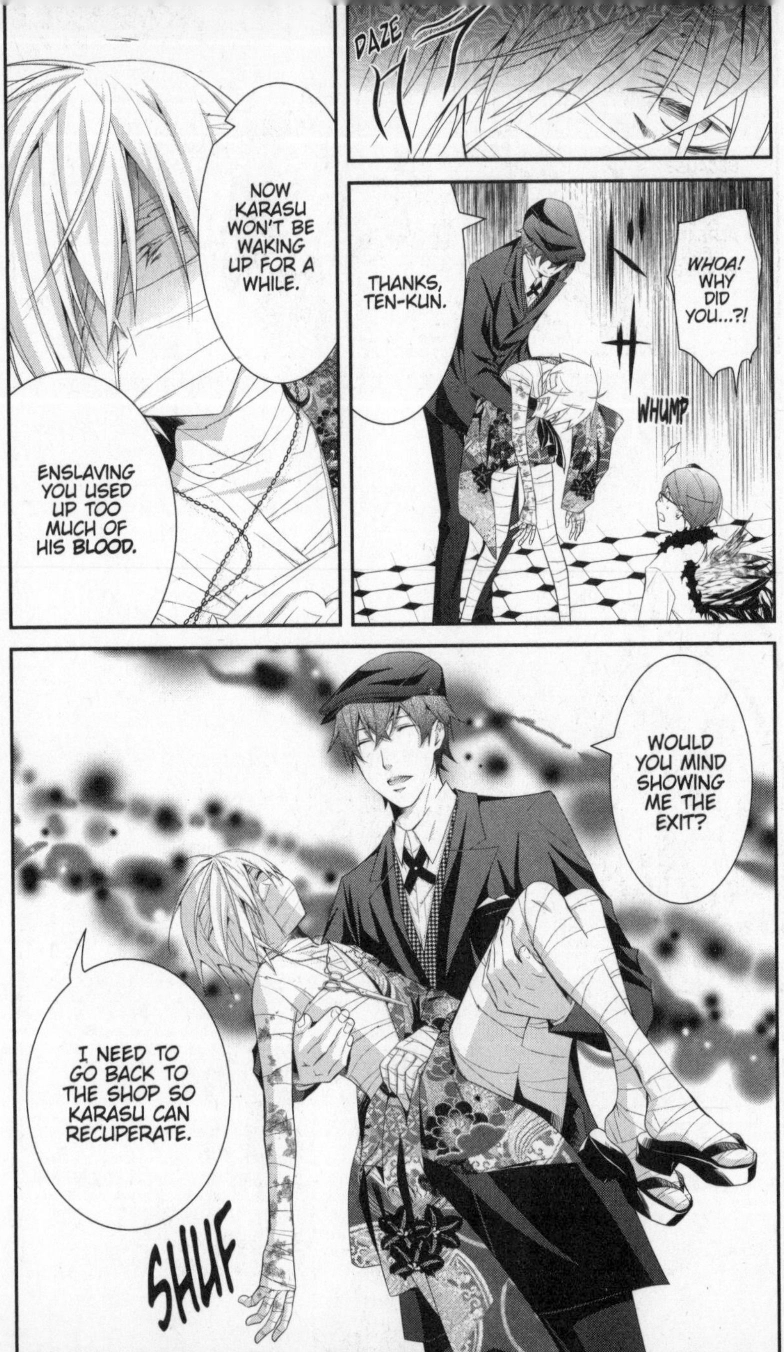
DAZE
WHOA! WHY DID YOU...?!
WHUMP
THANKS, TEN-KUN.
NOW KARASU WON'T BE WAKING UP FOR A WHILE.
ENSLAVING YOU USED UP TOO MUCH OF HIS BLOOD.
WOULD YOU MIND SHOWING ME THE EXIT?
I NEED TO GO BACK TO THE SHOP SO KARASU CAN RECUPERATE.
SHUF

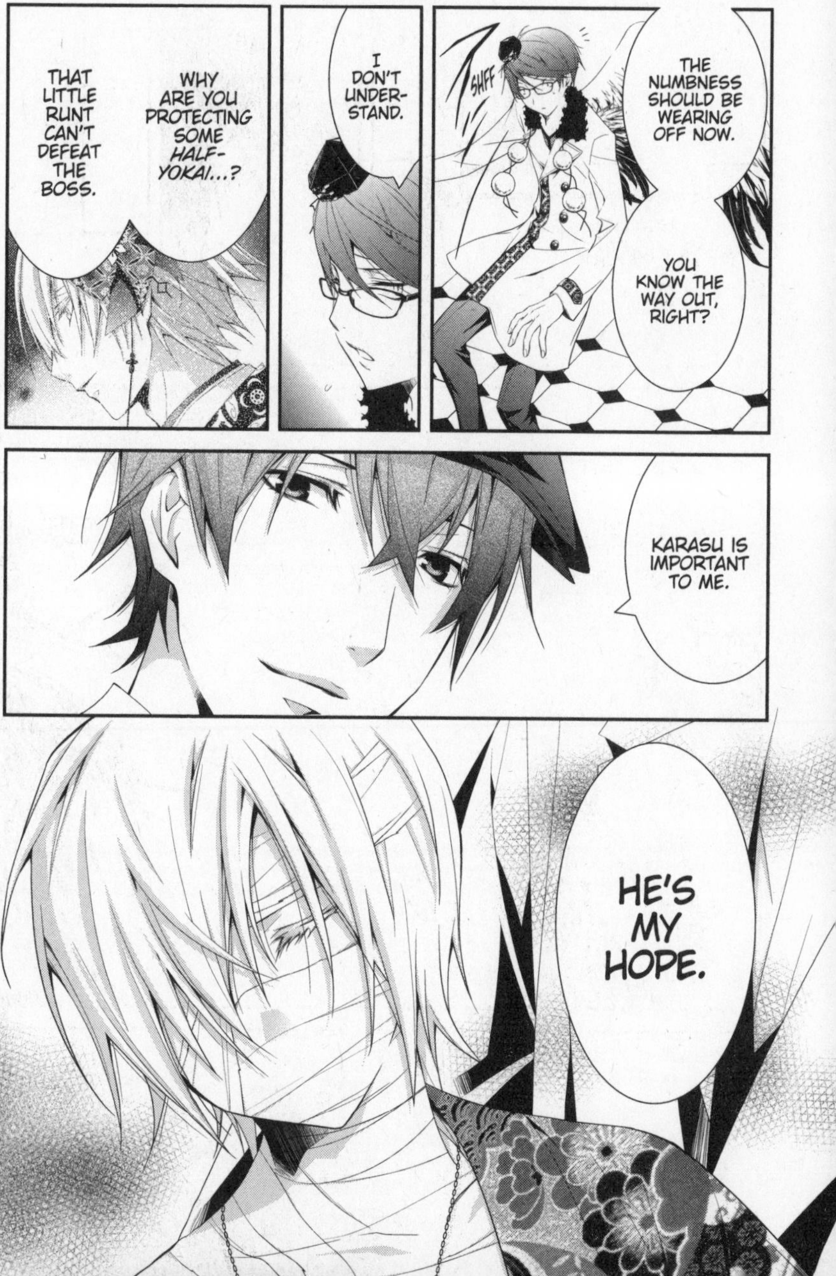
THE NUMBNESS SHOULD BE WEARING OFF NOW.
SHFF
YOU KNOW THE WAY OUT, RIGHT?
I DON'T UNDER-STAND.
WHY ARE YOU PROTECTING SOME *HALF-YOKAI*...?
THAT LITTLE RUNT CAN'T DEFEAT THE BOSS.
KARASU IS IMPORTANT TO ME.
HE'S MY HOPE.

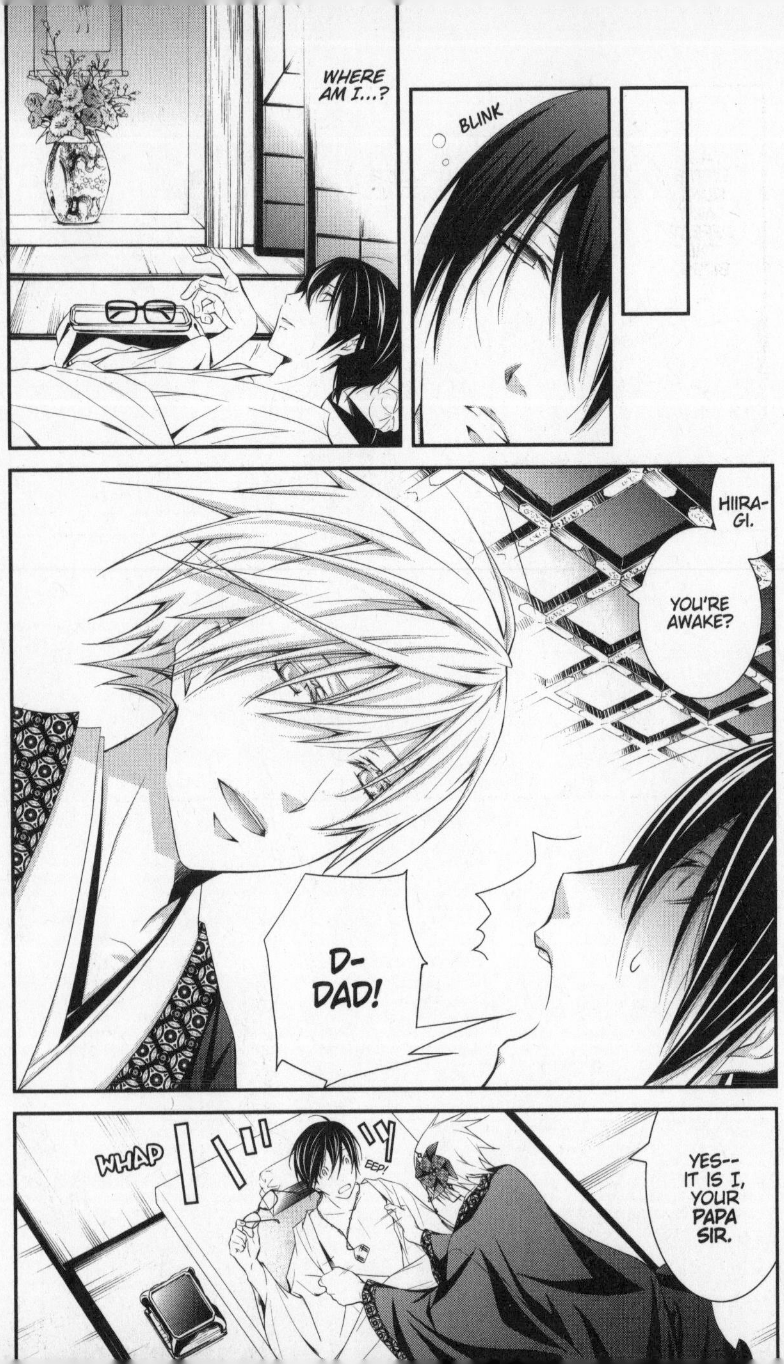
BLINK
WHERE AM I...?
HIIRA-GI.
YOU'RE AWAKE?
D-DAD!
YES--IT IS I, YOUR PAPA SIR.
EEP!
WHAP

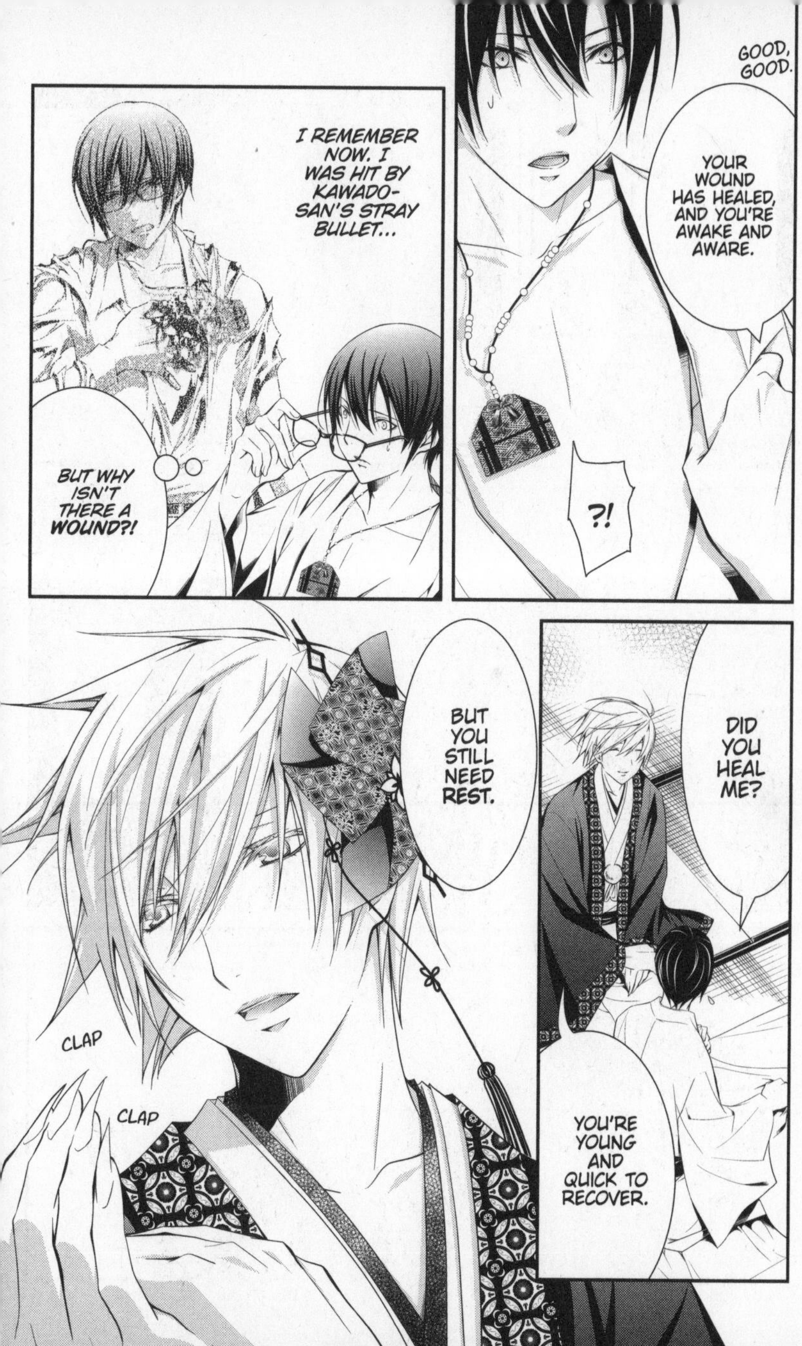
GOOD, GOOD.
YOUR WOUND HAS HEALED, AND YOU'RE AWAKE AND AWARE.
?!
I REMEMBER NOW. I WAS HIT BY KAWADO-SAN'S STRAY BULLET...
BUT WHY ISN'T THERE A WOUND?!
DID YOU HEAL ME?
YOU'RE YOUNG AND QUICK TO RECOVER.
BUT YOU STILL NEED REST.
CLAP
CLAP

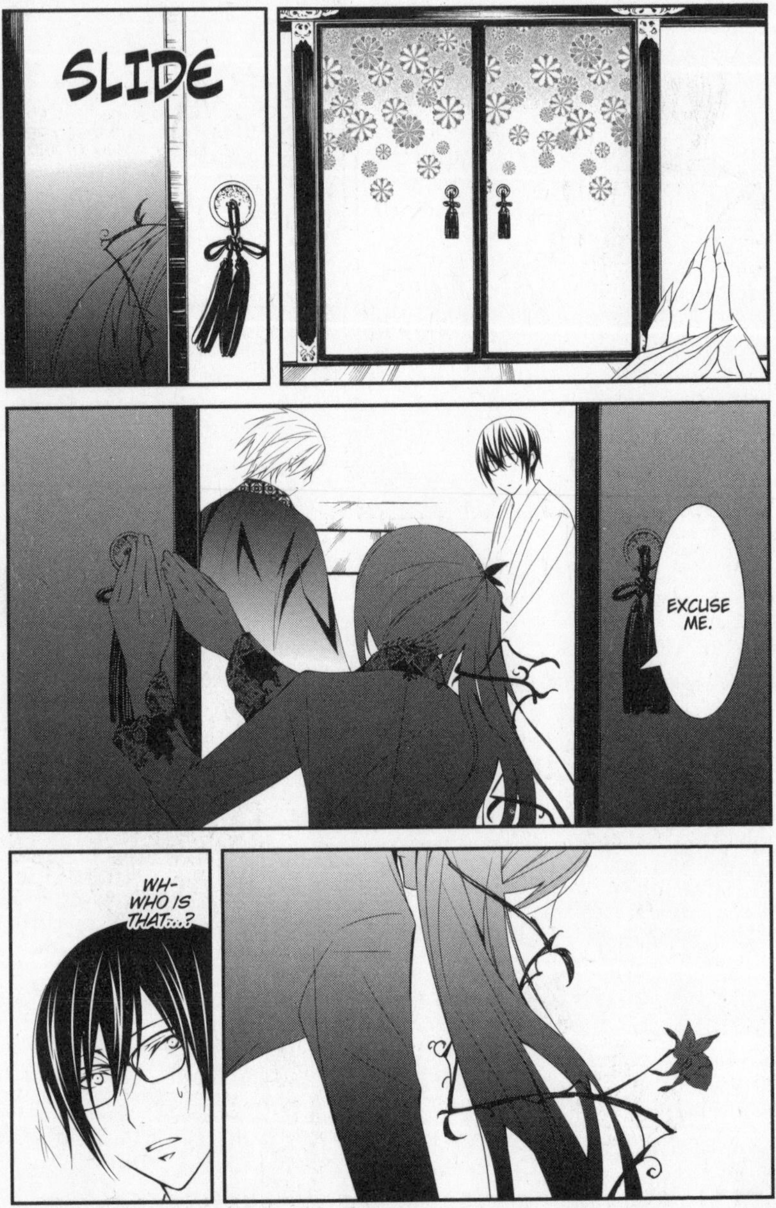
SLIDE
EXCUSE ME.
WH- WHO IS THAT...?

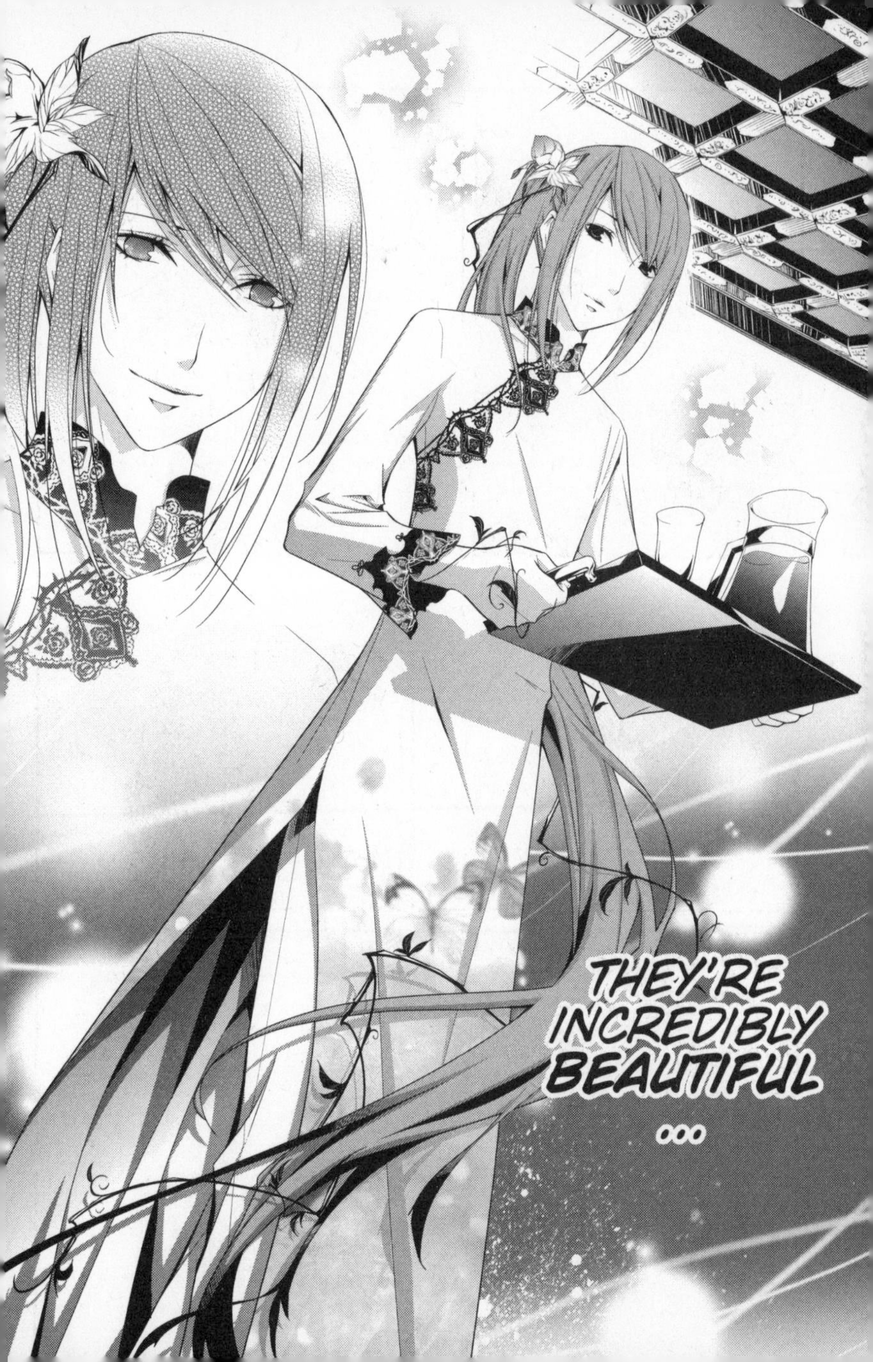
THEY'RE INCREDIBLY BEAUTIFUL ...

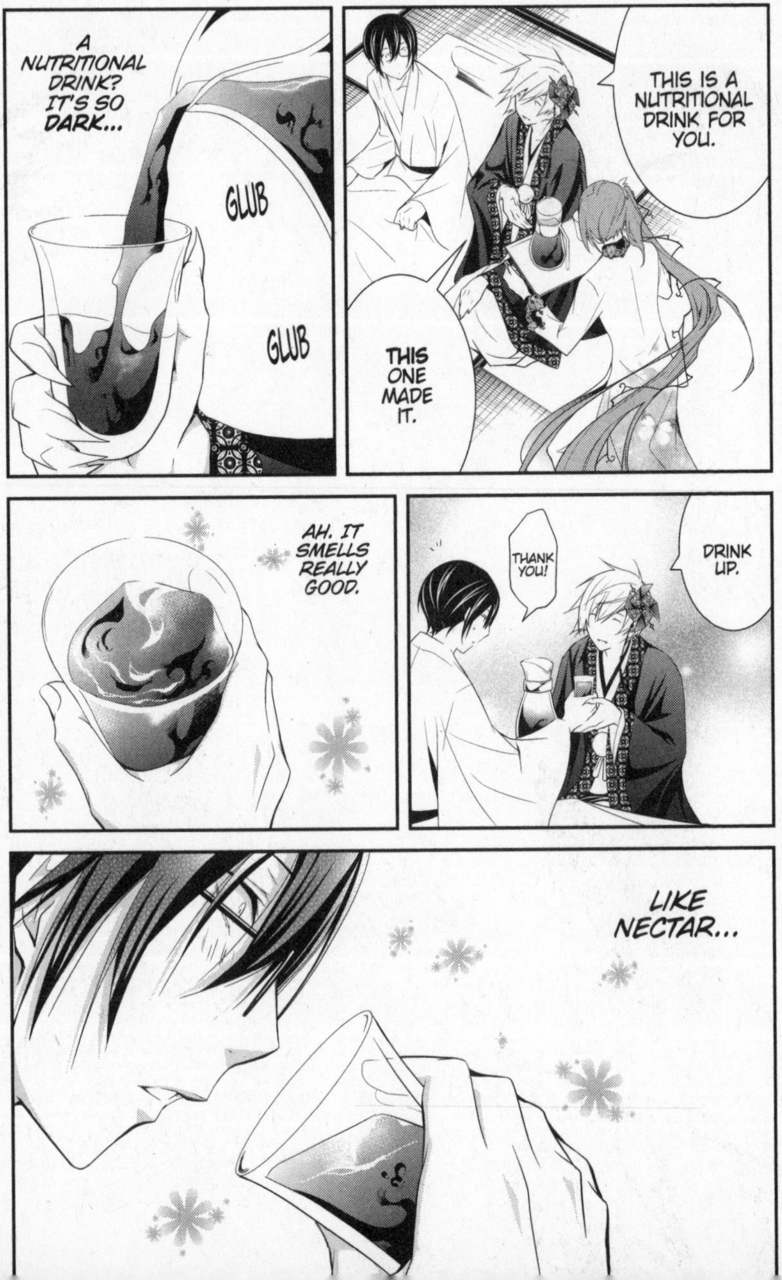
THIS IS A NUTRITIONAL DRINK FOR YOU.
THIS ONE MADE IT.
A NUTRITIONAL DRINK? IT'S SO DARK...
GLUB
GLUB
DRINK UP.
THANK YOU!
AH. IT SMELLS REALLY GOOD.
LIKE NECTAR...

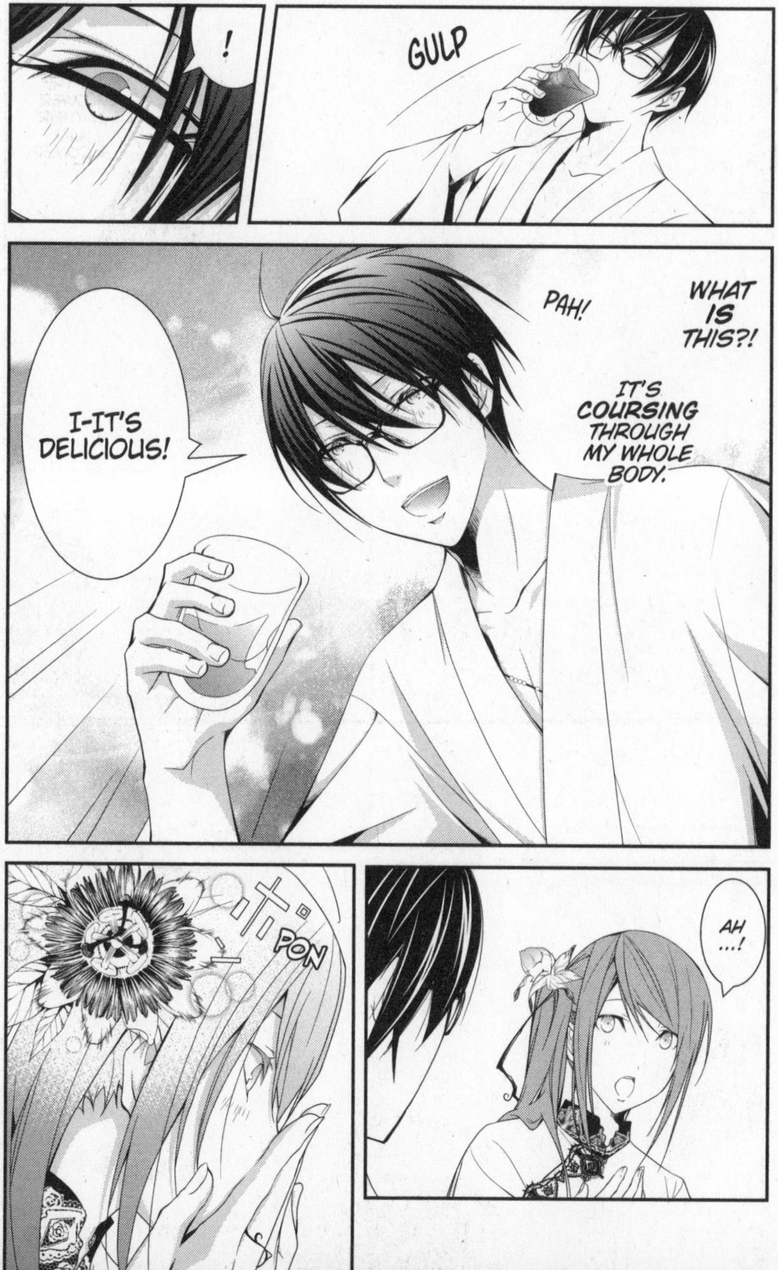
GULP
!
WHAT IS THIS?!
PAH!
IT'S COURSING THROUGH MY WHOLE BODY.
I-IT'S DELICIOUS!
AH ...!
PON

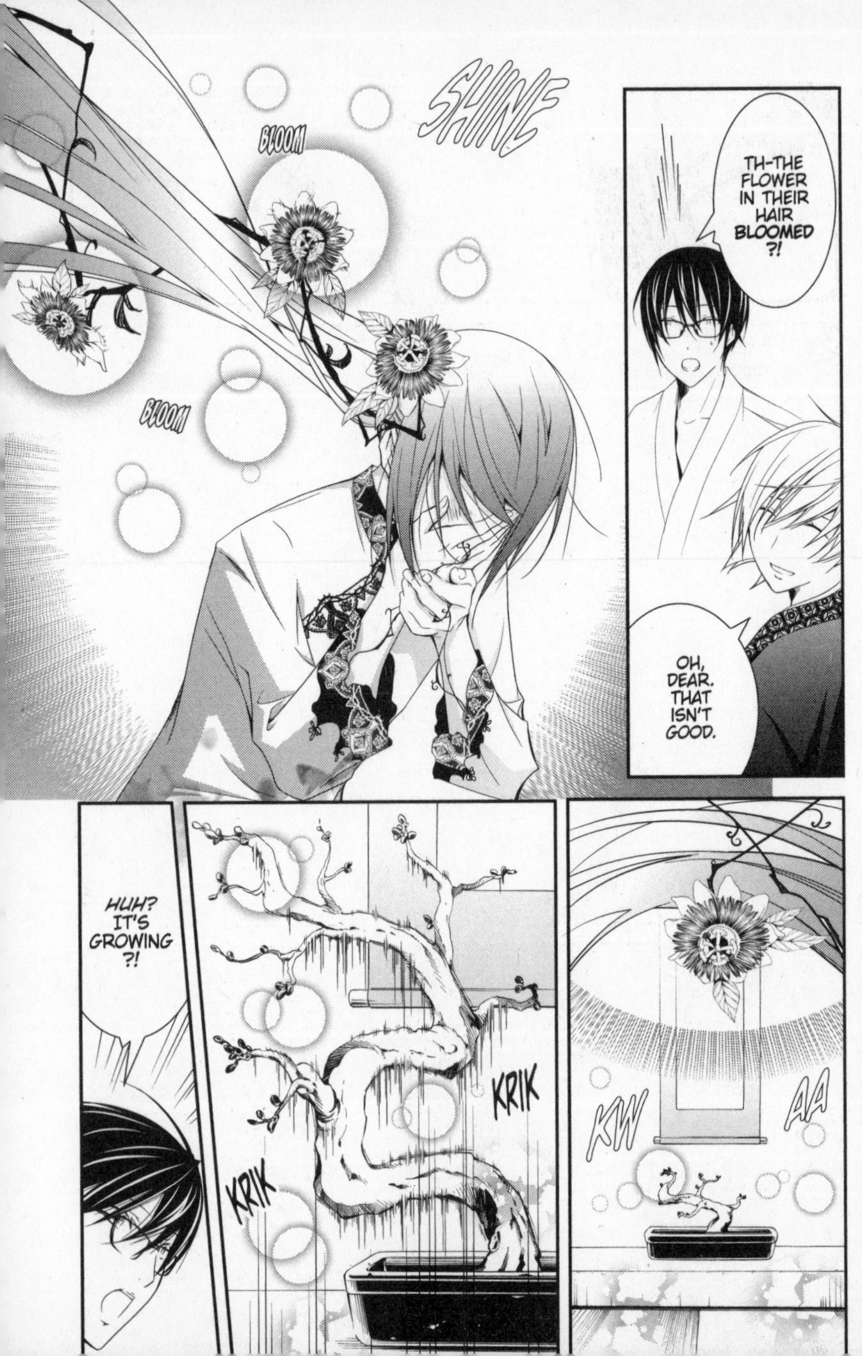
TH-THE FLOWER IN THEIR HAIR BLOOMED ?!
OH, DEAR. THAT ISN'T GOOD.
SHINE
BLOOM
BLOOM
KW
AA
KRIK
KRIK
HUH? IT'S GROWING ?!

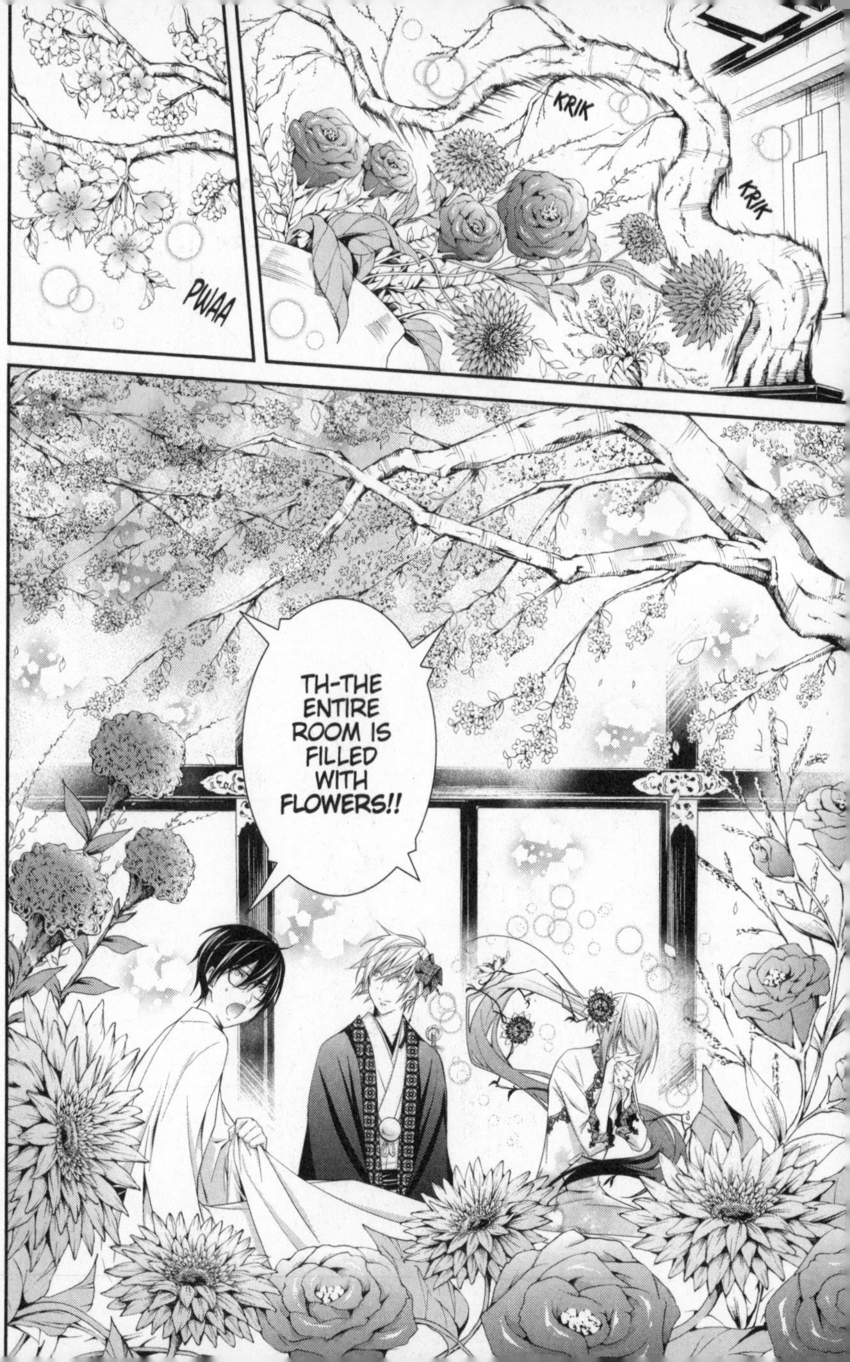
KRIK
KRIK
PWAA
TH-THE ENTIRE ROOM IS FILLED WITH FLOWERS!!

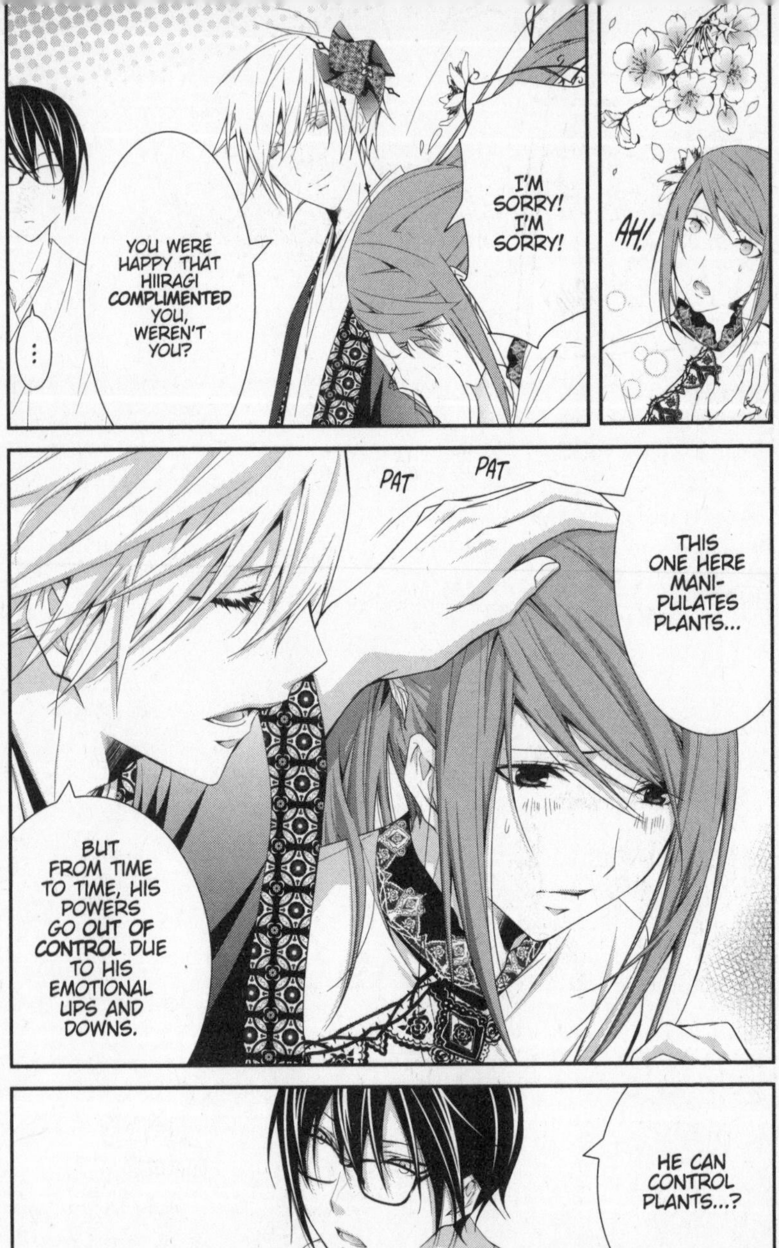
AH!
I'M SORRY! I'M SORRY!
YOU WERE HAPPY THAT HIIRAGI COMPLIMENTED YOU, WEREN'T YOU?
...
PAT
PAT
THIS ONE HERE MANI-PULATES PLANTS...
BUT FROM TIME TO TIME, HIS POWERS GO OUT OF CONTROL DUE TO HIS EMOTIONAL UPS AND DOWNS.
HE CAN CONTROL PLANTS...?

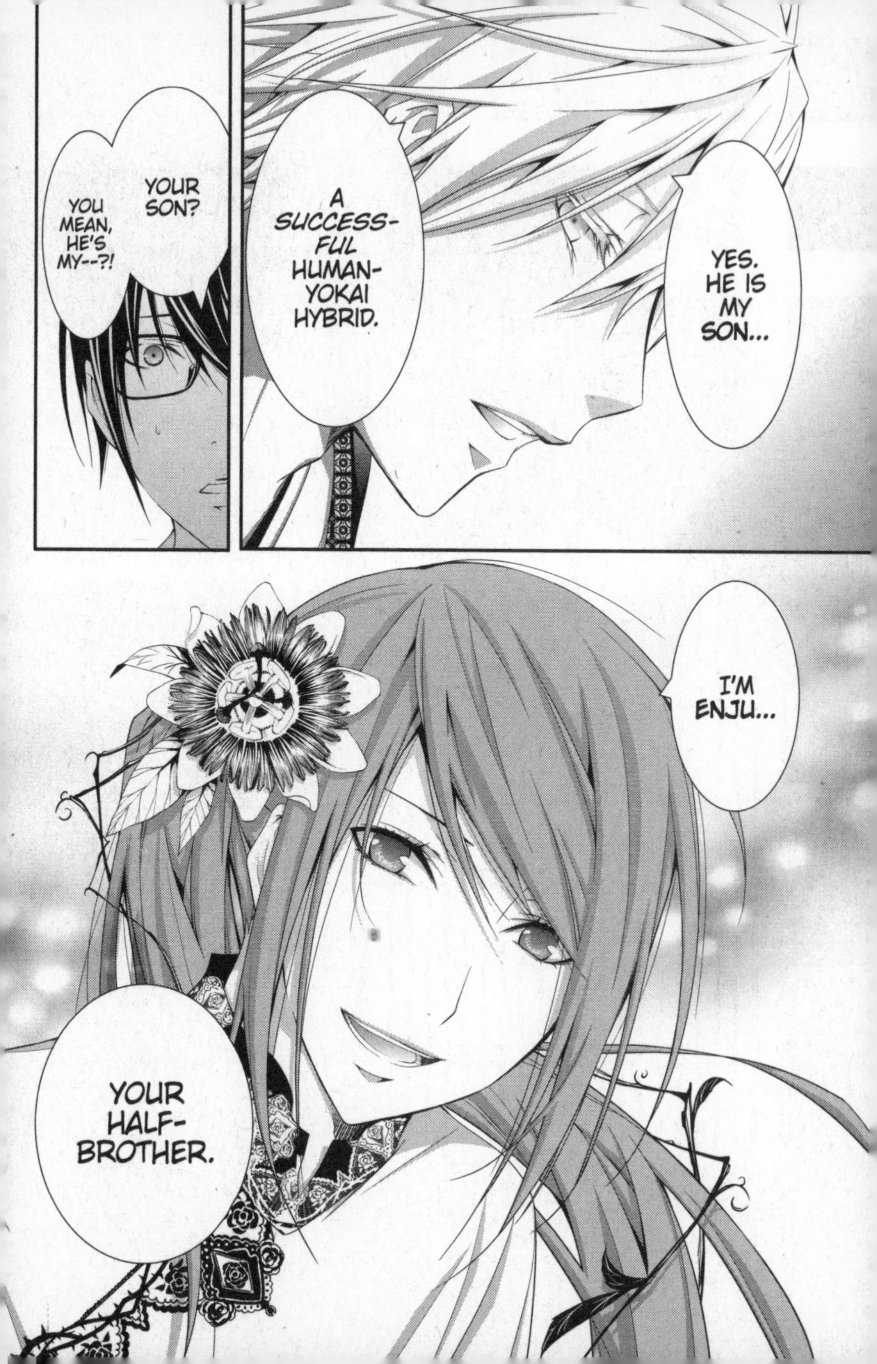
YES. HE IS MY SON...
A SUCCESSFUL HUMAN-YOKAI HYBRID.
YOUR SON?
YOU MEAN, HE'S MY--?!
I'M ENJU...
YOUR HALF-BROTHER.

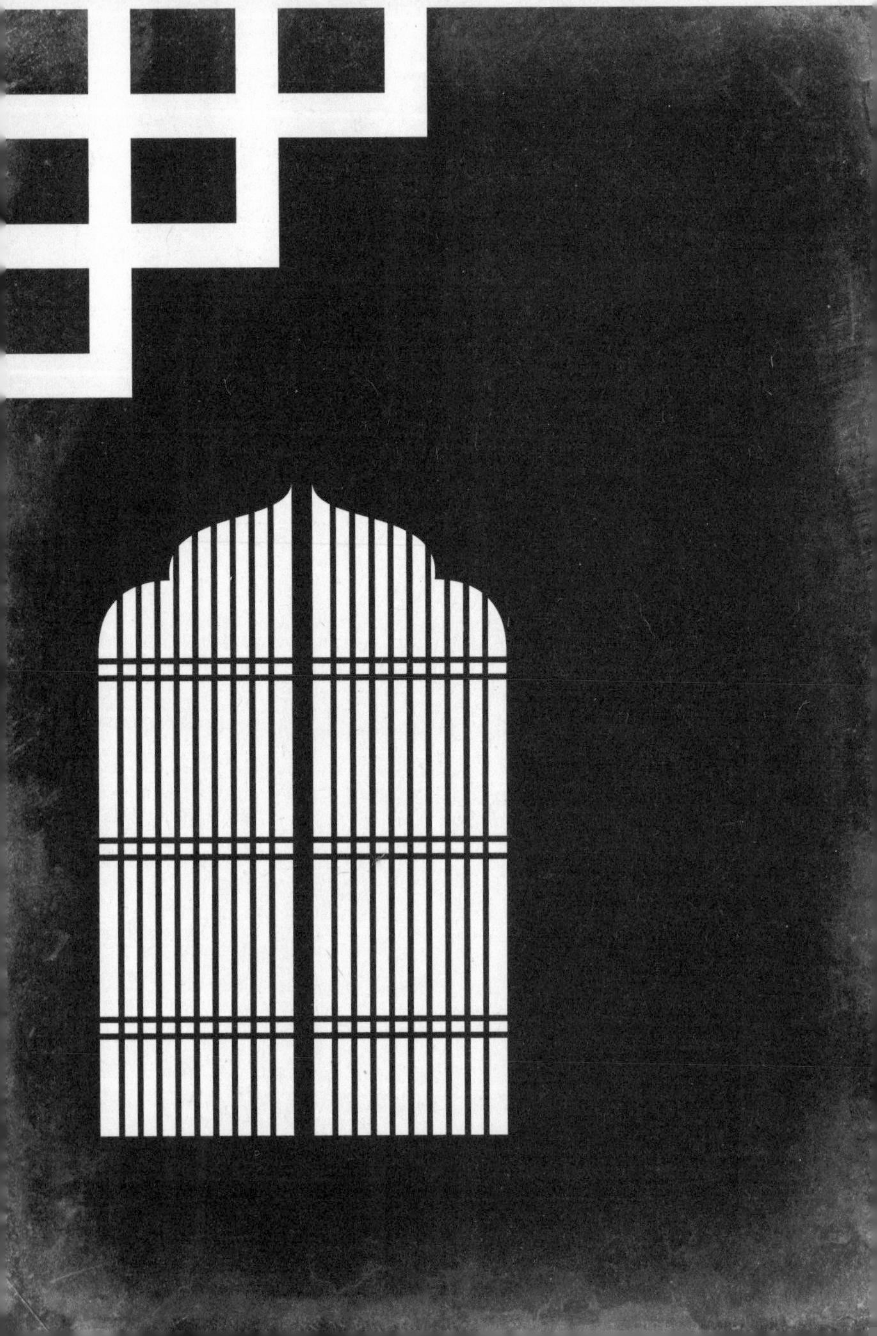

Yōkai Rental Shop

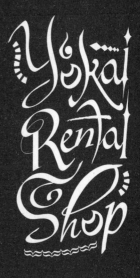

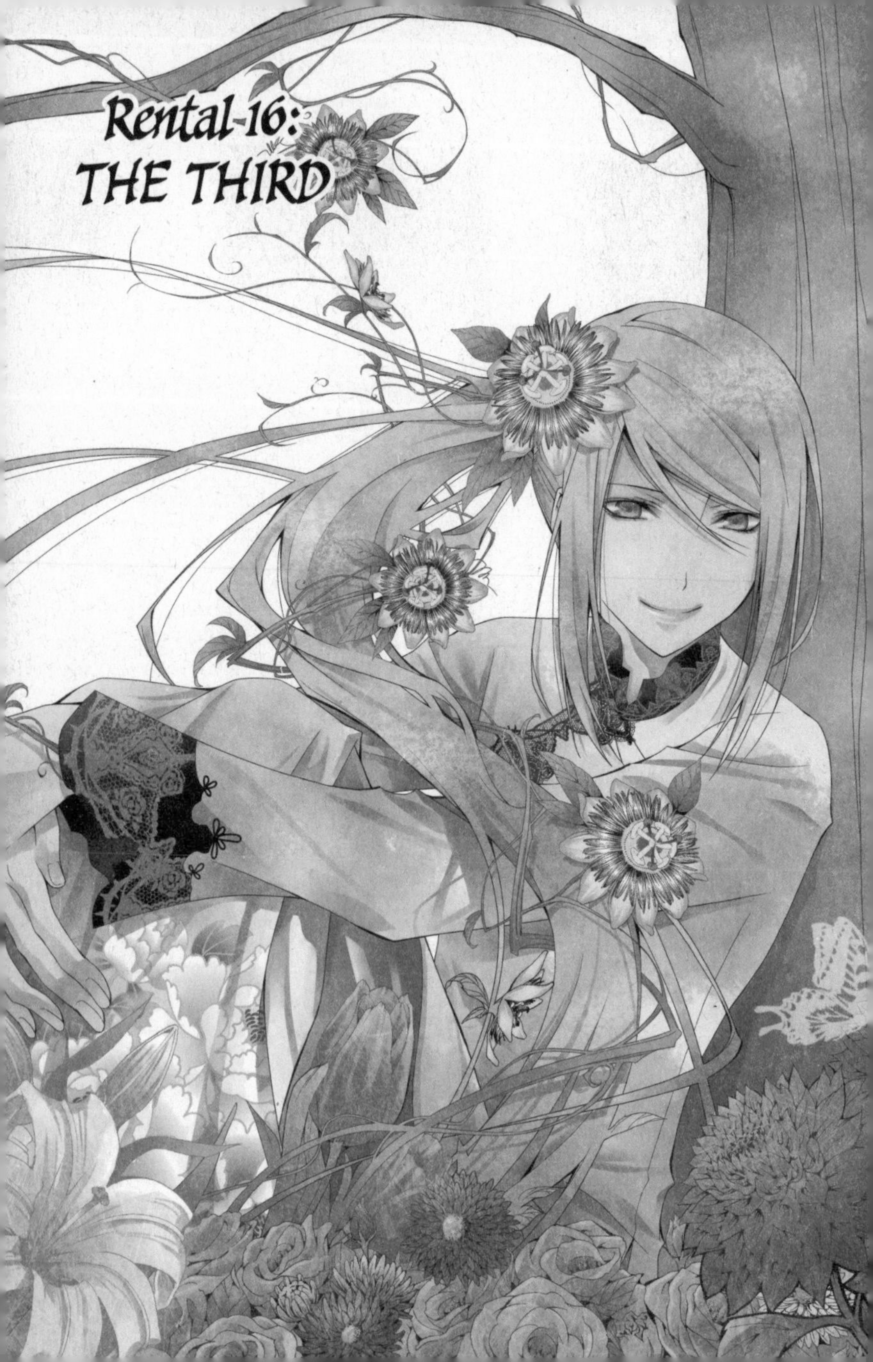
Rental-16:
THE THIRD

Yōkai Rental Shop

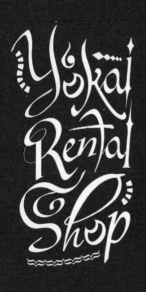

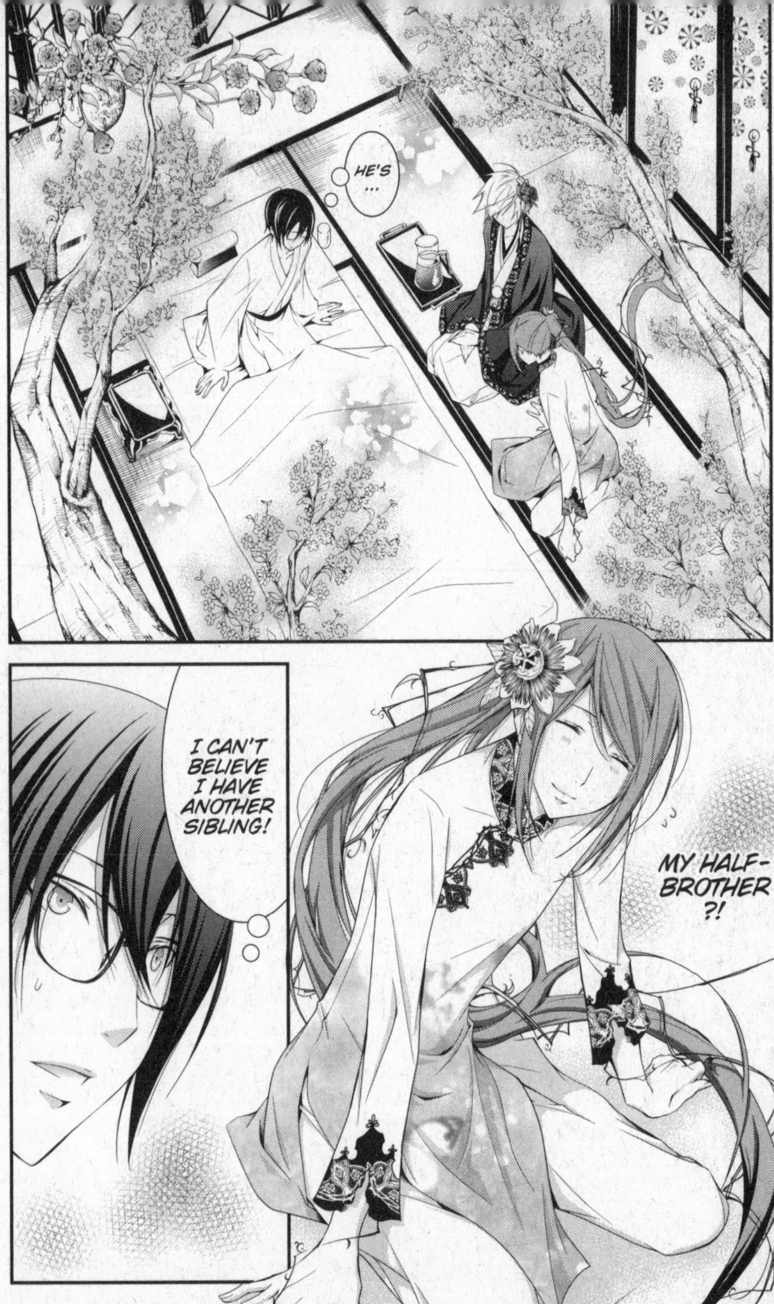
HE'S ...
MY HALF-BROTHER ?!
I CAN'T BELIEVE I HAVE ANOTHER SIBLING!

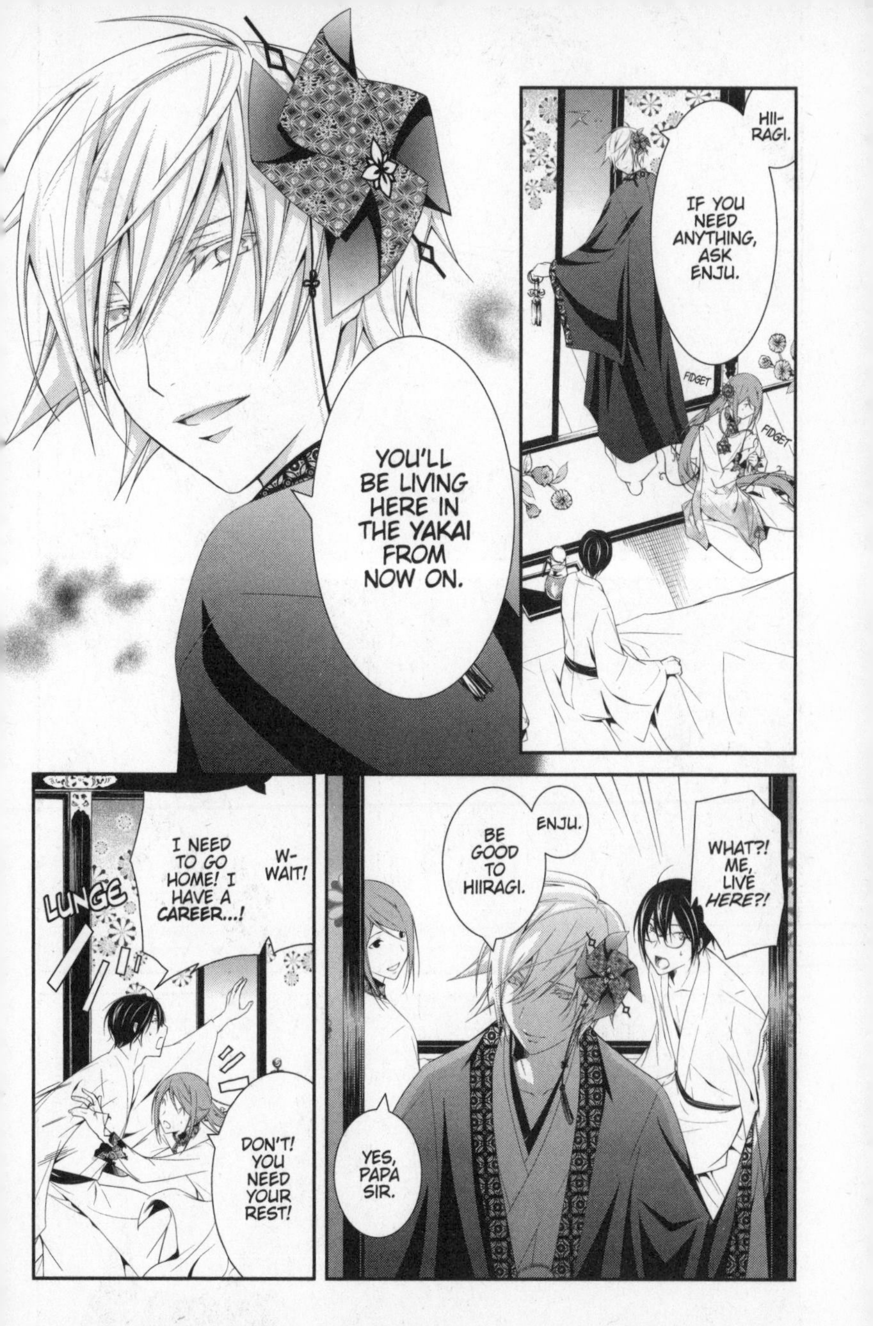
HIIRAGI.
IF YOU NEED ANYTHING, ASK ENJU.
FIDGET
FIDGET
YOU'LL BE LIVING HERE IN THE YAKAI FROM NOW ON.
WHAT?! ME, LIVE HERE?!
ENJU.
BE GOOD TO HIIRAGI.
YES, PAPA SIR.
W-WAIT!
I NEED TO GO HOME! I HAVE A CAREER...!
LUNGE
DON'T! YOU NEED YOUR REST!

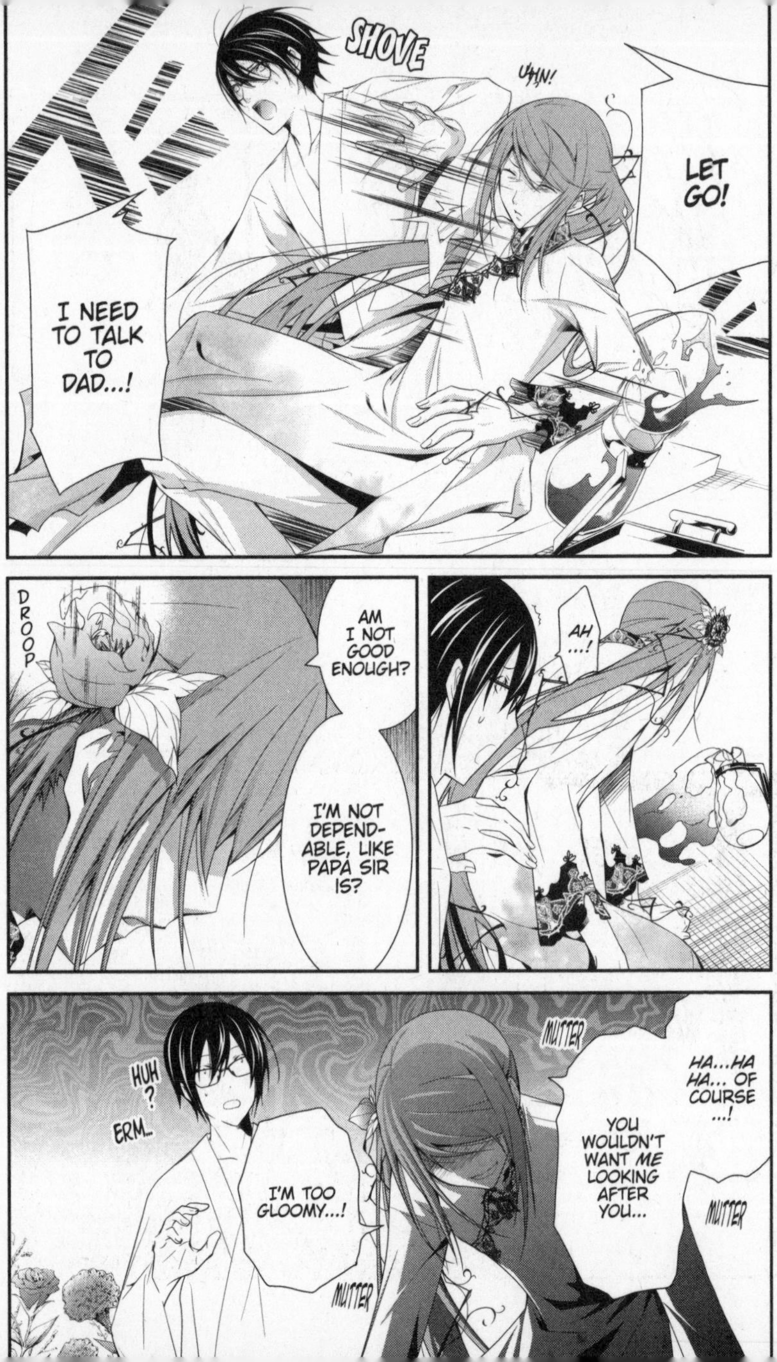
LET GO!
UHN!
SHOVE
I NEED TO TALK TO DAD...!
AH ...!
AM I NOT GOOD ENOUGH?
I'M NOT DEPENDABLE, LIKE PAPA SIR IS?
DROOP
HA...HA HA... OF COURSE ...!
MUTTER
YOU WOULDN'T WANT ME LOOKING AFTER YOU...
MUTTER
I'M TOO GLOOMY...!
MUTTER
HUH ?
ERM...

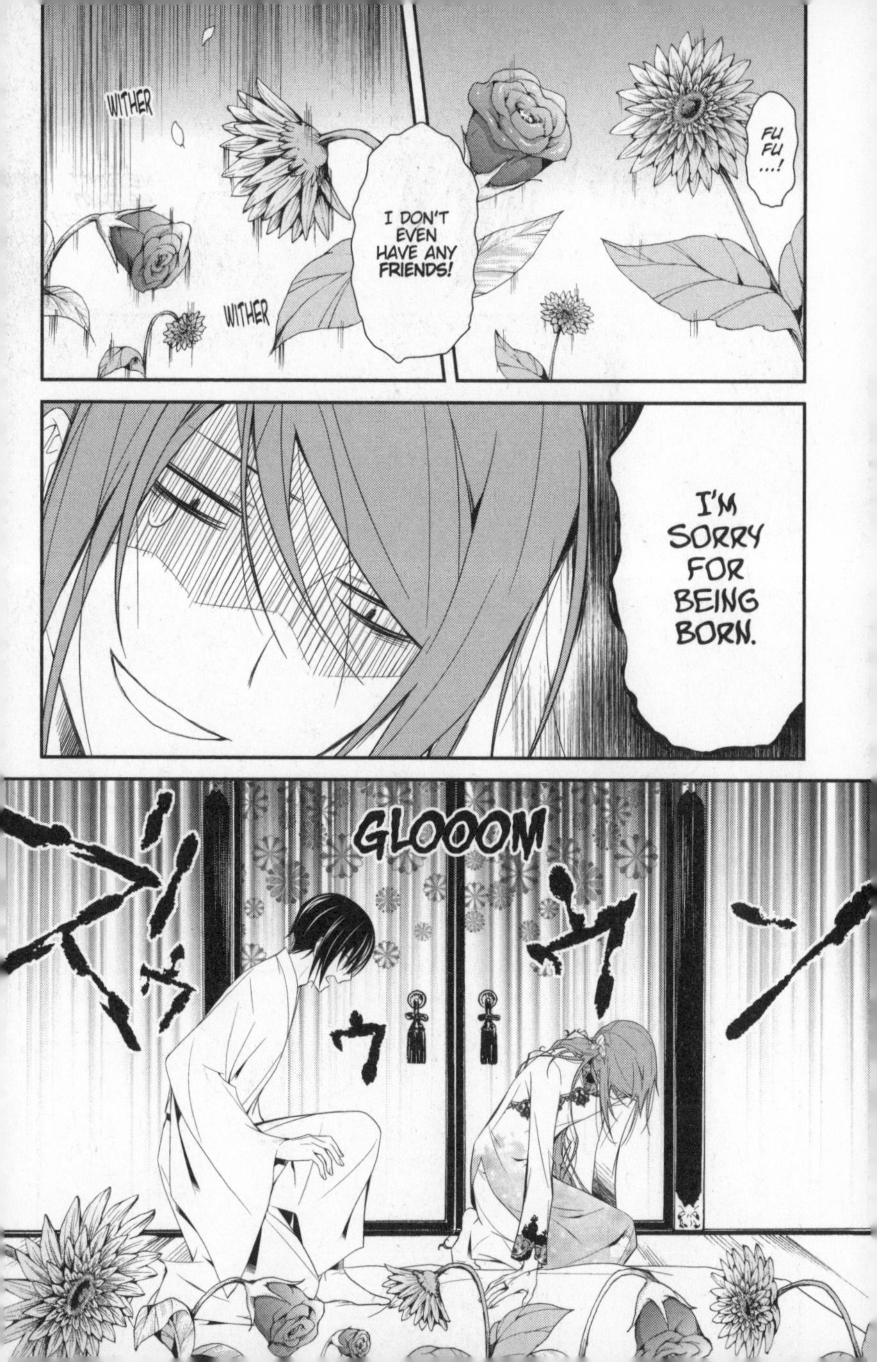
FU FU ...!
I DON'T EVEN HAVE ANY FRIENDS!
WITHER
WITHER
I'M SORRY FOR BEING BORN.
GLOOOM

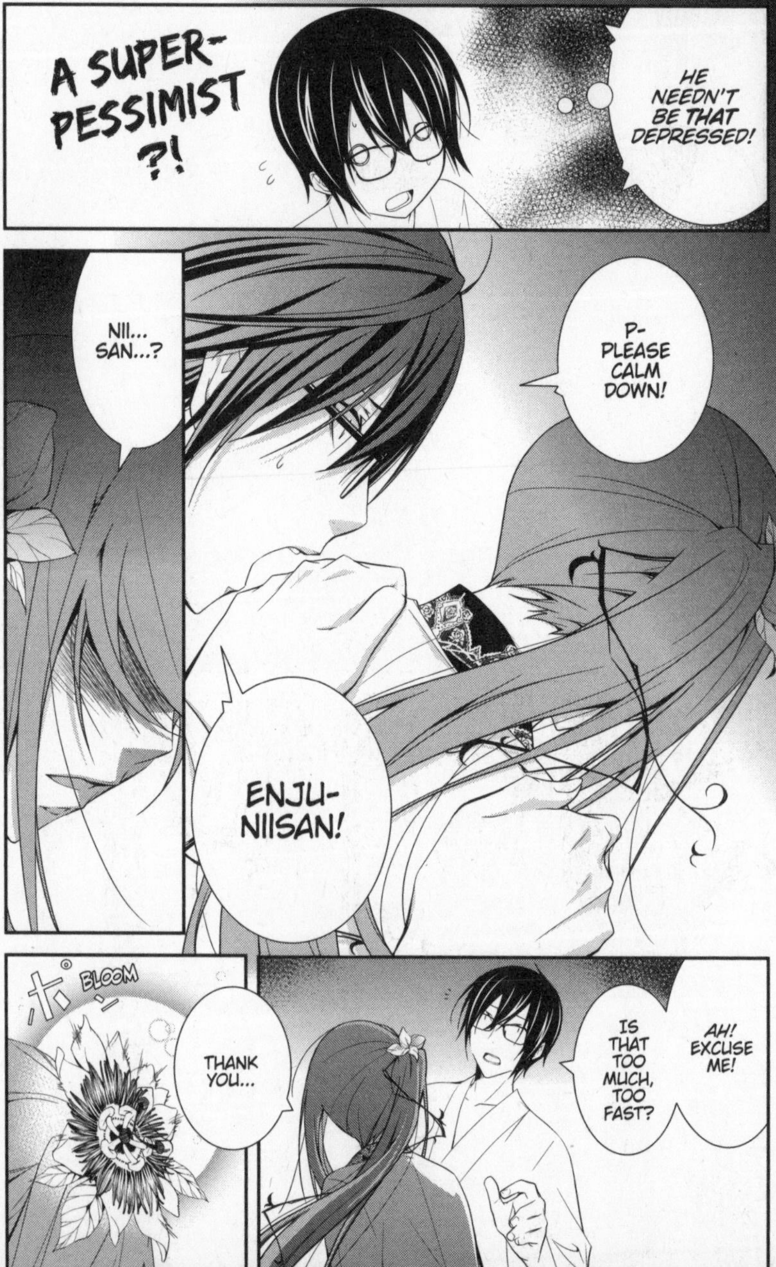
HE NEEDN'T BE THAT DEPRESSED!
A SUPER-PESSIMIST?!
P-PLEASE CALM DOWN!
ENJU-NIISAN!
NII... SAN...?
AH! EXCUSE ME!
IS THAT TOO MUCH, TOO FAST?
THANK YOU...
BLOOM

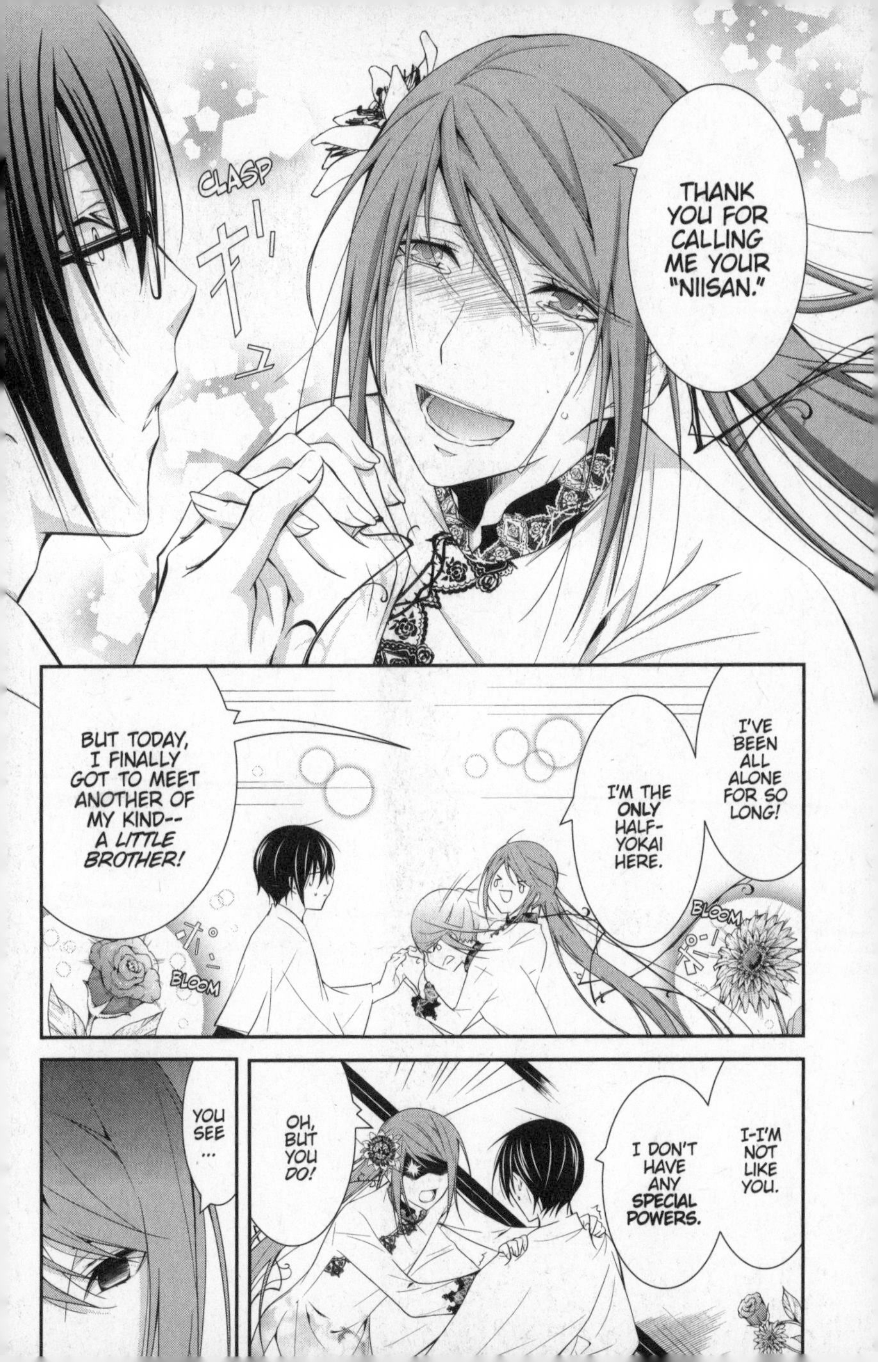
THANK YOU FOR CALLING ME YOUR "NIISAN."
CLASP
I'VE BEEN ALL ALONE FOR SO LONG!
I'M THE ONLY HALF-YOKAI HERE.
BUT TODAY, I FINALLY GOT TO MEET ANOTHER OF MY KIND-- A *LITTLE BROTHER!*
BLOOM
BLOOM
I-I'M NOT LIKE YOU.
I DON'T HAVE ANY SPECIAL POWERS.
OH, BUT YOU *DO!*
YOU SEE ...

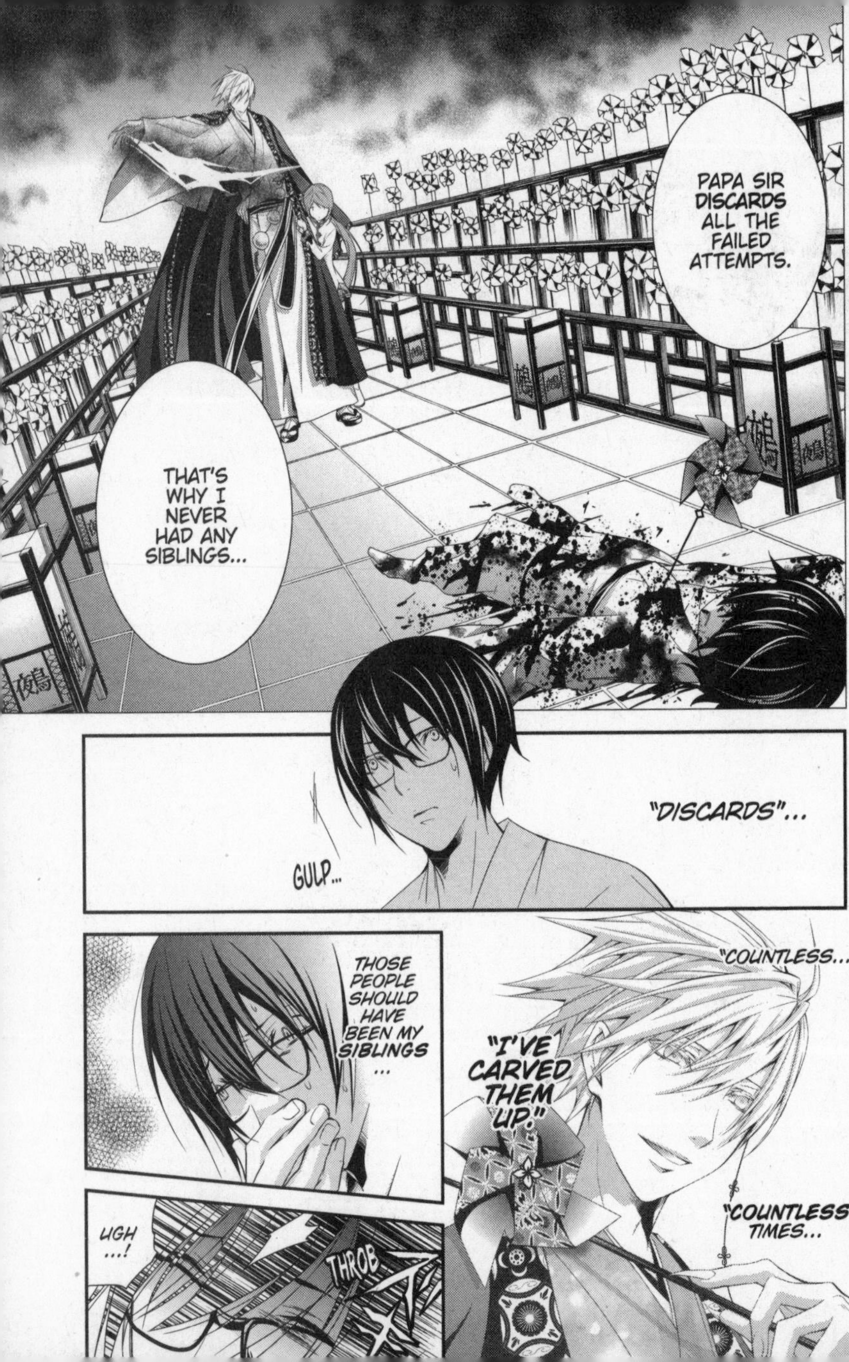
PAPA SIR DISCARDS ALL THE FAILED ATTEMPTS.
THAT'S WHY I NEVER HAD ANY SIBLINGS...
"DISCARDS"...
GULP...
"COUNTLESS...
"I'VE CARVED THEM UP."
"COUNTLESS TIMES...
THOSE PEOPLE SHOULD HAVE BEEN MY SIBLINGS ...
UGH ...!
THROB

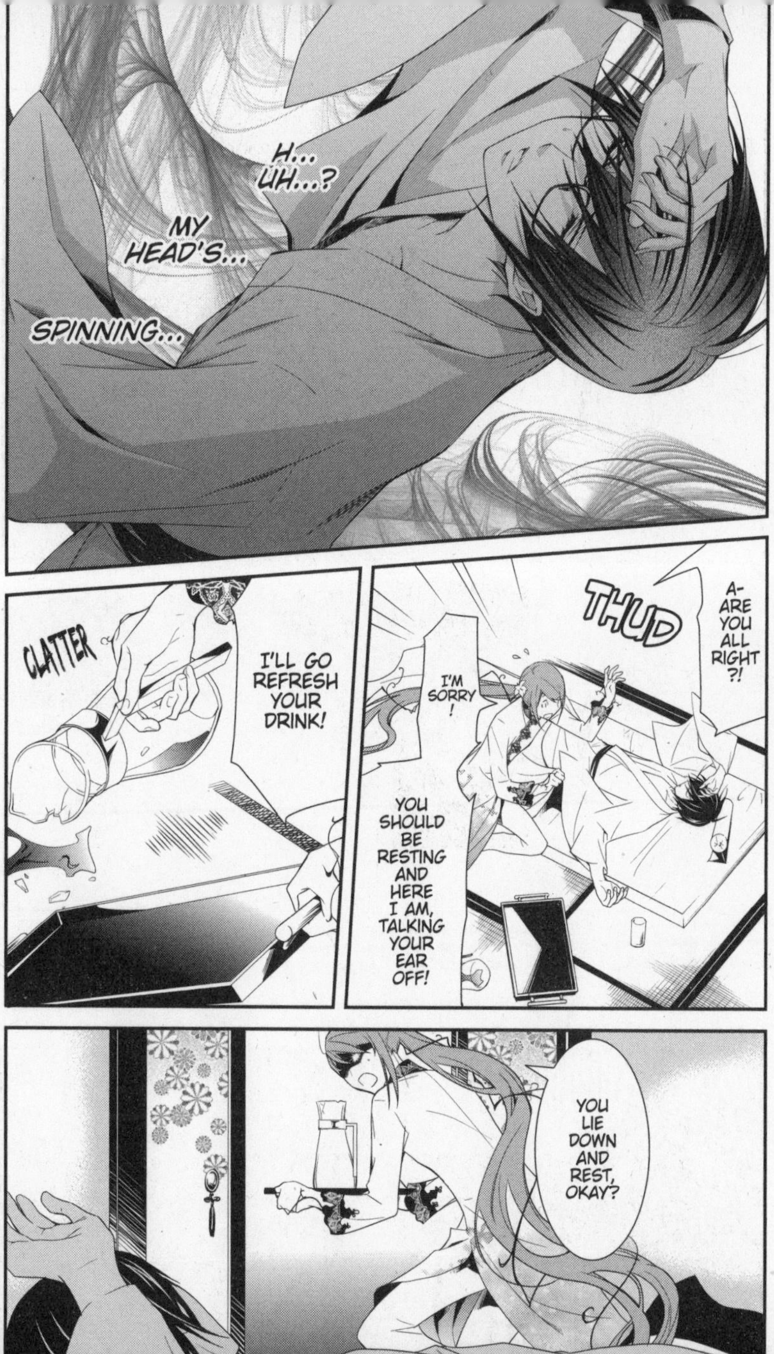
H... UH...?
MY HEAD'S...
SPINNING...
THUD
A-ARE YOU ALL RIGHT?!
I'M SORRY!
YOU SHOULD BE RESTING AND HERE I AM, TALKING YOUR EAR OFF!
I'LL GO REFRESH YOUR DRINK!
CLATTER
YOU LIE DOWN AND REST, OKAY?

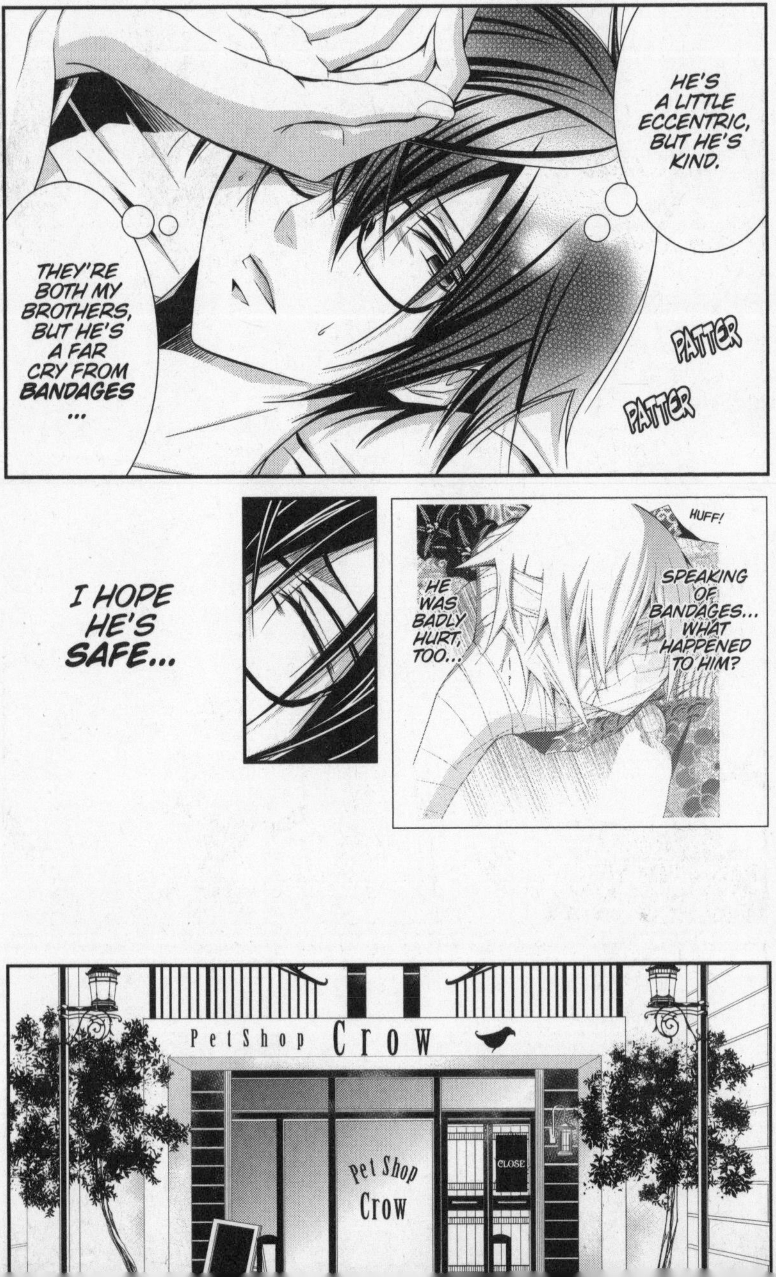
HE'S A LITTLE ECCENTRIC, BUT HE'S KIND.
THEY'RE BOTH MY BROTHERS, BUT HE'S A FAR CRY FROM BANDAGES ...
PATTER
PATTER
HUFF!
SPEAKING OF BANDAGES... WHAT HAPPENED TO HIM?
HE WAS BADLY HURT, TOO...
I HOPE HE'S SAFE...
PetShop Crow
CLOSE
Pet Shop Crow

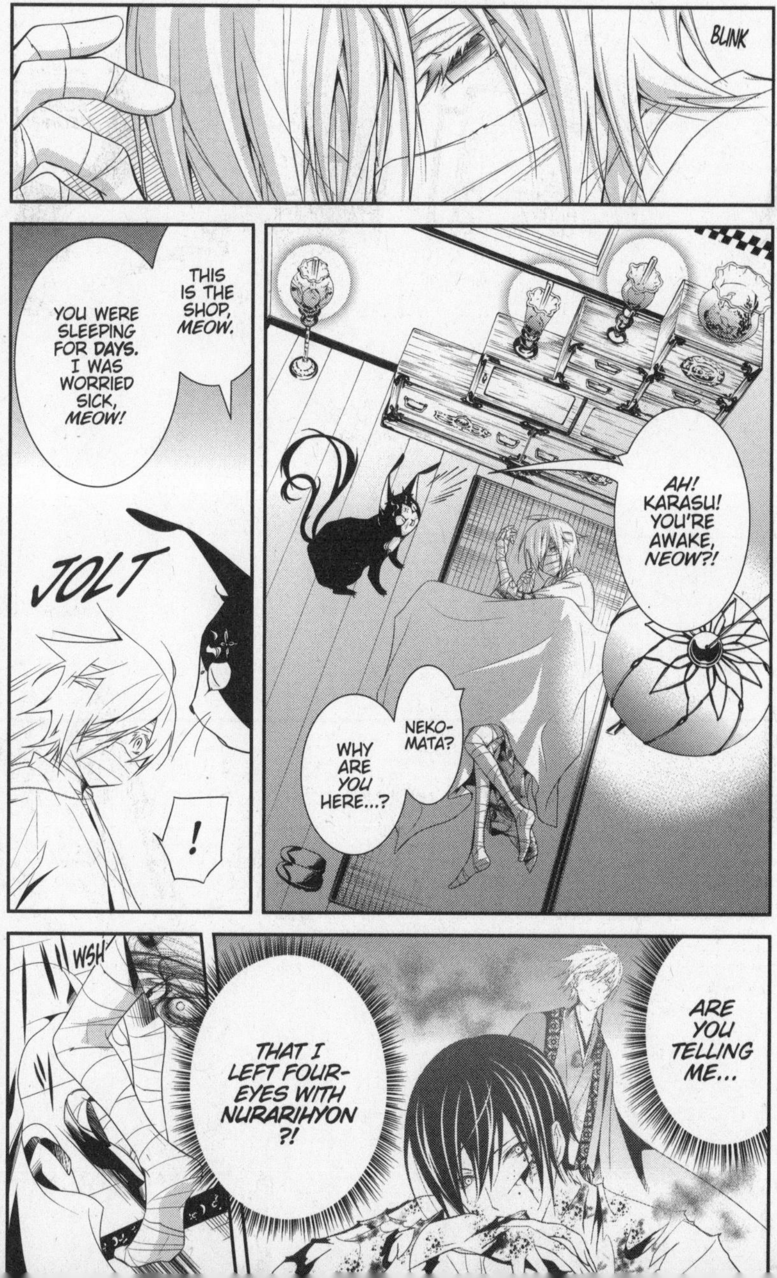
BLINK
AH! KARASU! YOU'RE AWAKE, NEOW?!
NEKO-MATA?
WHY ARE YOU HERE...?
THIS IS THE SHOP, MEOW.
YOU WERE SLEEPING FOR DAYS. I WAS WORRIED SICK, MEOW!
JOLT
!
ARE YOU TELLING ME...
THAT I LEFT FOUR-EYES WITH NURARIHYON?!
WSH

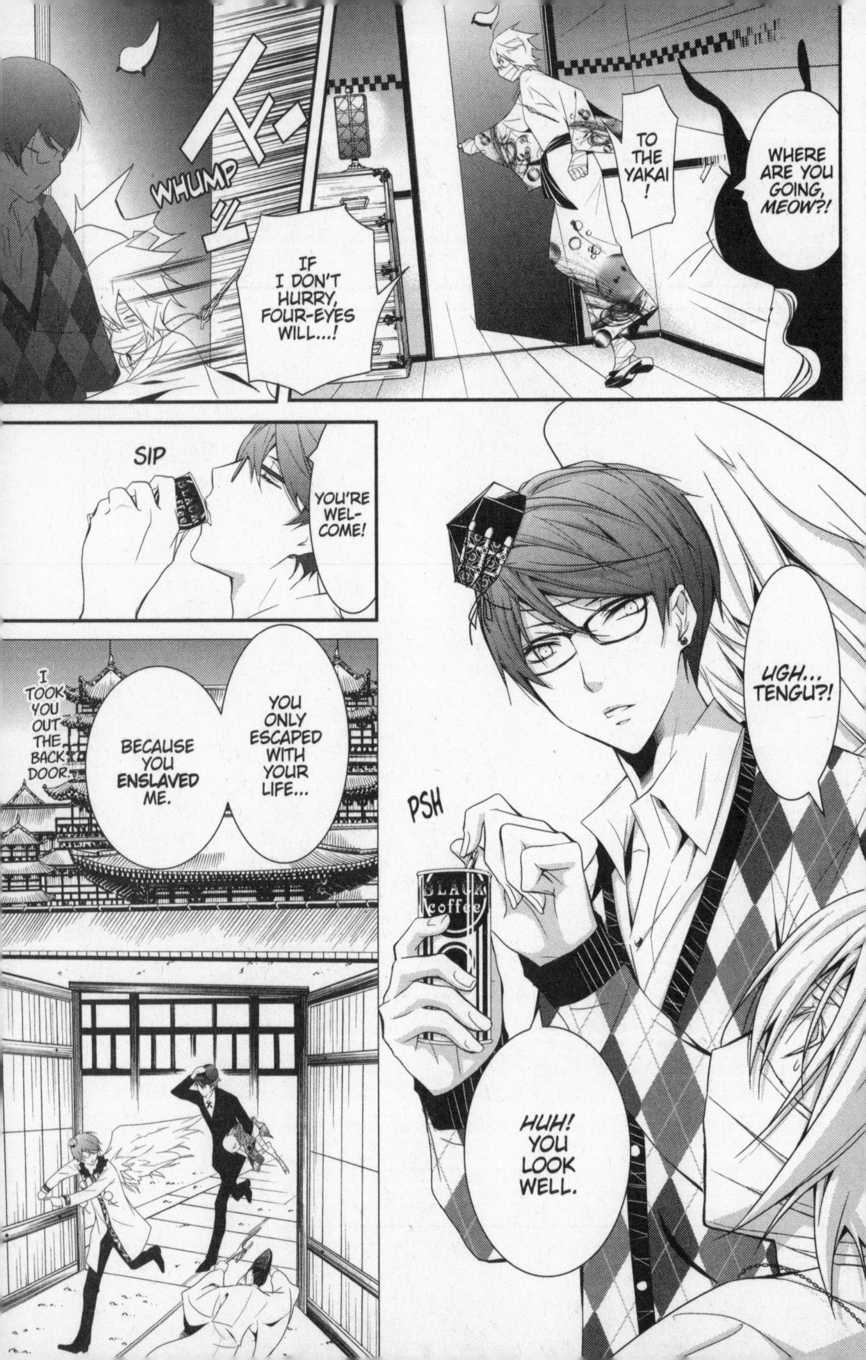
WHERE ARE YOU GOING, MEOW?!
TO THE YAKAI!
WHUMP
IF I DON'T HURRY, FOUR-EYES WILL...!
UGH... TENGU?!
PSH
HUH! YOU LOOK WELL.
SIP
YOU'RE WEL-COME!
YOU ONLY ESCAPED WITH YOUR LIFE...
BECAUSE YOU ENSLAVED ME.
I TOOK YOU OUT THE BACK DOOR.

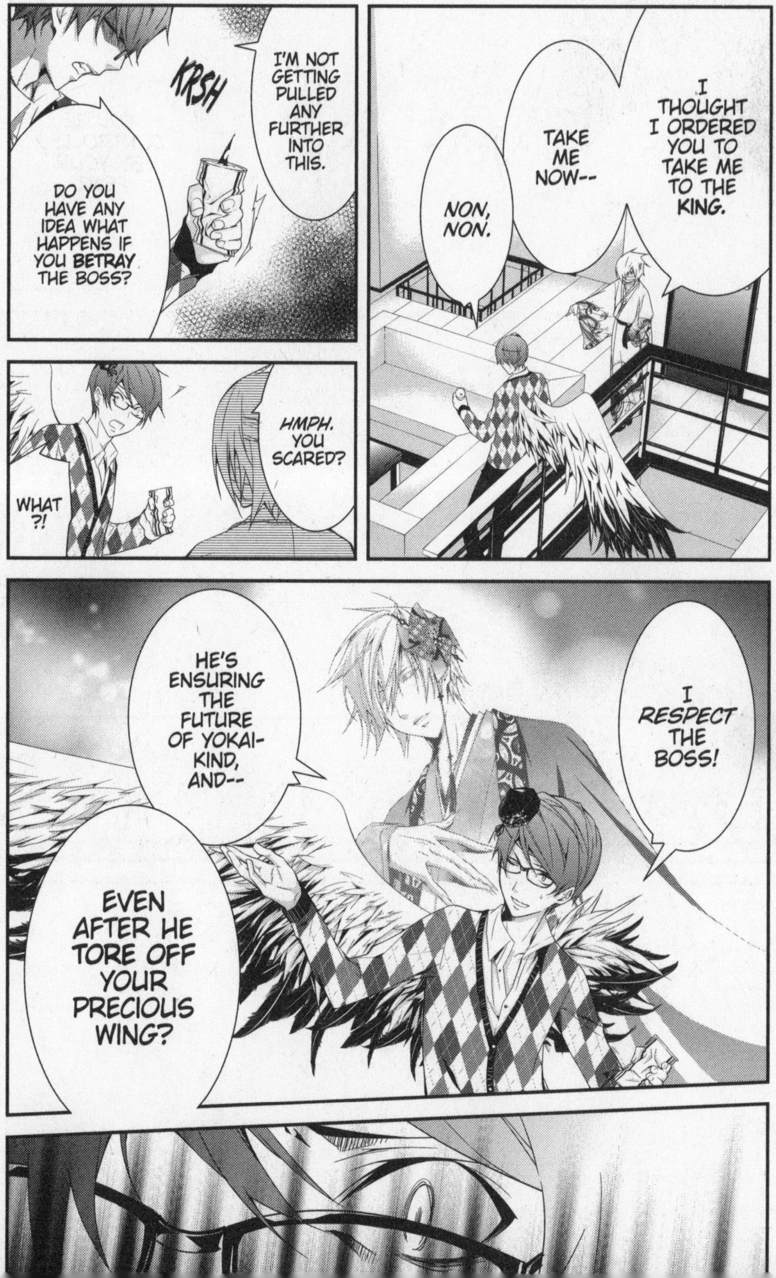
I THOUGHT I ORDERED YOU TO TAKE ME TO THE KING.
TAKE ME NOW--
NON, NON.
I'M NOT GETTING PULLED ANY FURTHER INTO THIS.
KRSH
DO YOU HAVE ANY IDEA WHAT HAPPENS IF YOU BETRAY THE BOSS?
HMPH. YOU SCARED?
WHAT?!
I RESPECT THE BOSS!
HE'S ENSURING THE FUTURE OF YOKAI-KIND, AND--
EVEN AFTER HE TORE OFF YOUR PRECIOUS WING?

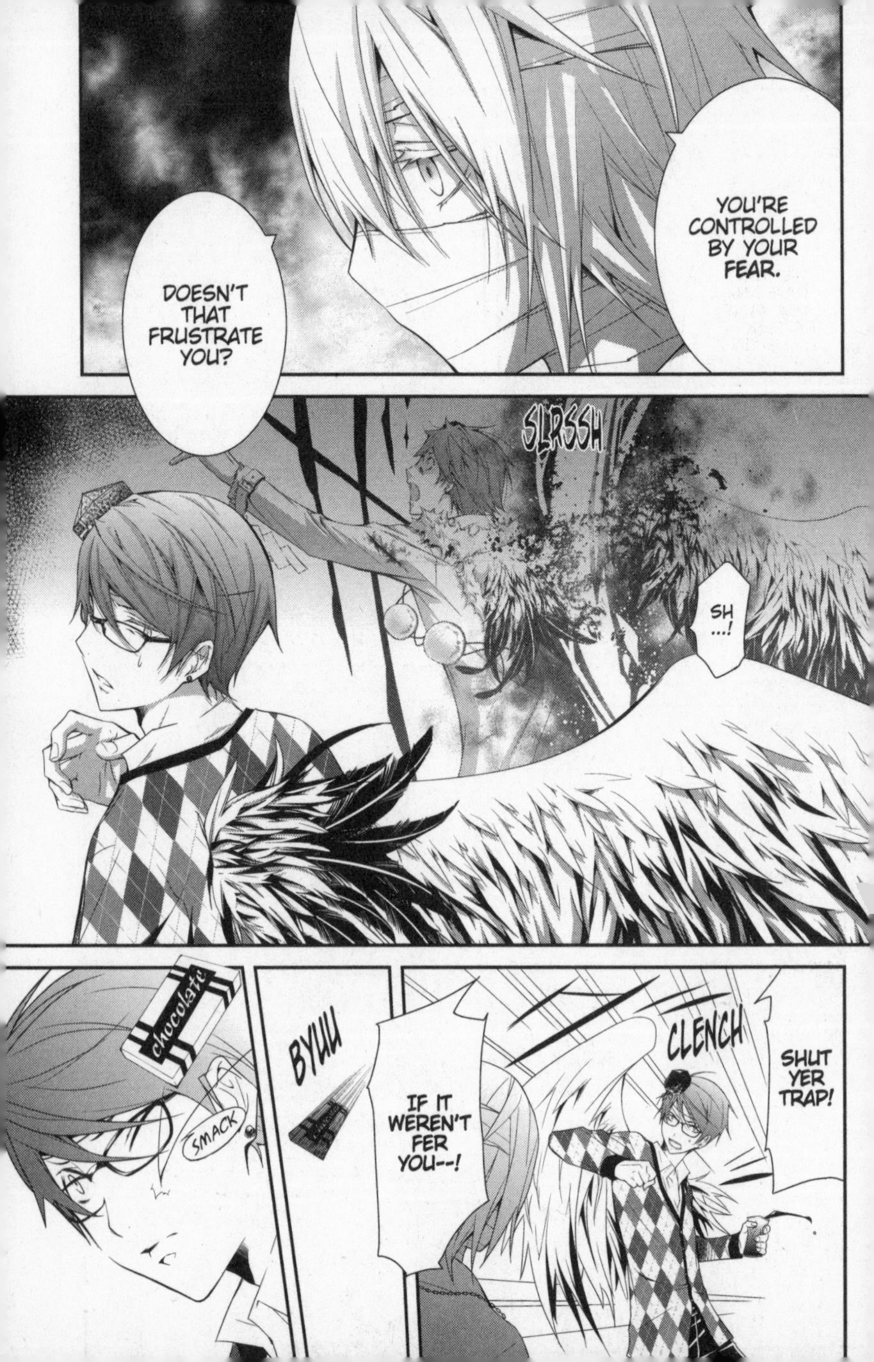
YOU'RE CONTROLLED BY YOUR FEAR.
DOESN'T THAT FRUSTRATE YOU?
SLRSSH
SH ...!
SHUT YER TRAP!
CLENCH
IF IT WEREN'T FER YOU--!
BYUU
chocolate
SMACK

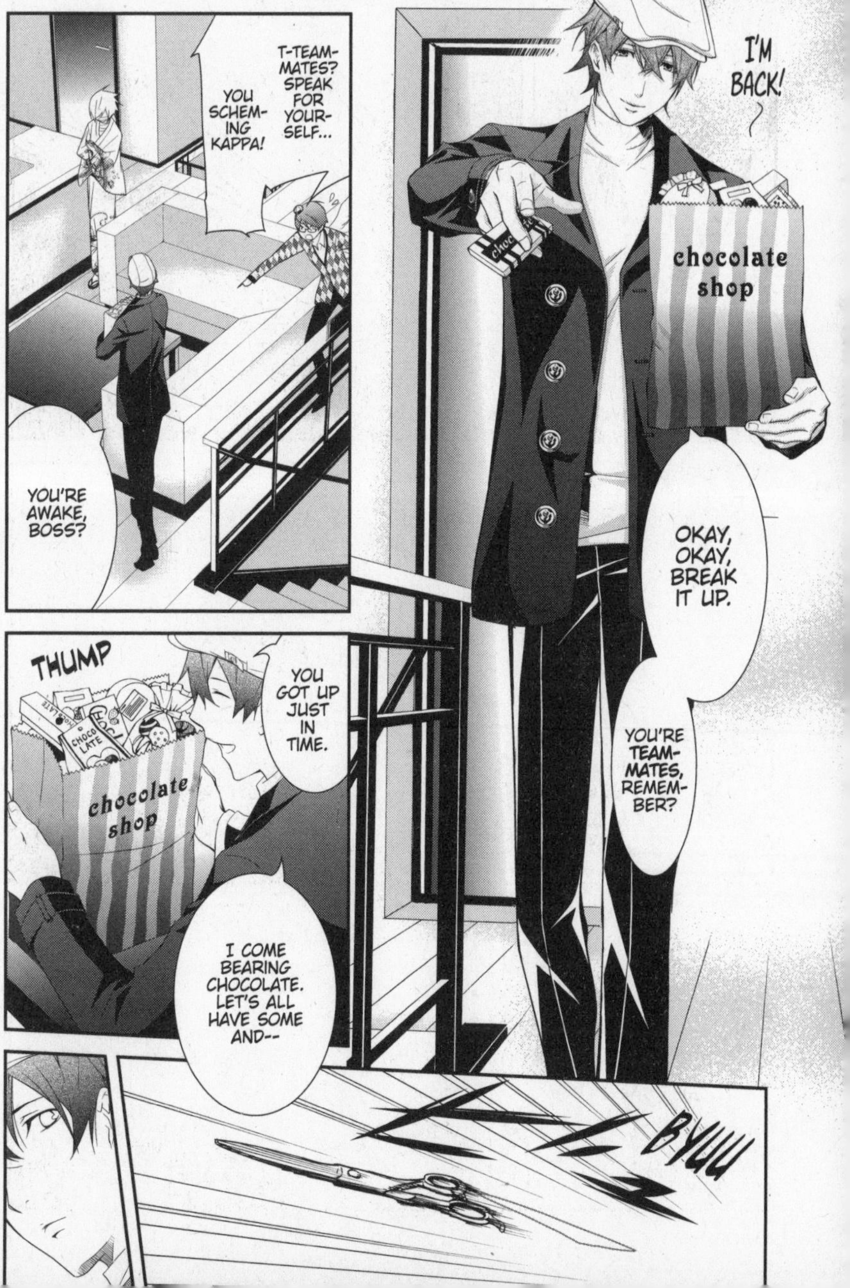
I'M BACK!
chocolate shop
OKAY, OKAY, BREAK IT UP.
YOU'RE TEAMMATES, REMEMBER?
T-TEAMMATES? SPEAK FOR YOURSELF...
YOU SCHEMING KAPPA!
YOU'RE AWAKE, BOSS?
YOU GOT UP JUST IN TIME.
THUMP
chocolate shop
I COME BEARING CHOCOLATE. LET'S ALL HAVE SOME AND--
BYUU

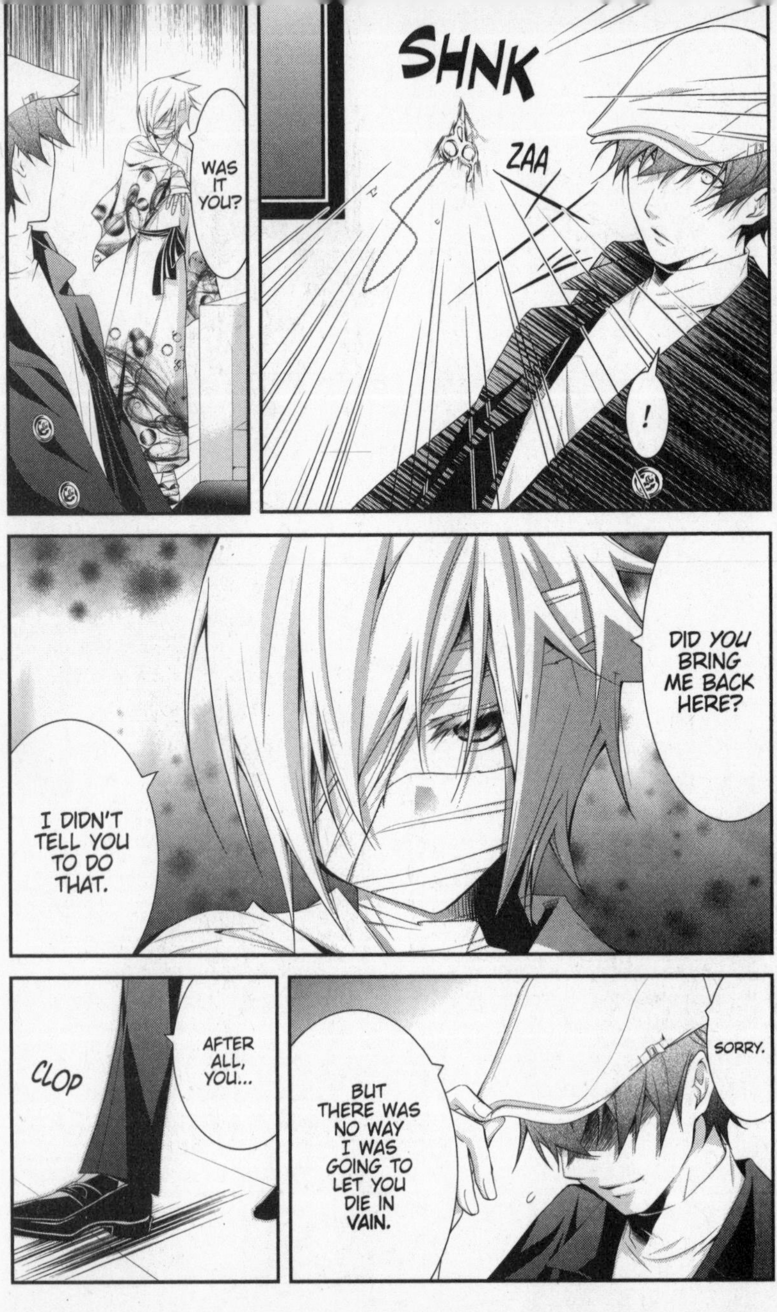
SHNK
ZAA
!
WAS IT YOU?
DID YOU BRING ME BACK HERE?
I DIDN'T TELL YOU TO DO THAT.
SORRY.
BUT THERE WAS NO WAY I WAS GOING TO LET YOU DIE IN VAIN.
AFTER ALL, YOU...
CLOP

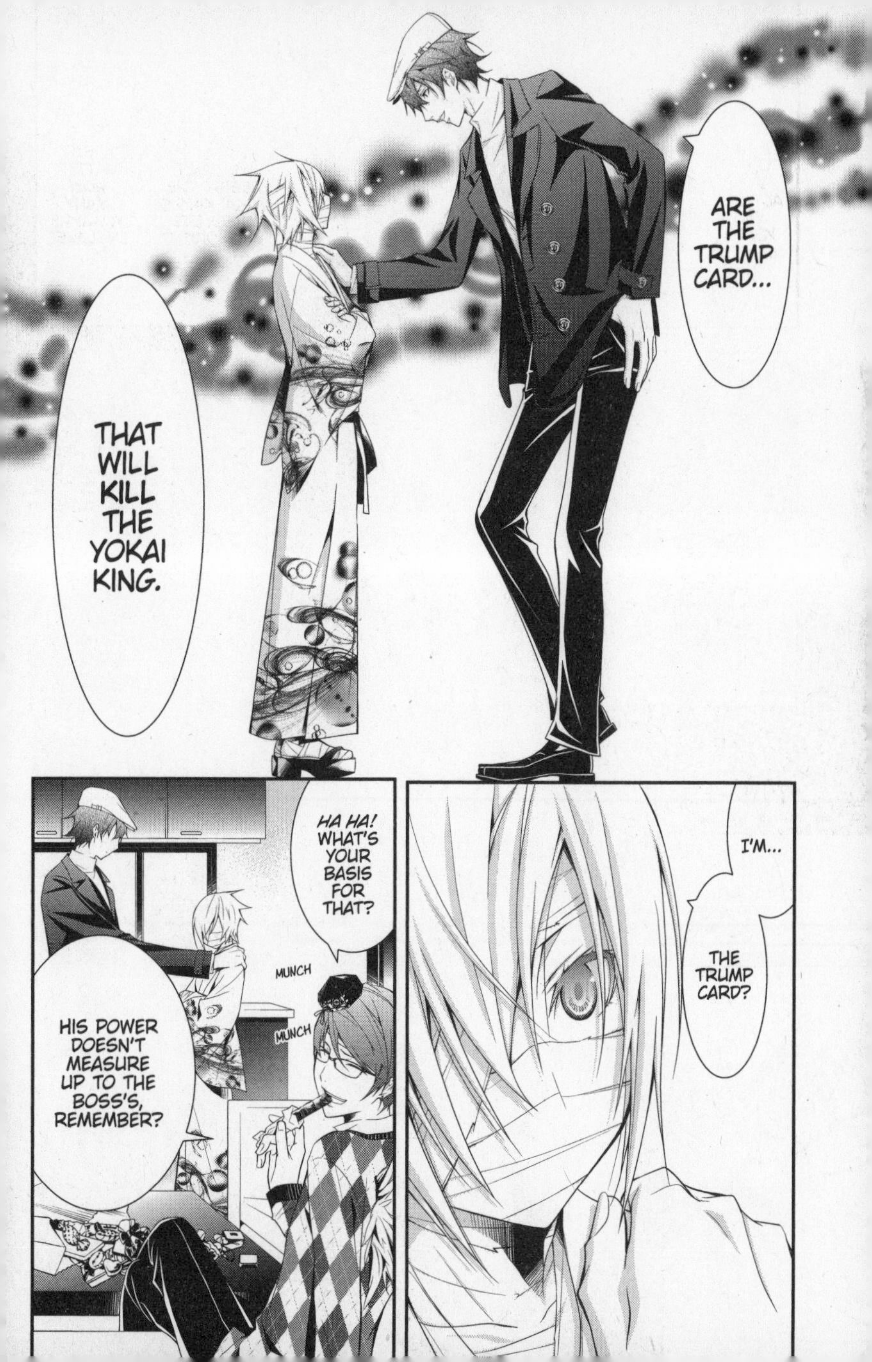
ARE THE TRUMP CARD...
THAT WILL KILL THE YOKAI KING.
I'M...
THE TRUMP CARD?
HA HA! WHAT'S YOUR BASIS FOR THAT?
MUNCH
MUNCH
HIS POWER DOESN'T MEASURE UP TO THE BOSS'S, REMEMBER?

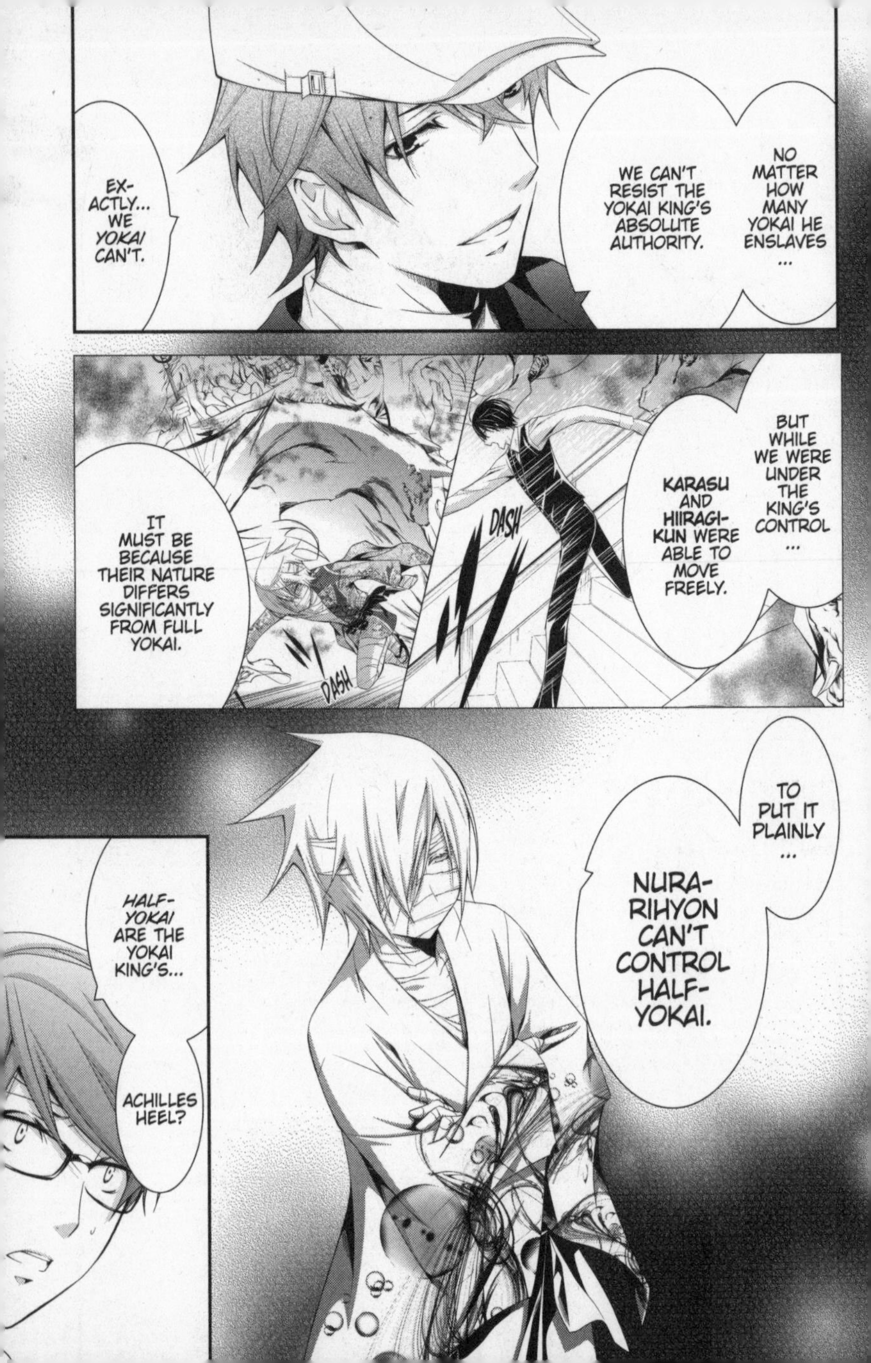
NO MATTER HOW MANY YOKAI HE ENSLAVES...
WE CAN'T RESIST THE YOKAI KING'S ABSOLUTE AUTHORITY.
EX-ACTLY... WE *YOKAI* CAN'T.
BUT WHILE WE WERE UNDER THE KING'S CONTROL...
KARASU AND HIIRAGI-KUN WERE ABLE TO MOVE FREELY.
DASH
DASH
IT MUST BE BECAUSE THEIR NATURE DIFFERS SIGNIFICANTLY FROM FULL YOKAI.
TO PUT IT PLAINLY...
NURA-RIHYON CAN'T CONTROL HALF-YOKAI.
HALF-YOKAI ARE THE YOKAI KING'S...
ACHILLES HEEL?

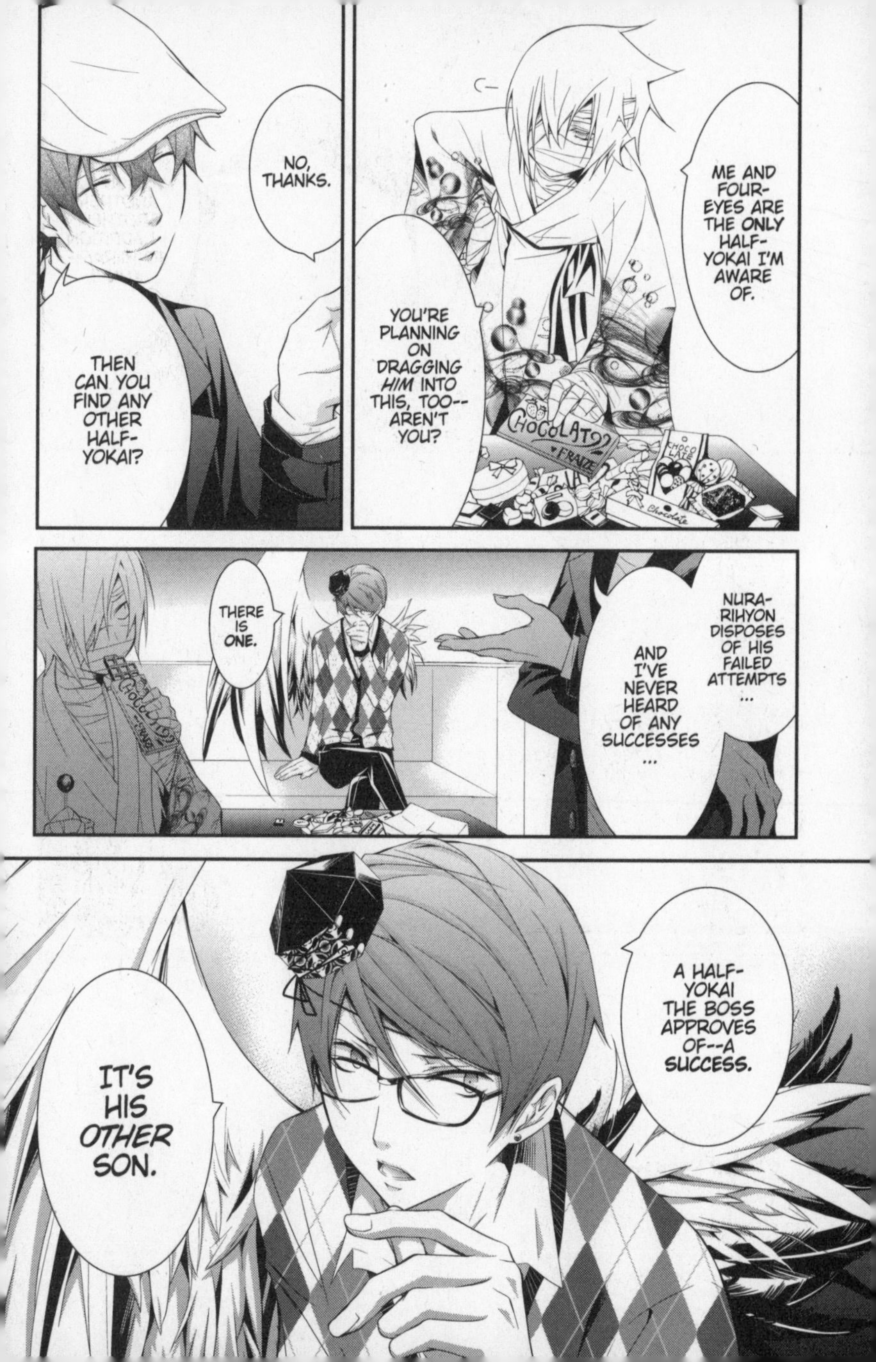
ME AND FOUR-EYES ARE THE ONLY HALF-YOKAI I'M AWARE OF.
YOU'RE PLANNING ON DRAGGING *HIM* INTO THIS, TOO--AREN'T YOU?
NO, THANKS.
THEN CAN YOU FIND ANY OTHER HALF-YOKAI?
NURA-RIHYON DISPOSES OF HIS FAILED ATTEMPTS...
AND I'VE NEVER HEARD OF ANY SUCCESSES...
THERE IS ONE.
A HALF-YOKAI THE BOSS APPROVES OF--A SUCCESS.
IT'S HIS *OTHER* SON.

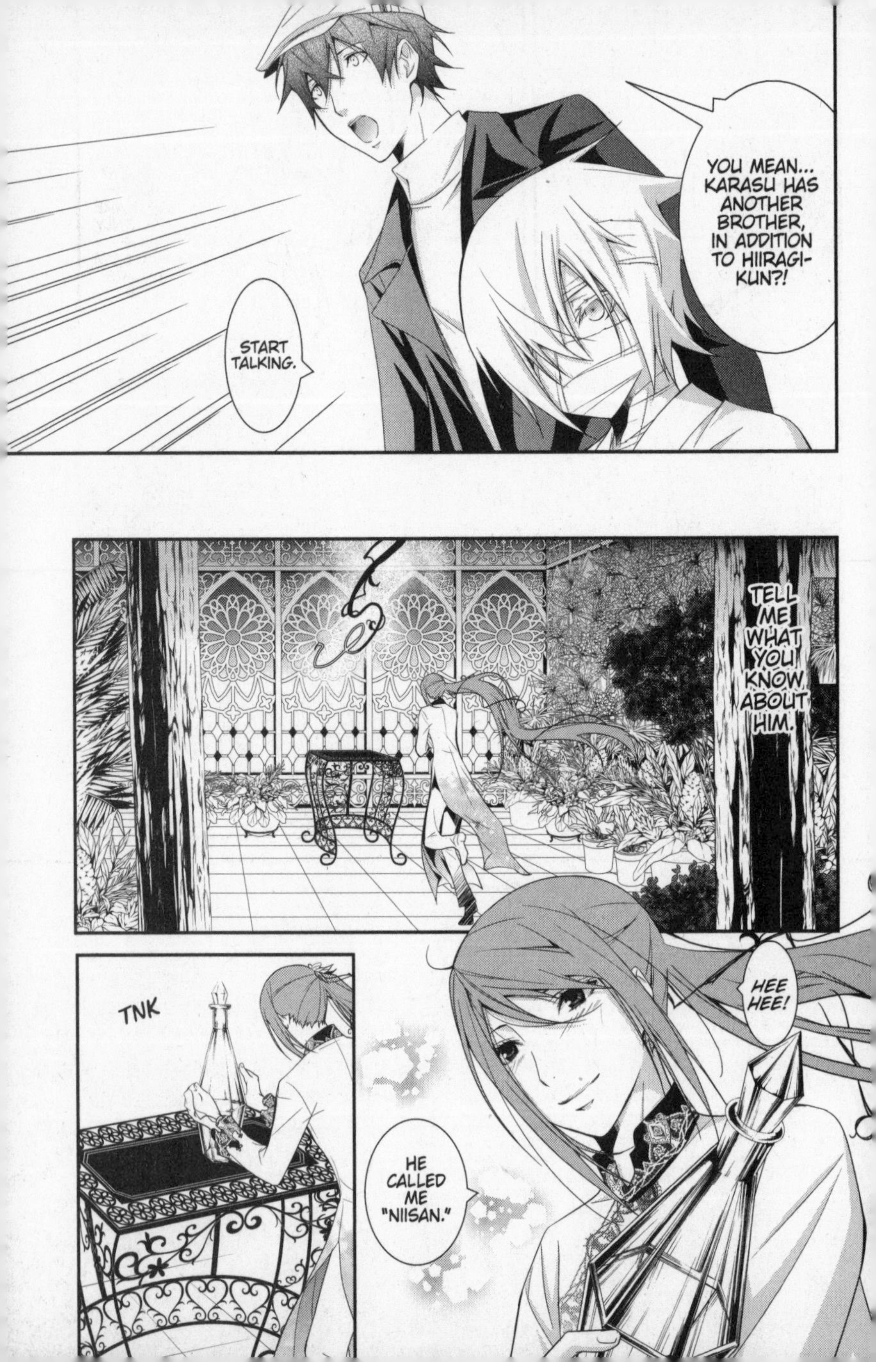
YOU MEAN... KARASU HAS ANOTHER BROTHER, IN ADDITION TO HIIRAGI-KUN?!
START TALKING.
TELL ME WHAT YOU KNOW ABOUT HIM.
HEE HEE!
HE CALLED ME "NIISAN."
TNK

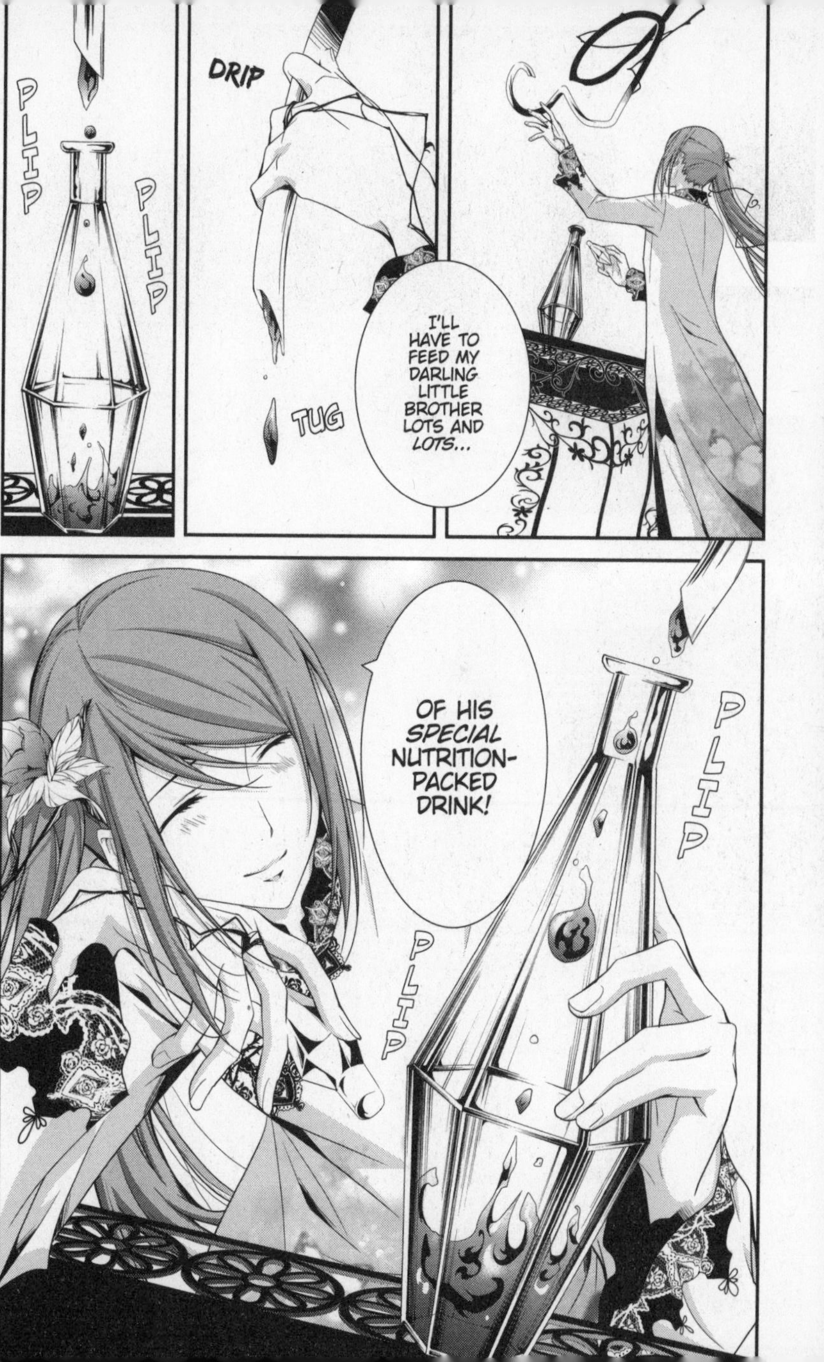
I'LL HAVE TO FEED MY DARLING LITTLE BROTHER LOTS AND *LOTS*...
DRIP
TUG
PLIP
PLIP
OF HIS *SPECIAL* NUTRITION-PACKED DRINK!
PLIP
PLIP

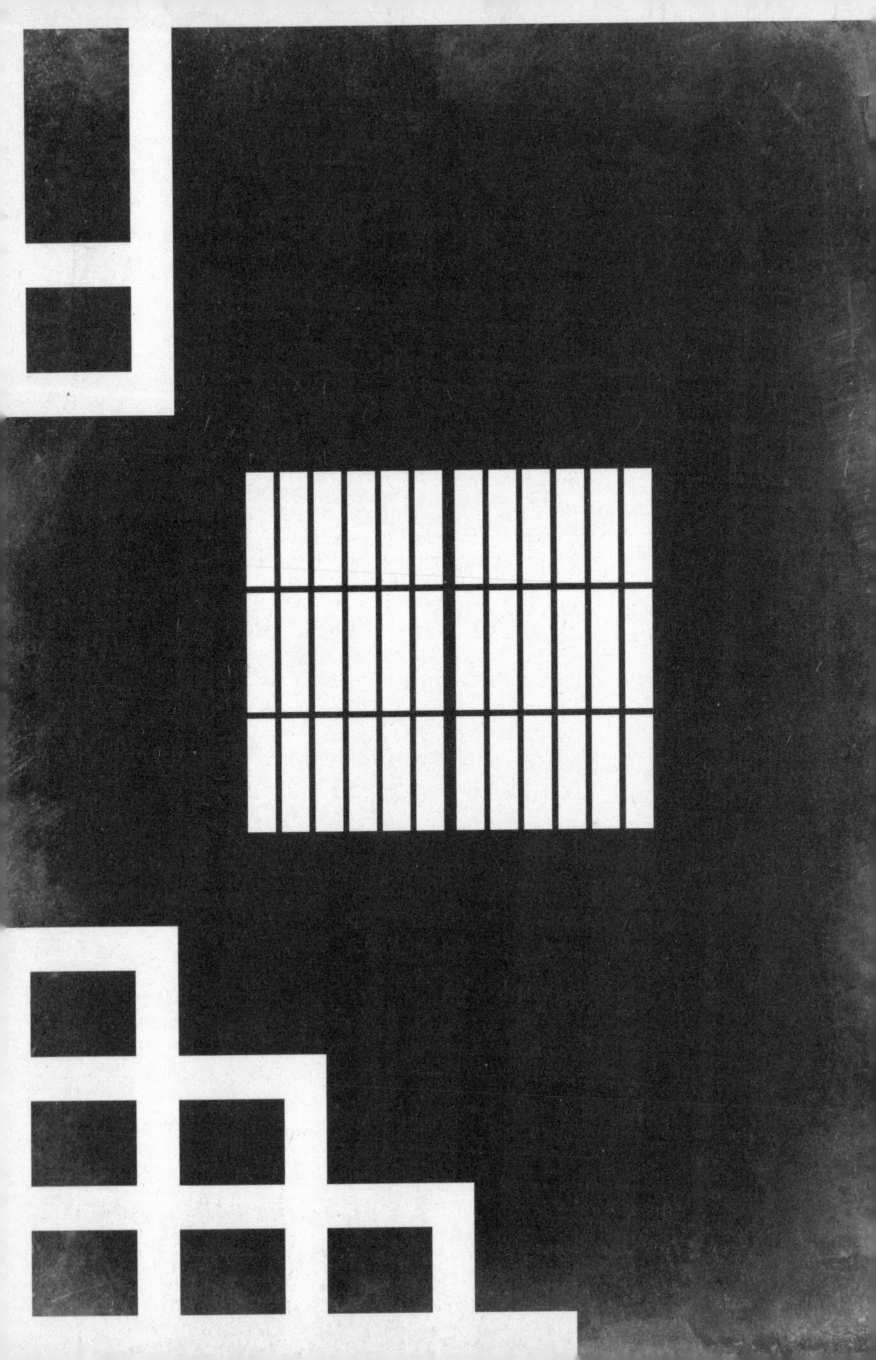

Yōkai Rental Shop

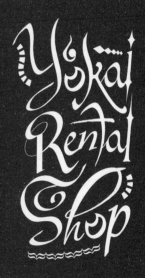

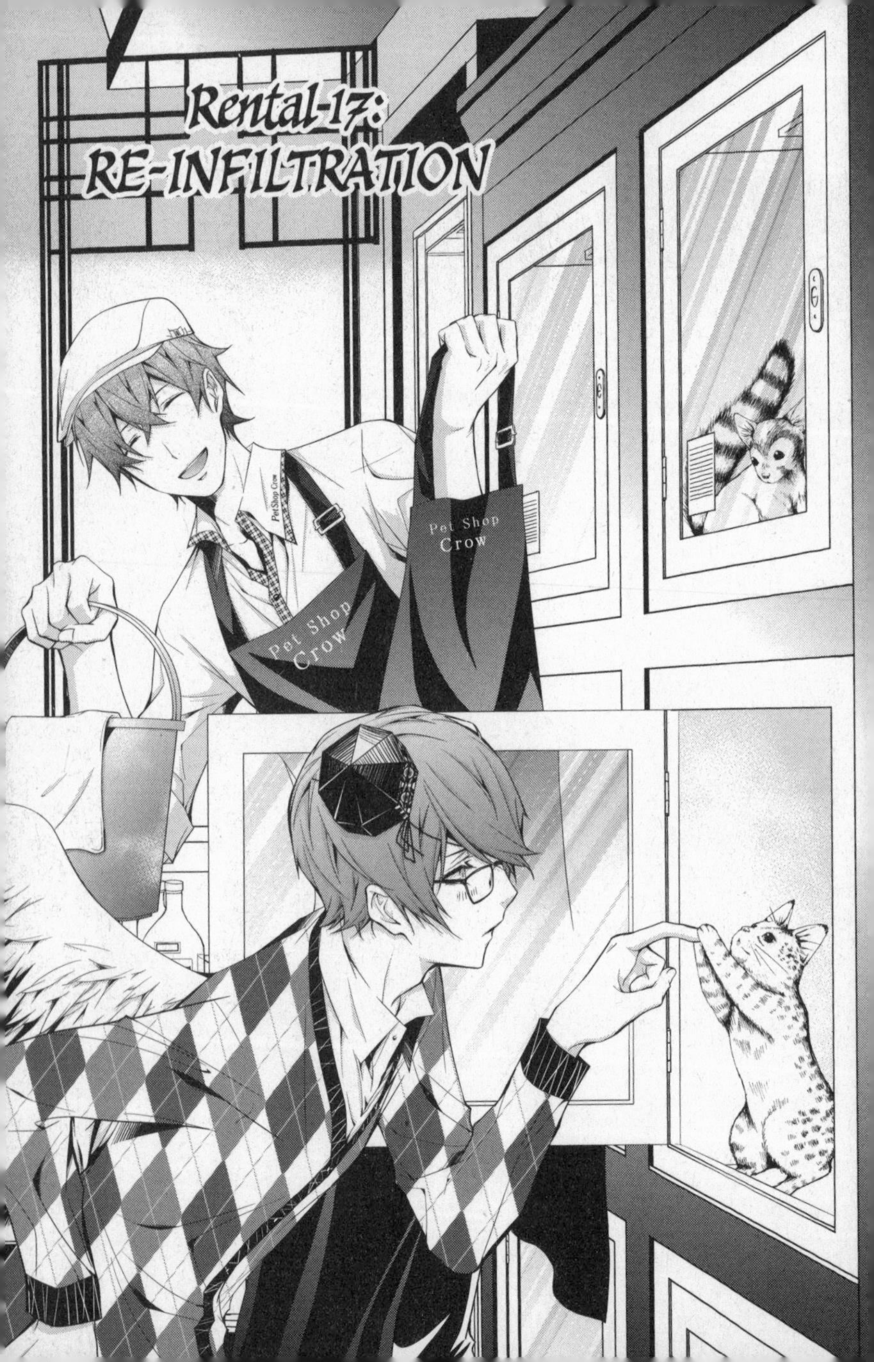
Rental-17:
RE-INFILTRATION
Pet Shop Crow
Pet Shop Crow
Pet Shop Crow

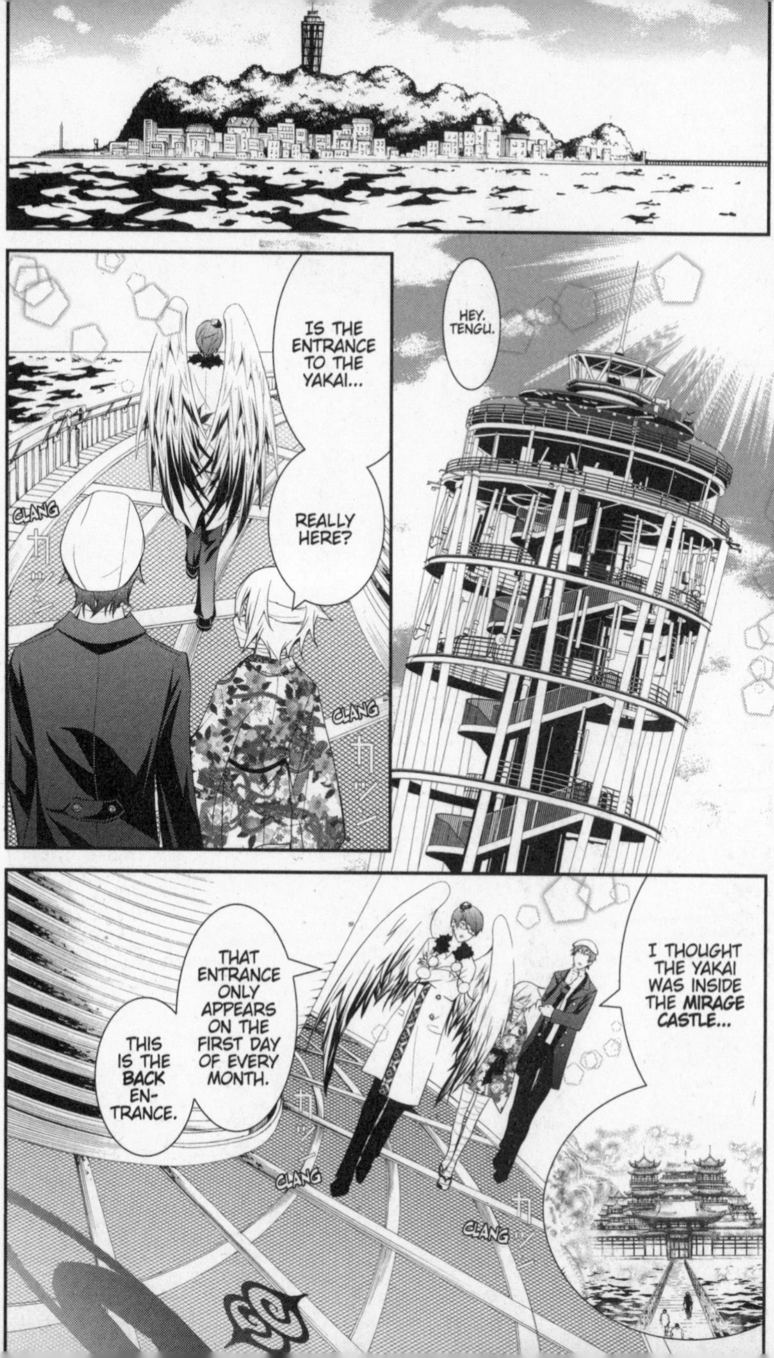
HEY. TENGU.
IS THE ENTRANCE TO THE YAKAI...
REALLY HERE?
CLANG
CLANG
I THOUGHT THE YAKAI WAS INSIDE THE MIRAGE CASTLE...
THAT ENTRANCE ONLY APPEARS ON THE FIRST DAY OF EVERY MONTH.
THIS IS THE BACK EN-TRANCE.
CLANG
CLANG

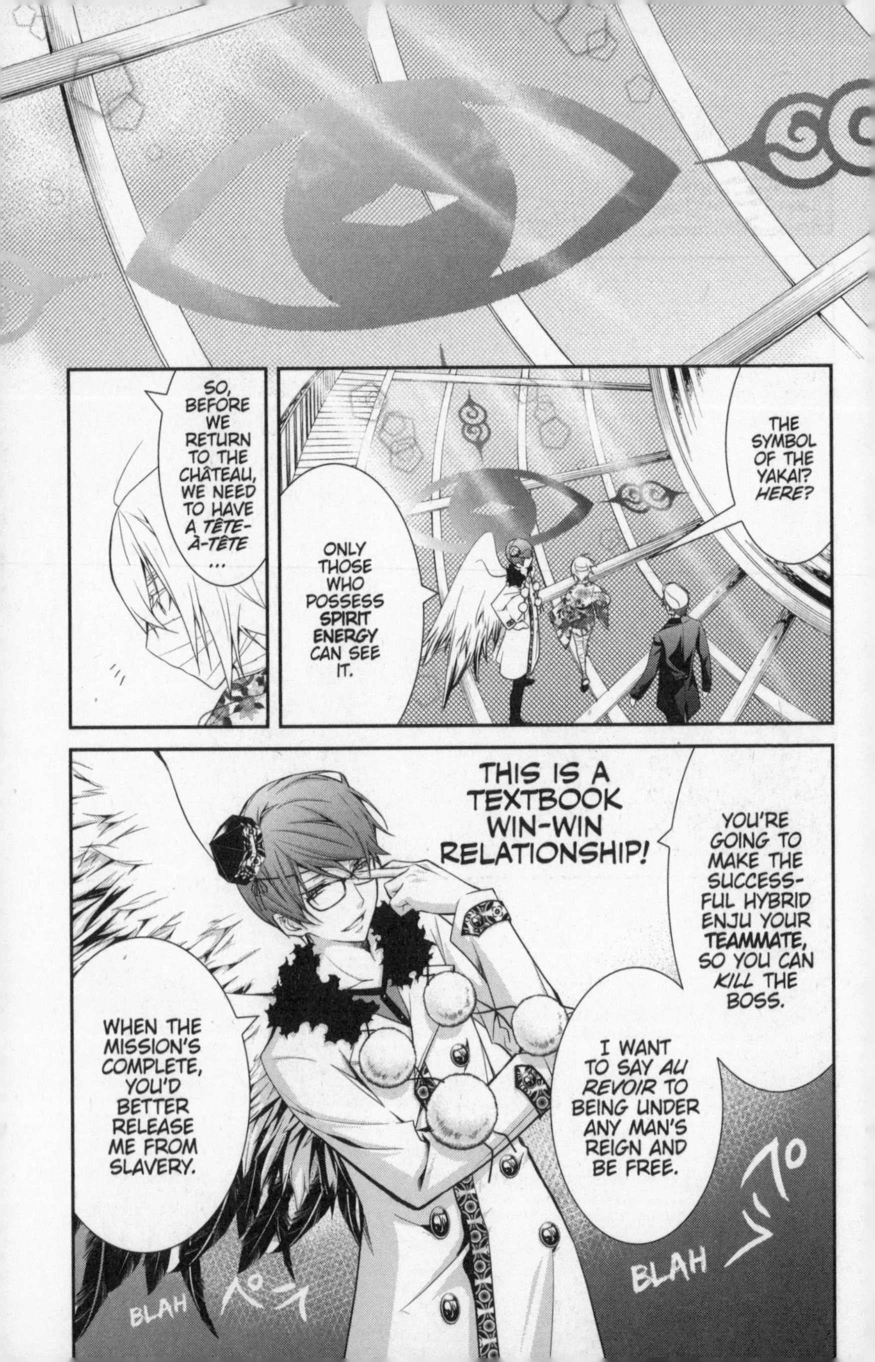

THE SYMBOL OF THE YAKAI? *HERE?*
ONLY THOSE WHO POSSESS SPIRIT ENERGY CAN SEE IT.
SO, BEFORE WE RETURN TO THE CHÂTEAU, WE NEED TO HAVE A *TÊTE-À-TÊTE*...
YOU'RE GOING TO MAKE THE SUCCESSFUL HYBRID ENJU YOUR TEAMMATE, SO YOU CAN *KILL* THE BOSS.
THIS IS A TEXTBOOK WIN-WIN RELATIONSHIP!
I WANT TO SAY *AU REVOIR* TO BEING UNDER ANY MAN'S REIGN AND BE FREE.
WHEN THE MISSION'S COMPLETE, YOU'D BETTER RELEASE ME FROM SLAVERY.
BLAH
BLAH

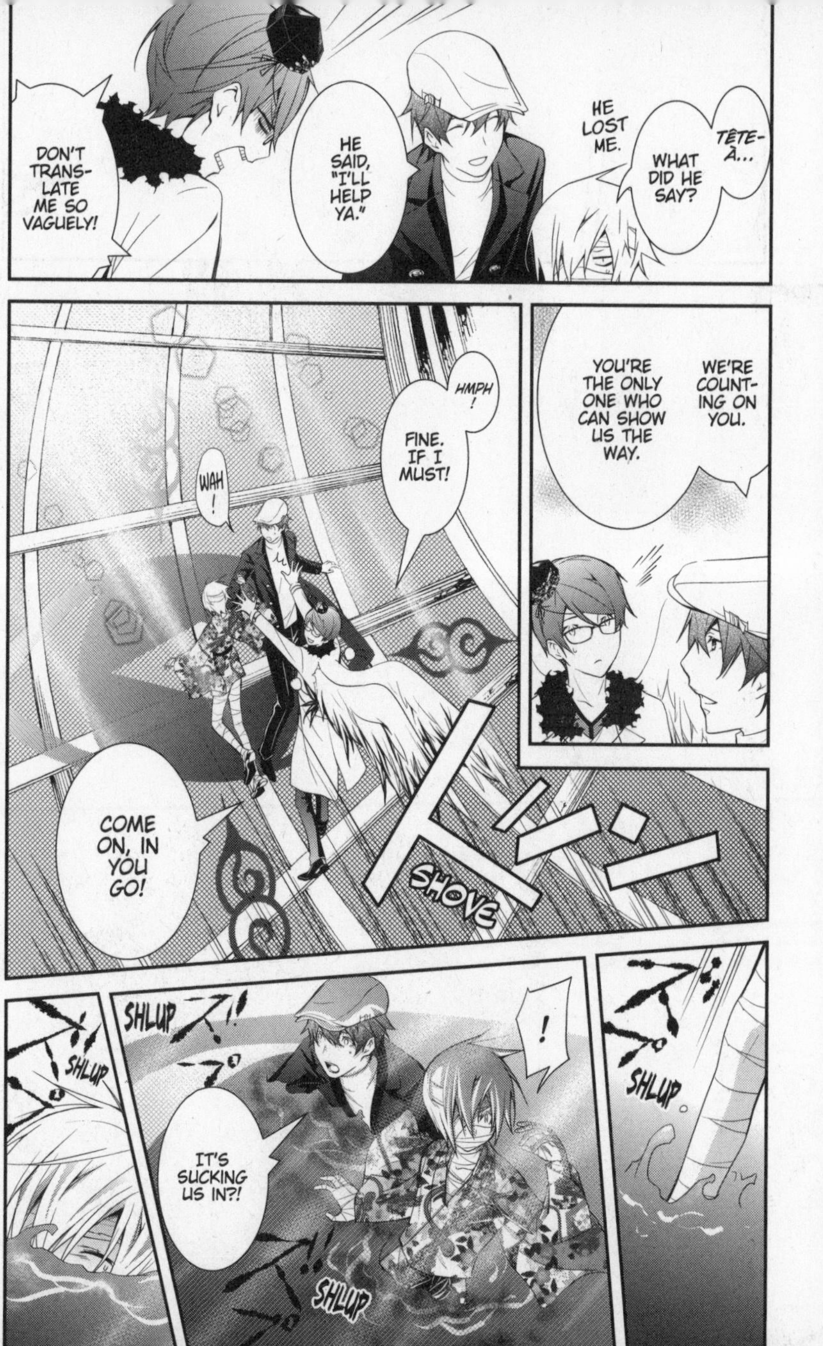
TÊTE-À...
WHAT DID HE SAY?
HE LOST ME.
HE SAID, "I'LL HELP YA."
DON'T TRANS-LATE ME SO VAGUELY!
WE'RE COUNT-ING ON YOU.
YOU'RE THE ONLY ONE WHO CAN SHOW US THE WAY.
HMPH!
FINE. IF I MUST!
WAH!
SHOVE
COME ON, IN YOU GO!
SHLUP
!
SHLUP
IT'S SUCKING US IN?!
SHLUP
SHLUP

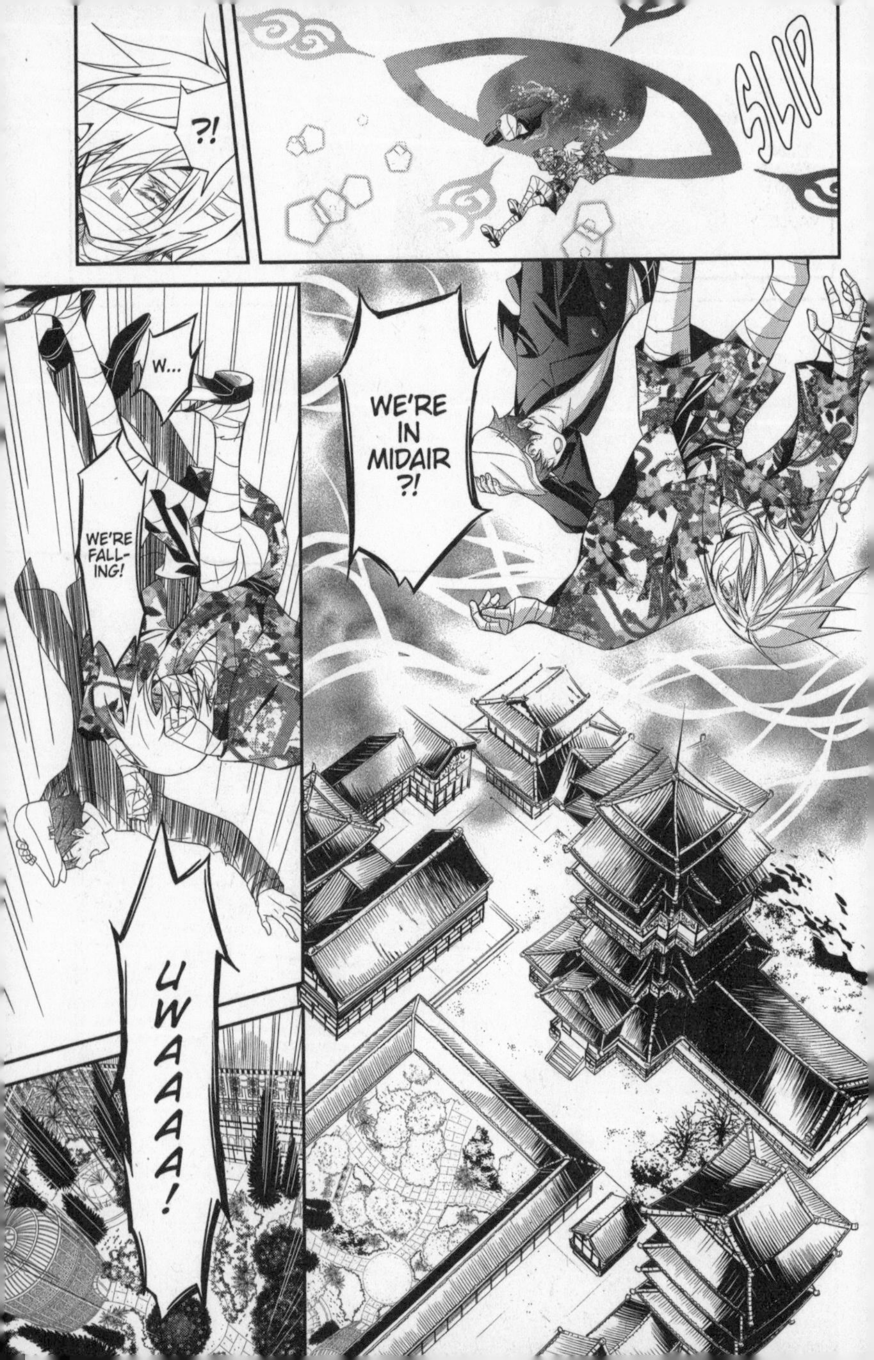
SLIP
?!
WE'RE IN MIDAIR ?!
W...
WE'RE FALLING!
UWAAAAAA!

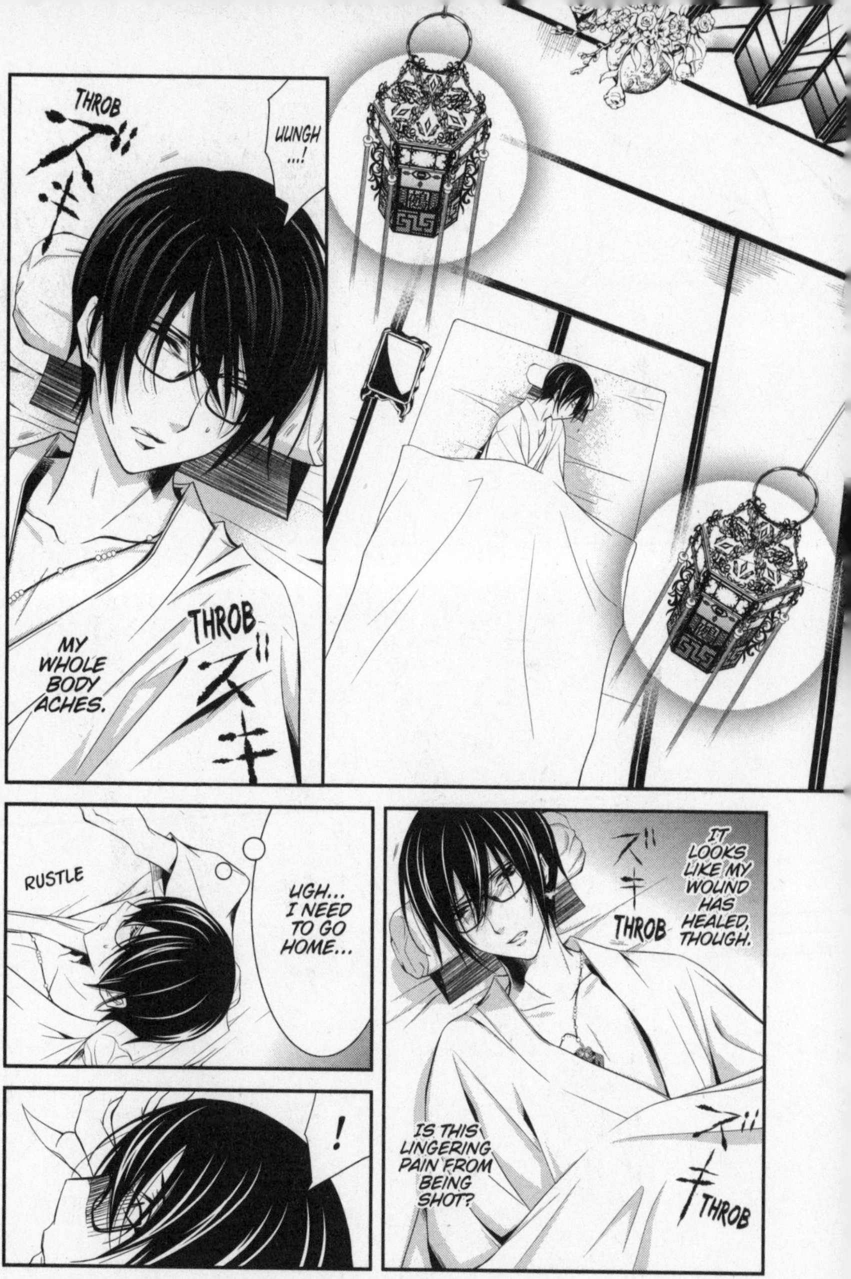
THROB
UUNGH ...!
MY WHOLE BODY ACHES.
THROB
IT LOOKS LIKE MY WOUND HAS HEALED, THOUGH.
THROB
IS THIS LINGERING PAIN FROM BEING SHOT?
THROB
RUSTLE
UGH... I NEED TO GO HOME...
!

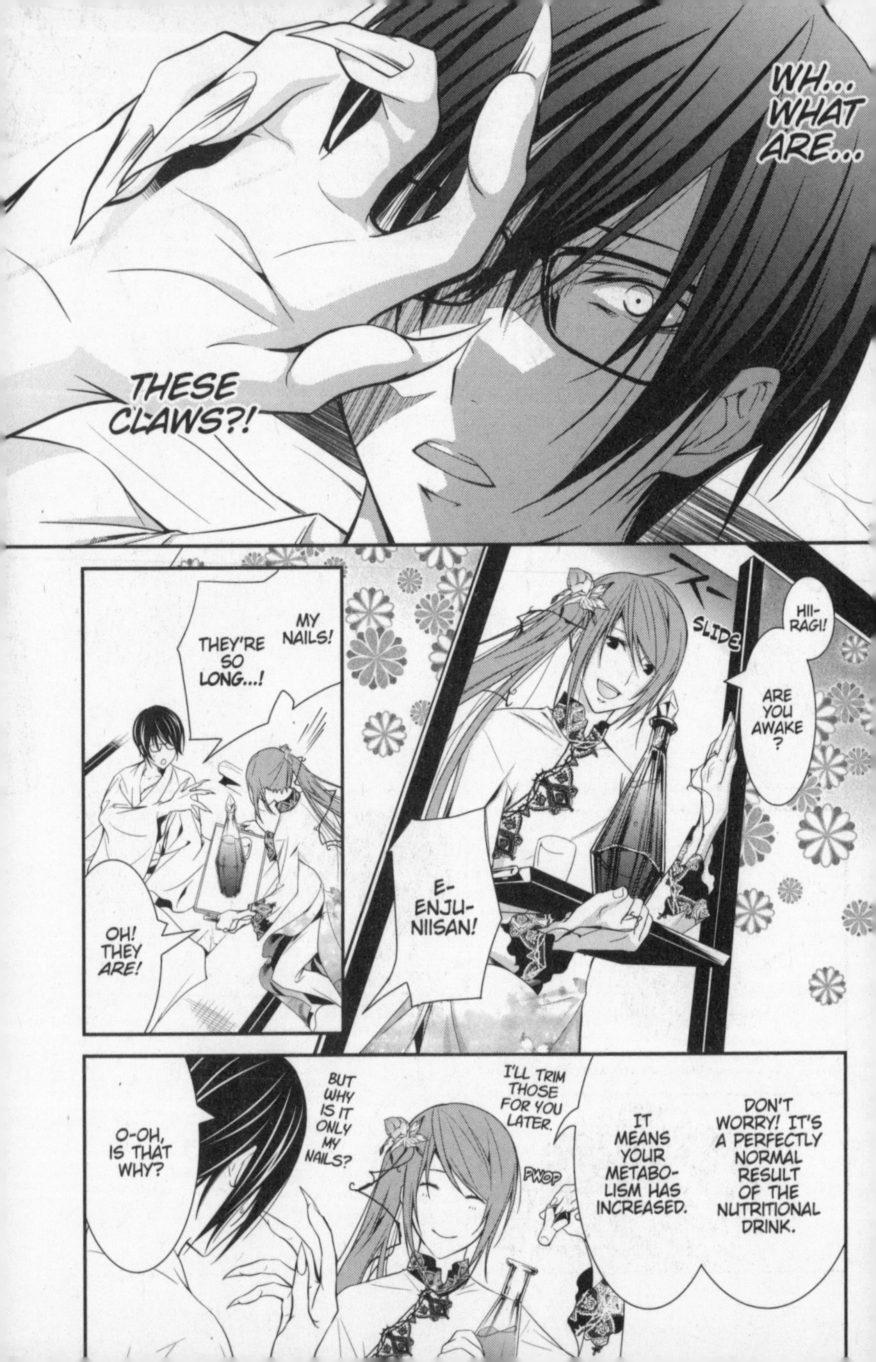
WH... WHAT ARE...
THESE CLAWS?!
SLIDE
HII-RAGI!
ARE YOU AWAKE?
E-ENJU-NIISAN!
MY NAILS!
THEY'RE SO LONG...!
OH! THEY ARE!
DON'T WORRY! IT'S A PERFECTLY NORMAL RESULT OF THE NUTRITIONAL DRINK.
IT MEANS YOUR METABOLISM HAS INCREASED.
PWOP
I'LL TRIM THOSE FOR YOU LATER.
BUT WHY IS IT ONLY MY NAILS?
O-OH, IS THAT WHY?

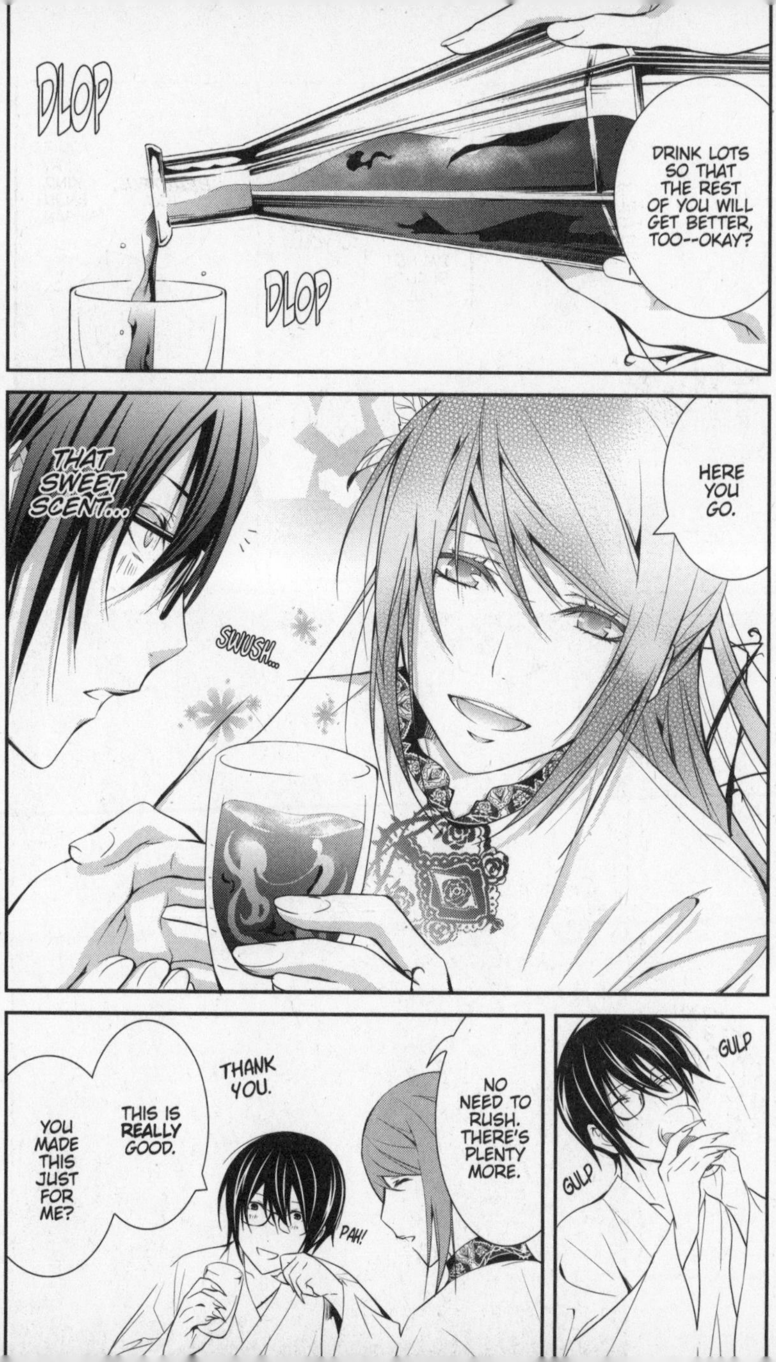
DRINK LOTS SO THAT THE REST OF YOU WILL GET BETTER, TOO--OKAY?
DLOP
DLOP
HERE YOU GO.
THAT SWEET SCENT...
SWUSH...
GULP
GULP
NO NEED TO RUSH. THERE'S PLENTY MORE.
THANK YOU.
PAH!
THIS IS REALLY GOOD.
YOU MADE THIS JUST FOR ME?

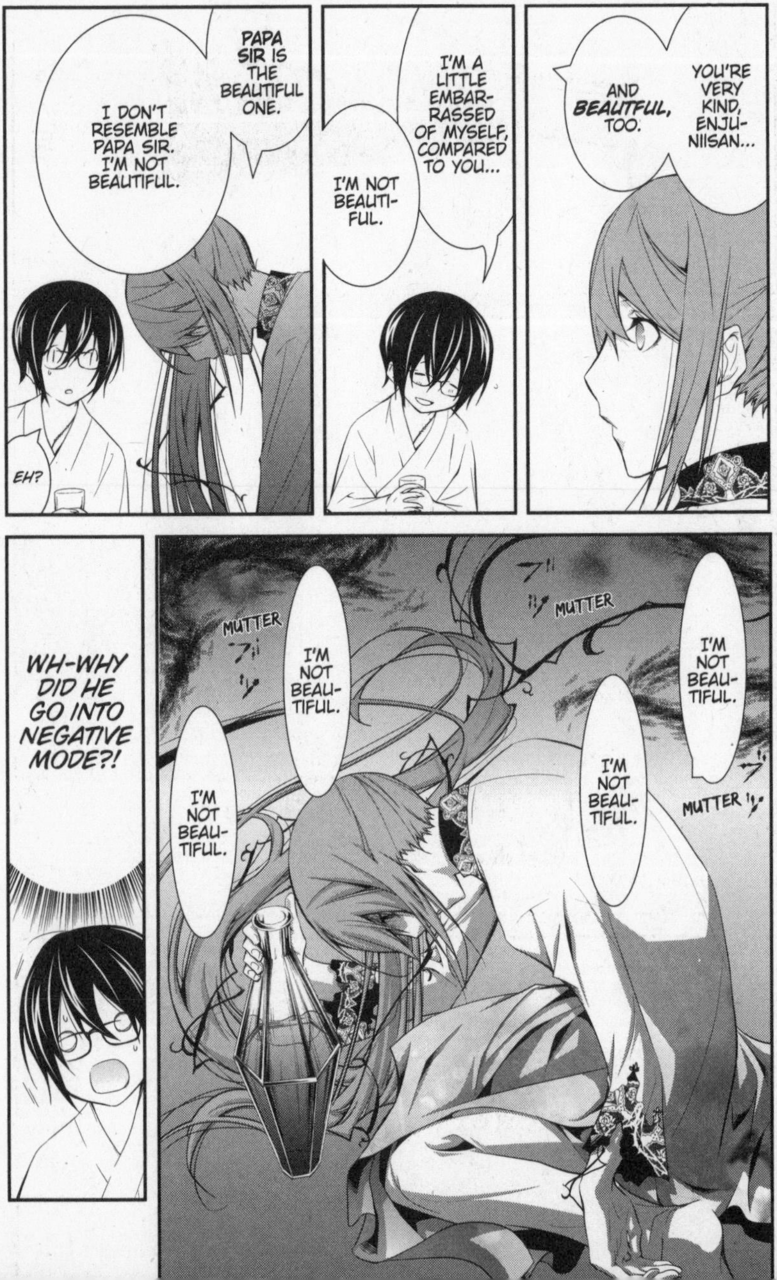
YOU'RE VERY KIND, ENJU-NIISAN...
AND BEAUTIFUL, TOO.
I'M A LITTLE EMBAR-RASSED OF MYSELF, COMPARED TO YOU...
I'M NOT BEAUTI-FUL.
PAPA SIR IS THE BEAUTIFUL ONE.
I DON'T RESEMBLE PAPA SIR. I'M NOT BEAUTIFUL.
EH?
MUTTER
I'M NOT BEAU-TIFUL.
MUTTER
I'M NOT BEAU-TIFUL.
MUTTER
I'M NOT BEAU-TIFUL.
I'M NOT BEAU-TIFUL.
WH-WHY DID HE GO INTO NEGATIVE MODE?!

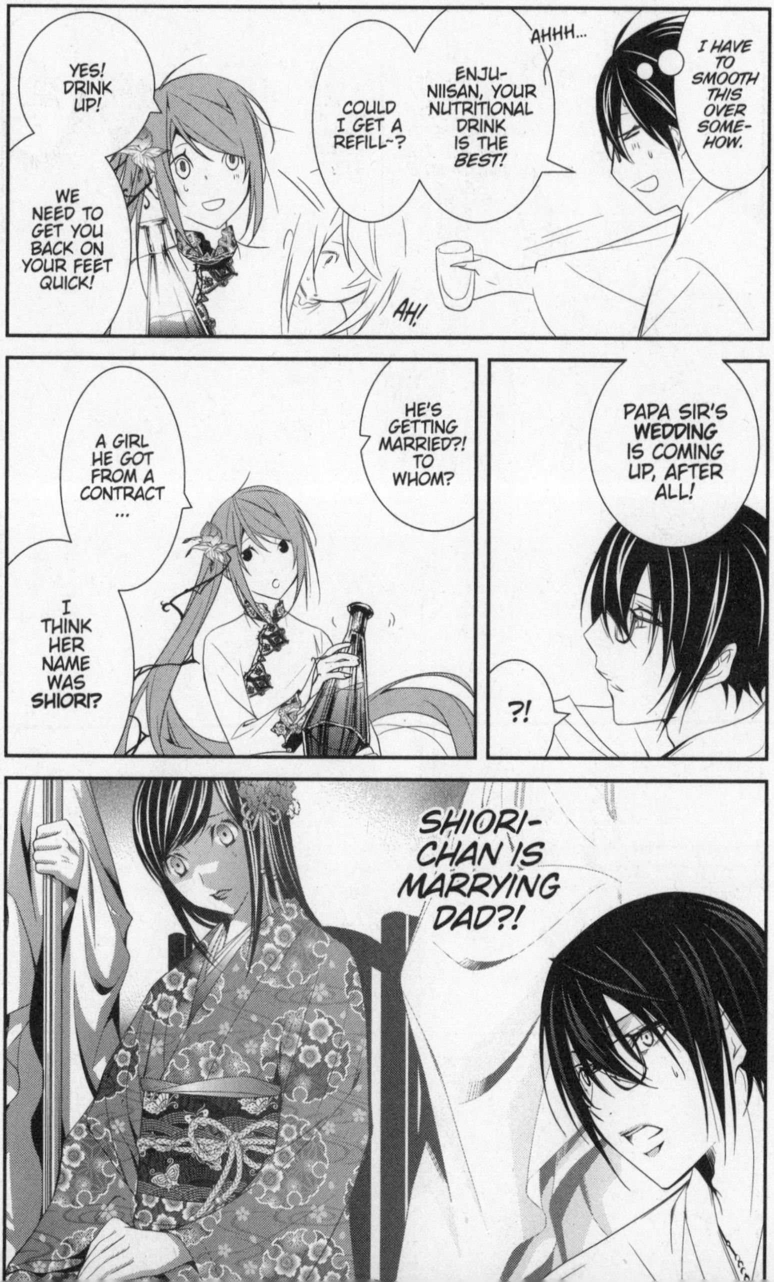
I HAVE TO SMOOTH THIS OVER SOME-HOW.
AHHH...
ENJU-NIISAN, YOUR NUTRITIONAL DRINK IS THE BEST!
COULD I GET A REFILL~?
AH!
YES! DRINK UP!
WE NEED TO GET YOU BACK ON YOUR FEET QUICK!
PAPA SIR'S WEDDING IS COMING UP, AFTER ALL!
?!
HE'S GETTING MARRIED?! TO WHOM?
A GIRL HE GOT FROM A CONTRACT ...
I THINK HER NAME WAS SHIORI?
SHIORI-CHAN IS MARRYING DAD?!

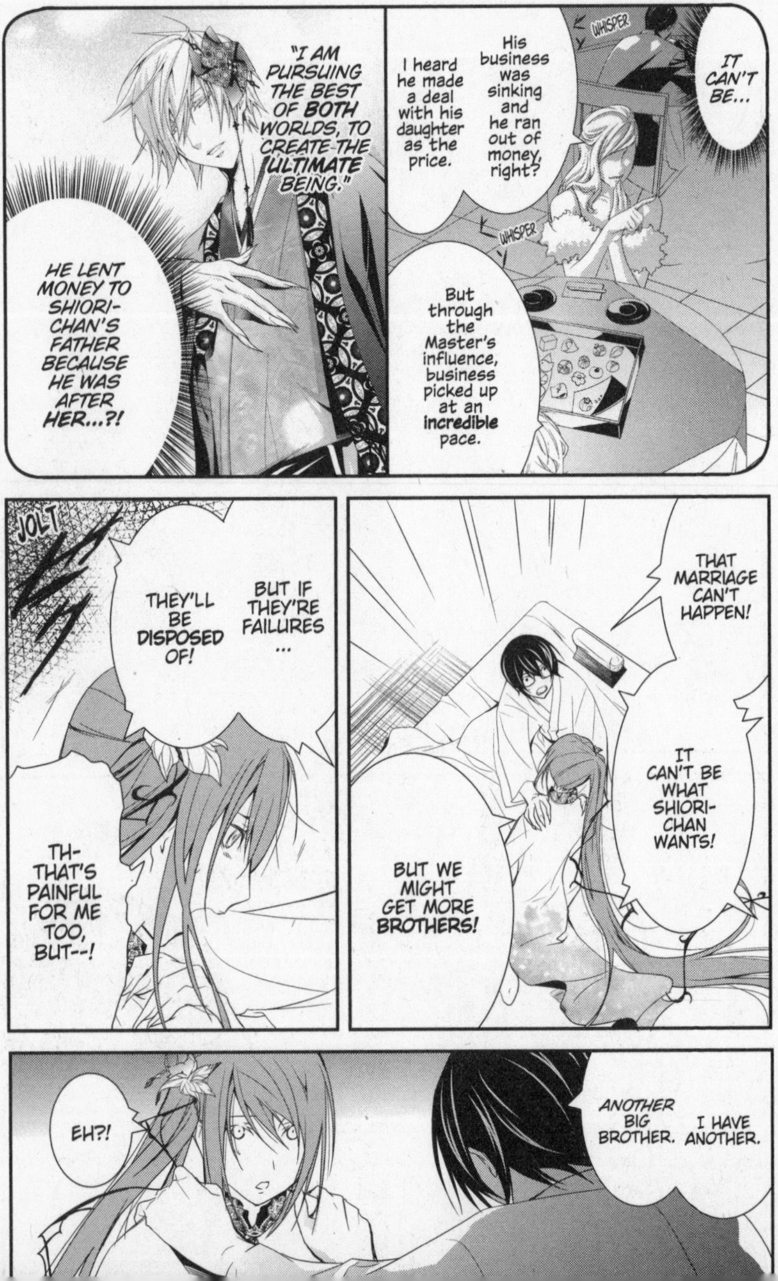
WHISPER
IT CAN'T BE...
His business was sinking and he ran out of money, right?
I heard he made a deal with his daughter as the price.
WHISPER
But through the Master's influence, business picked up at an incredible pace.
"I AM PURSUING THE BEST OF BOTH WORLDS, TO CREATE THE ULTIMATE BEING."
HE LENT MONEY TO SHIORI-CHAN'S FATHER BECAUSE HE WAS AFTER HER...?!
THAT MARRIAGE CAN'T HAPPEN!
IT CAN'T BE WHAT SHIORI-CHAN WANTS!
BUT WE MIGHT GET MORE BROTHERS!
JOLT
BUT IF THEY'RE FAILURES ...
THEY'LL BE DISPOSED OF!
TH-THAT'S PAINFUL FOR ME TOO, BUT--!
I HAVE ANOTHER.
ANOTHER BIG BROTHER.
EH?!

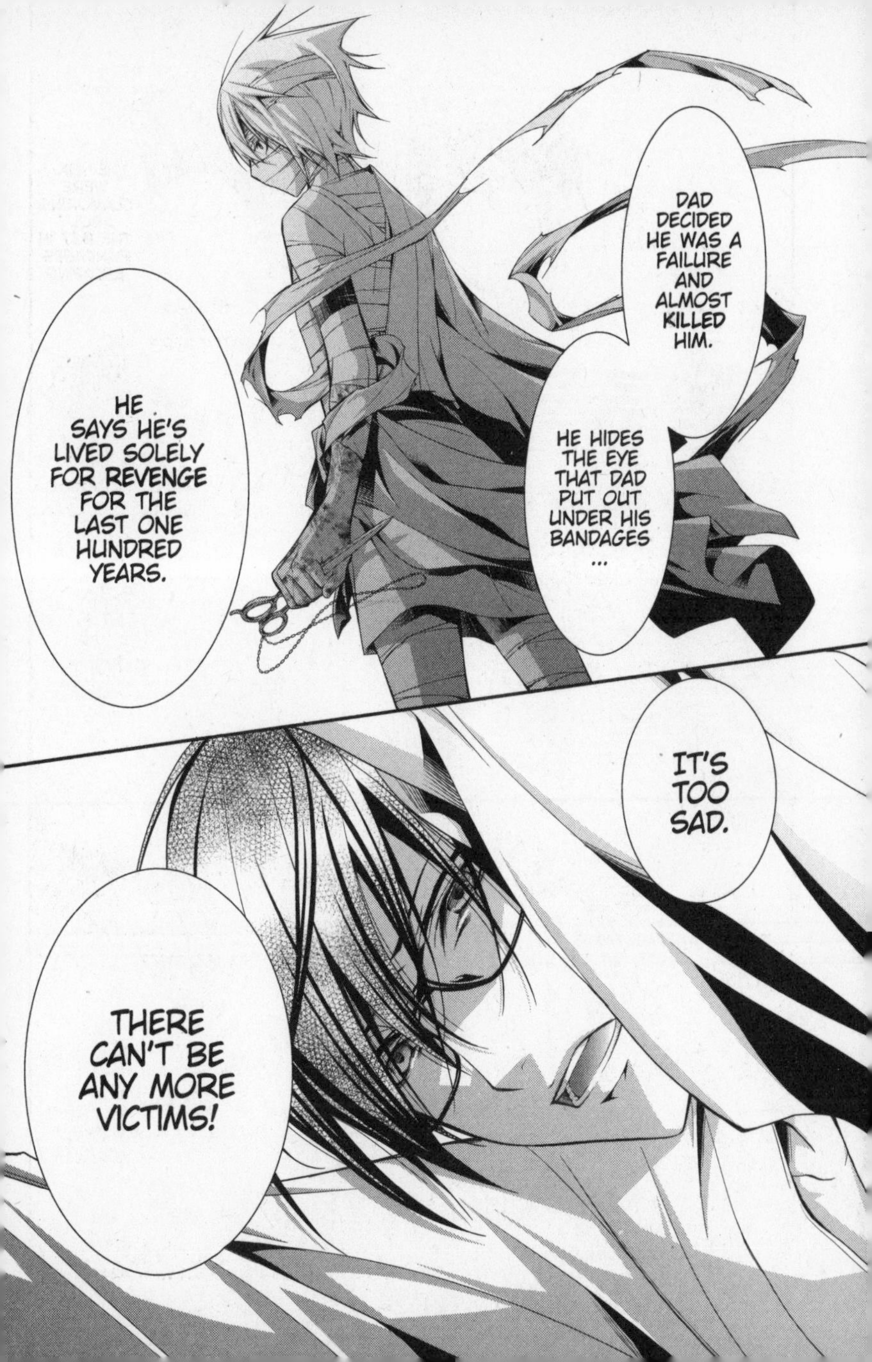
DAD DECIDED HE WAS A FAILURE AND ALMOST KILLED HIM.
HE HIDES THE EYE THAT DAD PUT OUT UNDER HIS BANDAGES...
HE SAYS HE'S LIVED SOLELY FOR REVENGE FOR THE LAST ONE HUNDRED YEARS.
IT'S TOO SAD.
THERE CAN'T BE ANY MORE VICTIMS!

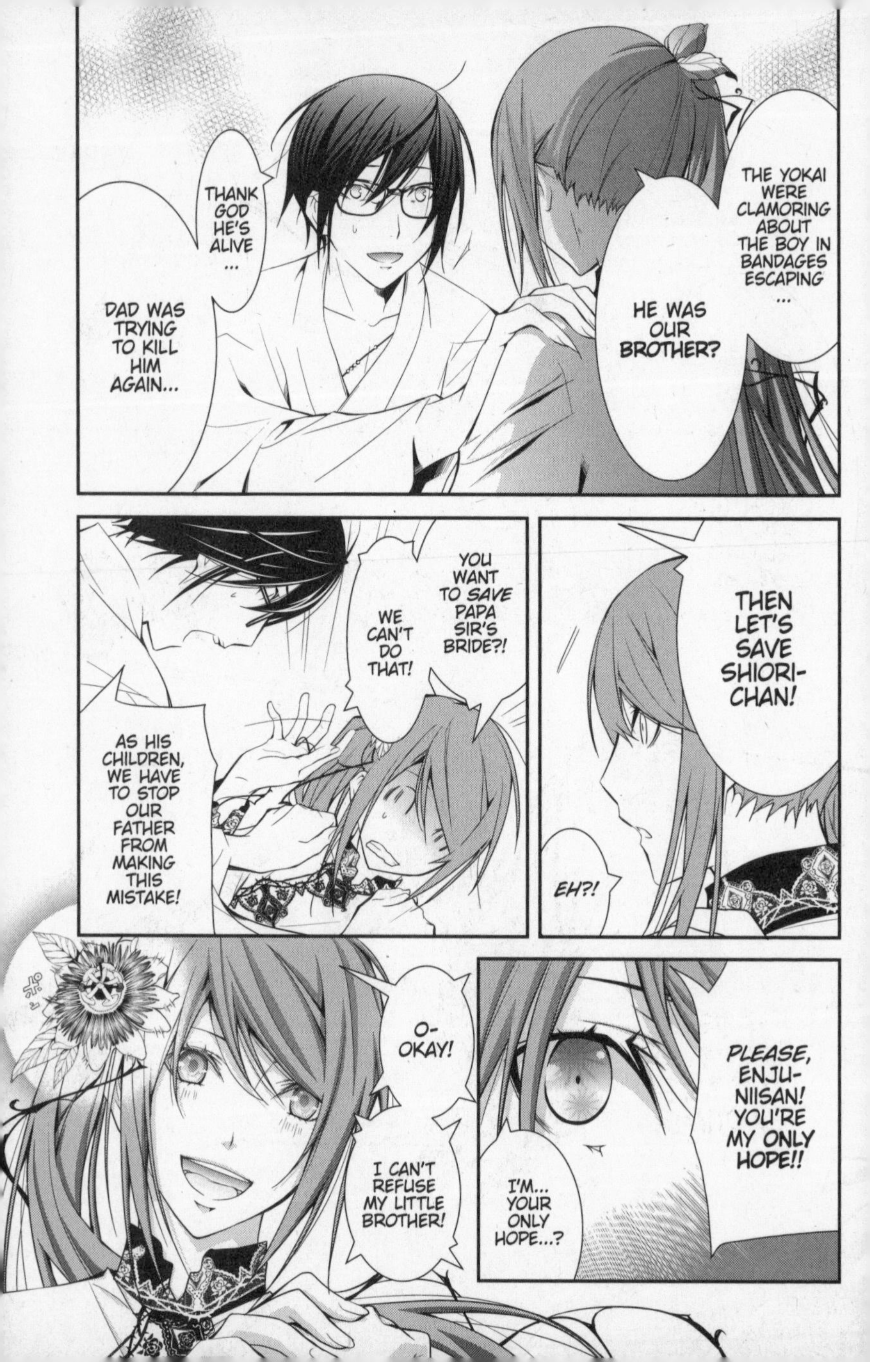
THE YOKAI WERE CLAMORING ABOUT THE BOY IN BANDAGES ESCAPING ...
HE WAS OUR BROTHER?
THANK GOD HE'S ALIVE ...
DAD WAS TRYING TO KILL HIM AGAIN...
THEN LET'S SAVE SHIORI-CHAN!
EH?!
YOU WANT TO SAVE PAPA SIR'S BRIDE?!
WE CAN'T DO THAT!
AS HIS CHILDREN, WE HAVE TO STOP OUR FATHER FROM MAKING THIS MISTAKE!
PLEASE, ENJU-NIISAN! YOU'RE MY ONLY HOPE!!
I'M... YOUR ONLY HOPE...?
O-OKAY!
I CAN'T REFUSE MY LITTLE BROTHER!

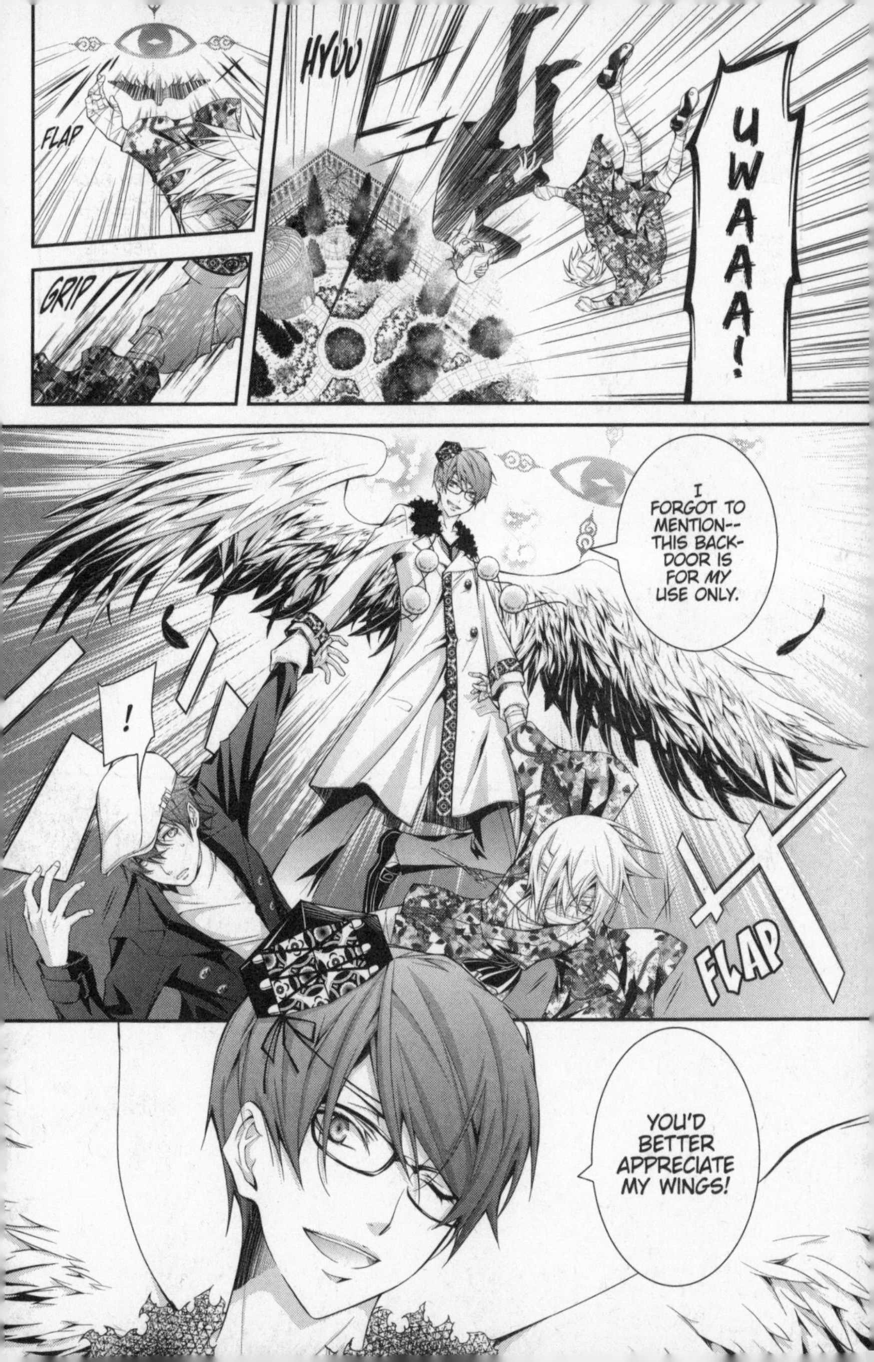

UWAAA!
HYUU
FLAP
GRIP
I FORGOT TO MENTION-- THIS BACKDOOR IS FOR MY USE ONLY.
!
FLAP
YOU'D BETTER APPRECIATE MY WINGS!

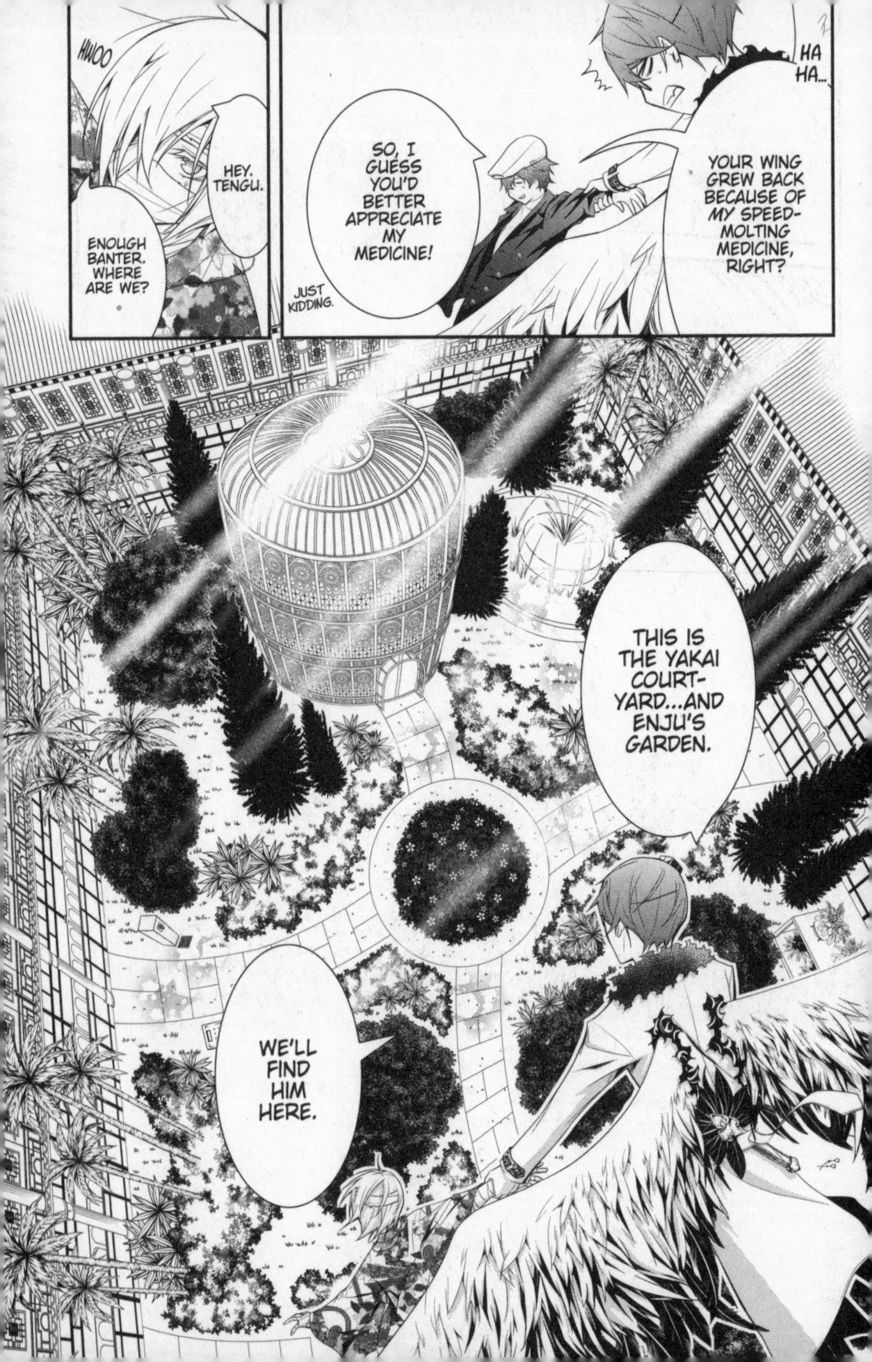
HA HA...
YOUR WING GREW BACK BECAUSE OF MY SPEED-MOLTING MEDICINE, RIGHT?
SO, I GUESS YOU'D BETTER APPRECIATE MY MEDICINE!
JUST KIDDING.
HWOO
HEY. TENGU.
ENOUGH BANTER. WHERE ARE WE?
THIS IS THE YAKAI COURT-YARD...AND ENJU'S GARDEN.
WE'LL FIND HIM HERE.

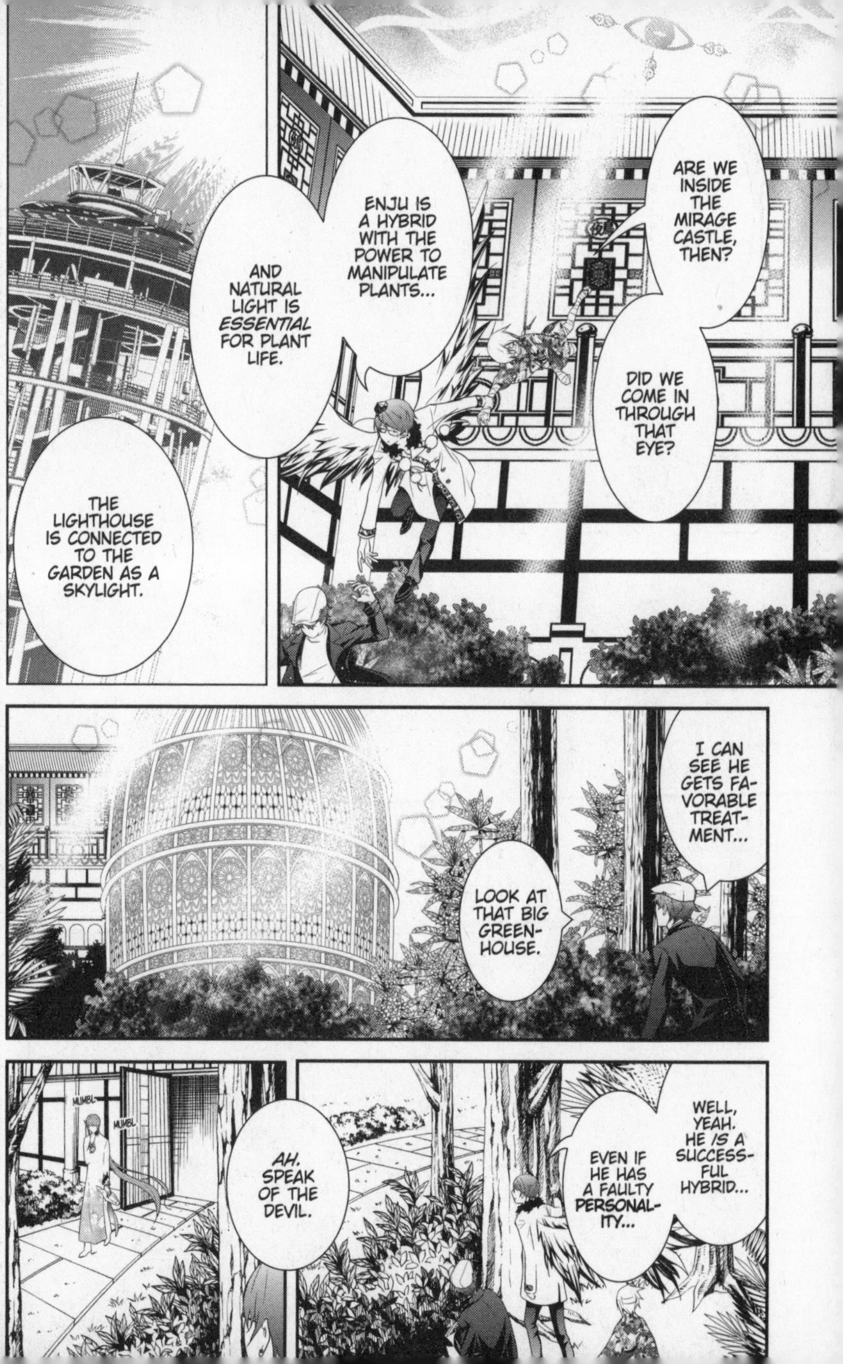
ARE WE INSIDE THE MIRAGE CASTLE, THEN?
DID WE COME IN THROUGH THAT EYE?
ENJU IS A HYBRID WITH THE POWER TO MANIPULATE PLANTS...
AND NATURAL LIGHT IS *ESSENTIAL* FOR PLANT LIFE.
THE LIGHTHOUSE IS CONNECTED TO THE GARDEN AS A SKYLIGHT.
I CAN SEE HE GETS FA-VORABLE TREAT-MENT...
LOOK AT THAT BIG GREEN-HOUSE.
WELL, YEAH. HE *IS* A SUCCESS-FUL HYBRID...
EVEN IF HE HAS A FAULTY PERSONAL-ITY...
AH. SPEAK OF THE DEVIL.
MUMBL
MUMBL

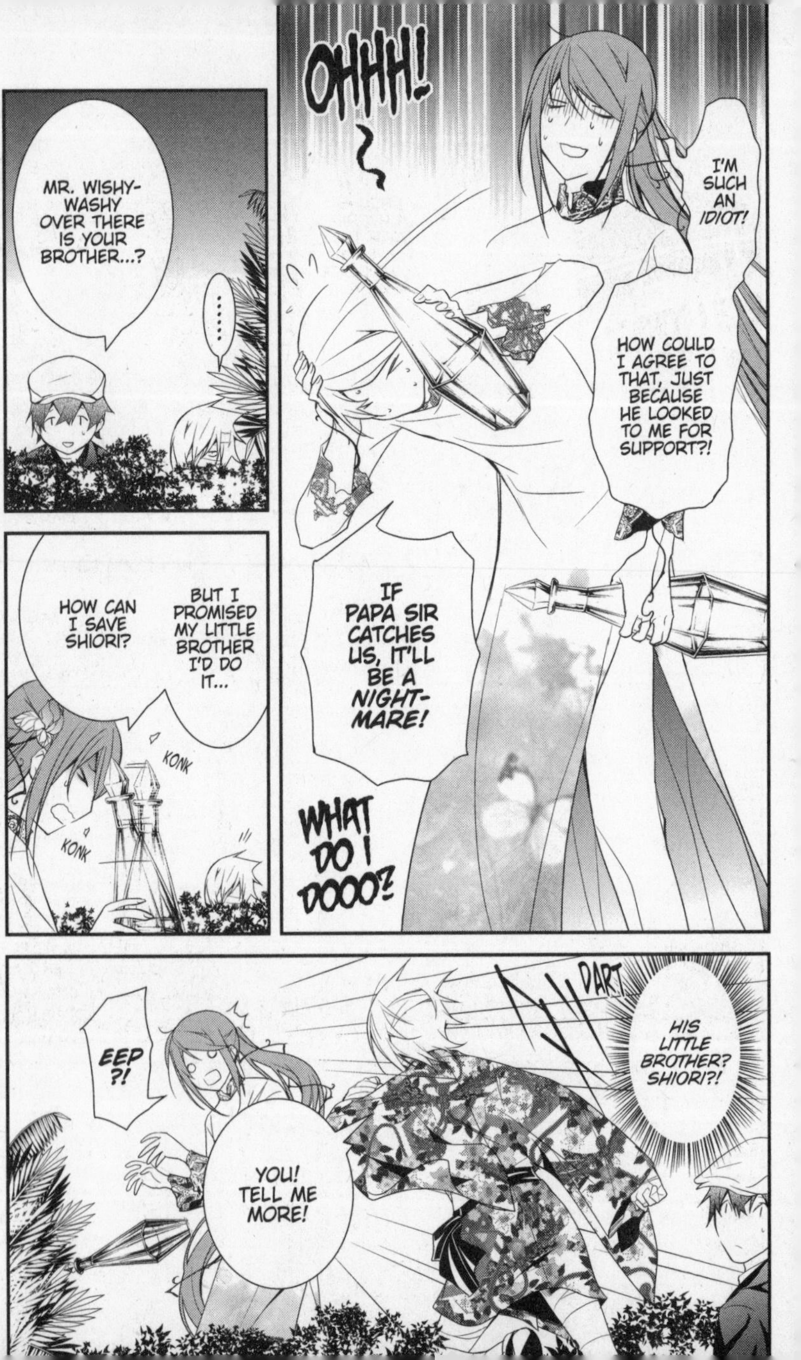
I'M SUCH AN IDIOT!
OHHH!
HOW COULD I AGREE TO THAT, JUST BECAUSE HE LOOKED TO ME FOR SUPPORT?!
IF PAPA SIR CATCHES US, IT'LL BE A NIGHT-MARE!
WHAT DO I DOOO?!
MR. WISHY-WASHY OVER THERE IS YOUR BROTHER...?
......
BUT I PROMISED MY LITTLE BROTHER I'D DO IT...
HOW CAN I SAVE SHIORI?
KONK
KONK
DART
HIS LITTLE BROTHER? SHIORI?!
EEP?!
YOU! TELL ME MORE!

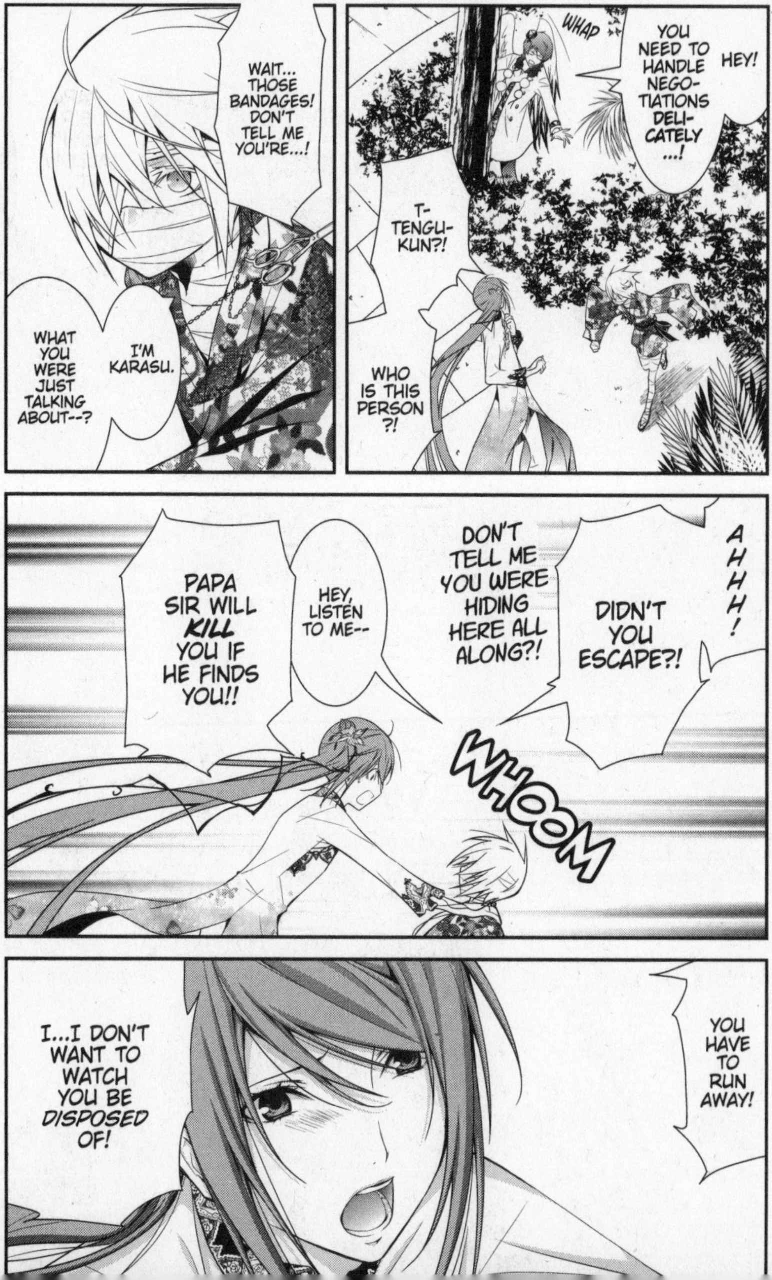
HEY!
YOU NEED TO HANDLE NEGO-TIATIONS DELI-CATELY ...!
WHAP
T-TENGU-KUN?!
WHO IS THIS PERSON ?!
WAIT... THOSE BANDAGES! DON'T TELL ME YOU'RE...!
I'M KARASU.
WHAT YOU WERE JUST TALKING ABOUT--?
AHHHH!
DIDN'T YOU ESCAPE?!
DON'T TELL ME YOU WERE HIDING HERE ALL ALONG?!
HEY, LISTEN TO ME--
PAPA SIR WILL *KILL* YOU IF HE FINDS YOU!!
WHOOM
YOU HAVE TO RUN AWAY!
I...I DON'T WANT TO WATCH YOU BE *DISPOSED* OF!

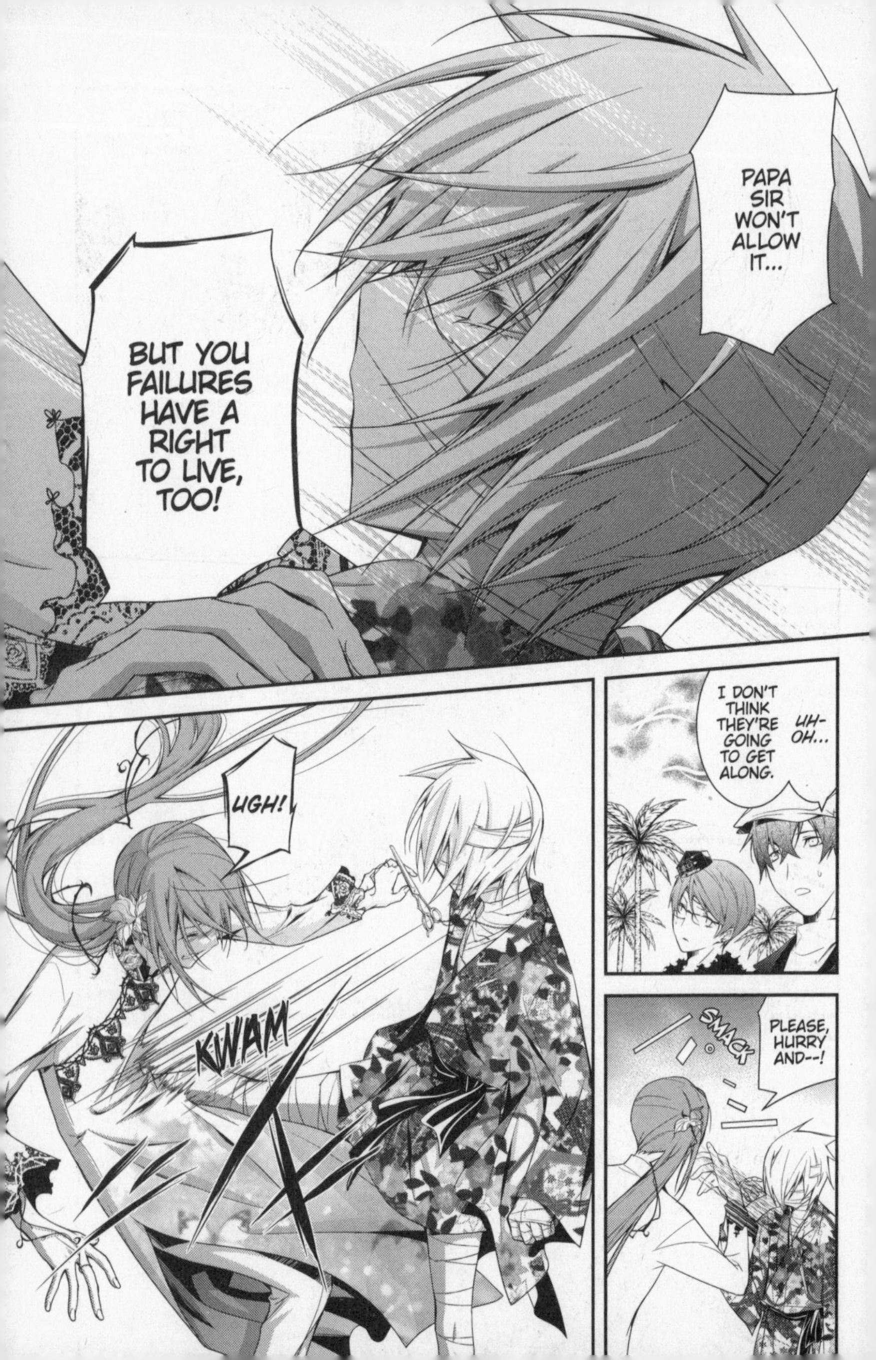
PAPA SIR WON'T ALLOW IT...
BUT YOU FAILURES HAVE A RIGHT TO LIVE, TOO!
UH-OH...
I DON'T THINK THEY'RE GOING TO GET ALONG.
SMACK
PLEASE, HURRY AND--!
UGH!
KWAM

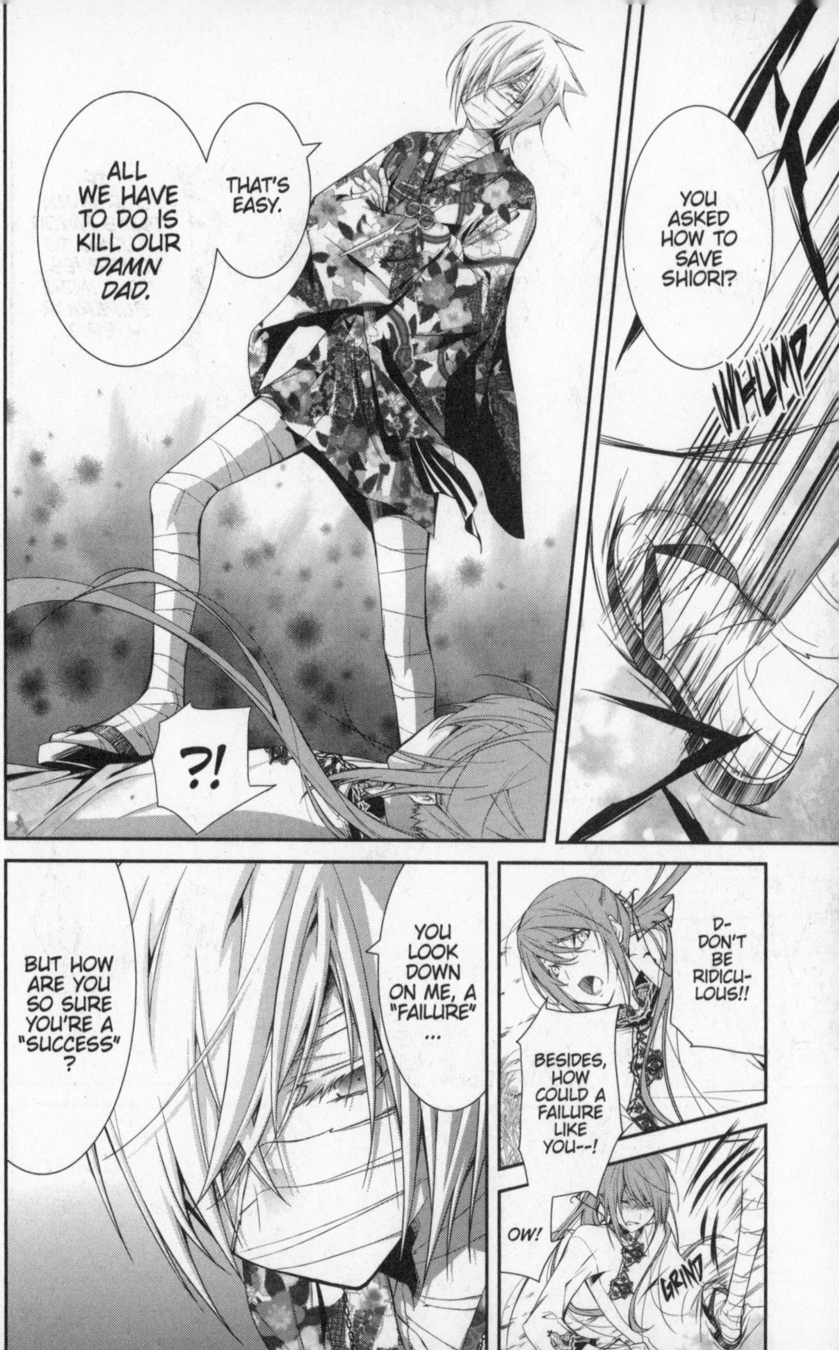
YOU ASKED HOW TO SAVE SHIORI?
WHUMP
THAT'S EASY.
ALL WE HAVE TO DO IS KILL OUR DAMN DAD.
?!
D-DON'T BE RIDICULOUS!!
BESIDES, HOW COULD A FAILURE LIKE YOU--!
OW!
GRIND
YOU LOOK DOWN ON ME, A "FAILURE"...
BUT HOW ARE YOU SO SURE YOU'RE A "SUCCESS"?

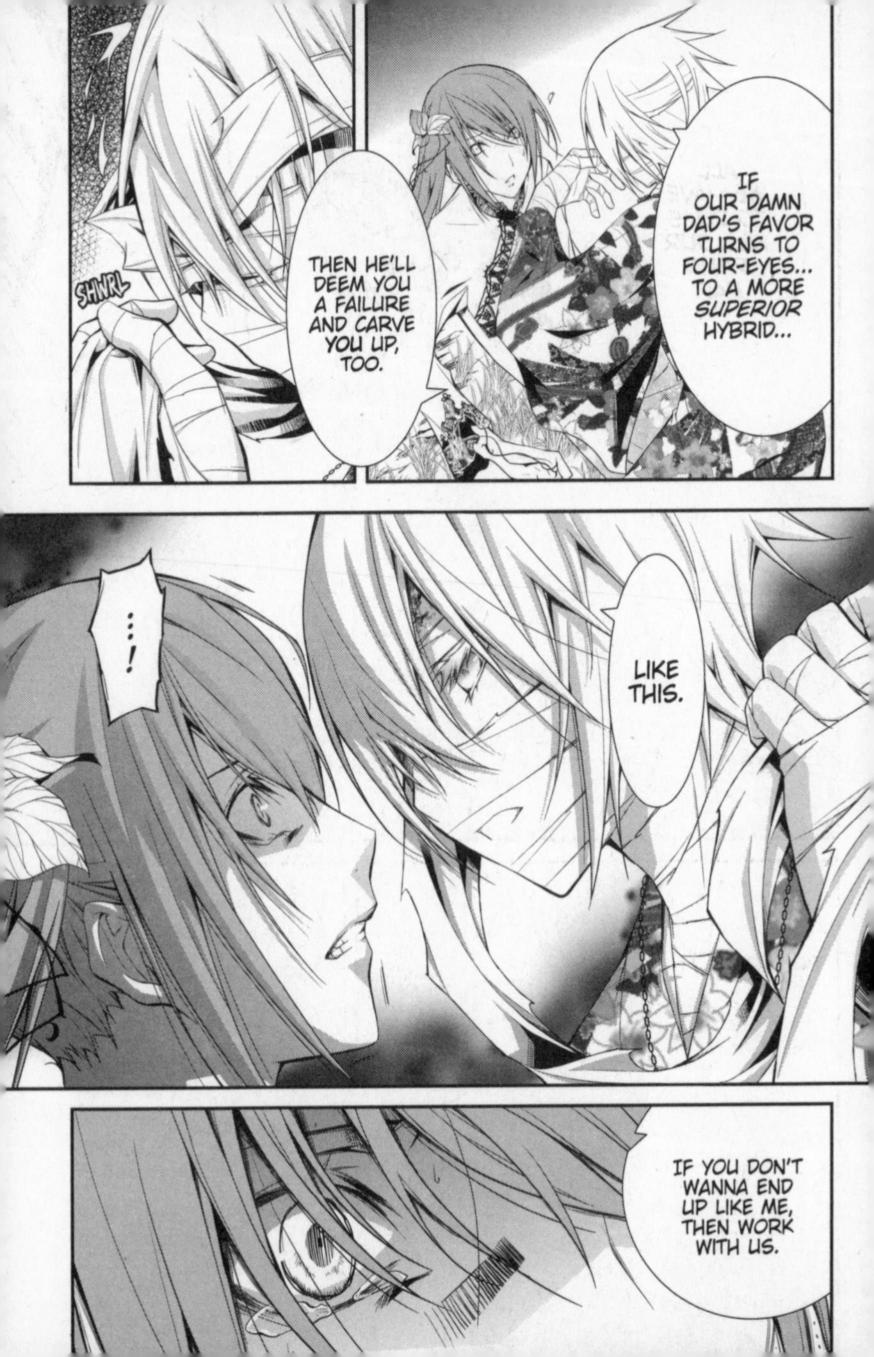
IF OUR DAMN DAD'S FAVOR TURNS TO FOUR-EYES... TO A MORE *SUPERIOR* HYBRID...
THEN HE'LL DEEM YOU A FAILURE AND CARVE YOU UP, TOO.
SHWRL
LIKE THIS.
...!
IF YOU DON'T WANNA END UP LIKE ME, THEN WORK WITH US.

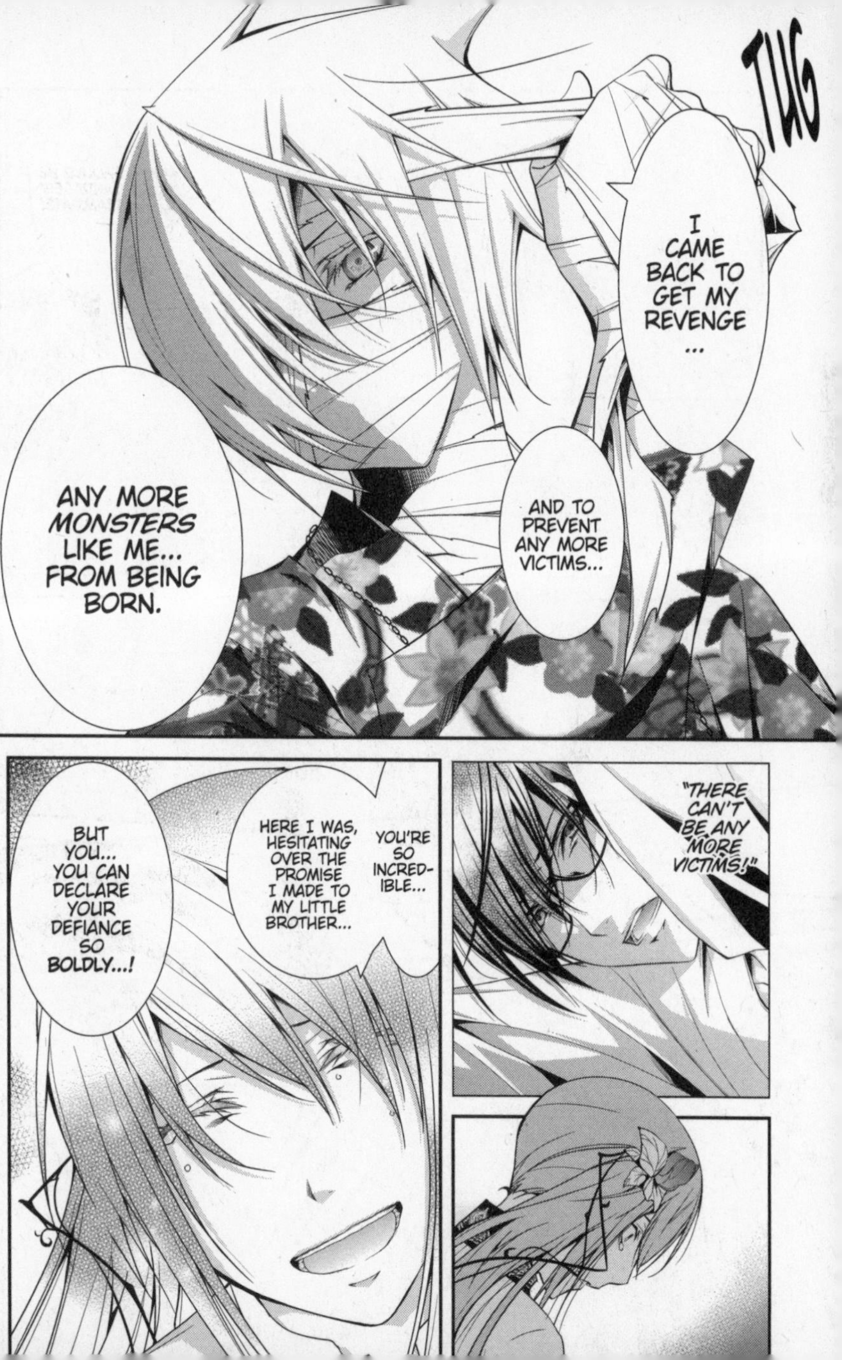
TUG
I CAME BACK TO GET MY REVENGE ...
AND TO PREVENT ANY MORE VICTIMS...
ANY MORE MONSTERS LIKE ME... FROM BEING BORN.
"THERE CAN'T BE ANY MORE VICTIMS!"
YOU'RE SO INCREDIBLE...
HERE I WAS, HESITATING OVER THE PROMISE I MADE TO MY LITTLE BROTHER...
BUT YOU... YOU CAN DECLARE YOUR DEFIANCE SO BOLDLY...!

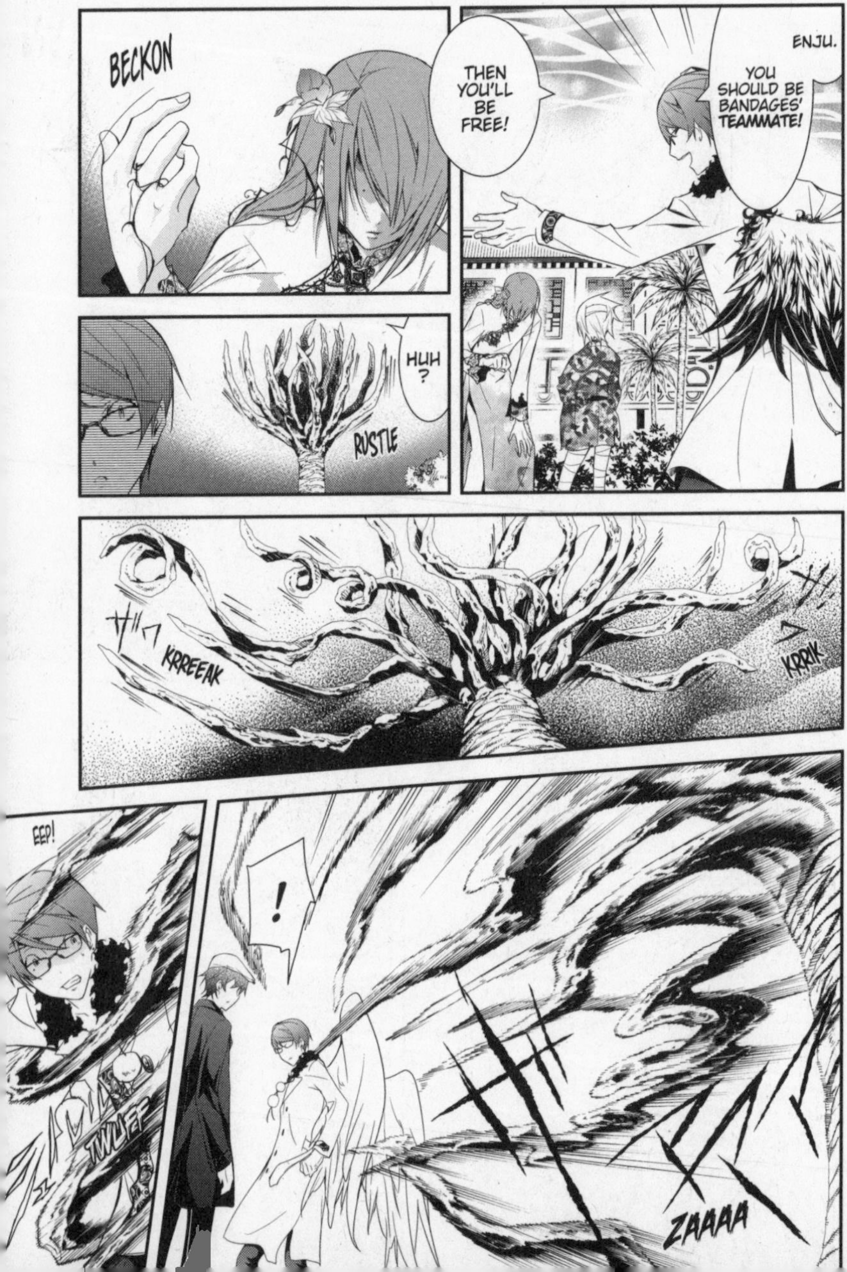
ENJU.
YOU SHOULD BE BANDAGES' TEAMMATE!
THEN YOU'LL BE FREE!
BECKON
HUH?
RUSTLE
KRRIK
KRREEAK
!
ZAAAA
EEP!
TWUFF

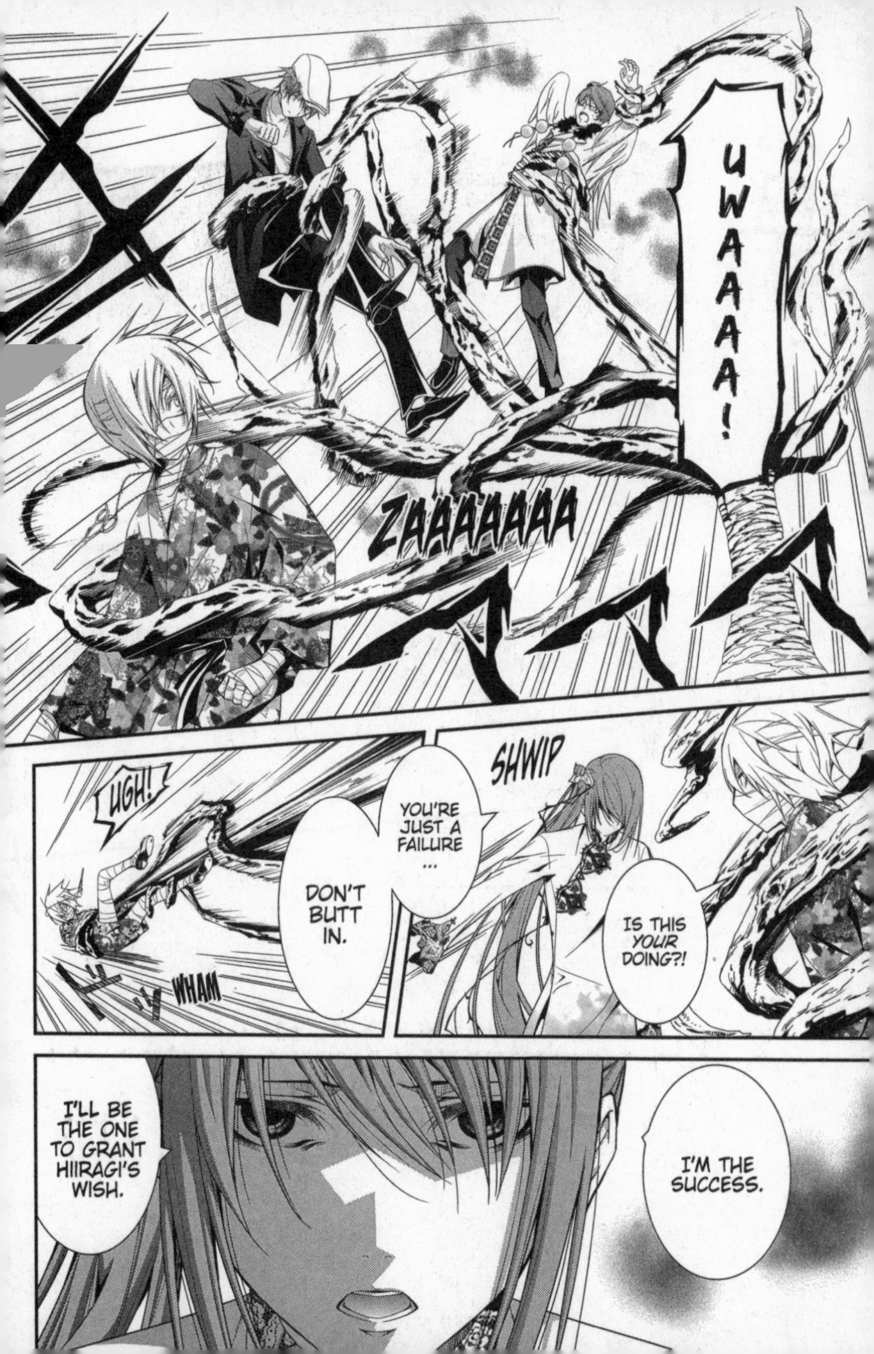
UWAAAAA!
ZAAAAAAA
SHWIP
IS THIS *YOUR* DOING?!
YOU'RE JUST A FAILURE ...
UGH!
DON'T BUTT IN.
WHAM
I'M THE SUCCESS.
I'LL BE THE ONE TO GRANT HIIRAGI'S WISH.

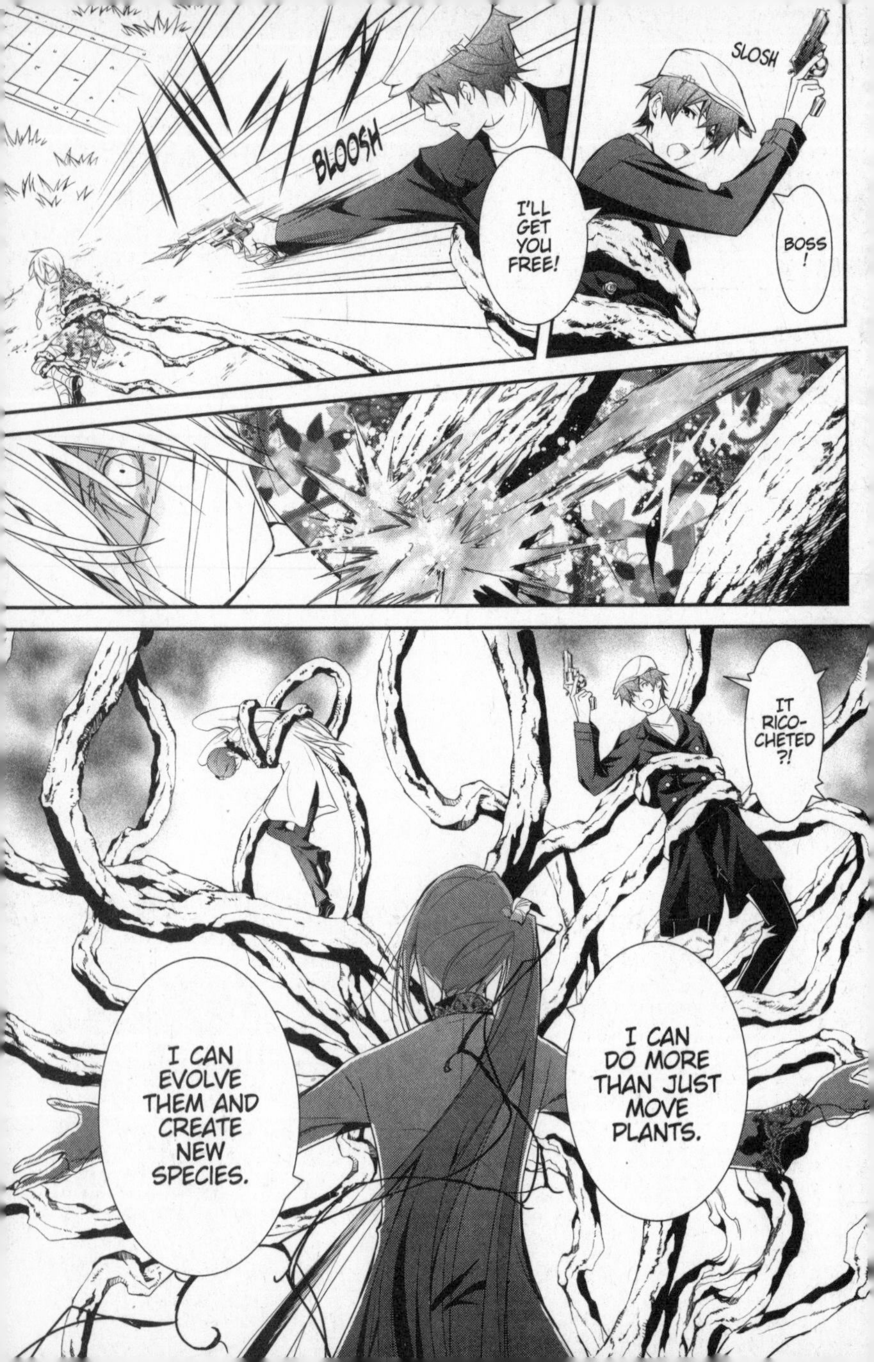
SLOSH
BOSS!
I'LL GET YOU FREE!
BLOOSH
IT RICOCHETED?!
I CAN DO MORE THAN JUST MOVE PLANTS.
I CAN EVOLVE THEM AND CREATE NEW SPECIES.

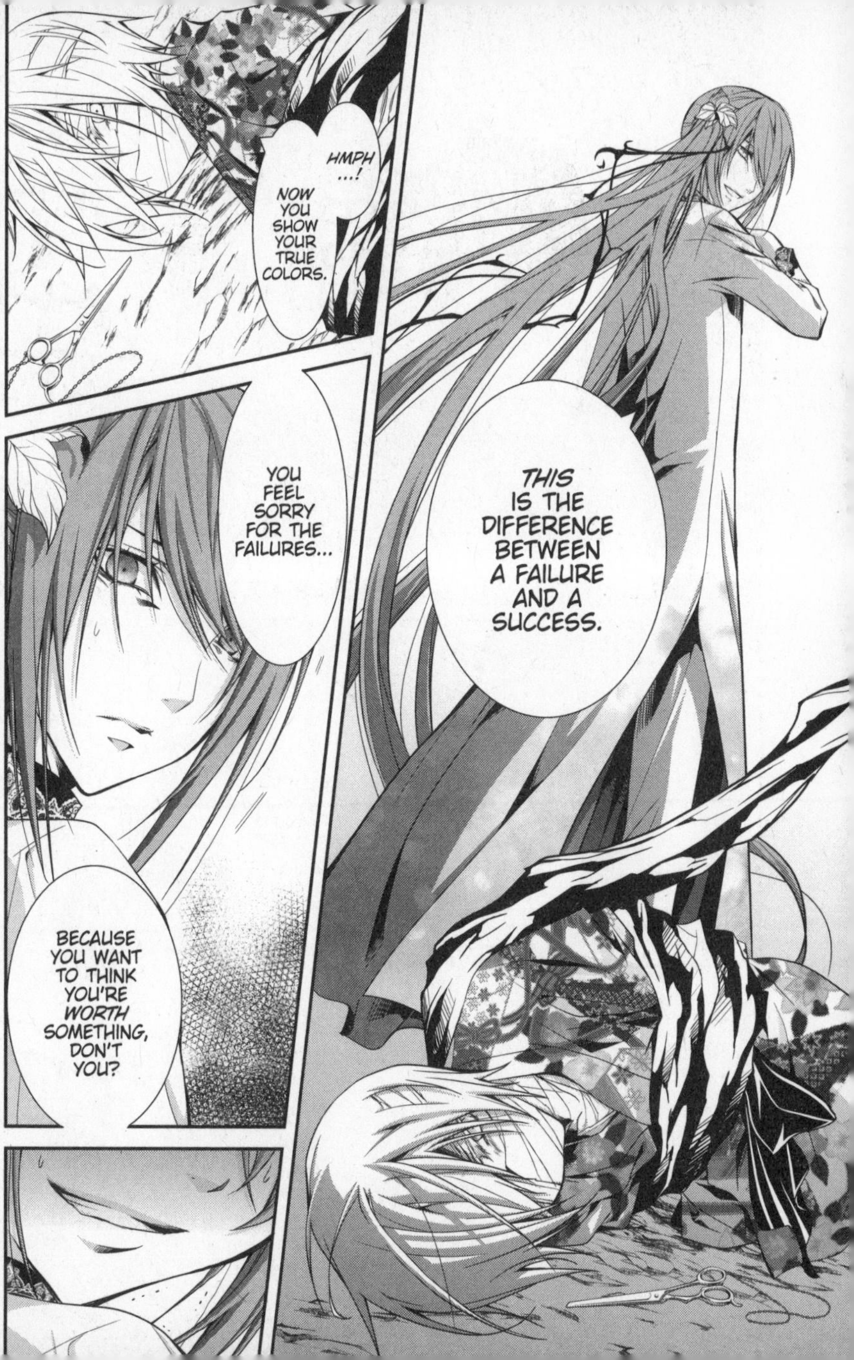
THIS IS THE DIFFERENCE BETWEEN A FAILURE AND A SUCCESS.
HMPH...! NOW YOU SHOW YOUR TRUE COLORS.
YOU FEEL SORRY FOR THE FAILURES...
BECAUSE YOU WANT TO THINK YOU'RE WORTH SOMETHING, DON'T YOU?

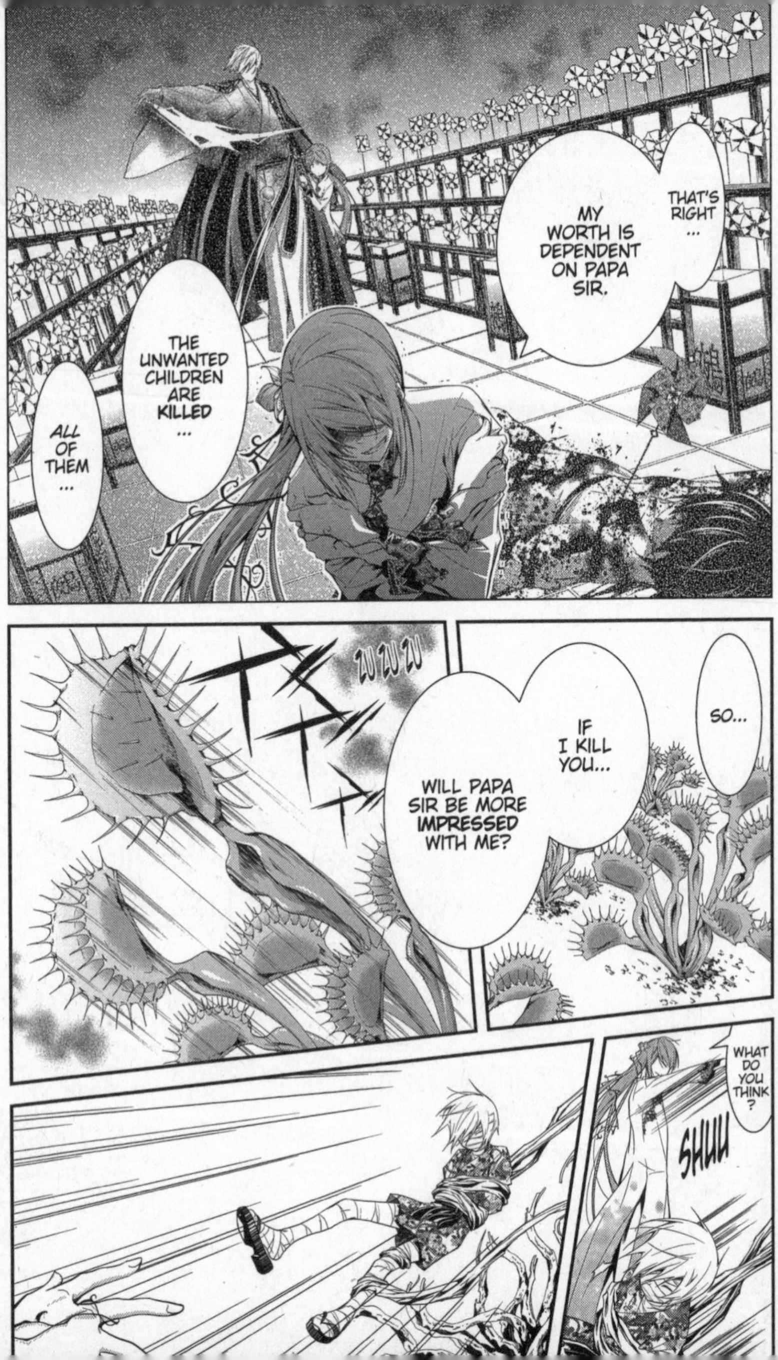
THAT'S RIGHT ...
MY WORTH IS DEPENDENT ON PAPA SIR.
THE UNWANTED CHILDREN ARE KILLED ...
ALL OF THEM ...
SO...
IF I KILL YOU...
WILL PAPA SIR BE MORE IMPRESSED WITH ME?
ZU ZU ZU
WHAT DO YOU THINK?
SHUU

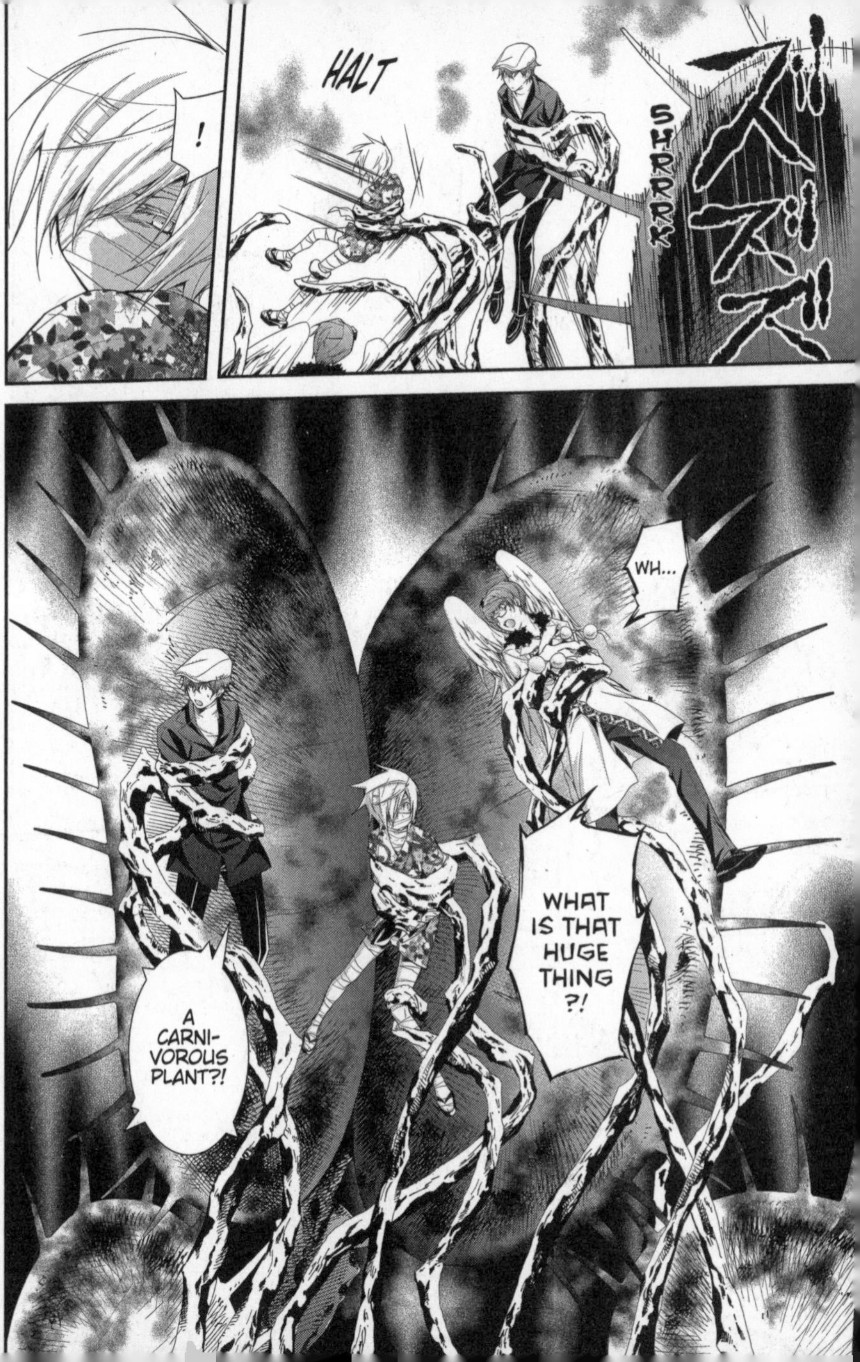
ズズズ!!
SHRRRK
HALT
!
WH...
WHAT IS THAT HUGE THING?!
A CARNIVOROUS PLANT?!

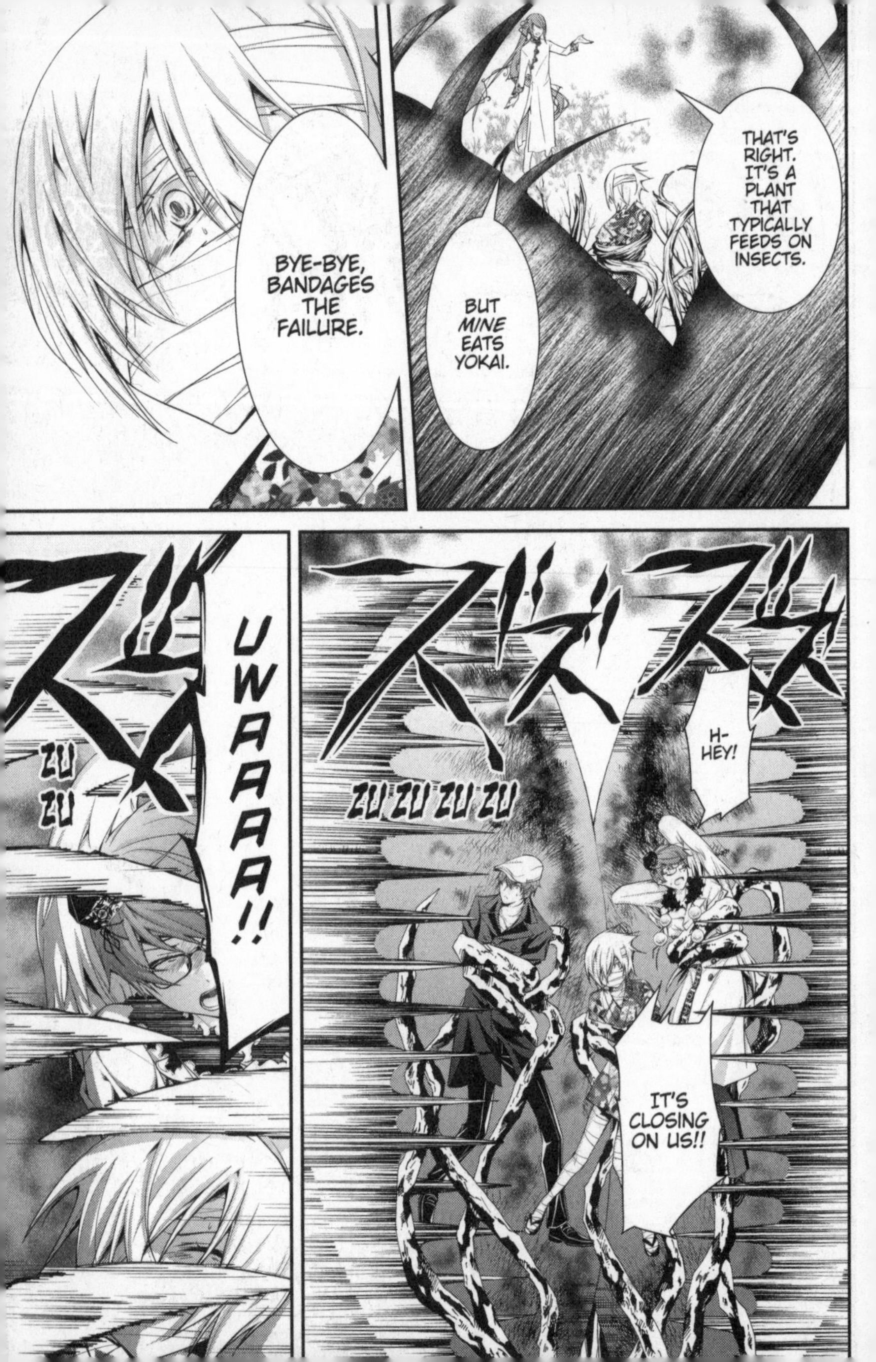
THAT'S RIGHT. IT'S A PLANT THAT TYPICALLY FEEDS ON INSECTS.
BUT *MINE* EATS YOKAI.
BYE-BYE, BANDAGES THE FAILURE.
ZU ZU ZU ZU
H-HEY!
IT'S CLOSING ON US!!
ZU ZU
UWAAAAAA!!

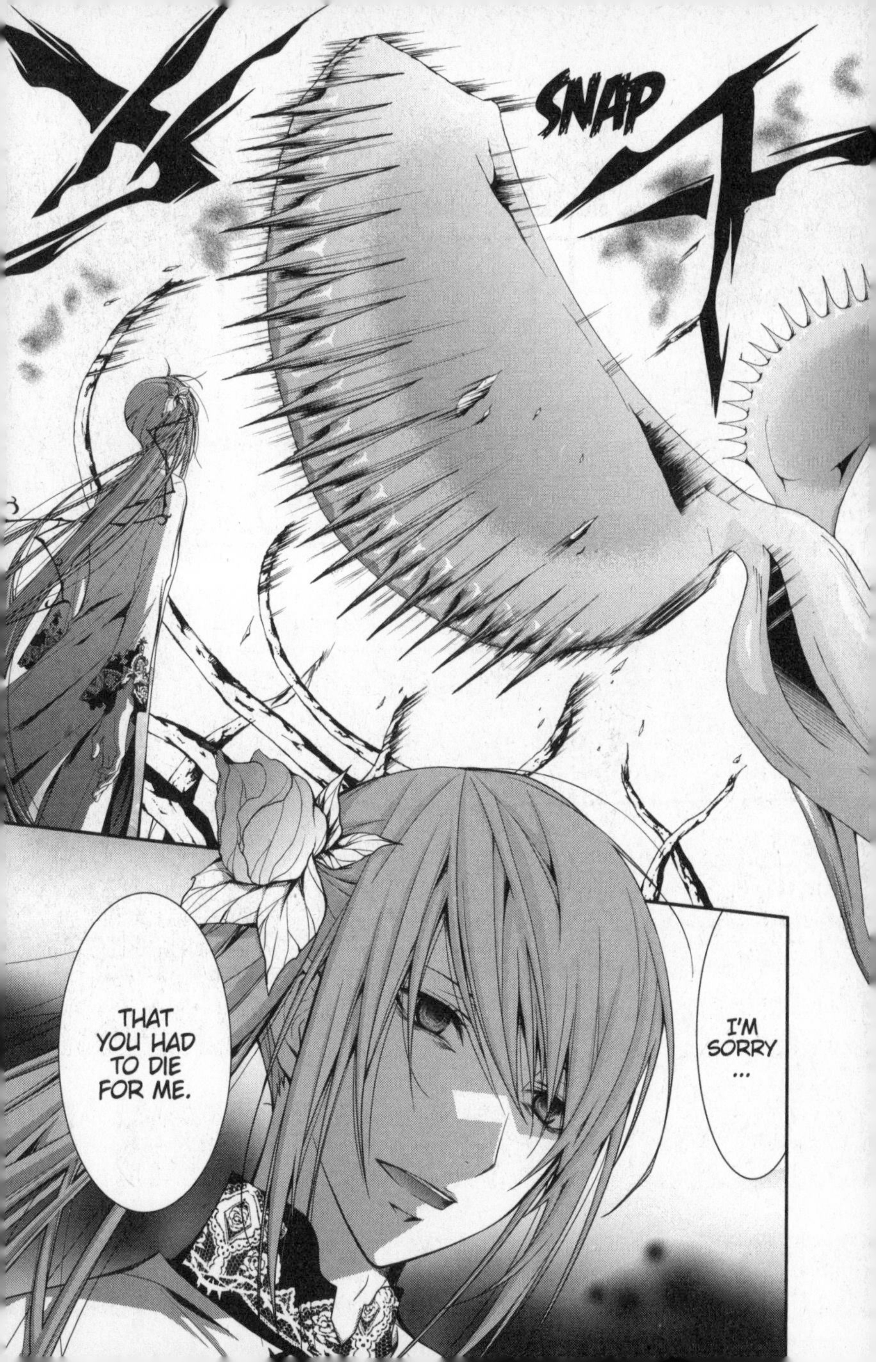
SNAP
I'M SORRY ...
THAT YOU HAD TO DIE FOR ME.

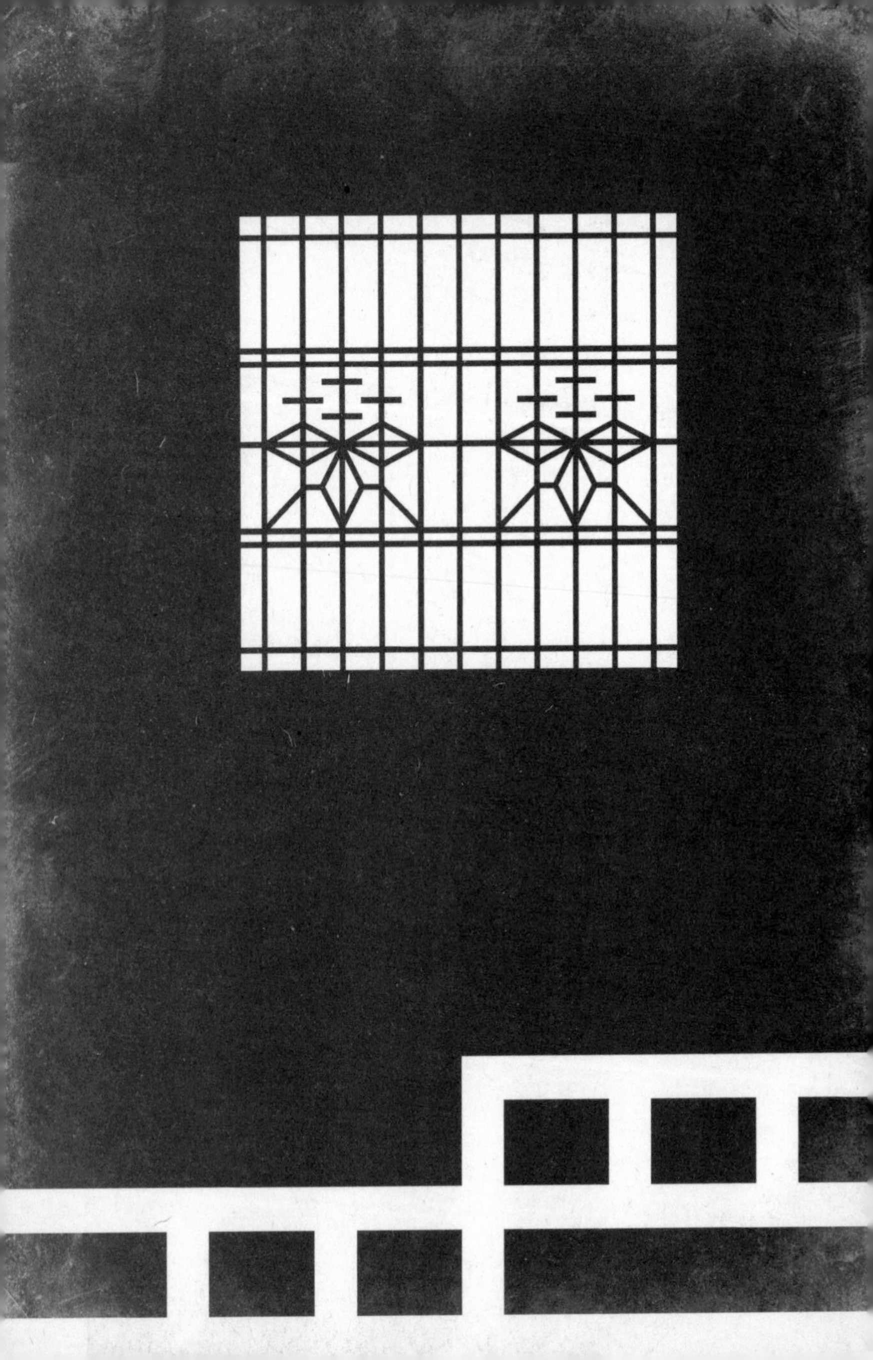

Yōkai Rental Shop

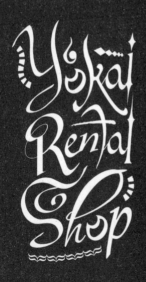

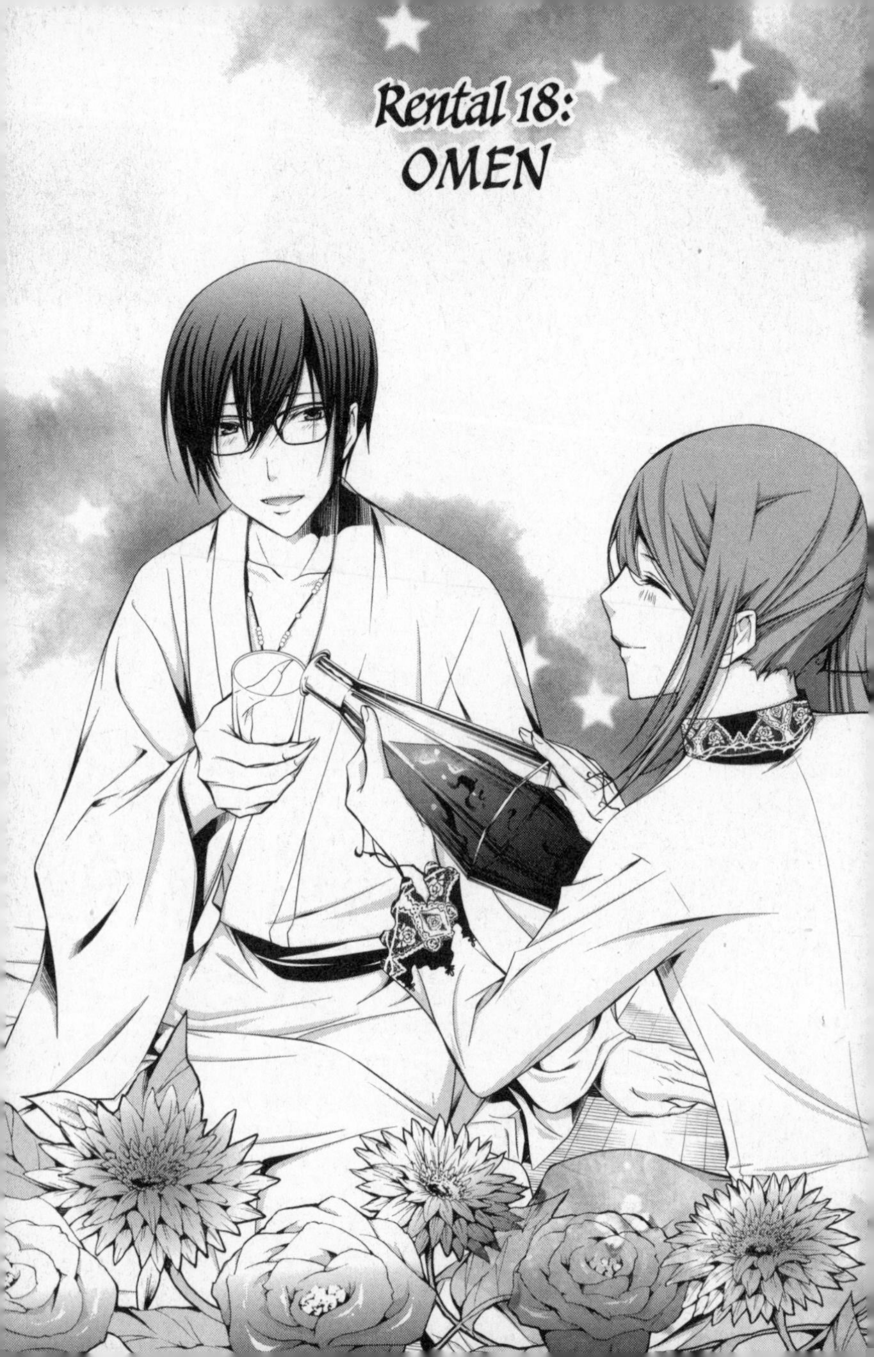
Rental 18:
OMEN

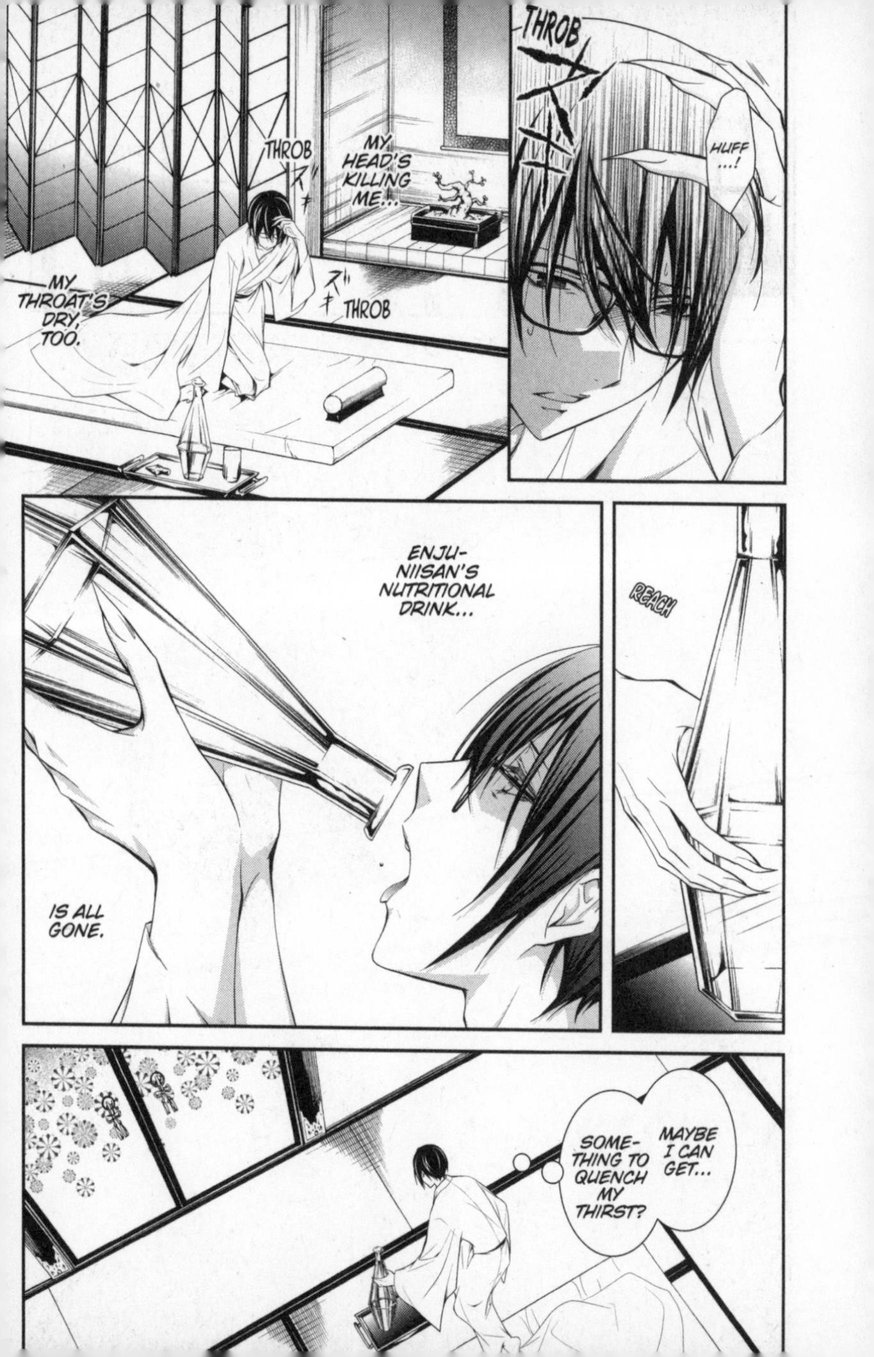
THROB
HUFF ...!
THROB
ズキ
MY HEAD'S KILLING ME...
MY THROAT'S DRY, TOO.
ズキ
THROB
REACH
ENJU-NIISAN'S NUTRITIONAL DRINK...
IS ALL GONE.
MAYBE I CAN GET...
SOME-THING TO QUENCH MY THIRST?

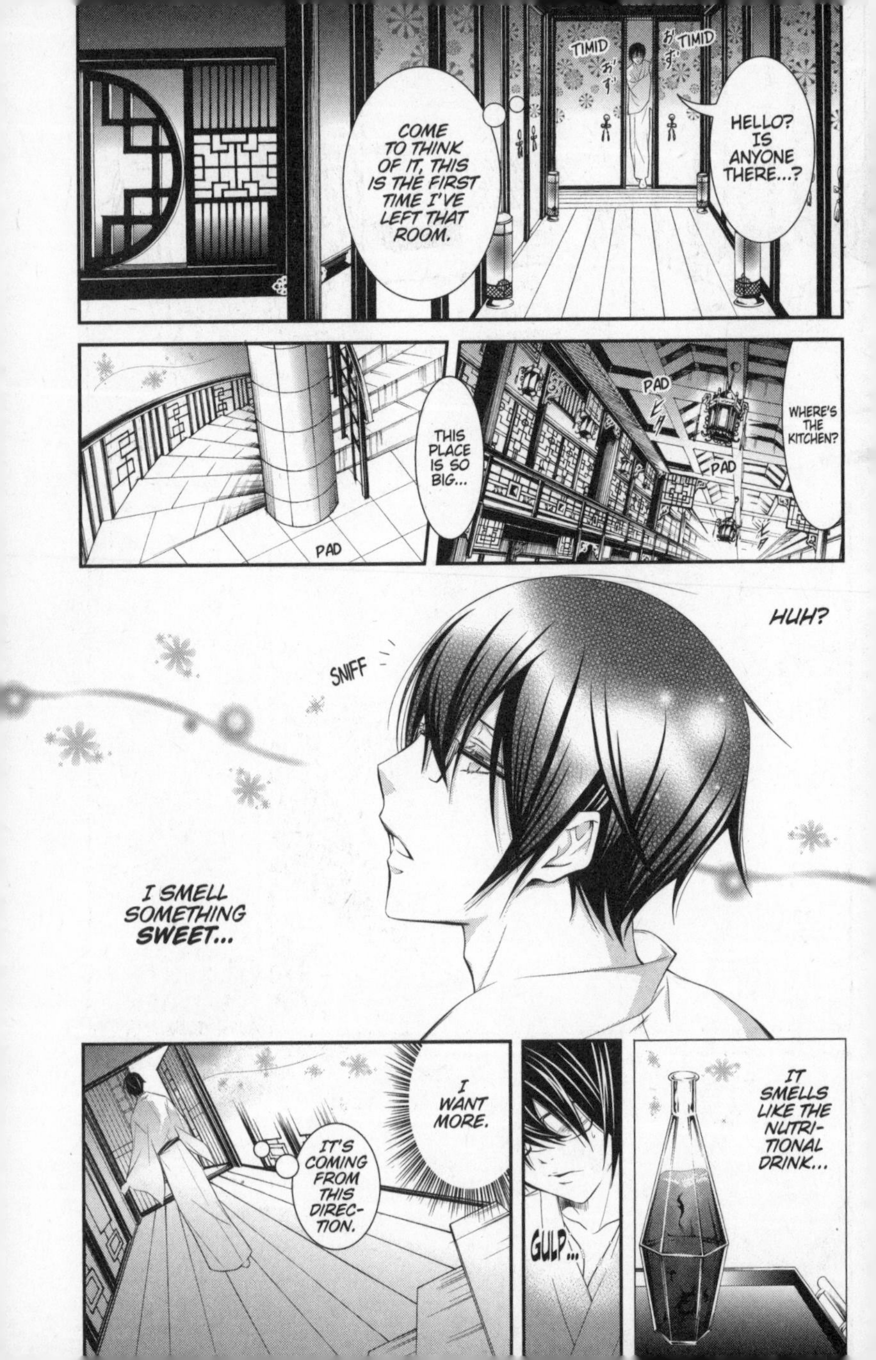
TIMID
TIMID
HELLO? IS ANYONE THERE...?
COME TO THINK OF IT, THIS IS THE FIRST TIME I'VE LEFT THAT ROOM.
WHERE'S THE KITCHEN?
PAD
PAD
THIS PLACE IS SO BIG...
PAD
HUH?
SNIFF
I SMELL SOMETHING SWEET...
IT SMELLS LIKE THE NUTRI-TIONAL DRINK...
GULP...
I WANT MORE.
IT'S COMING FROM THIS DIREC-TION.

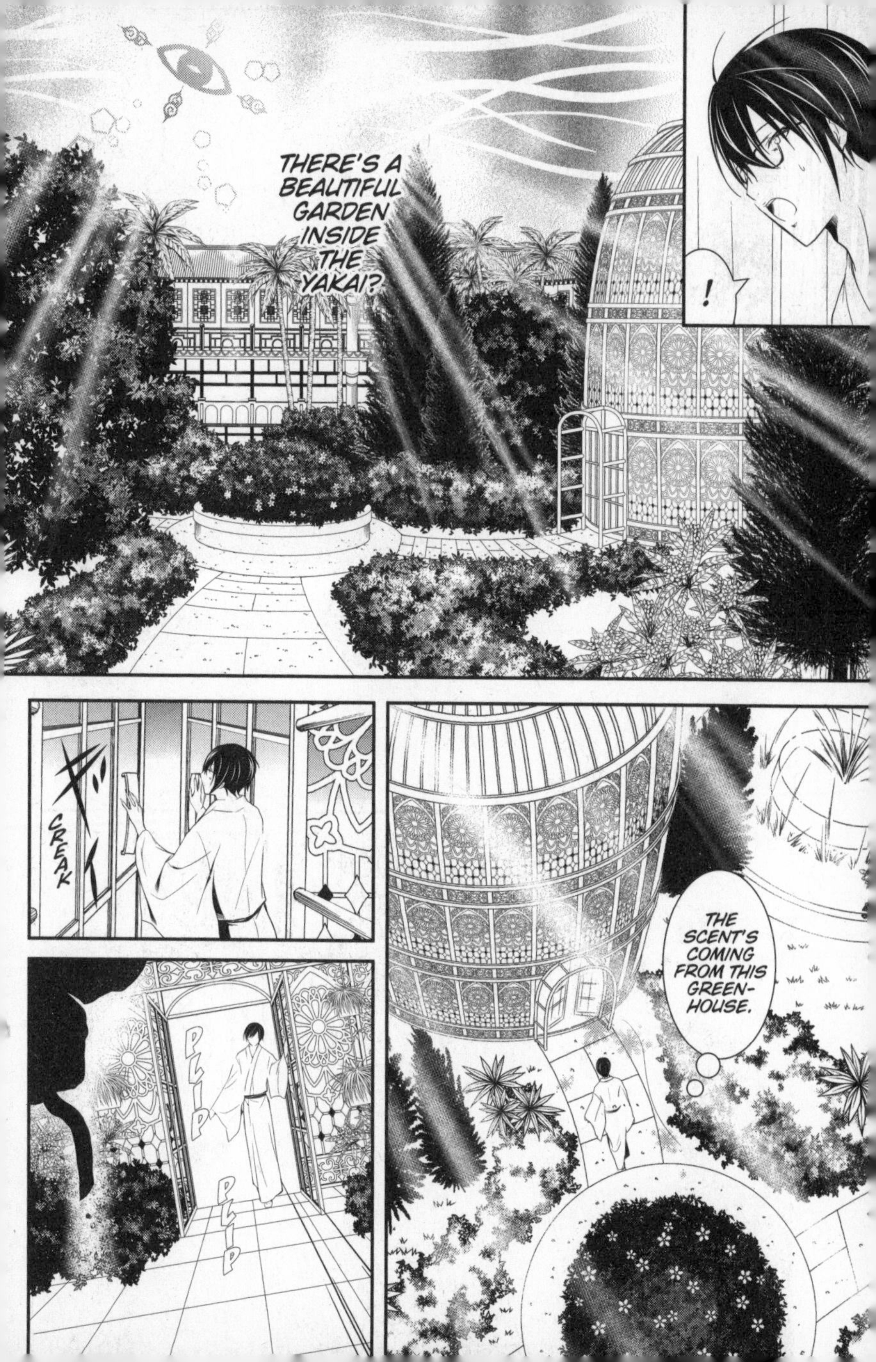
!
THERE'S A BEAUTIFUL GARDEN INSIDE THE YAKAI?
THE SCENT'S COMING FROM THIS GREEN-HOUSE.
CREAK
PLIP
PLIP

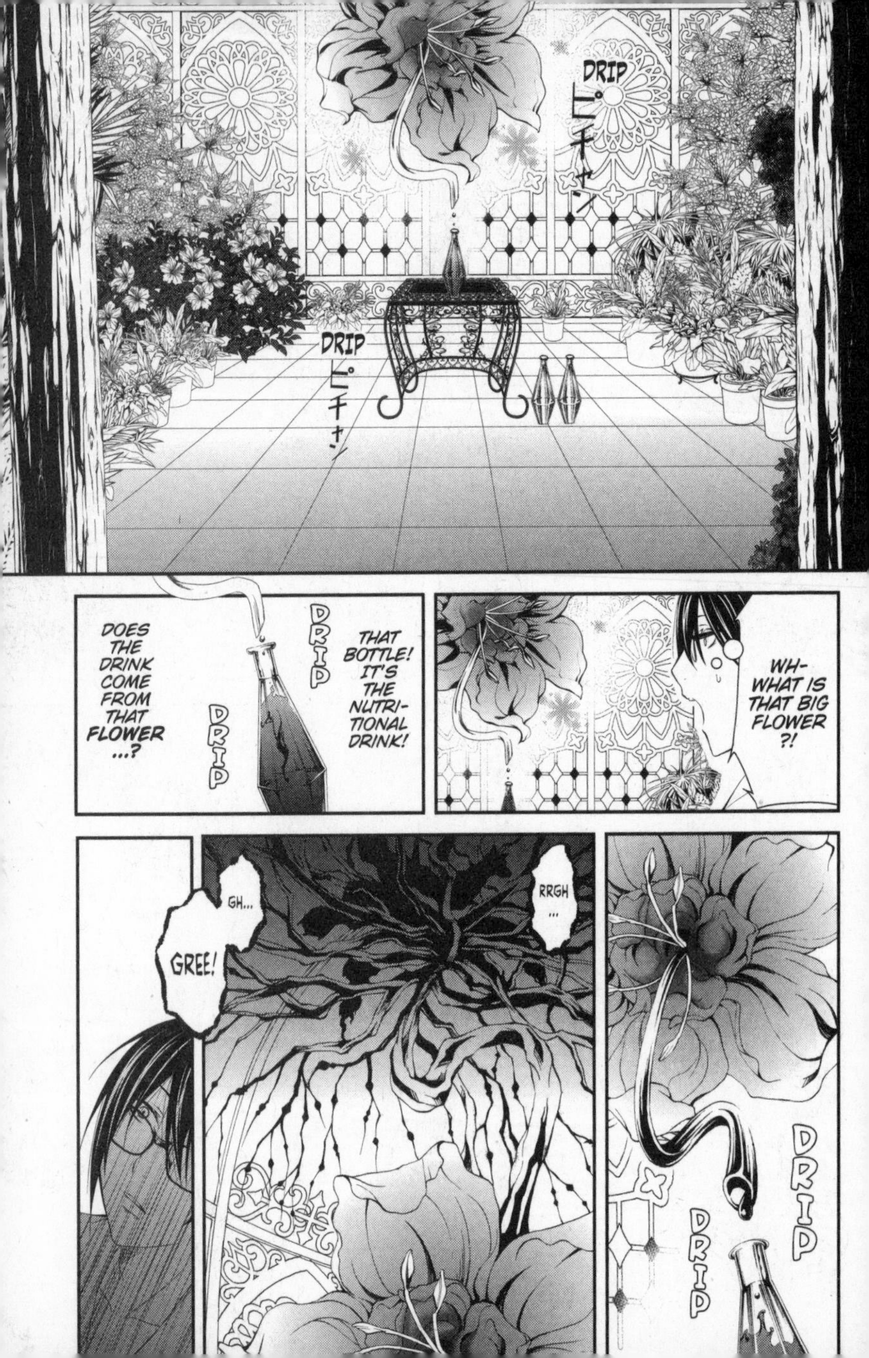
DRIP
ピチャン
DRIP
ピチャン
WH- WHAT IS THAT BIG FLOWER ?!
THAT BOTTLE! IT'S THE NUTRITIONAL DRINK!
DRIP
DRIP
DOES THE DRINK COME FROM THAT FLOWER ...?
DRIP
DRIP
RRGH ...
GH...
GREE!

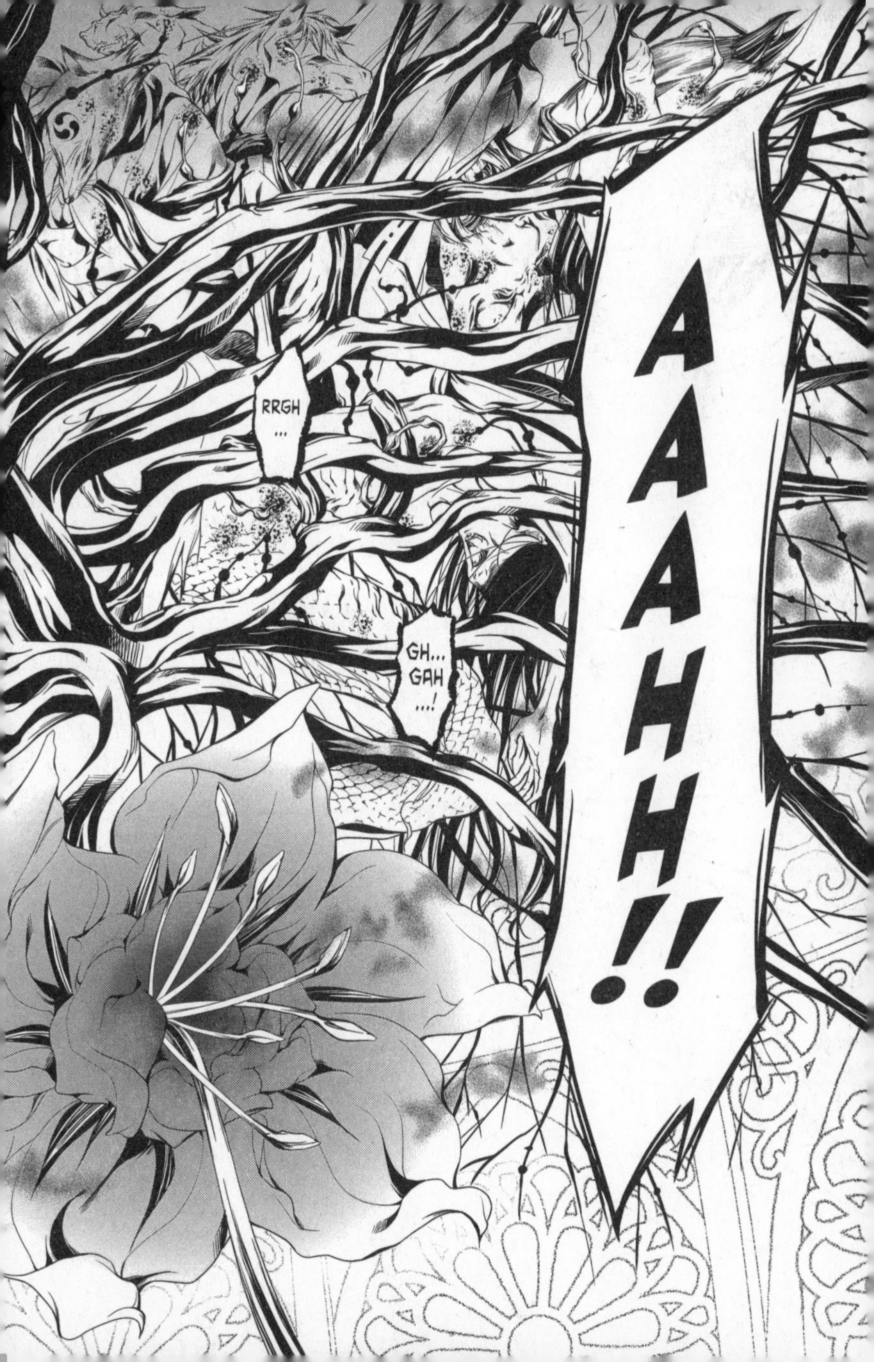
AAAHH!!
GH... GAH ...!
RRGH ...

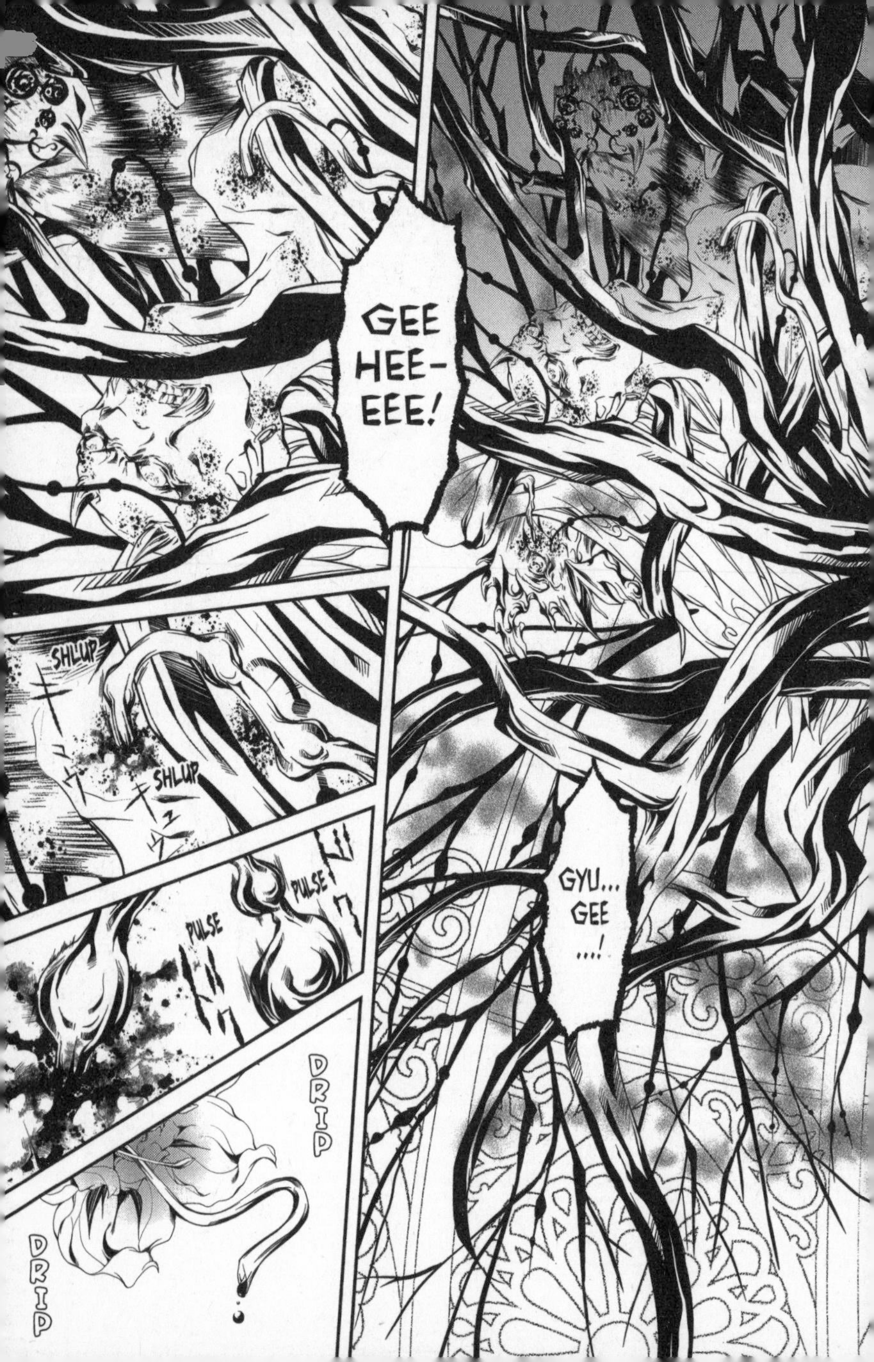
GEE HEE-EEE!
GYU... GEE ...!
SHLUP
SHLUP
PULSE
PULSE
DRIP
DRIP

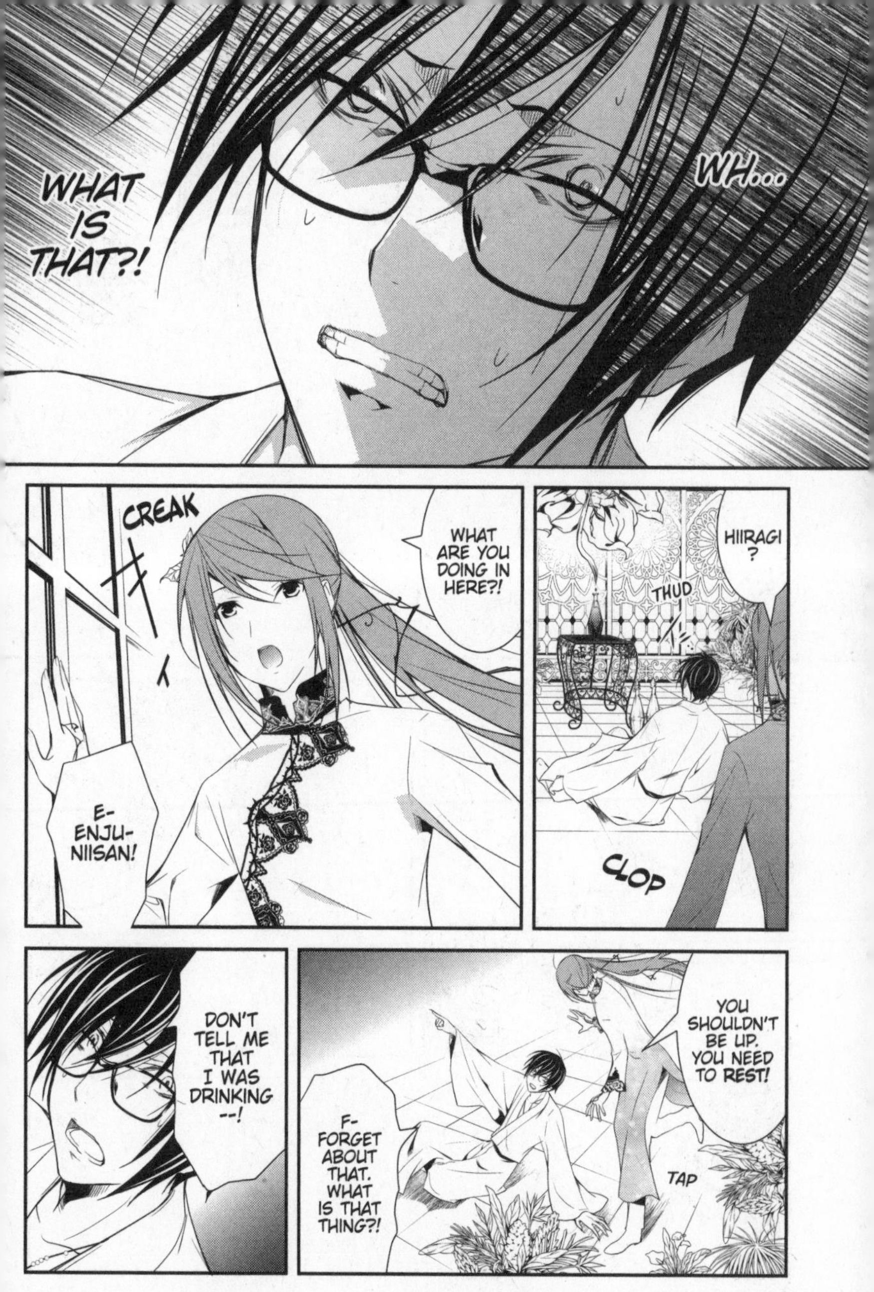
WH...
WHAT IS THAT?!
HIIRAGI?
THUD
CLOP
WHAT ARE YOU DOING IN HERE?!
CREAK
E-ENJU-NIISAN!
YOU SHOULDN'T BE UP. YOU NEED TO REST!
F-FORGET ABOUT THAT. WHAT IS THAT THING?!
TAP
DON'T TELL ME THAT I WAS DRINKING--!

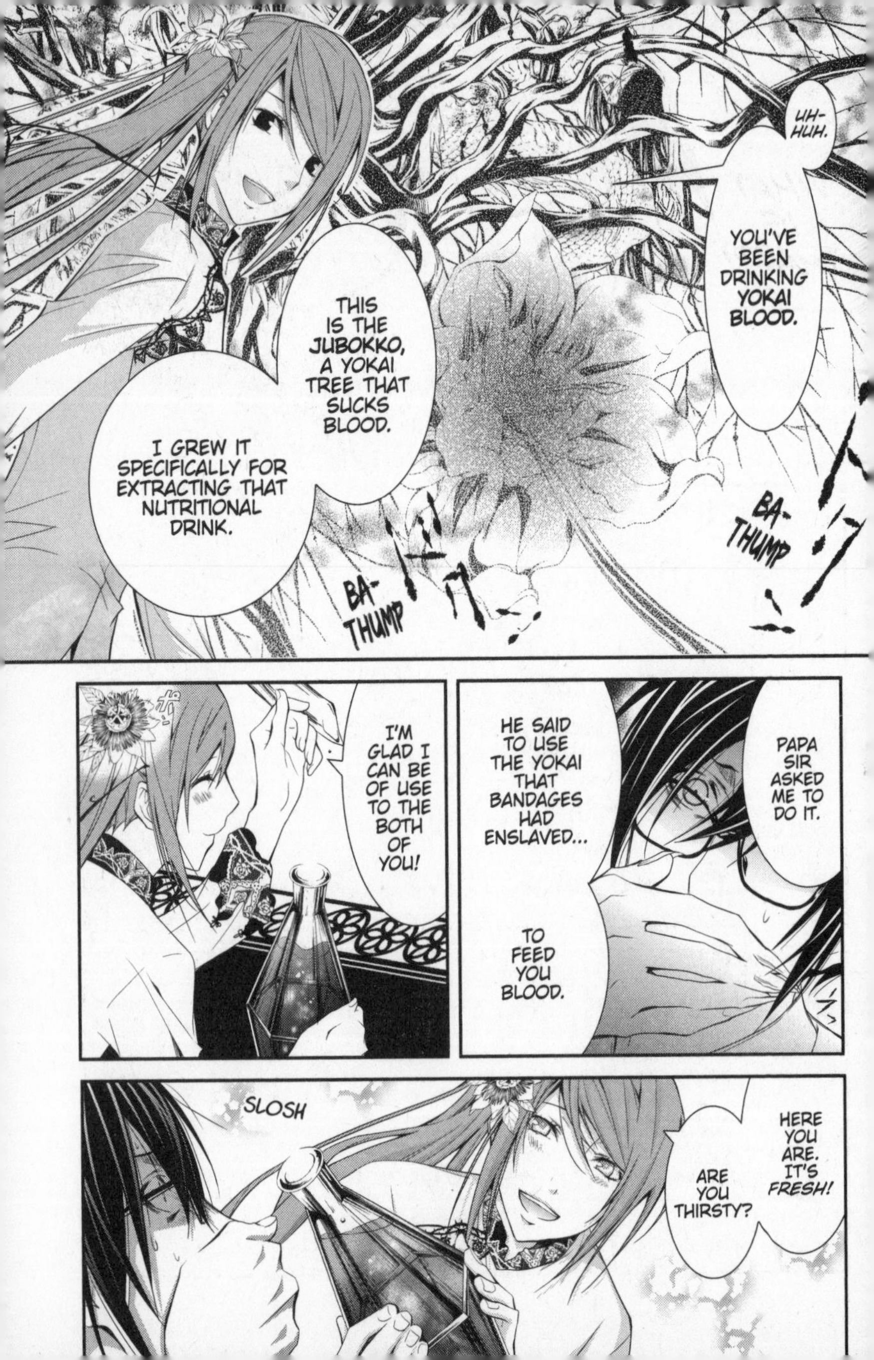
UH-HUH.
YOU'VE BEEN DRINKING YOKAI BLOOD.
THIS IS THE JUBOKKO, A YOKAI TREE THAT SUCKS BLOOD.
I GREW IT SPECIFICALLY FOR EXTRACTING THAT NUTRITIONAL DRINK.
BA-THUMP
BA-THUMP
PAPA SIR ASKED ME TO DO IT.
HE SAID TO USE THE YOKAI THAT BANDAGES HAD ENSLAVED...
TO FEED YOU BLOOD.
I'M GLAD I CAN BE OF USE TO THE BOTH OF YOU!
HERE YOU ARE. IT'S FRESH!
ARE YOU THIRSTY?
SLOSH

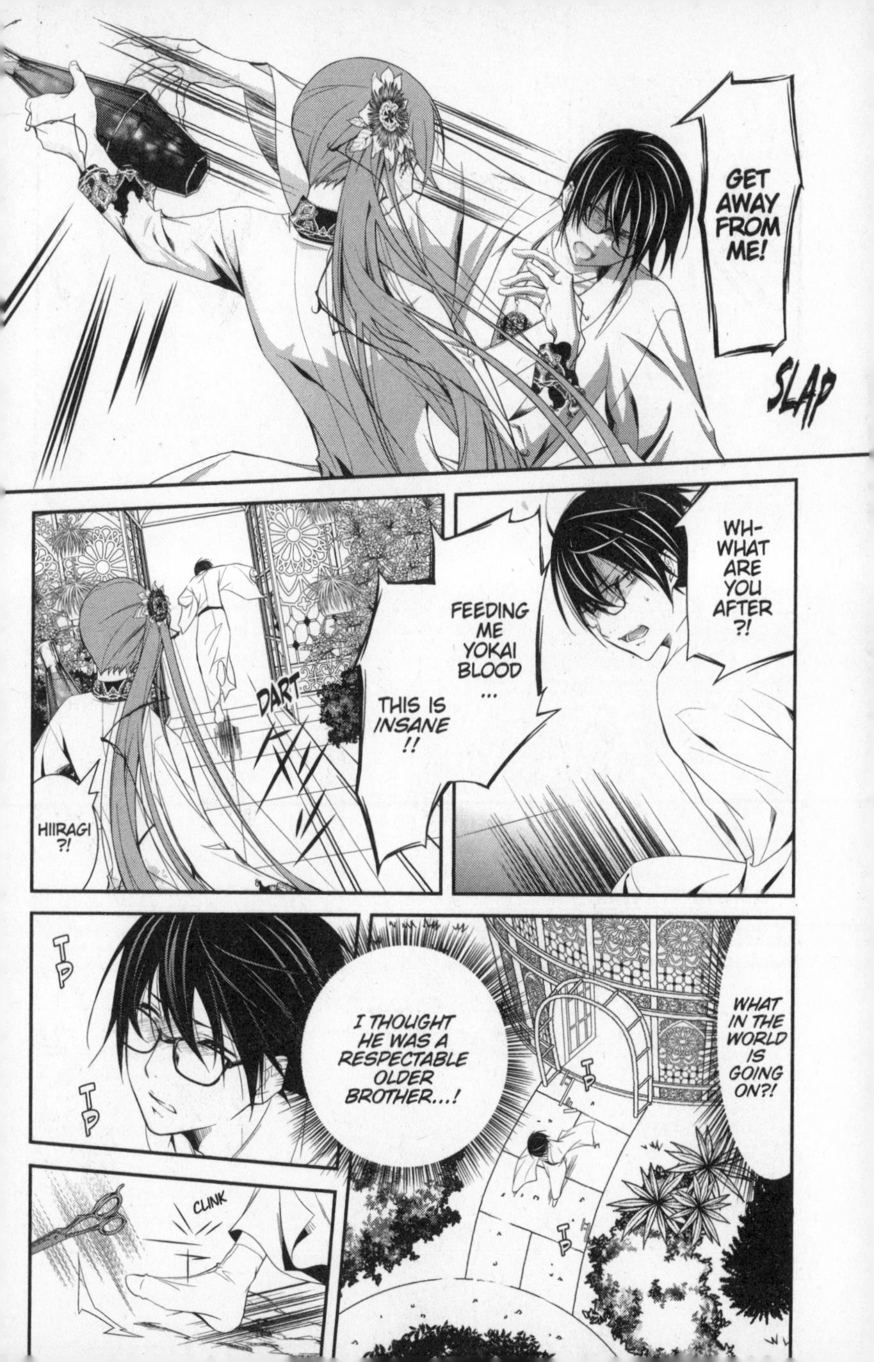
GET AWAY FROM ME!
SLAP
WH-WHAT ARE YOU AFTER?!
FEEDING ME YOKAI BLOOD...
THIS IS INSANE!!
DART
HIIRAGI?!
WHAT IN THE WORLD IS GOING ON?!
TP
TP
I THOUGHT HE WAS A RESPECTABLE OLDER BROTHER...!
TP
TP
CLINK

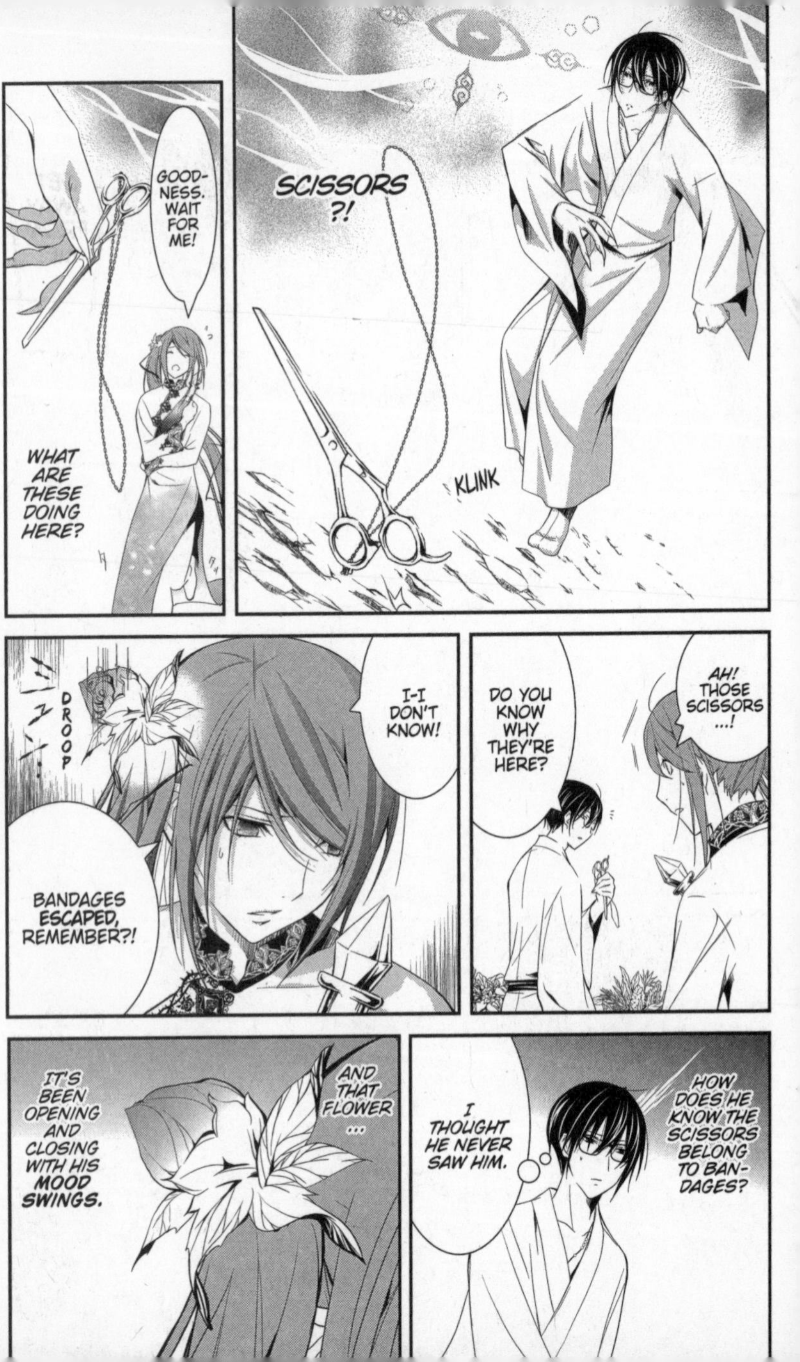
SCISSORS ?!
KLINK
GOODNESS. WAIT FOR ME!
WHAT ARE THESE DOING HERE?
AH! THOSE SCISSORS ...!
DO YOU KNOW WHY THEY'RE HERE?
I-I DON'T KNOW!
DROOP
BANDAGES ESCAPED, REMEMBER?!
HOW DOES HE KNOW THE SCISSORS BELONG TO BANDAGES?
I THOUGHT HE NEVER SAW HIM.
AND THAT FLOWER ...
IT'S BEEN OPENING AND CLOSING WITH HIS MOOD SWINGS.

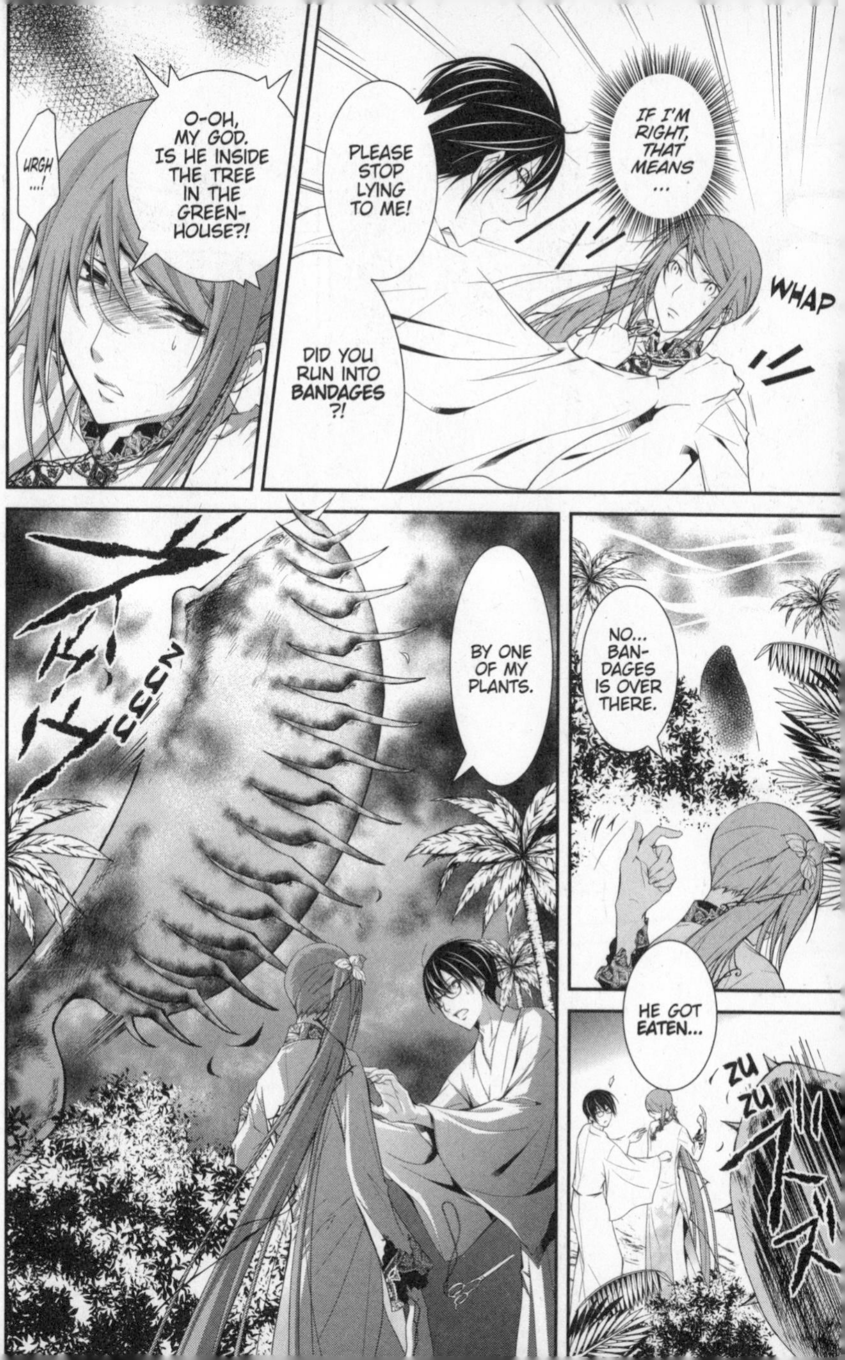
IF I'M RIGHT, THAT MEANS...
WHAP
PLEASE STOP LYING TO ME!
DID YOU RUN INTO BANDAGES?!
O-OH, MY GOD. IS HE INSIDE THE TREE IN THE GREEN-HOUSE?!
URGH...!
NO... BAN-DAGES IS OVER THERE.
HE GOT EATEN...
ZU
ZU
BY ONE OF MY PLANTS.

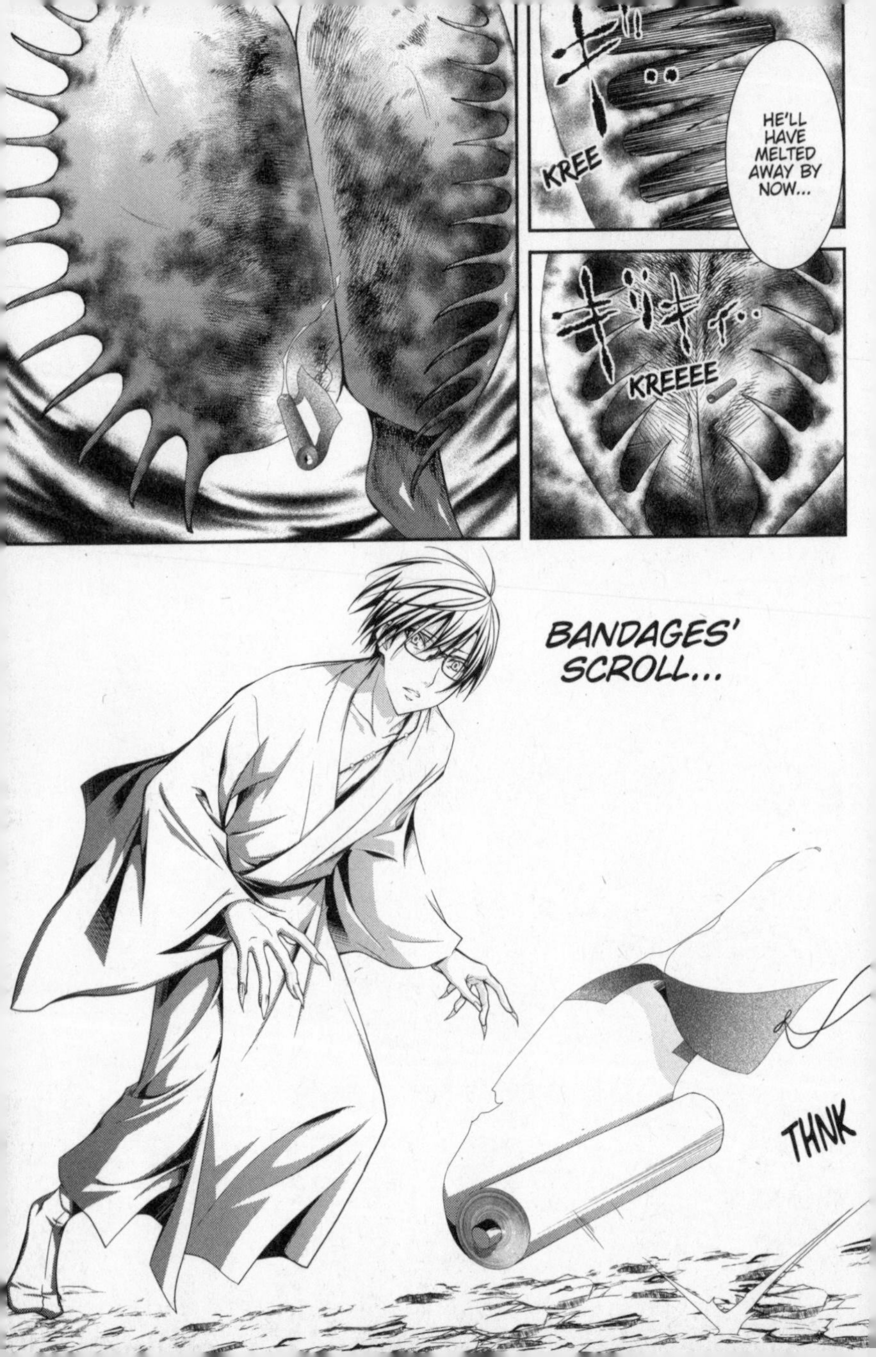
HE'LL HAVE MELTED AWAY BY NOW...
KREE
KREEEE
BANDAGES' SCROLL...
THNK

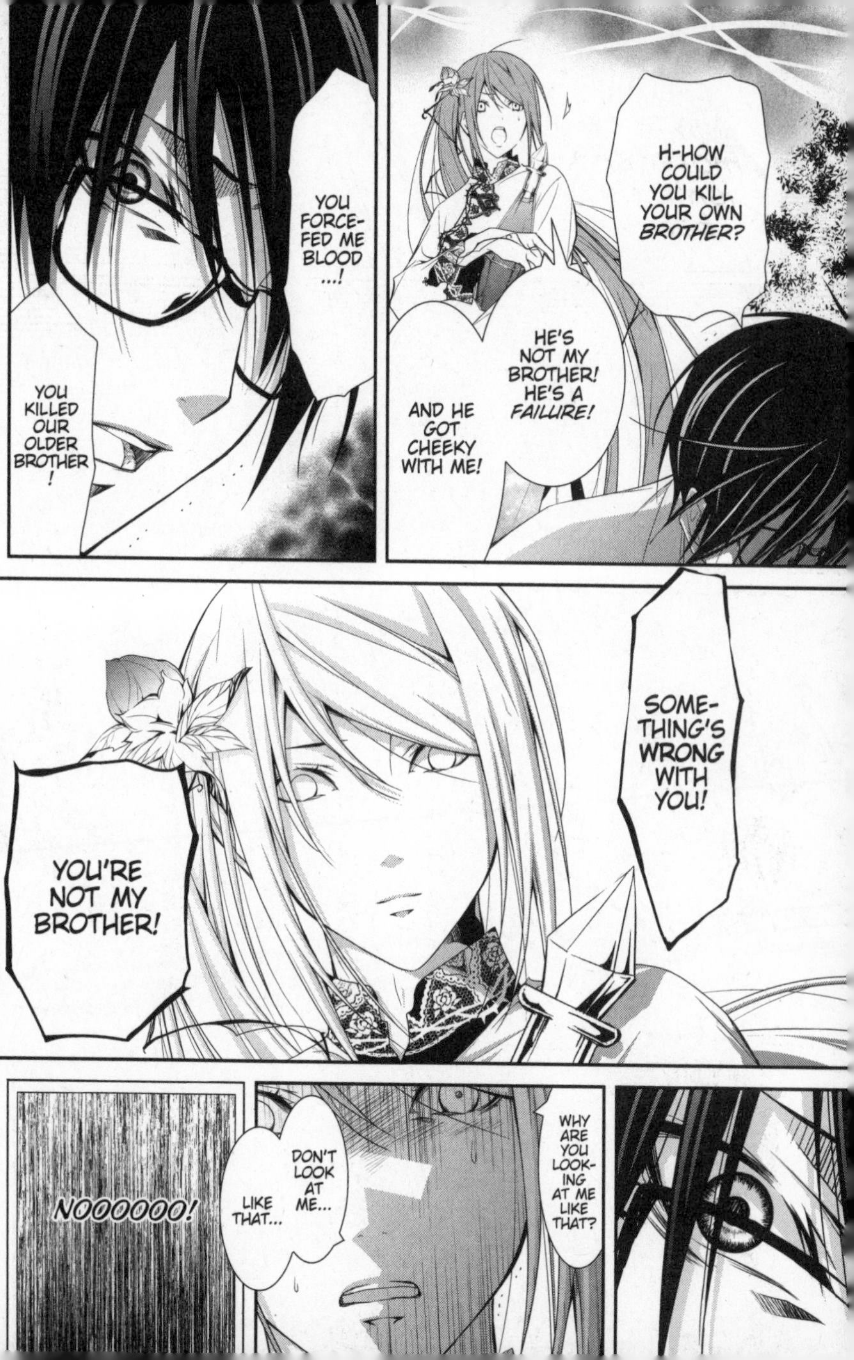
H-HOW COULD YOU KILL YOUR OWN *BROTHER?*
HE'S NOT MY BROTHER! HE'S A *FAILURE!*
AND HE GOT CHEEKY WITH ME!
YOU FORCE-FED ME BLOOD ...!
YOU KILLED OUR OLDER BROTHER!
SOME-THING'S WRONG WITH YOU!
YOU'RE NOT MY BROTHER!
WHY ARE YOU LOOK-ING AT ME LIKE THAT?
DON'T LOOK AT ME...
LIKE THAT...
NOOOOOO!

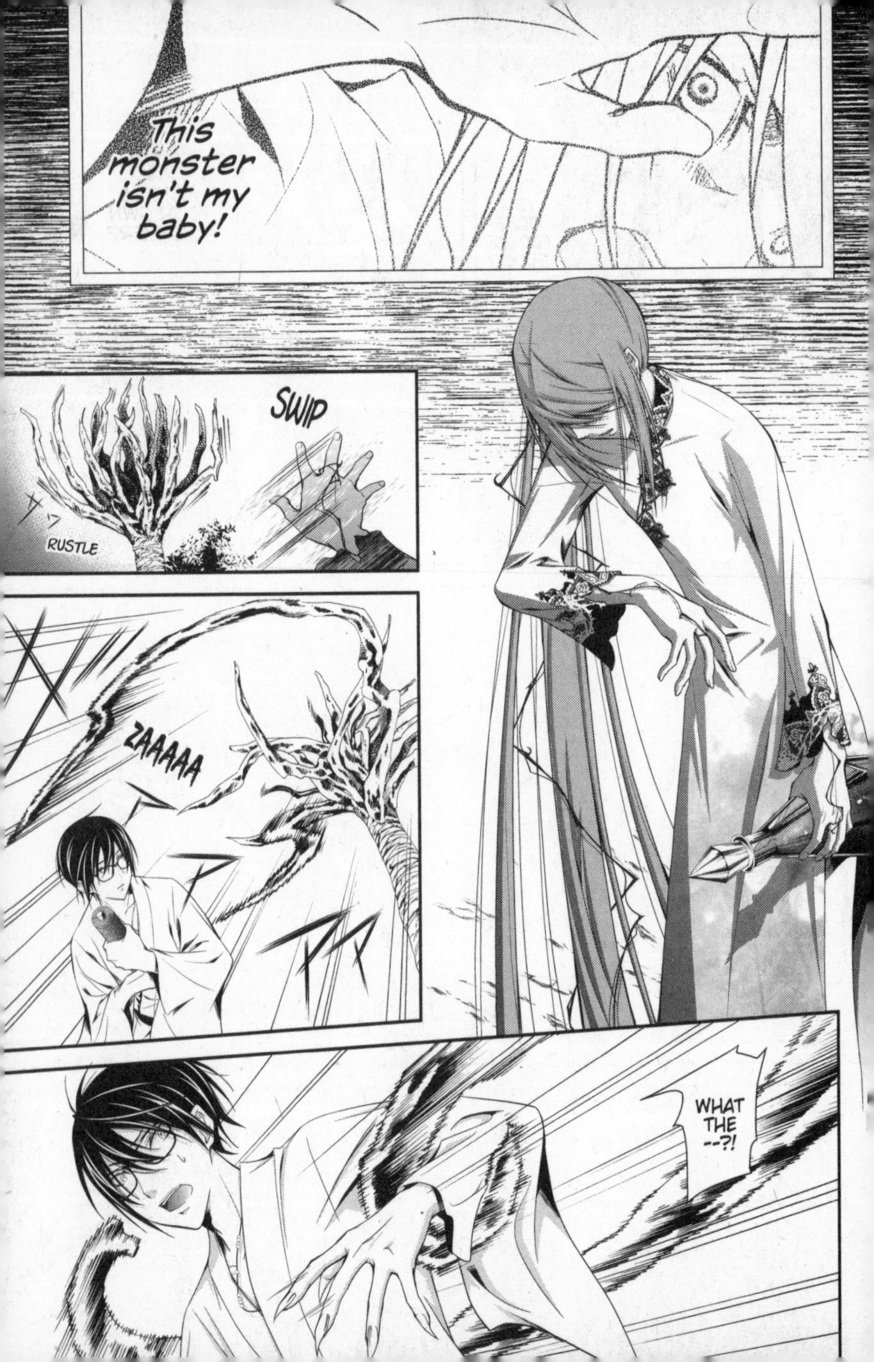
This monster isn't my baby!
SWIP
RUSTLE
ZAAAAA
WHAT THE --?!

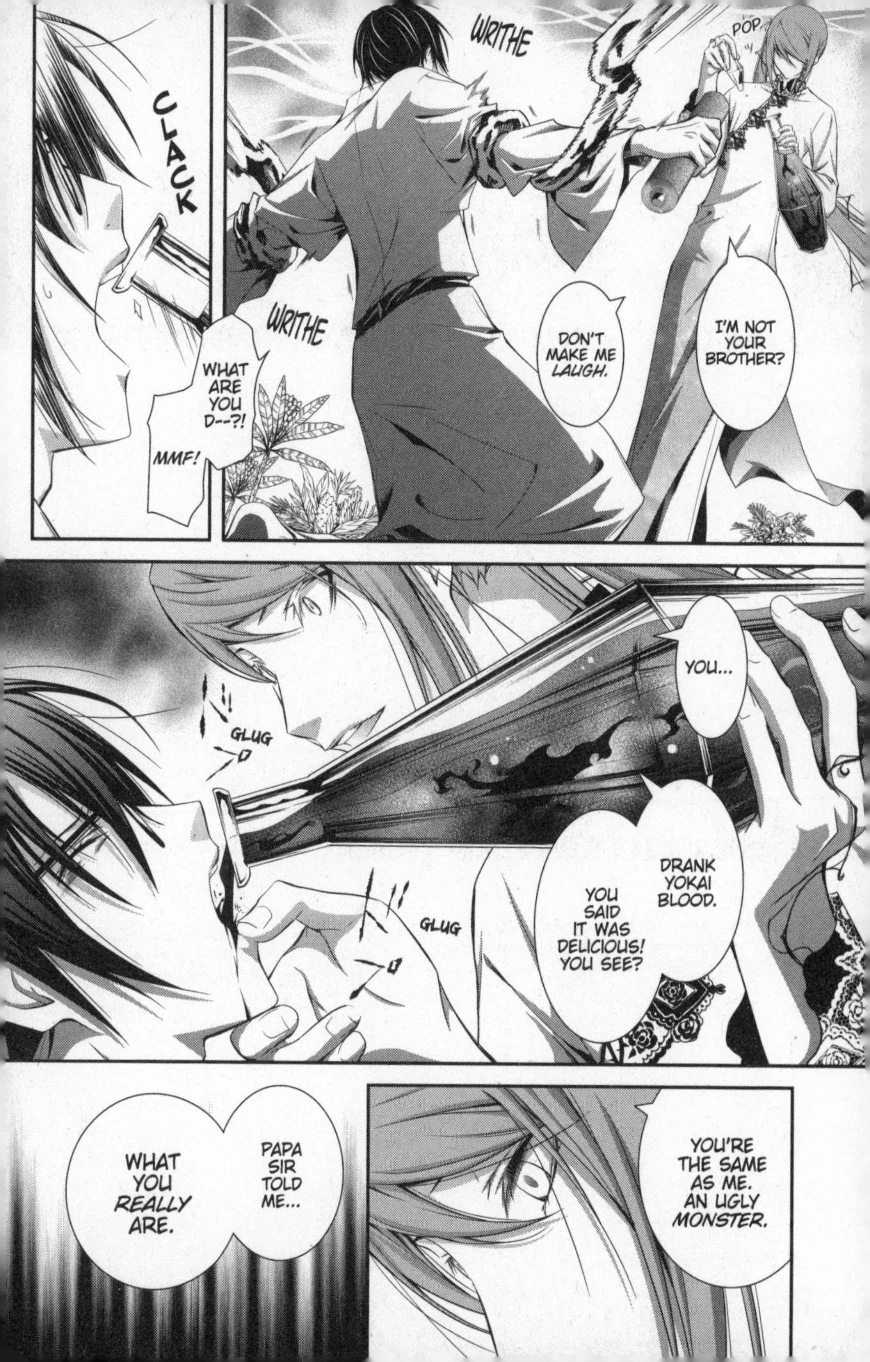

POP
WRITHE
I'M NOT YOUR BROTHER?
DON'T MAKE ME *LAUGH.*
WRITHE
CLACK
WHAT ARE YOU D--?!
MMF!
YOU...
DRANK YOKAI BLOOD.
YOU SAID IT WAS DELICIOUS! YOU SEE?
GLUG
GLUG
YOU'RE THE SAME AS ME. AN UGLY *MONSTER.*
PAPA SIR TOLD ME...
WHAT YOU *REALLY* ARE.

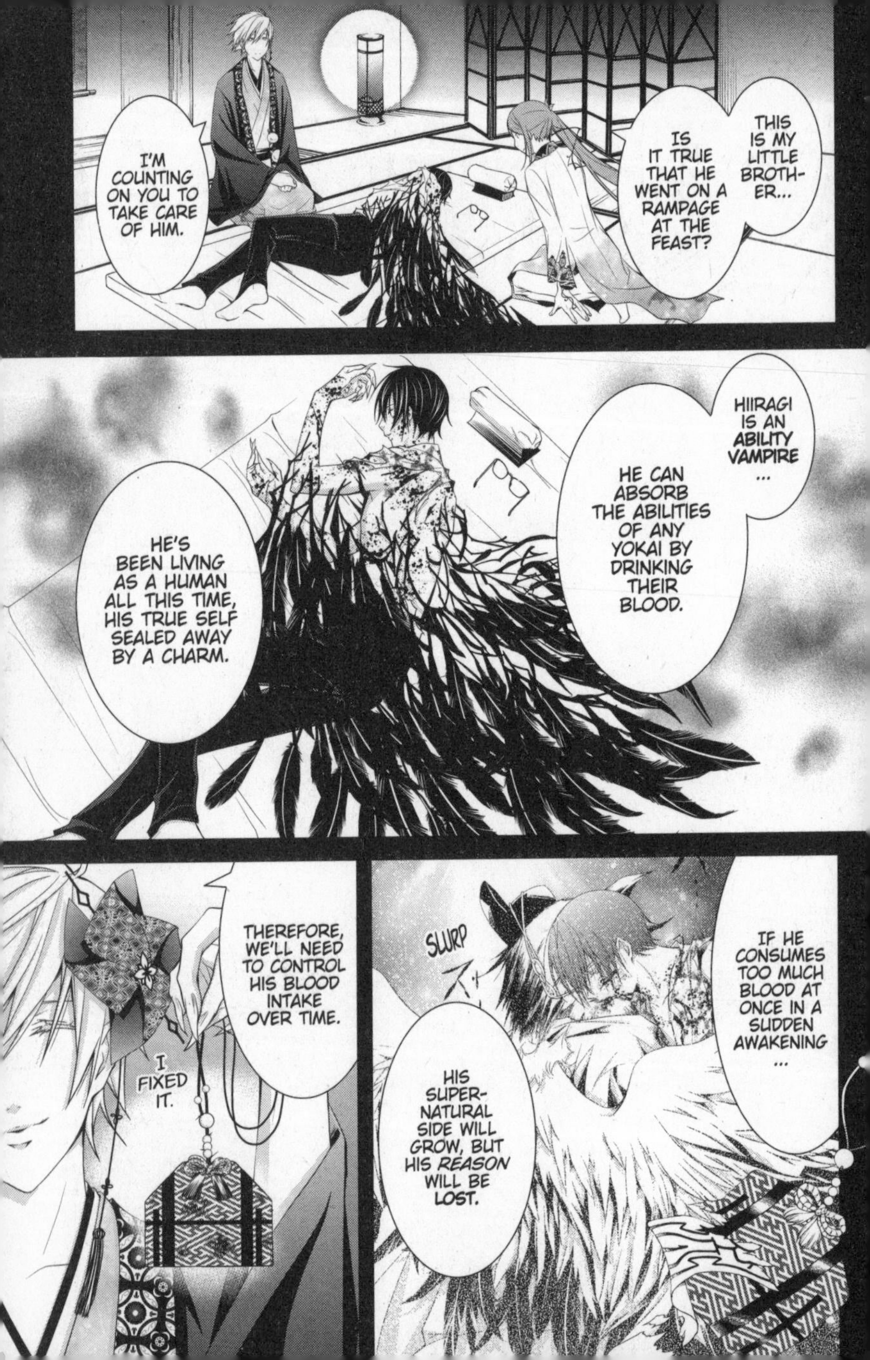
THIS IS MY LITTLE BROTH-ER...
IS IT TRUE THAT HE WENT ON A RAMPAGE AT THE FEAST?
I'M COUNTING ON YOU TO TAKE CARE OF HIM.
HIIRAGI IS AN **ABILITY VAMPIRE** ...
HE CAN ABSORB THE ABILITIES OF ANY YOKAI BY DRINKING THEIR BLOOD.
HE'S BEEN LIVING AS A HUMAN ALL THIS TIME, HIS TRUE SELF SEALED AWAY BY A CHARM.
IF HE CONSUMES TOO MUCH BLOOD AT ONCE IN A SUDDEN AWAKENING ...
SLURP
HIS SUPER-NATURAL SIDE WILL GROW, BUT HIS *REASON* WILL BE **LOST.**
THEREFORE, WE'LL NEED TO CONTROL HIS BLOOD INTAKE OVER TIME.
I FIXED IT.

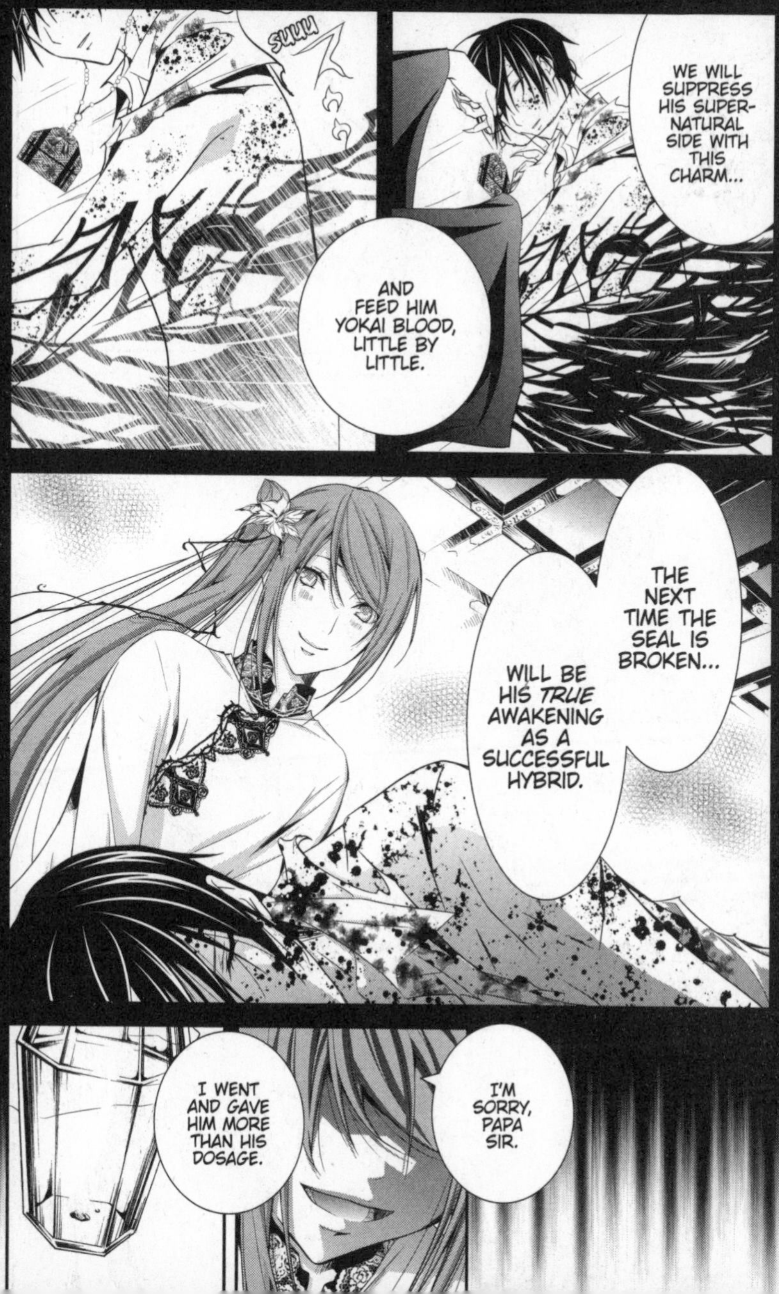
WE WILL SUPPRESS HIS SUPER-NATURAL SIDE WITH THIS CHARM...
AND FEED HIM YOKAI BLOOD, LITTLE BY LITTLE.
SUUU
THE NEXT TIME THE SEAL IS BROKEN...
WILL BE HIS *TRUE* AWAKENING AS A SUCCESSFUL HYBRID.
I'M SORRY, PAPA SIR.
I WENT AND GAVE HIM MORE THAN HIS DOSAGE.

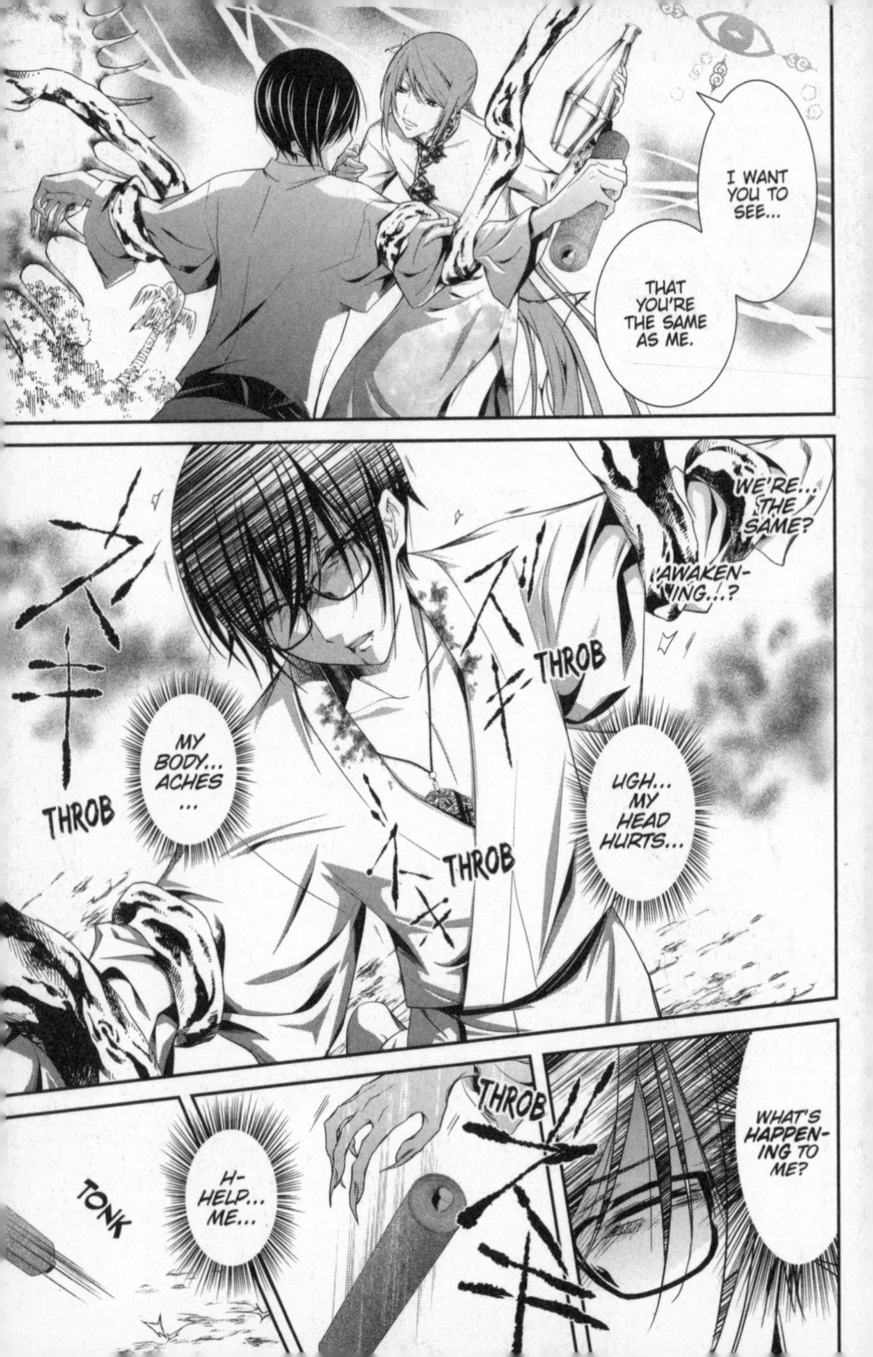
I WANT YOU TO SEE...
THAT YOU'RE THE SAME AS ME.
WE'RE... THE SAME?
AWAKEN-ING...?
THROB
UGH... MY HEAD HURTS...
THROB
MY BODY... ACHES ...
THROB
WHAT'S HAPPEN-ING TO ME?
THROB
H-HELP... ME...
TONK

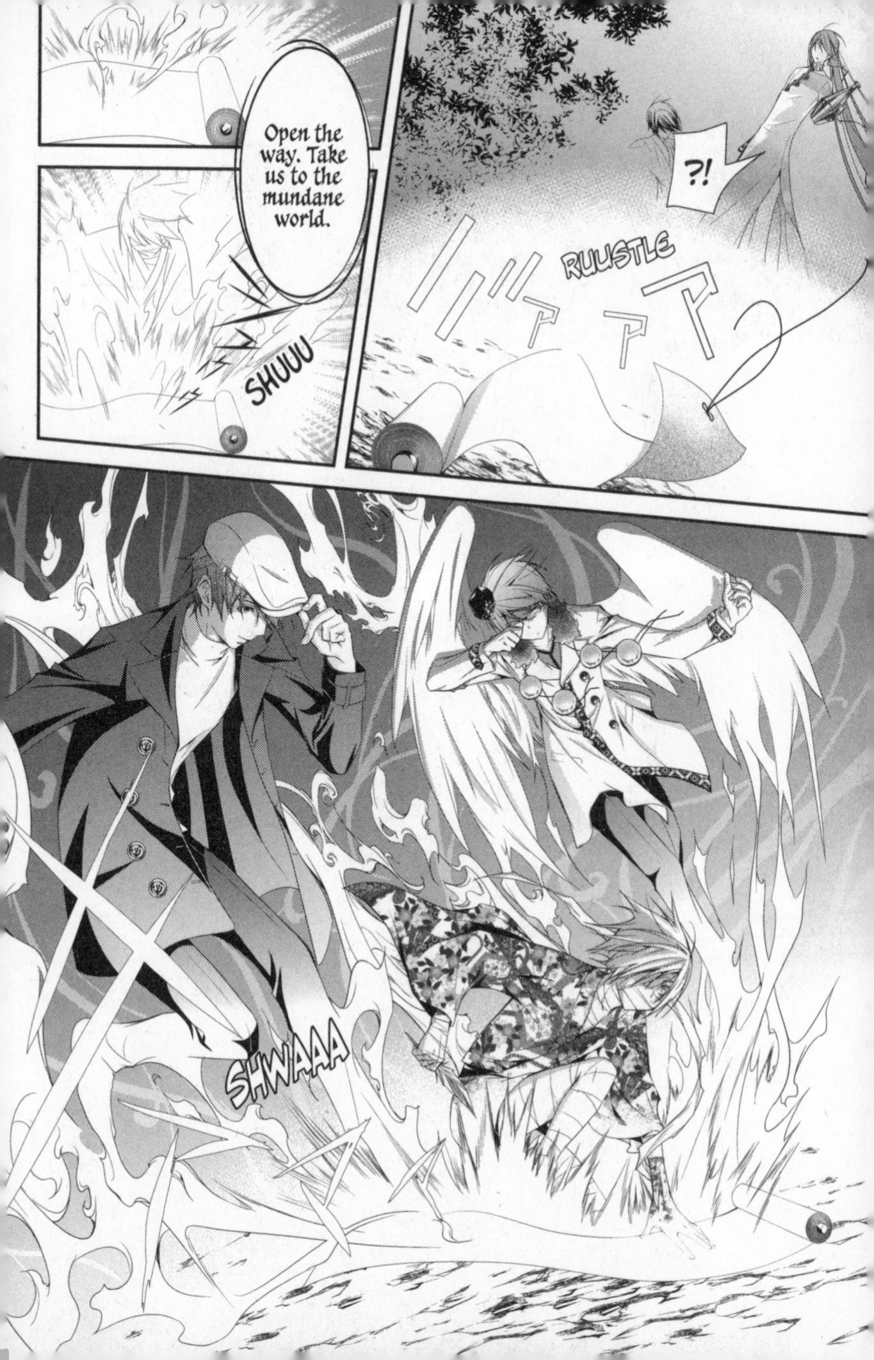
?!
RUUSTLE
Open the way. Take us to the mundane world.
SHUUU
SHWAAA

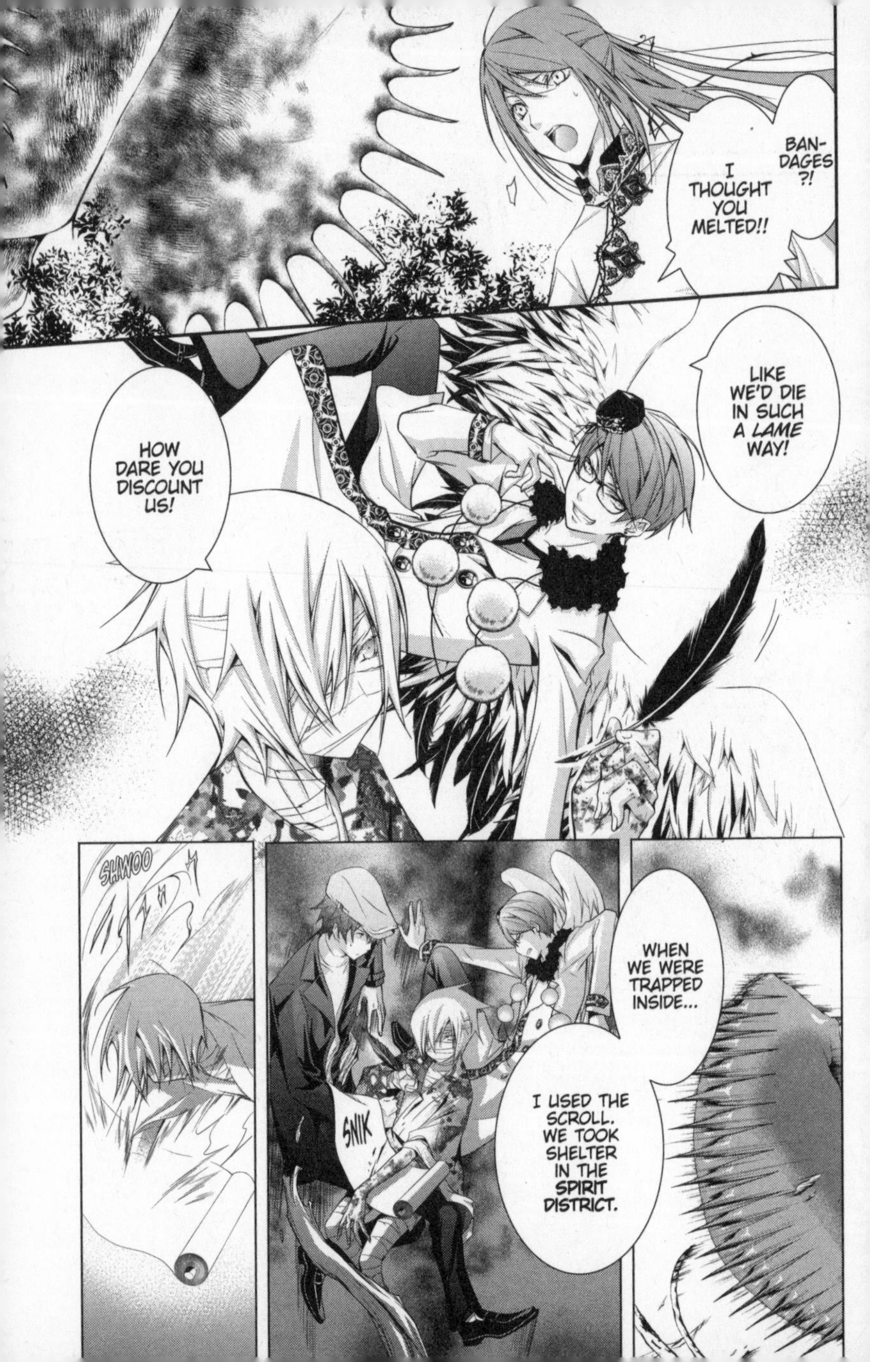
BAN-DAGES ?!
I THOUGHT YOU MELTED!!
LIKE WE'D DIE IN SUCH A *LAME* WAY!
HOW DARE YOU DISCOUNT US!
WHEN WE WERE TRAPPED INSIDE...
I USED THE SCROLL. WE TOOK SHELTER IN THE **SPIRIT DISTRICT.**
SNIK
SHWOO

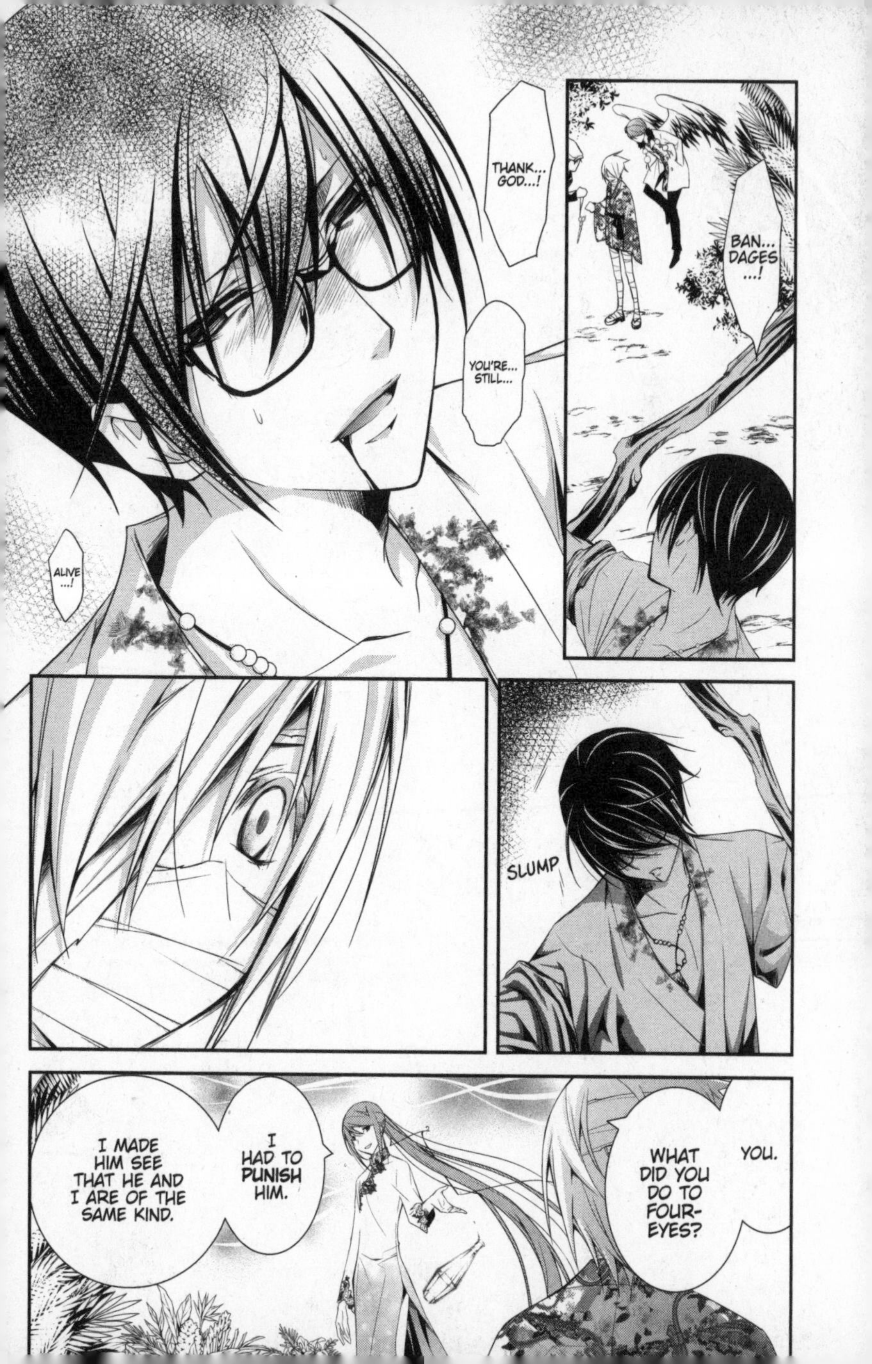
BAN... DAGES ...!
THANK... GOD...!
YOU'RE... STILL...
ALIVE ...!
SLUMP
YOU.
WHAT DID YOU DO TO FOUR-EYES?
I HAD TO PUNISH HIM.
I MADE HIM SEE THAT HE AND I ARE OF THE SAME KIND.

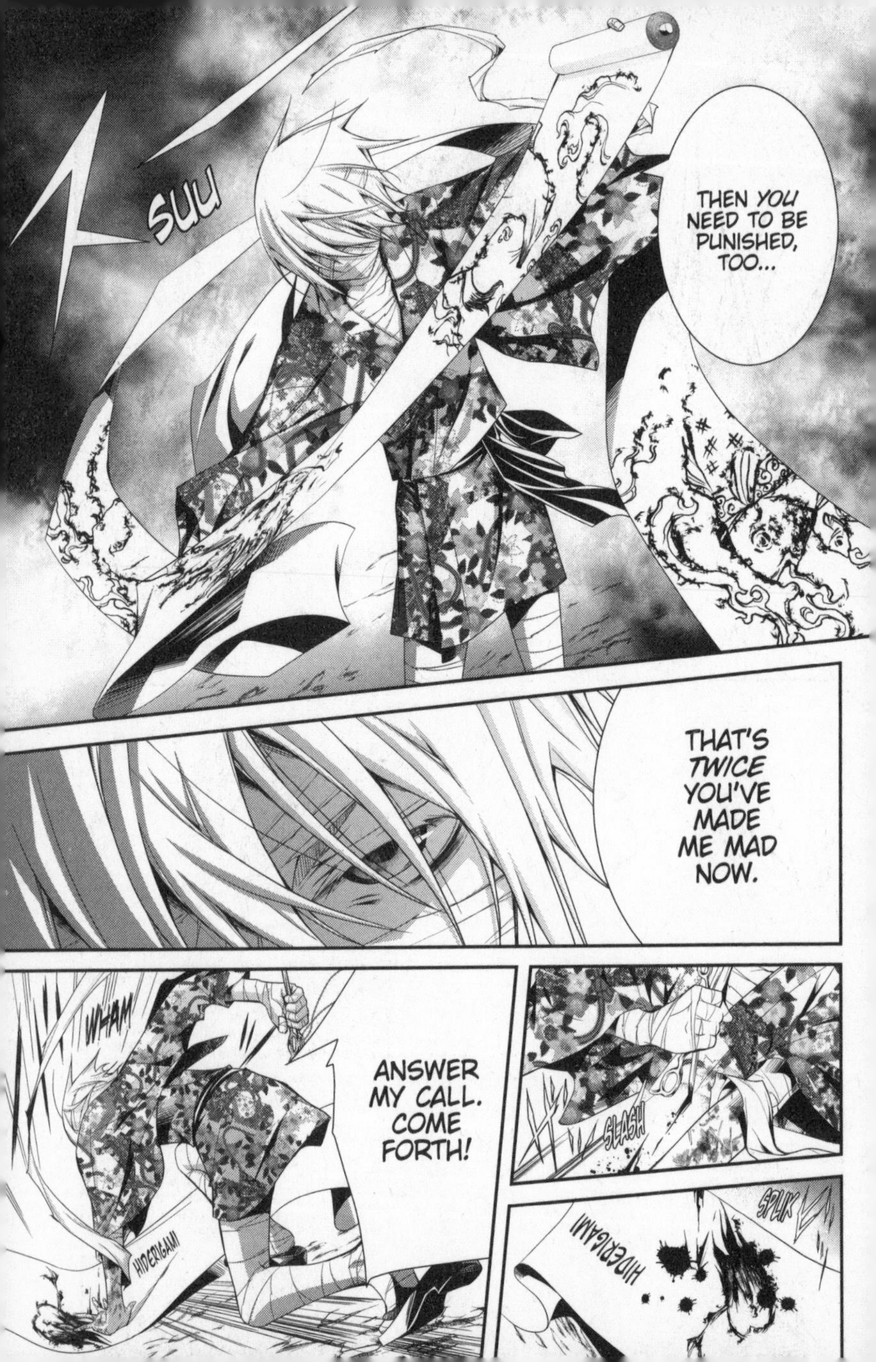
THEN *YOU* NEED TO BE PUNISHED, TOO...
SUU
THAT'S *TWICE* YOU'VE MADE ME MAD NOW.
SLASH
SPLIK
HIDERIGAMI
WHAM
ANSWER MY CALL. COME FORTH!
HIDERIGAMI

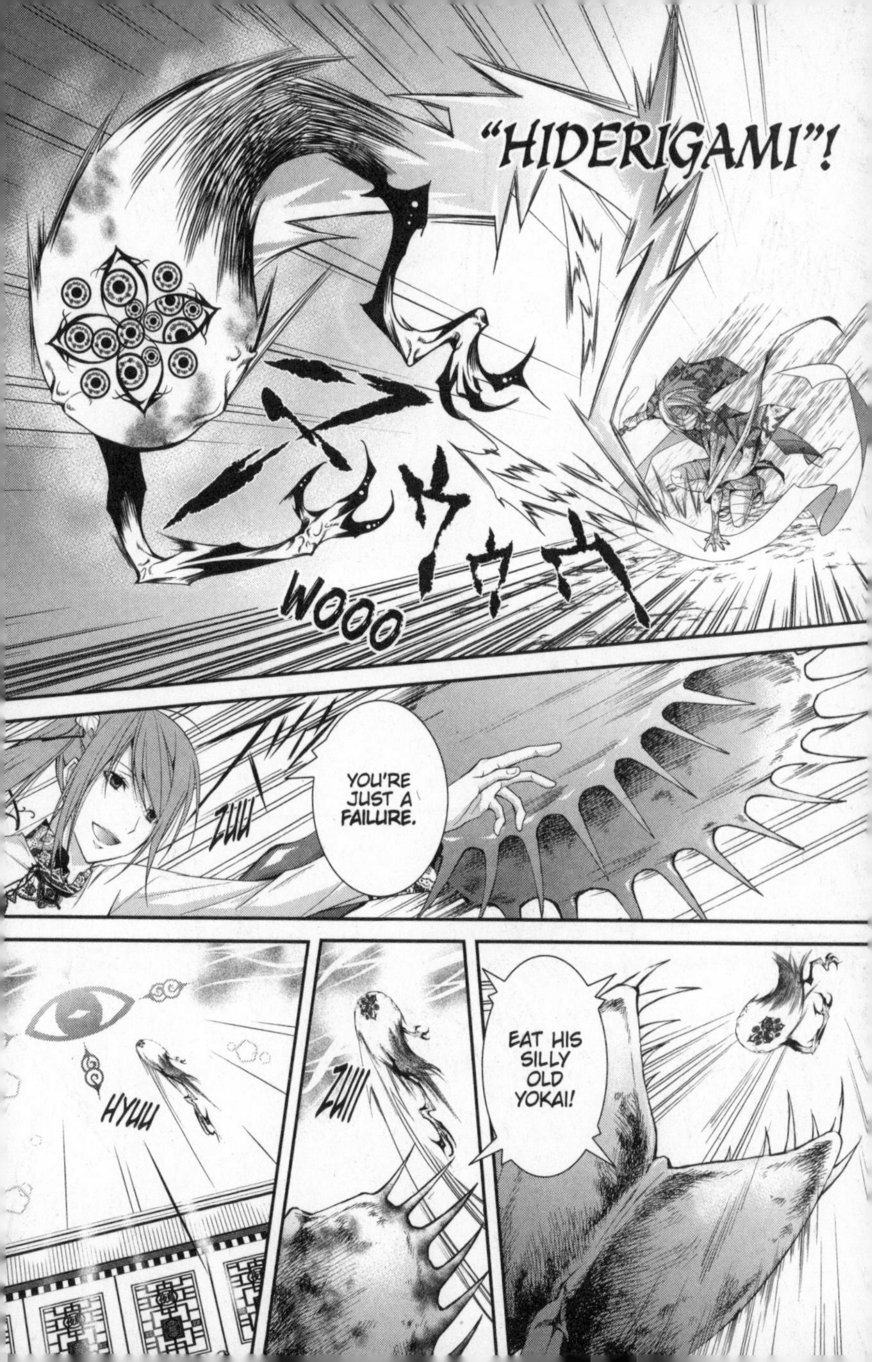
"HIDERIGAMI"!
WOOO
YOU'RE JUST A FAILURE.
ZUU
EAT HIS SILLY OLD YOKAI!
ZUII
HYUU

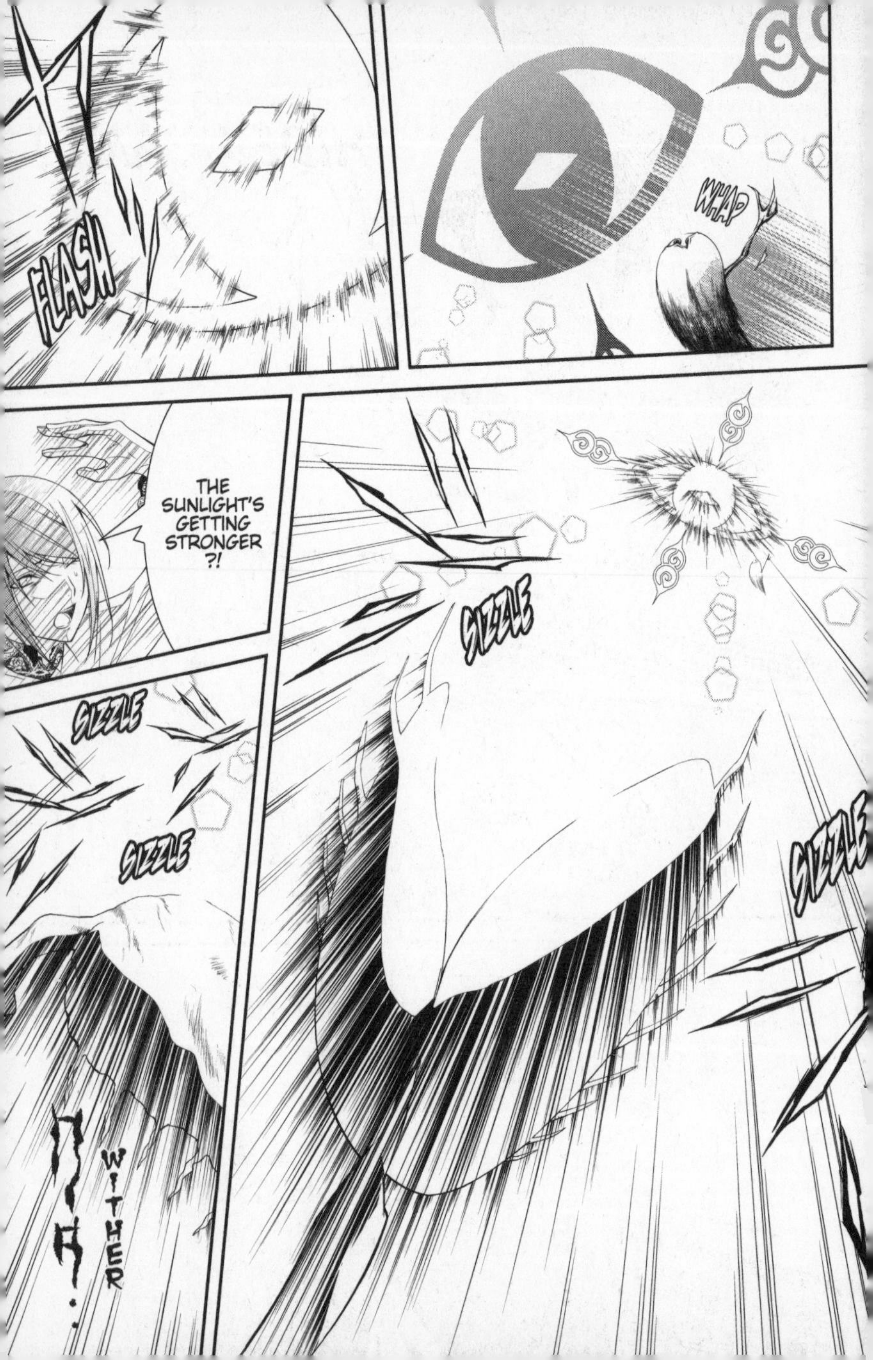
WHAP
FLASH
SIZZLE
SIZZLE
THE SUNLIGHT'S GETTING STRONGER ?!
SIZZLE
SIZZLE
WITHER

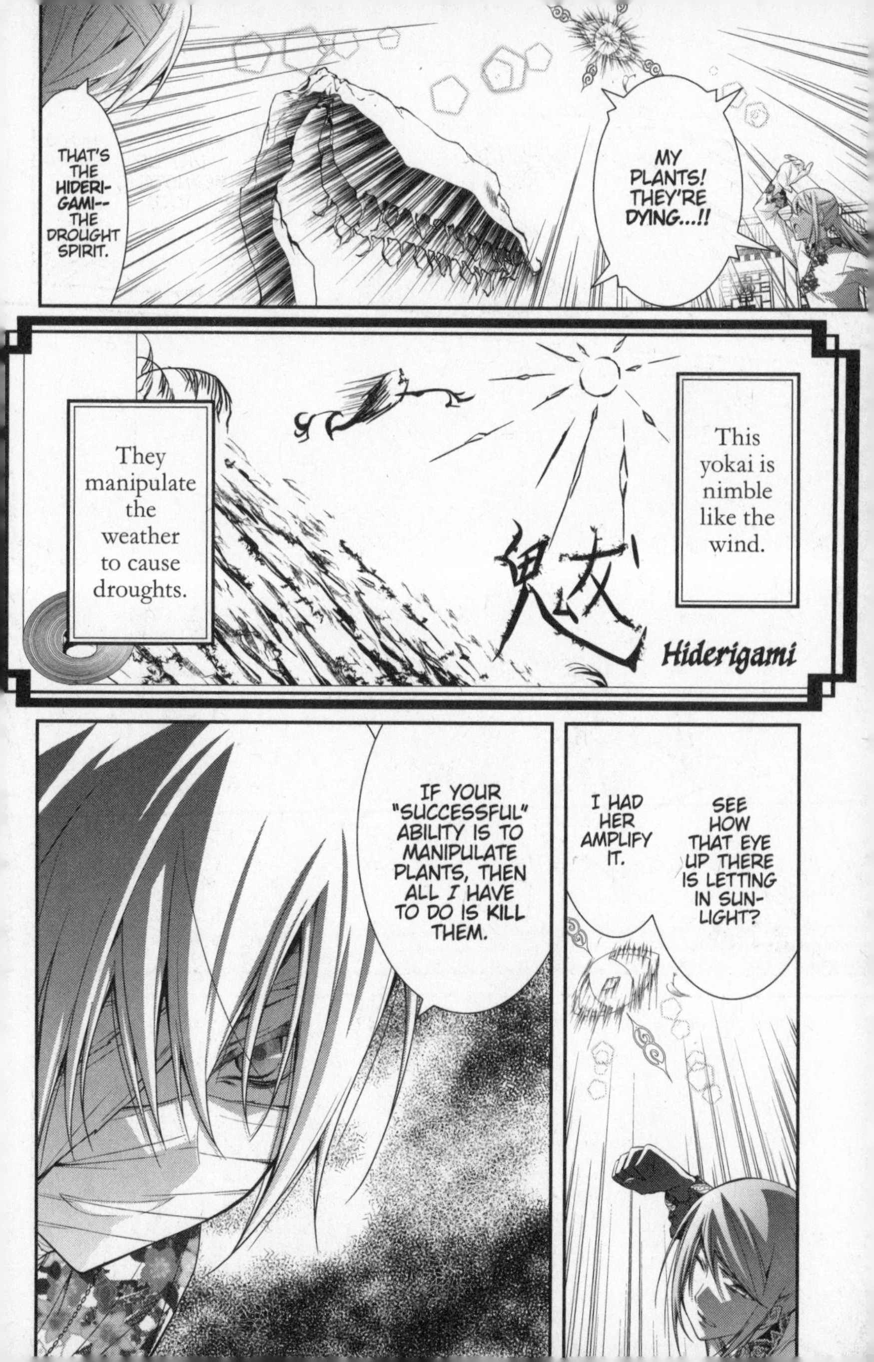
MY PLANTS! THEY'RE DYING...!!
THAT'S THE HIDERIGAMI--THE DROUGHT SPIRIT.
This yokai is nimble like the wind.
魃
Hiderigami
They manipulate the weather to cause droughts.
SEE HOW THAT EYE UP THERE IS LETTING IN SUNLIGHT?
I HAD HER AMPLIFY IT.
IF YOUR "SUCCESSFUL" ABILITY IS TO MANIPULATE PLANTS, THEN ALL *I* HAVE TO DO IS KILL THEM.

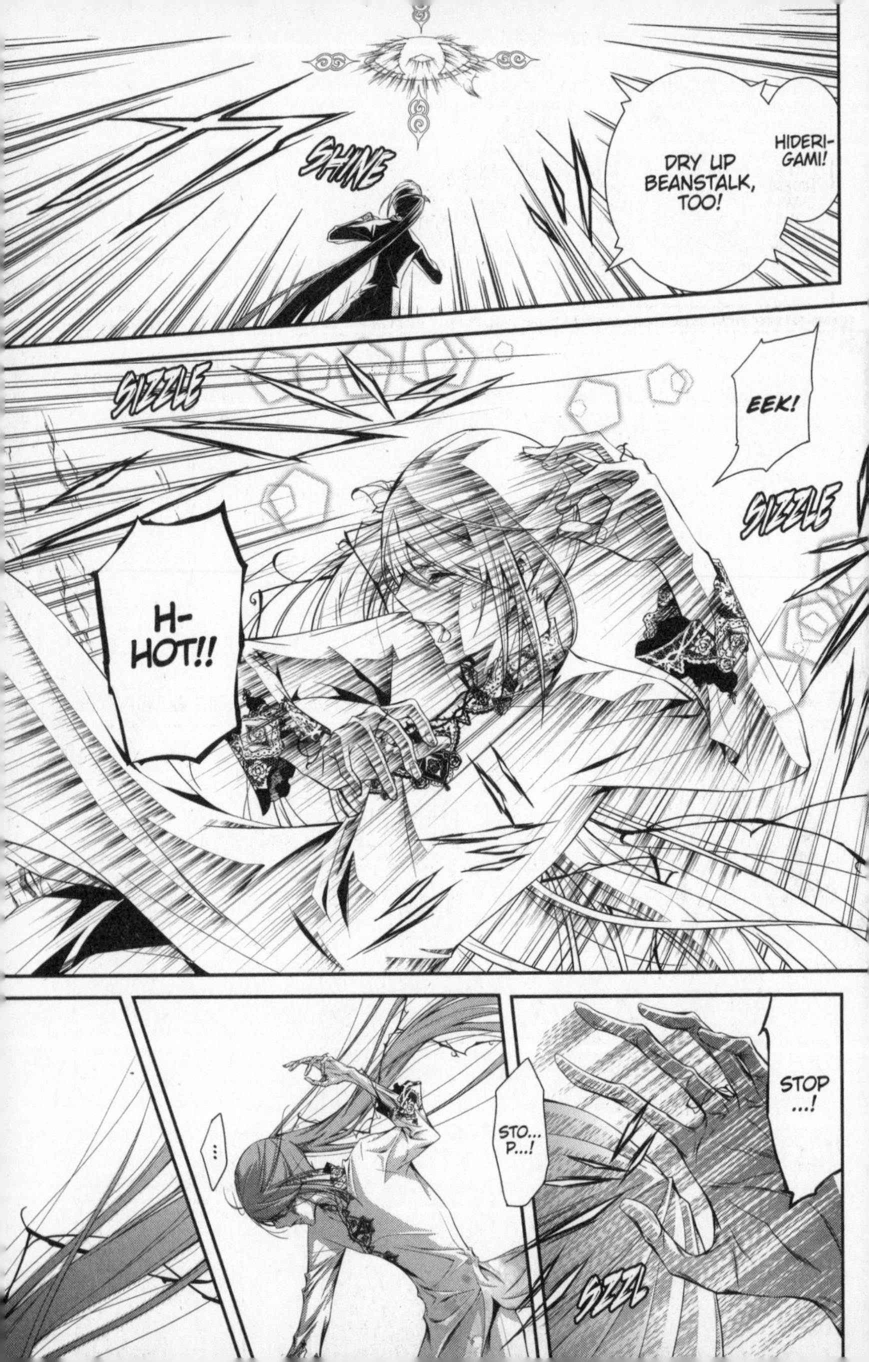
HIDERI-GAMI!
DRY UP BEANSTALK, TOO!
SHINE
EEK!
SIZZLE
H-HOT!!
SIZZLE
STOP ...!
SIZZL
STO... P...!
...

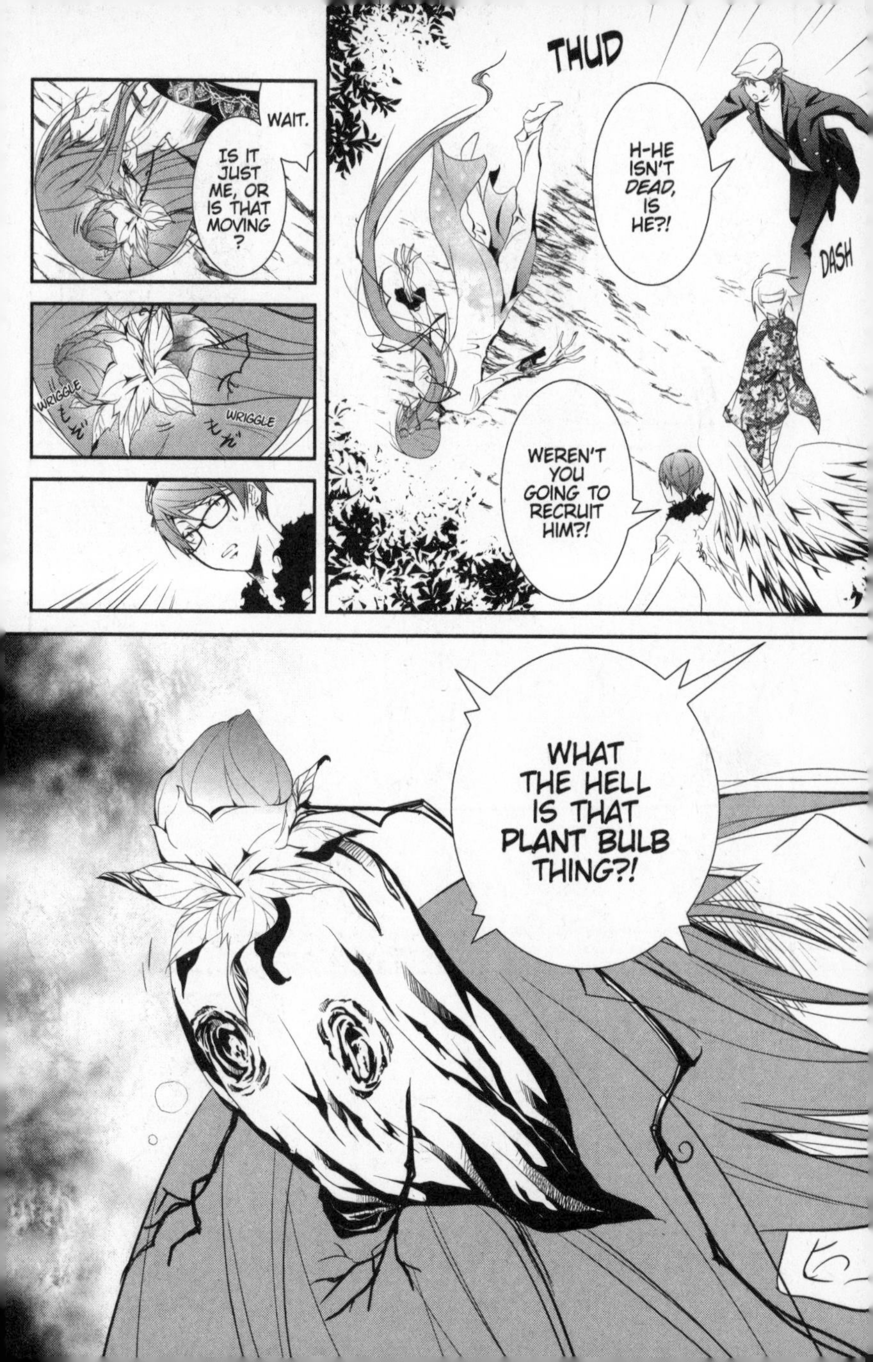
THUD
H-HE ISN'T DEAD, IS HE?!
DASH
WEREN'T YOU GOING TO RECRUIT HIM?!
WAIT.
IS IT JUST ME, OR IS THAT MOVING?
WRIGGLE
WRIGGLE
WHAT THE HELL IS THAT PLANT BULB THING?!

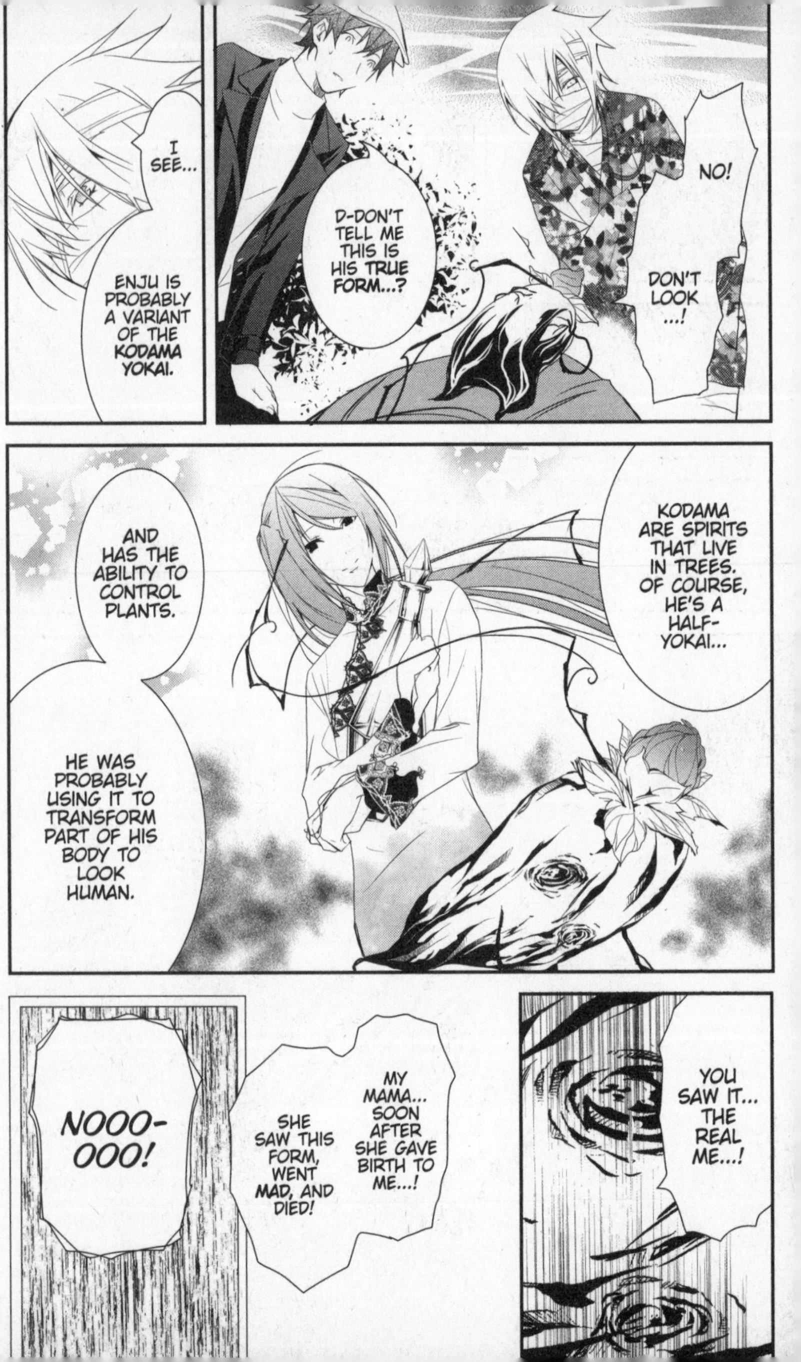
NO!
DON'T LOOK ...!
D-DON'T TELL ME THIS IS HIS TRUE FORM...?
I SEE...
ENJU IS PROBABLY A VARIANT OF THE KODAMA YOKAI.
KODAMA ARE SPIRITS THAT LIVE IN TREES. OF COURSE, HE'S A HALF-YOKAI...
AND HAS THE ABILITY TO CONTROL PLANTS.
HE WAS PROBABLY USING IT TO TRANSFORM PART OF HIS BODY TO LOOK HUMAN.
YOU SAW IT... THE REAL ME...!
MY MAMA... SOON AFTER SHE GAVE BIRTH TO ME...!
SHE SAW THIS FORM, WENT MAD, AND DIED!
NOOO-OOO!

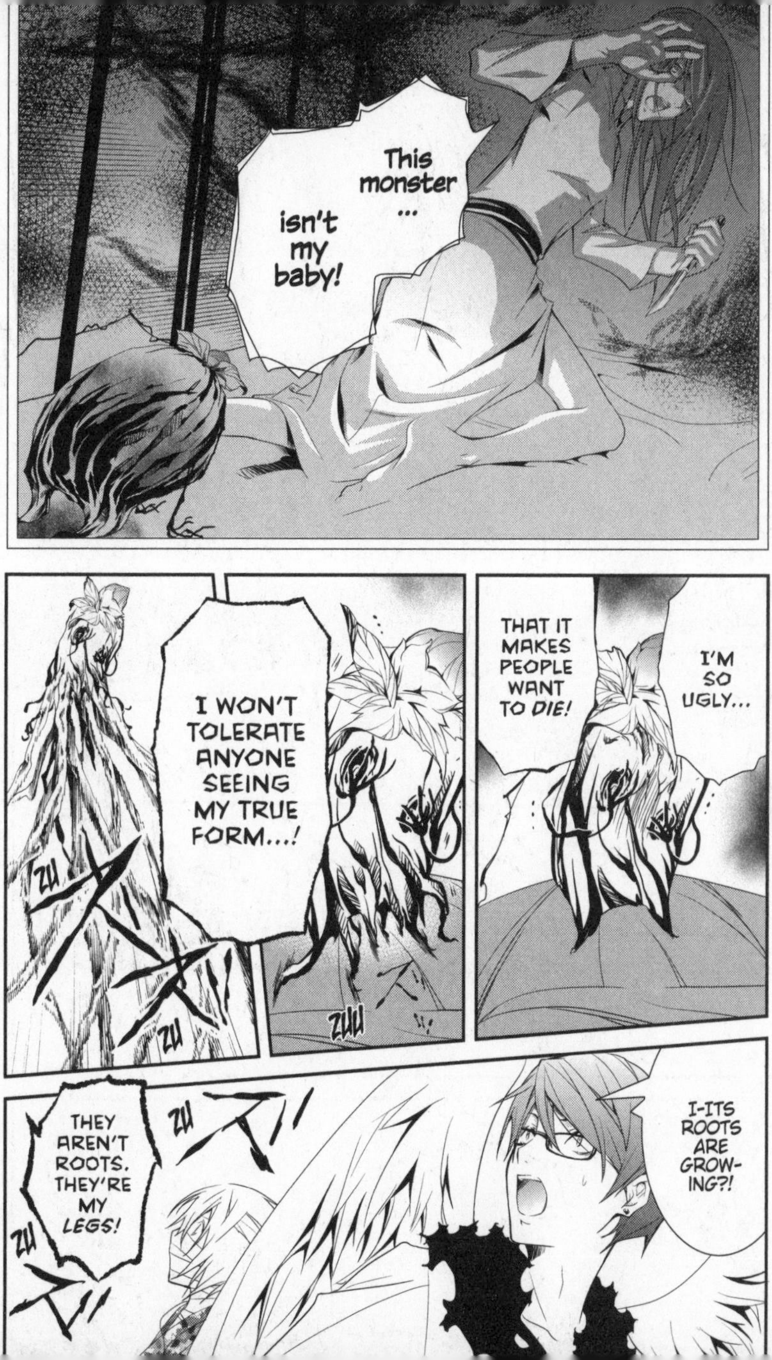
This monster...
isn't my baby!
I'M SO UGLY...
THAT IT MAKES PEOPLE WANT TO *DIE!*
I WON'T TOLERATE ANYONE SEEING MY TRUE FORM...!
ZUU
ZU
ZU
I-ITS ROOTS ARE GROW-ING?!
THEY AREN'T ROOTS. THEY'RE MY *LEGS!*
ZU
ZU

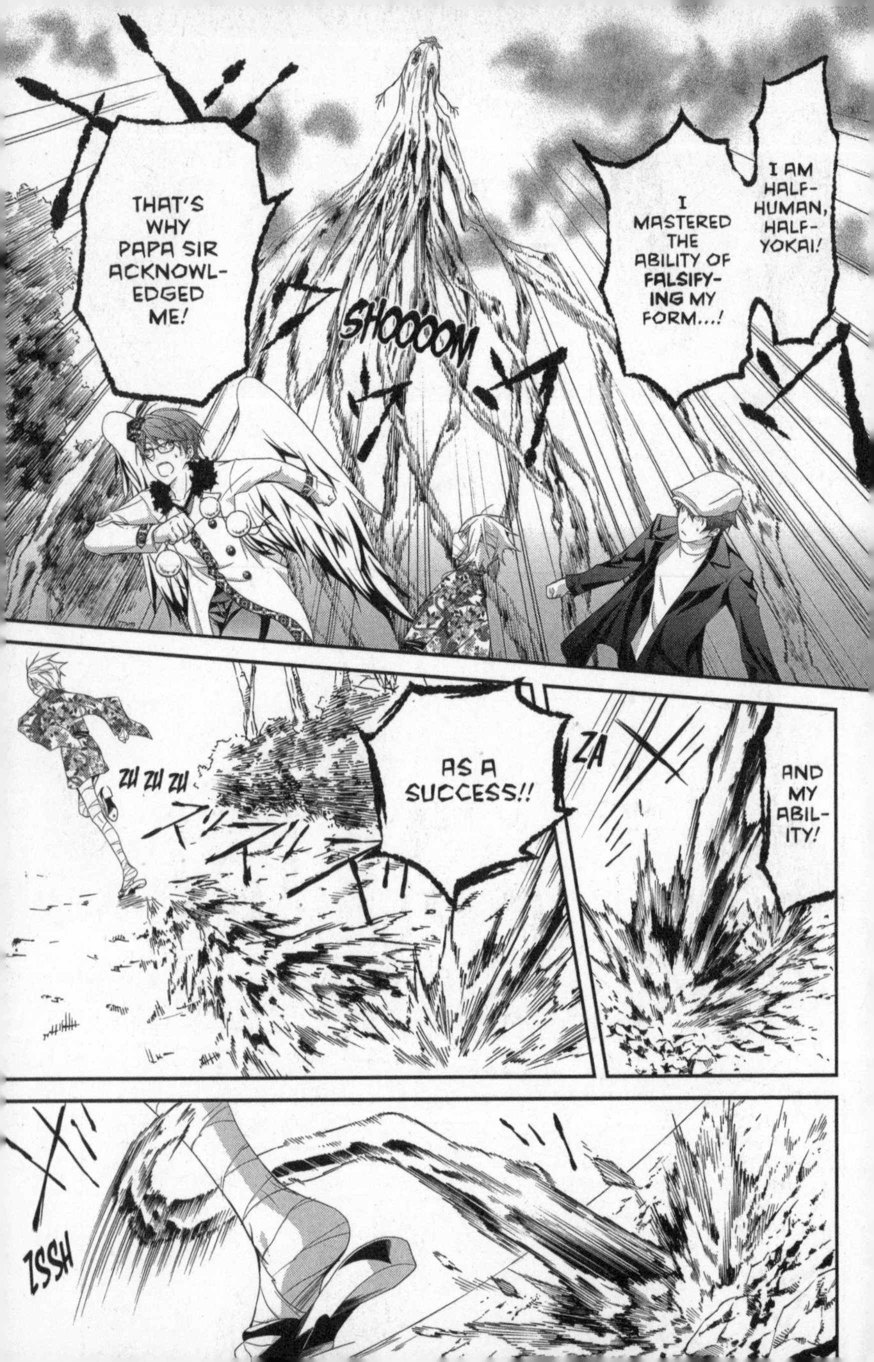
I AM HALF-HUMAN, HALF-YOKAI!
I MASTERED THE ABILITY OF FALSIFYING MY FORM...!
SHOOOOM
THAT'S WHY PAPA SIR ACKNOWLEDGED ME!
AND MY ABILITY!
ZA
AS A SUCCESS!!
ZU ZU ZU
ZSSH

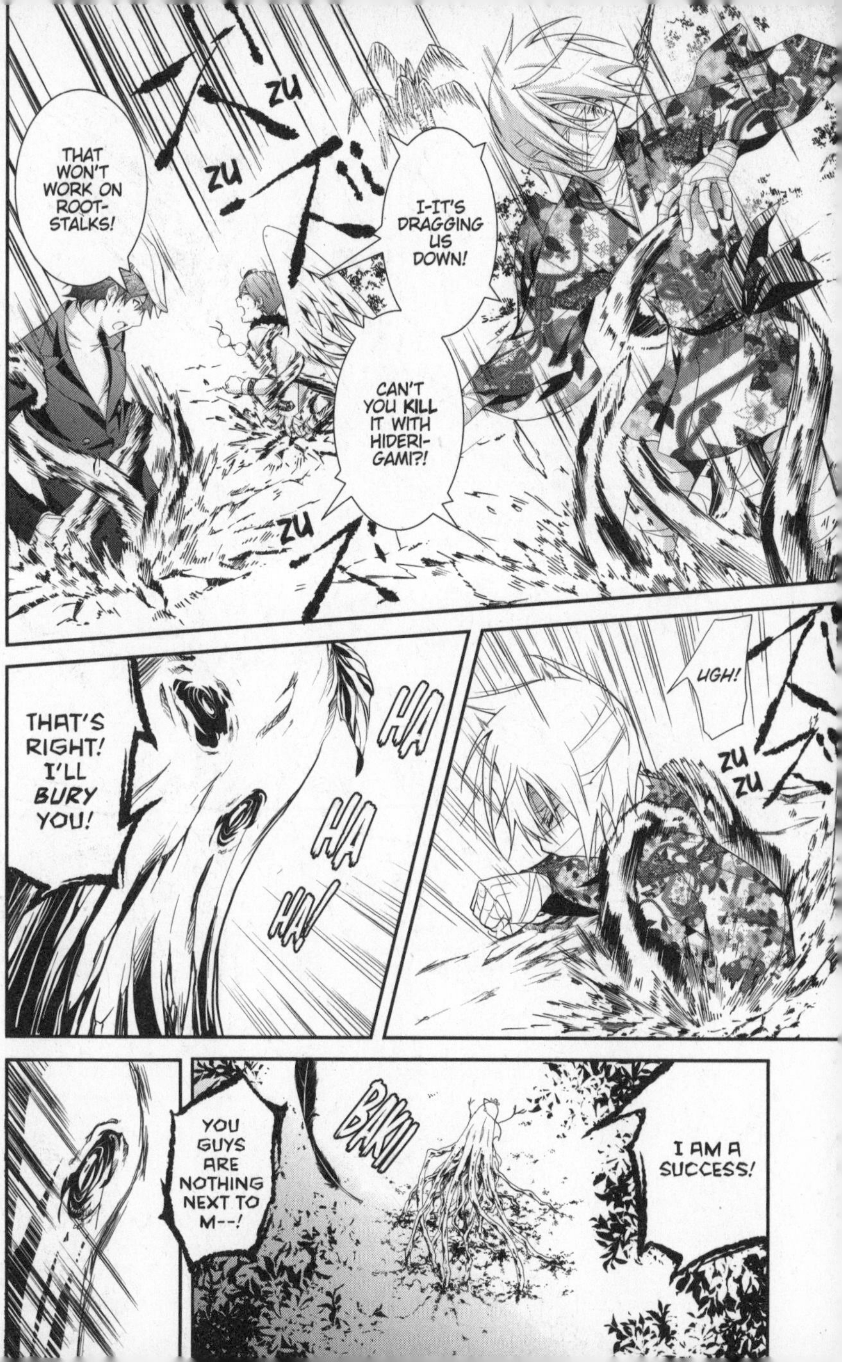
ZU
ZU
I-IT'S DRAGGING US DOWN!
CAN'T YOU KILL IT WITH HIDERI-GAMI?!
THAT WON'T WORK ON ROOT-STALKS!
ZU
UGH!
ZU ZU
HA HA HA!
THAT'S RIGHT! I'LL BURY YOU!
I AM A SUCCESS!
BAKI
YOU GUYS ARE NOTHING NEXT TO M--!

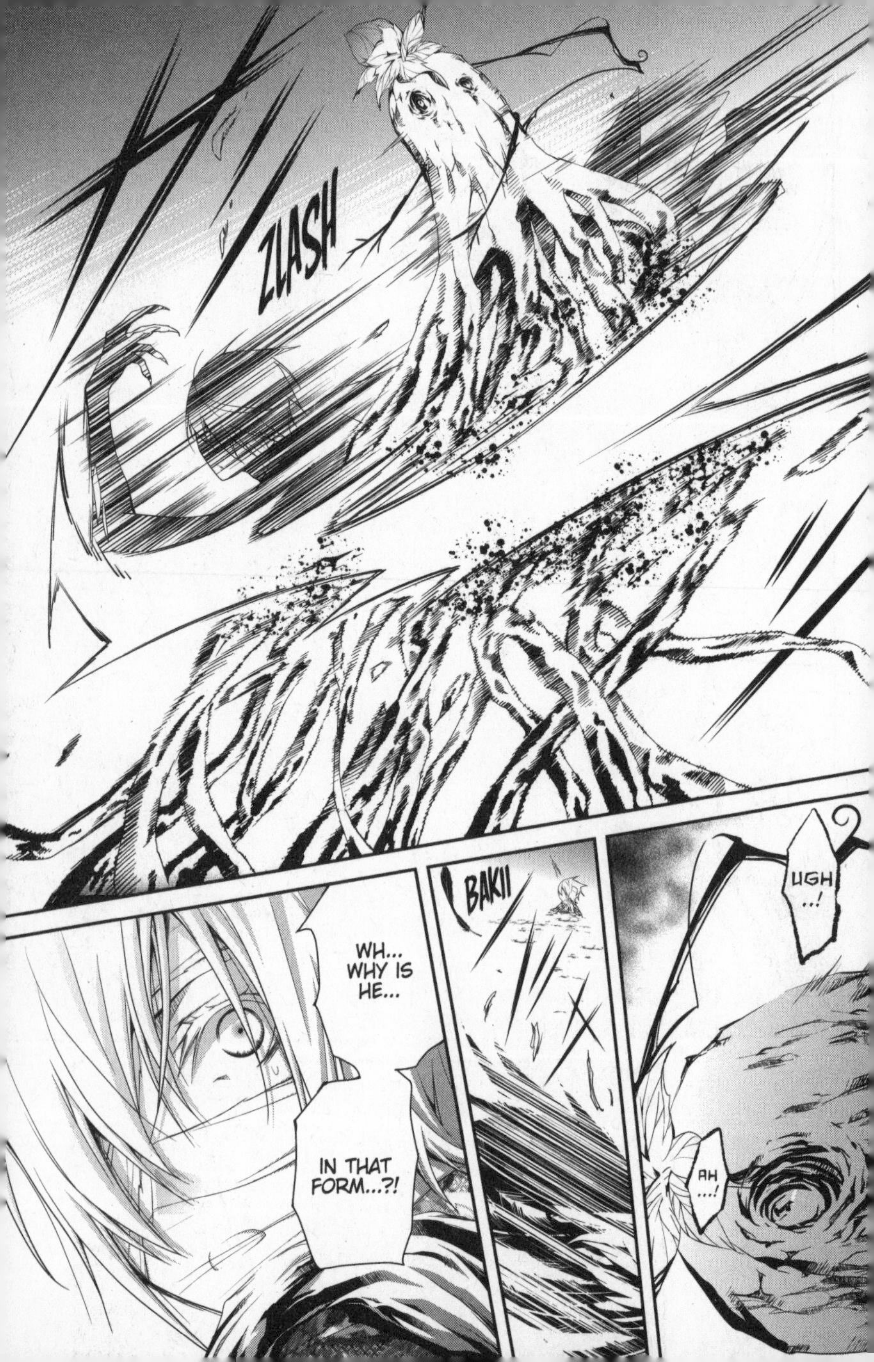
ZLASH
UGH ...!
AH ...!
BAKII
WH... WHY IS HE...
IN THAT FORM...?!

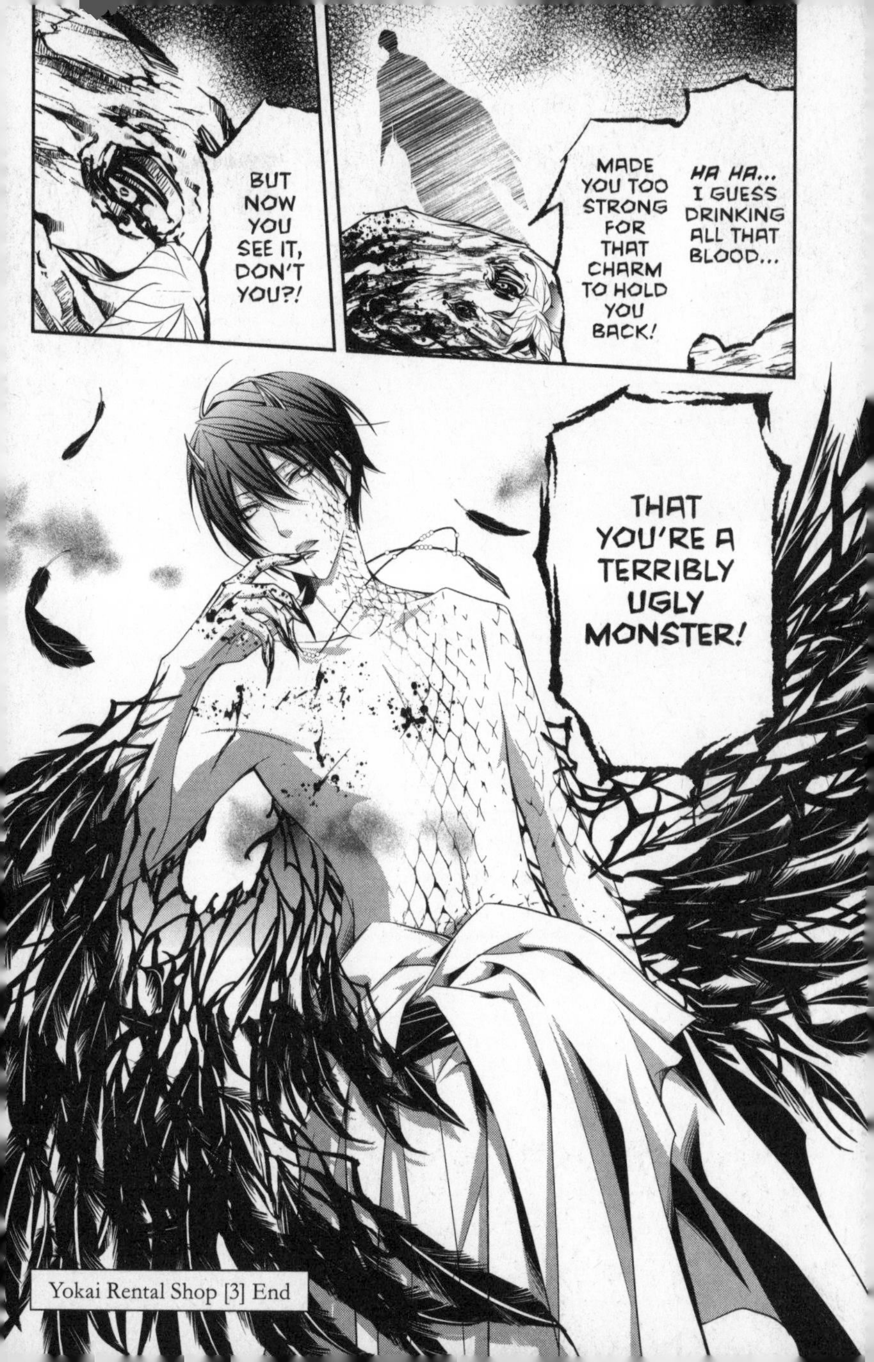
HA HA... I GUESS DRINKING ALL THAT BLOOD...
MADE YOU TOO STRONG FOR THAT CHARM TO HOLD YOU BACK!
BUT NOW YOU SEE IT, DON'T YOU?!
THAT YOU'RE A TERRIBLY UGLY MONSTER!

Yokai Rental Shop [3] End

[AFTERWORD]

Hello. Shin Mashiba here. Thank you very much for picking up volume 3. Oldest brother Bandages, middle brother Plant Bulb, and baby brother Pitiful... Now we have the full set of all three half-brothers, and the next volume will be the final book. I hope you'll watch over these brothers and their father until the end to see what happens to them.

[Assistants]

◇ Wan Wan Shiroi-sama <black inks, screen tones>
◇ Riru Shirayukii-sama <shadow tones>
◇ MOAI-sama <information>
◇ Maru-sama <backgrounds>
◇ Mori-sama <backgrounds>
◇ Katou-sama <backgrounds>

Lately I've been giving a lot of work instructions centered on the images in my head, yet my assistants still manage do a good job understanding what I'm trying to convey, somehow. You're all a huge help.

[Square Enix]

◇ My editor, Kumaoka-sama
◇ The editor-in-chief
◇ Everyone who was involved

I'm indebted to you, even for things outside of my manga series. I'm truly thankful for all your guidance and advice.

[Main Reference Books]

Nihon youkai daijiten (Japanese Yokai Dictionary) / Illustrations: Mizuki Shigeru / Compilation: Murakami Kenji (Kadokawa Shoten)
Zusetsu Nihon youkai taizen (Illustrated Compendium of Japanese Yokai) / Author: Mizuki Shigeru (Kodansha)
Youkai zukan (Yokai Picture Scroll)/ Writing: Kyogoku Natsuhiko / Editing and commentary: Tada Katsumi (Kokusho Kankokai)

次巻予告

NEXT VOLUME PREVIEW

The dark fantasy of scars and bonds...

His yokai blood awakened, Hiiragi transforms into an "ability vampire," becoming an irrational monster--and this time, he attacks Kawado, Tengu, and even Karasu... to light!

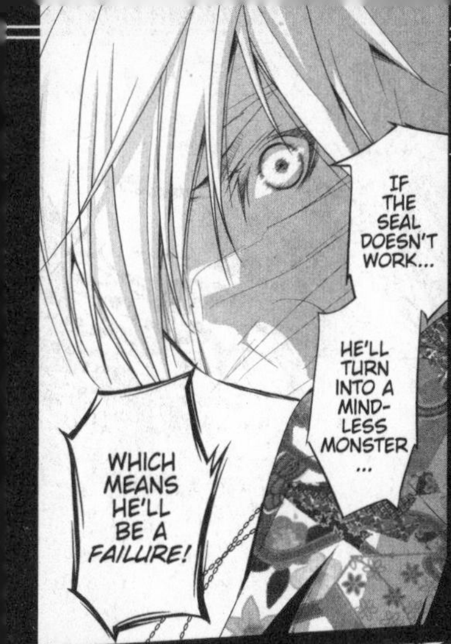
IF THE SEAL DOESN'T WORK...
HE'LL TURN INTO A MIND-LESS MONSTER...
WHICH MEANS HE'LL BE A FAILURE!

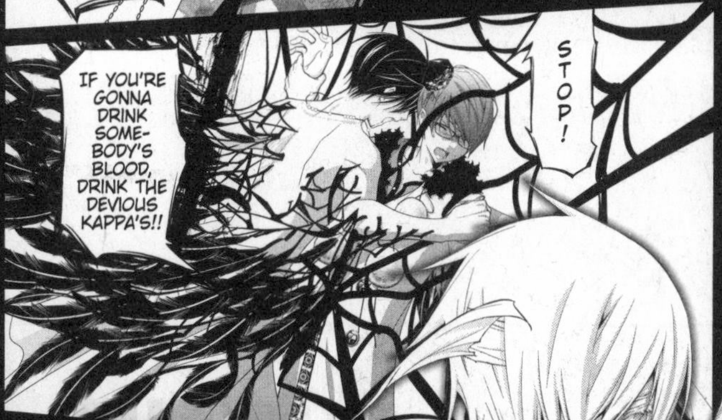
STOP!
IF YOU'RE GONNA DRINK SOME-BODY'S BLOOD, DRINK THE DEVIOUS KAPPA'S!!

"THIS...

IS THE ONLY WAY...

TO STOP HIM..."

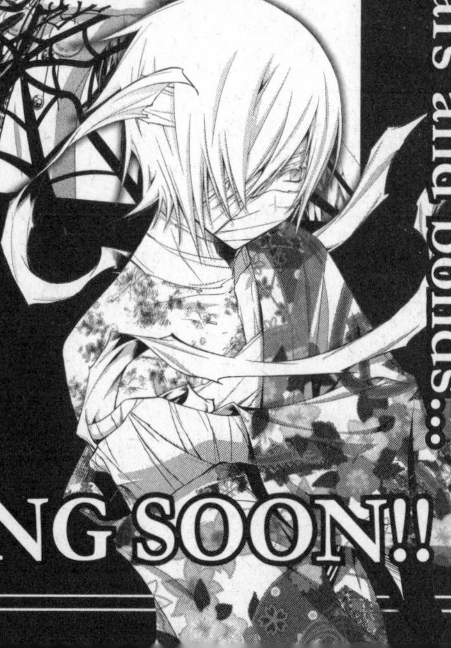

COMING SOON!!

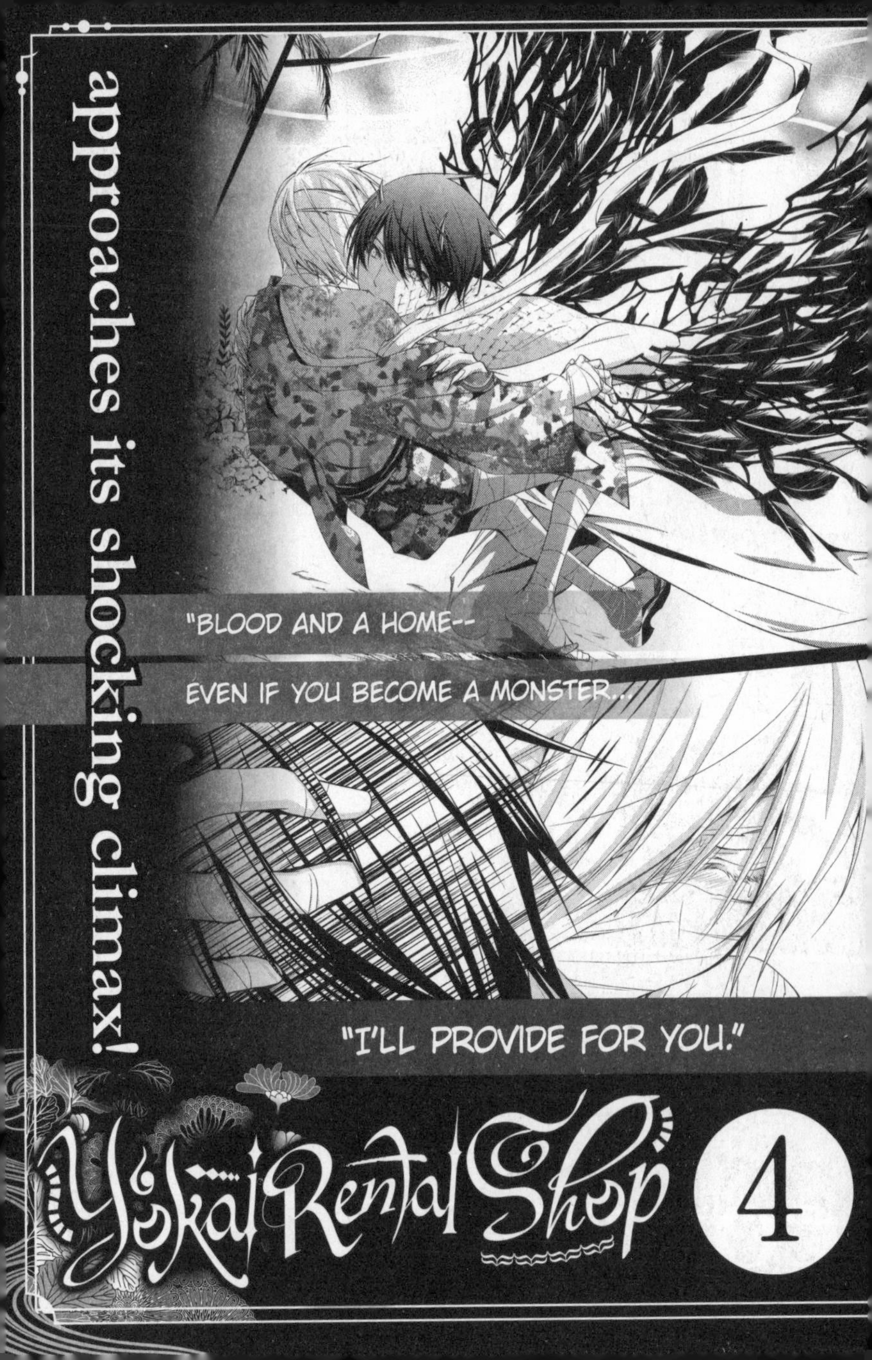
"BLOOD AND A HOME--
EVEN IF YOU BECOME A MONSTER...
"I'LL PROVIDE FOR YOU."
Yōkai Rental Shop 4
approaches its shocking climax!

Yōkai Rental Shop

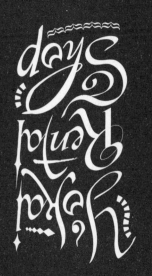

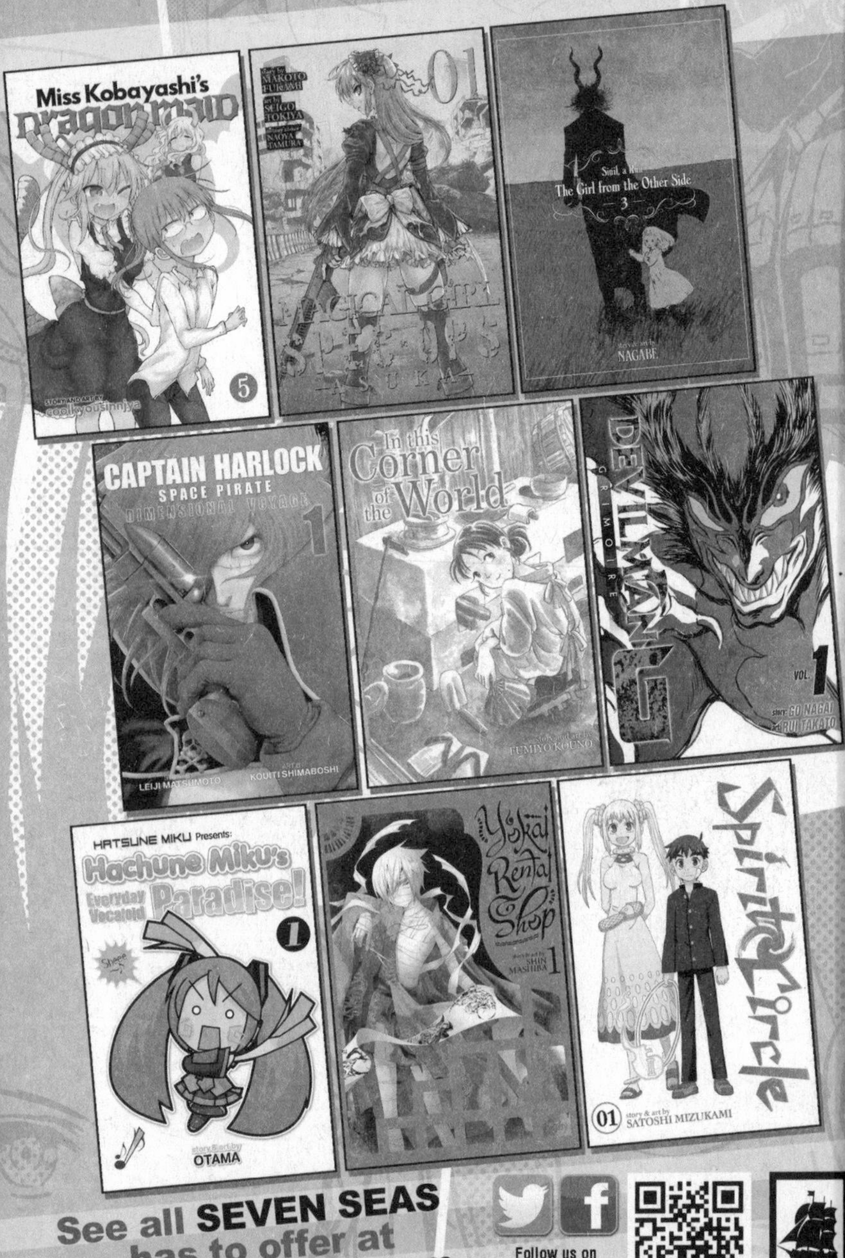
Miss Kobayashi's Dragon Maid
5
Magical Girl Spec-Ops Asuka
01
The Girl from the Other Side
Siúil, a Rún
3
story & art by NAGABE
CAPTAIN HARLOCK
SPACE PIRATE
DIMENSIONAL VOYAGE
1
LEIJI MATSUMOTO
KOUITI SHIMABOSHI
In this Corner of the World
FUMIYO KOUNO
DEVILMAN GRIMOIRE
VOL. 1
GO NAGAI
RUI TAKATO
HATSUNE MIKU Presents:
Hachune Miku's Everyday Vocaloid Paradise!
1
OTAMA
Yokai Rental Shop
SHIN MASHIBA
1
Spirit Circle
01
story & art by SATOSHI MIZUKAMI

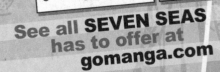

SEVEN SEAS ENTERTAINMENT PRESENTS

Yokai Rental Shop

story and art by SHIN MASHIBA

VOLUME 3

TRANSLATION
Amanda Haley

ADAPTATION
Julia Kinsman

LETTERING AND LAYOUT
Rina Mapa

COVER DESIGN
Nicky Lim

PROOFREADER
Danielle King
B. Lana Guggenheim

EDITOR
Jenn Grunigen

PRODUCTION ASSISTANT
CK Russell

PRODUCTION MANAGER
Lissa Pattillo

EDITOR-IN-CHIEF
Adam Arnold

PUBLISHER
Jason DeAngelis

YOKAI NIISAN VOL. 3
©2017 Shin Mashiba / SQUARE ENIX CO., LTD.
First published in Japan in 2017 by SQUARE ENIX CO., LTD.
English translation rights arranged with SQUARE ENIX CO., LTD. and
SEVEN SEAS ENTERTAINMENT, LLC. through Tuttle-Mori Agency, Inc.
Translation © 2017 by SQUARE ENIX CO., LTD.

No portion of this book may be reproduced or transmitted in any form without
written permission from the copyright holders. This is a work of fiction. Names,
characters, places, and incidents are the products of the author's imagination or
are used fictitiously. Any resemblance to actual events, locales, or persons, living
or dead, is entirely coincidental.

Seven Seas books may be purchased in bulk for promotional, educational, or
business use. Please contact your local bookseller or the Macmillan Corporate
and Premium Sales Department at 1-800-221-7945, extension 5442, or by e-mail
at MacmillanSpecialMarkets@macmillan.com.

Seven Seas and the Seven Seas logo are trademarks of
Seven Seas Entertainment, LLC. All rights reserved.

ISBN: 978-1-626927-90-2

Printed in Canada

First Printing: May 2018

10 9 8 7 6 5 4 3 2 1

FOLLOW US ONLINE: **www.sevenseasentertainment.com**

READING DIRECTIONS

This book reads from *right to left*, Japanese style. If this is your first time reading manga, you start reading from the top right panel on each page and take it from there. If you get lost, just follow the numbered diagram here. It may seem backwards at first, but you'll get the hang of it! Have fun!!

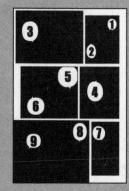

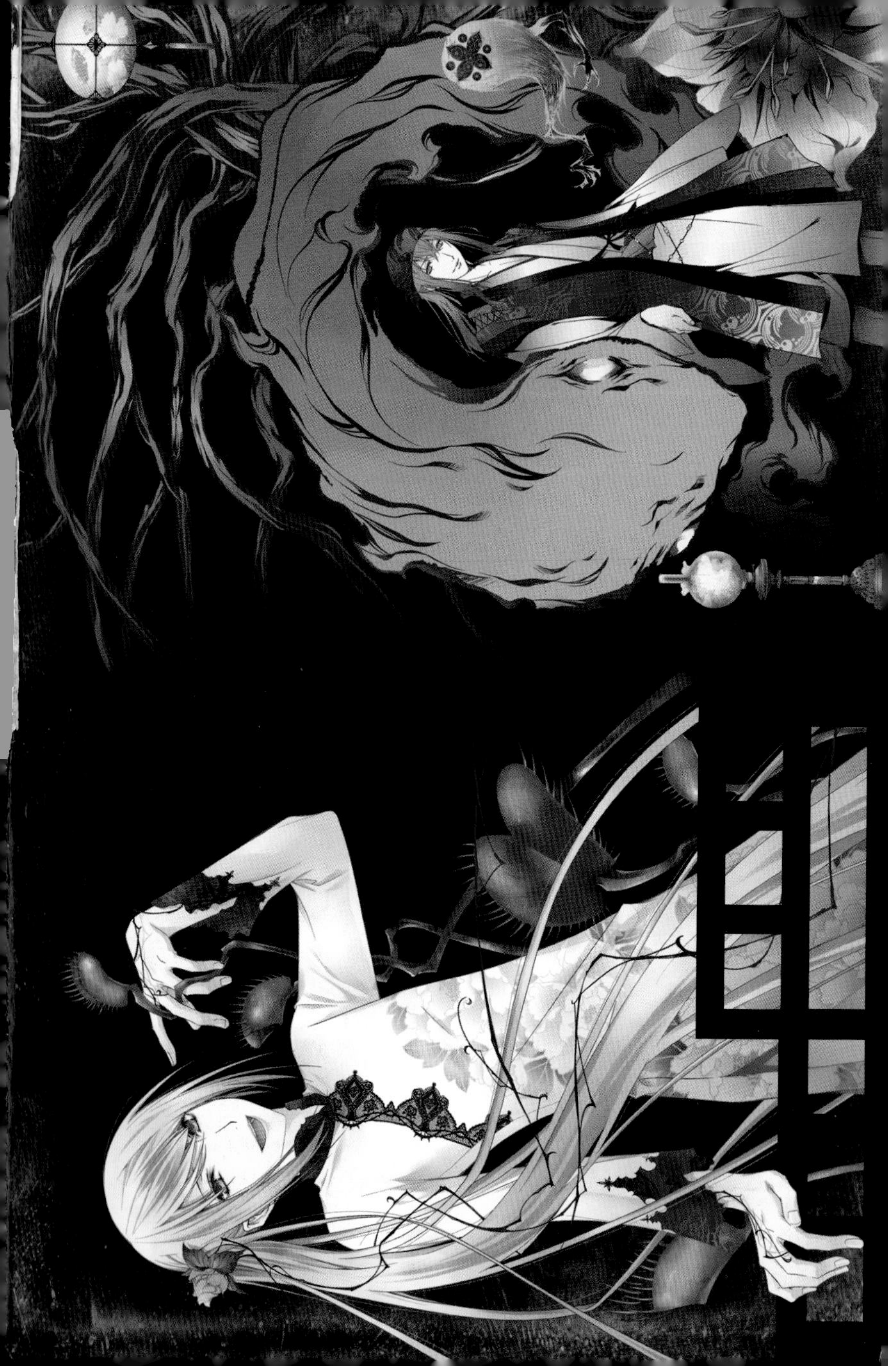

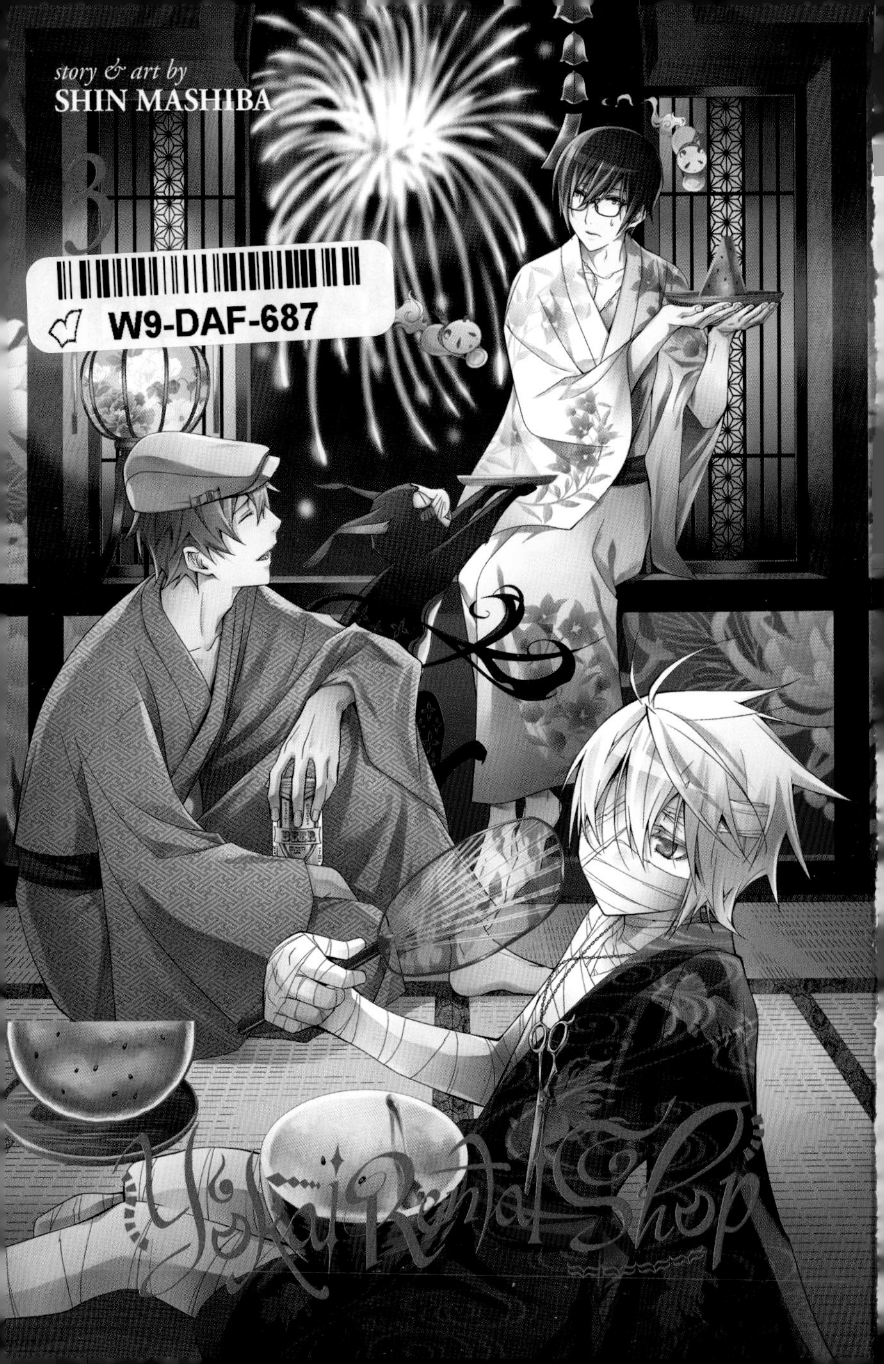
story & art by
SHIN MASHIBA
3
Yokai Rental Shop